Essentials of Data Science and Analytics

Essentials of Data Science and Analytics

Statistical Tools, Machine Learning, and R-Statistical Software Overview

Amar Sahay

BEP

BUSINESS EXPERT PRESS

Leader in applied, concise business books

Essentials of Data Science and Analytics:
Statistical Tools, Machine Learning, and R-Statistical Software Overview

Copyright © Business Expert Press, LLC, 2021.

Cover design by Charlene Kronstedt

Interior design by Exeter Premedia Services Private Ltd., Chennai, India

First published in 2021 by
Business Expert Press, LLC
222 East 46th Street, New York, NY 10017
www.businessexpertpress.com

ISBN-13: 978-1-63157-345-3 (paperback)
ISBN-13: 978-1-63157-346-0 (e-book)

Business Expert Press Quantitative Approaches to Decision Making
Collection

Collection ISSN: 2163-9515 (print)
Collection ISSN: 2163-9582 (electronic)

First edition: 2021

10 9 8 7 6 5 4 3 2 1

Description

This text provides a comprehensive overview of Data Science. With continued advancement in storage and computing technologies, data science has emerged as one of the most desired fields in driving business decisions. Data science employs techniques and methods from many other fields such as statistics, mathematics, computer science, and information science. Besides the methods and theories drawn from several fields, data science uses visualization techniques using specially designed big data software and statistical programming language, such as R programming, and Python. Data science has wide applications in the areas of Machine Learning (ML) and Artificial Intelligence (AI). The book has four parts divided into different chapters. These chapters explain the core of data science. Part I of the book introduces the field of data science, different disciplines it comprises of, and the scope with future outlook and career prospects. This section also explains analytics, business analytics, and business intelligence and their similarities and differences with data science. Since the data is at the core of data science, Part II is devoted to explaining the data, big data, and other features of data. One full chapter is devoted to data analysis, creating visuals, pivot table, and other applications using Excel with Office 365. Part III explains the statistics behind data science. It uses several chapters to explain the statistics and its importance, numerical and data visualization tools and methods, probability, and probability distribution applications in data science. Other chapters in the Part III are sampling, estimation, and hypothesis testing. All these are integral part of data science applications. Part IV of the book provides the basics of Machine Learning (ML) and R-statistical software. Data science has wide applications in the areas of Machine Learning (ML) and Artificial Intelligence (AI) and R-statistical software is widely used by data science professionals. The book also outlines a brief history, the body of knowledge, skills, and education requirements for data scientist and data science professionals. Some statistics on job growth and prospects are also summarized. A career in data science is ranked at the third best job in America for 2020 by Glassdoor and was ranked the number one best job from 2016 to 2019.[29]

Primary Audience

The book is appropriate for majors in data science, analytics, business, statistics and data analysis majors, graduate students in business, MBAs, professional MBAs, and working people in business and industry who are interested in learning and applying data science in making effective business decisions. Data science is a vast area and the tools of data science are proven to be effective in making timely business decisions and predicting the future outcomes in this current competitive business environment.

The book is designed with a wide variety of audience in mind. It takes a unique approach of presenting the body of knowledge and integrating such knowledge to different areas of data science, analytics, and predictive modeling. The importance and applications of data science tools in analyzing and solving different problems is emphasized throughout the book. It takes a simple yet unique learner-centered approach in teaching data science and predictive, knowledge, and skills requires as well as the tools. The students in Information Systems interested in data science will also find the book to be useful.

Scope

This book may be used as a suggested reading for professionals in interested in data science and can also be used as a real-world applications text in data science analytics, and business intelligence.

Because of its subject matter and content, the book may also be adopted as a suggested reading in undergraduate and graduate data science, data analytics, statistics, data analysis courses, and MBA, and professional MBA courses. The businesses are now data-driven where the decisions are made using real data both collected over time and current real-time data. Data analytics is now an integral part of businesses and a number of companies rely on data, analytics, and business intelligence, and machine learning and artificial intelligence (AI) applications in making effective and timely business decisions. The professionals involved in data science and analytics, big data, visual analytics, information systems and business intelligence, business and data analytics will find this book useful.

Keywords

data science; data analytics; business analytics; business intelligence; data analysis; decision making; descriptive analytics; predictive analytics; prescriptive analytics; statistical analysis; quantitative techniques; data mining; predictive modeling; regression analysis; modeling; time-series forecasting; optimization; simulation; machine learning; neural networks; artificial intelligence

Contents

Preface

This book is about Data Science, one of the fastest growing fields with applications in almost all disciplines. The book provides a comprehensive overview of data science.

Data science is a data-driven decision making approach that uses several different areas, methods, algorithms, models, and disciplines with a purpose of extracting insights and knowledge from structured and unstructured data. These insights are helpful in applying algorithms and models to make decisions. The models in data science are used in predictive analytics to predict future outcomes. Machine learning and artificial intelligence (AI) are major application areas of data science.

Data science is a multidisciplinary field that provides the knowledge and skills to understand, process, and visualize data in the initial stages followed by applications of statistics, modelling, mathematics, and technology to address and solve analytically complex problems using structured and unstructured data. At the core of data science is data. It is about using this data in creative and effective ways to help businesses in making data-driven business decisions. Data science is about extracting knowledge and insights from data. Businesses and processes today are run using data. The amount of data collected now is in massive scale and is usually referred as the age of *Big Data*. The rapid advancement in technology is making it possible to collect, store, and process volumes of data rapidly. It is about using this data effectively using visualization, statistical analysis, and modeling tools that can help businesses driving business decisions.

The knowledge of statistics in data science is as important as the applications of computer science. Companies now collect massive amounts of data from exabytes to zettabytes, which are both structured and unstructured. The advancement in technology and the computing capabilities have made it possible to process and analyze this huge data with smarter storage spaces.

Data science is a multidisciplinary field that involves the ability to understand, process, and visualize data in the initial stages followed by applications of statistics, modeling, mathematics, and technology to address and solve analytically complex problems using structured and unstructured data. At the core of data science is data. It is about using this data in creative and effective ways to help businesses in making data-driven business decisions.

The field of data science is vast and has a wide scope. The terms *data science, data analytics, business analytics,* and *business intelligence* are often used interchangeably even by the professions in the fields. All these areas are somewhat related with the field of data science having the largest scope. This book tries to outline the tools, techniques, and applications of data science and explain the similarities and differences of this field with data analytics, analytics, business analytics, and business intelligence.

The knowledge of statistics in data science is as important as the applications of computer science. Statistics is the science of data and variation. Statistics and data analysis, and statistical analysis constitute major applications of data science. Therefore, a significant part of this book emphasizes the statistical concepts needed to apply data science in real world. It provides a solid foundation of statistics applied to data science. Data visualization and other descriptive and inferential tools—the knowledge of which are critical for data science professionals are discussed in detail. The book also introduces the basics of machine learning that is now a major part of data science and introduces the statistical programming language R, which is widely used by data scientists. A chapter by chapter synopsis is provided.

Chapter 1 provides an overview of data science by defining and outlining the tools and techniques. It describes the differences and similarities between data science and data analytics. This chapter also discusses the role of statistics in data science, a brief history of data science, knowledge and skills for data science professionals, and a broad view of data science with associated areas. The body of knowledge essential for data science, and different tools technologies used in data science are also parts of this chapter. Finally, the chapter looks into the future outlook of data science and carrier career path for data scientists along with future outlook of data science as a field. The major topics discussed in Chapter 1 are: (a) broad view of data science with associated areas, (b) data science body of knowledge, (c) technologies used in data science, (d) future outlook, and (d) career path for data science professional and data scientist.

The other concepts related to data science including analytics, business analytics, and business intelligence (BI) are discussed in subsequent chapters. Data science continues to evolve as one of the most sought-after areas by companies. The job outlook for this area continues to be one of the highest of all field.

The discussion topic of Chapter 2 is analytics and business analytics. One of the major areas of data science is analytics and business analytics. These terms are often used interchangeably with data science. We outline the differences between the two along with the explanation of different types of analytics and the tools used in each one. The decision-making process in data science heavily makes use of analytics and business analytics tools and these are integral parts of data analysis. We, therefore, felt it necessary to explain and describe the role of analytics in data science. Analytics is the science of analysis—the processes by which we analyze data, draw conclusions, and make decisions. Business analytics (BA) covers a vast area. It is a complex field that encompasses visualization, statistics and modeling, optimization, simulation-based modeling, and statistical analysis. It uses descriptive, predictive, and prescriptive analytics including text and speech analytics, web analytics, and other application-based analytics and much more. This chapter also discusses different predictive models and predictive analytics. Flow diagrams outlining the tools of each of the descriptive, predictive, and prescriptive analytics presented in this chapter. The decision-making tools in analytics are part of data science.

Chapter 3 draws a comparison between the business intelligence (BI) and business analytics. Business analytics, data, analytics, and advanced analytics fall under the broad area of business intelligence (BI). The broad scope of BI and the distinction between the BI and business analytics (BA) tools are outlined in this chapter.

Chapter 4 is devoted to the study of collection, presentation, and various classification of data. Data science is about the study of data.

Data are of various types and are collected using different means. This chapter explained the types of data and their classification with examples. Companies collect massive amounts of data. The volume of data collected and analyzed by businesses is so large that it is referred to as "Big Data." The volume, variety, and the speed (velocity) with which data are collected requires specialized tools and techniques including specially designed big data software for analysis.

In Chapter 5, we introduce Excel, a widely available and used software for data visualization and analysis. A number of graphs and charts with stepwise instructions are presented. There are several packages available as add-ins to Excel to enhance its capabilities. The chapter presents basic to more involved features and capabilities. The chapter is divided into sections including "Getting Stated with Excel" followed by several applications including formatting data as a table, filtering and sorting data, and simple calculations. Other applications in this chapter are analyzing data using pivot_table/pivot chart, descriptive statistics using Excel, visualizing data using Excel charts and graphs, visualizing categorical data—bar charts, pie charts, cross tabulation, exploring the relationship between two and three variables—scatter plot bubble graph, and time-series plot. Excel is very widely used software application program in data science.

Chapters 6 and 7 deal with basics of statistical analysis for data science. Statistics, data analysis, and analytics are at the core of data science applications. Statistics involves making decisions from the data. Making effective decisions using statistical methods and data require the understanding of three areas of statistics: (1) descriptive statistics, (2) probability and probability distributions, and (3) inferential statistics. Descriptive statistics involves describing the data using graphical and numerical methods. Graphical and numerical methods are used to create visual representation of the variables or data and to calculate various statistics to describe the data. Graphical tools are also helpful in identifying the patterns in the data. This chapter discusses data visualization tools. A number of graphical techniques are explained with their applications.

There has been an increasing amount of pressure on businesses to provide high-quality products and services. This is critical to improving their market share in this highly competitive market. Not only it is critical for businesses to meet and exceed customer needs and requirements, it is also important for businesses to process and analyze a large amount of data (in real time, in many cases). Data visualization, processing, analysis, and using data timely and effectively are needed to drive business decisions and also make timely data-driven decisions. The processing and analysis of large data sets comes under the emerging field known as big data, data mining, and analytics.

To process these massive amounts of data, data mining uses statistical techniques and algorithms and extracts nontrivial, implicit, previously unknown, and potentially useful patterns. Because applications of data mining tools are growing, there will be more of a demand for professionals trained in data science and analytics. The knowledge discovered from this data in order to make intelligent data driven decisions is referred to as business intelligence (BI) and business analytics. These are hot topics in business and leadership circles today as it uses a set of techniques and processes which aid in fact-based decision making. These concepts are discussed in various chapters of the book.

Much of the data analysis and statistical techniques we discuss in Chapters 6 and 7 are prerequisites to fully understanding data science and business analytics.

In Chapter 8, we discuss numerical methods that describe several measures critical to data science and analysis. The calculated measures are also known as statistics when calculated from the sample data. We explained the measures of central tendency, measures of position, and measures of variation. We also discussed empirical rule that relates the mean and standard deviation and aid in the understanding of what it means for a data to be normal. Finally, in this chapter, we study the statistics that measure the association between two variables—covariance and correlation coefficient. All these measures along with the visual tools are essential part of data analysis.

In data analytics and data science, probability and probability distributions play an important role in decision making. These are essential parts of drawing conclusion from the data and are used in problems involving inferential statistics. Chapter 9 provides a comprehensive review of probability.

Chapter 10 discusses the concepts of random variable and discrete probability distributions. The distributions play an important role in the decision-making process. Several discrete probability distributions including the binomial, Poisson, hypergeometric, and geometric distributions were discussed with applications. The second part of this chapter deals with continuous probability distribution. The emphasis is on normal distribution. The normal distribution is perhaps the most important distribution in statistics and plays a very important role in statistics and data analysis. The basis of quality programs such as, Six Sigma is the normal distribution. The chapter also provides a brief explanation of exponential distribution. This distribution has wide applications in modeling and reliability engineering.

Chapter 11 introduces the concepts of sampling and sampling distribution. In statistical analysis, we almost always rely on sample to draw conclusion about the population. The chapter also explains the concepts of standard error and the concept of central limit theorem.

Chapter 12 discusses the concepts of estimation, confidence intervals, and hypothesis testing. The concept of sampling theory is important in studying these applications. Samples are used to make inferences about the population, and this can be done through sampling distribution. The probability distribution of a sample statistic is called its *sampling distribution*. We explained the *central limit theorem*. We also discussed several examples of formulating and testing hypothesis about the population mean and population proportion. Hypothesis tests are used in assessing the validity of regression methods. They form the basis of many of the assumptions underlying the regression analysis to be discussed in the coming chapters.

Chapter 13 provides the basics of machine learning. It is a widely used method in data science and is used in designing systems that can learn, adjust, and improve based on the data fed to them without being explicitly programmed. Machine Learning is used to create models from huge amount of data commonly referred to as *big data*. It is closely related to artificial intelligence (AI). In fact, it is an application of artificial intelligence (AI). Machine learning algorithms are based on teaching a computer how to learn from the training data. The algorithms learn and improve as more data flows through the system. Fraud detection, e-mail spam, and GPS systems are some examples of machine learning applications.

Machine learning tasks are typically classified into two broad categories: supervised learning and unsupervised learning. These concepts are described in this chapter.

Finally, in Chapter 14, we introduce R statistical software. R is a powerful and widely used software for data analysis and machine learning applications. This chapter introduced the software and provided the basic statistical features, and instructions on how to download R and R studio. The software can be downloaded to run on all major operating systems including Windows, Mac OS X, and Unix. It is supported by R Foundation for Statistical Computing. R statistical analysis programming language was designed for statistical computing and graphics and is widely used by statisticians, data mining,[36] and data science professionals for data analysis. R is perhaps one of the most widely used and powerful programming platforms for statistical programming and applied machine learning. It is widely used for data science and analysis application and is a desired skill for data science professionals.

The book provides a comprehensive overview of data science and the tools and technology used in this field. The mastery of the concepts in this book are critical in the practice of data science. Data science is a growing field. It continues to evolve as one of the most sought-after areas by companies. A career in data science is ranked at the third best job in America for 2020 by Glassdoor and was ranked the number one best job from 2016 to 2019. Data scientists have a median salary of $118,370 per year or $56.91 per hour. These are based on level of education and experience in the field. Job growth in this field is also above average, with a projected increase of 16 percent from 2018 to 2028.

Salt Lake City, Utah, U.S.A.

amar@xmission.com

amar@realleansixsigmaquality.com

Acknowledgments

I would like to thank the reviewers who took the time to provide excellent insights, which helped shape this book. I wish to thank many people who have helped to make this book a reality. I have benefited from numerous authors and researchers and their excellent work in the areas of data science and analytics.

I would especially like to thank Mr. Karun Mehta, a friend and engineer whom I miss so much. I greatly appreciate the numerous hours he spent in correcting, formatting, and supplying distinctive comments. The book would not be possible without his tireless effort. Karun has been a wonderful friend, counsel, and advisor.

I am very thankful to Prof. Edward Engh for his thoughtful advice and counsel.

I would like to express my gratitude to Prof. Susumu Kasai, Professor of CSIS for reviewing and administering invaluable suggestions.

Thanks to all of my students for their input in making this book possible. They have helped me pursue a dream filled with lifelong learning. This book will not be a reality without them.

I am indebted to senior acquisitions editor, Scott Isenberg; Charlene Kronstedt, director of production, Sheri Dean, director of marketing, all the reviewers, and the publishing team at Business Expert Press for their counsel and support during the preparation of this book. I also wish to thank Mark Ferguson, Editor, for reviewing the manuscript and providing helpful suggestions for improvement. I acknowledge the help and support of Exeter Premedia Services, Chennai, India team for their help with editing and publishing.

I would like to thank my parents who always emphasized the importance of what education brings to the world. Lastly, I would like to express a special appreciation to my lovely wife Nilima, to my daughter Neha, and her husband Dave, my daughter Smita, and my son Rajeev—both engineers for their creative comments and suggestions. And finally, to our beautiful Priyanka for her lovely smiles. I am grateful to all for their love, support, and encouragement.

PART I

Data Science, Analytics, and Business Analytics

CHAPTER 1

Data Science and Its Scope

Chapter Highlights

- Introduction
- What Is Data Science?
- Objective and Overview of Chapters
- What Is Data Science?
- Another Look at Data Science
- Data Science and Statistics
- Role of Statistics in Data Science
- Data Science: A Brief History
- Difference between Data Science and Data Analytics
- Knowledge and Skills for Data Science Professionals
- Some Technologies used in Data Science
- Career Path for Data Science Professional and Data Scientist
- Future Outlook
- Summary

Introduction

Data science is about extracting knowledge and insights from data. The tools and techniques of data science are used to drive business and process decisions. It can be seen as a major data-driven decision-making approach to decision making. Data science is a multidisciplinary field that involves the ability to understand, process, and visualize data in the initial stages followed by applications of statistics, modeling, mathematics, and technology to address and solve analytically complex problems using structured and unstructured data. At the core of data science is data. It is about using this data in creative and effective ways to help businesses in making data-driven business decisions.

The knowledge of statistics in data science is as important as the applications of computer science. Companies now collect massive amounts of data from exabytes to zettabytes, which are both structured and unstructured. The advancement in technology and the computing capabilities have made it possible to store, process, and analyze this huge data with smarter storage spaces.

Data science is applied to extract information from both structured and unstructured data.[1,2]

Unstructured data is usually not organized in a structured manner and may contain qualitative or categorical elements, such as dates, categories, and so on, and are text heavy. They also contain numbers and other forms of measurements. Compared to structured data, the unstructured data contain irregularities. The ambiguities in unstructured data make it difficult to apply traditional tools of statistics and data analysis. Structured data are usually stored in clearly defined fields in databases. The software applications and programs are designed to process such data. In recent years, a number of newly developed tools and software programs have emerged that are capable of analyzing big and unstructured data. One of the earliest applications of unstructured data is in analyzing text data using text-mining and other methods.

Recently, unstructured data is becoming more prevalent. In 1998, Merrill Lynch said, "unstructured data comprises the vast majority of data found in an organization, some estimates run as high as 80%."[1] Here are some other predictions: As of 2012, IDC (International Data Group)[3] and Dell EMC[4] project that data will grow to 40 zettabytes by 2020, resulting in a 50-fold growth from the beginning of 2010.[4] More recently, IDC and Seagate predict that the global datasphere will grow to 163 zettabytes by 2025[5] and majority of that will be unstructured. The *Computer World* magazine[7] states that unstructured information might account for more than 70 to 80 percent of all data in in organizations. (https://en.wikipedia.org/wiki/Unstructured_data)[8]

Objective and Overview of Chapters

The objective of this book is to provide an introductory overview of data science, understand what data science is, and why data science is such an important field. We will also explore and outline the role of data scientists/professionals and what they do.

The initial chapters of the book introduce data science and closely related areas. The terms data science, data analytics, business analytics, and business intelligence are often used interchangeably even by the professions in the fields. Therefore, Chapter 1, which provides an overview of data science, is followed by two chapters that explain the relationship between data science, analytics, and business intelligence. Analytics itself is wide area and different forms of analytics including descriptive, predictive, and prescriptive analytics are used by companies to drive major business decisions. Chapters 2 and 3 outline the differences and similarities between data science, analytics, and business intelligence. Chapter 2 also outlines the tools of descriptive, predictive, and prescriptive analytics along with the most recent and emerging technologies of machine learning and artificial intelligence. Since the field is data science is about the data, a chapter is devoted to data and data types. Chapter 4 provides definitions of data, different forms of data, and their types followed by some tools and techniques for working with data. One of the major objectives of data science is to make sense from the massive amounts of data companies collect. One of the ways of making sense from data is to apply data visualization or graphical techniques used in data analysis. Understanding other tools and techniques for working with data are also important. A chapter is devoted to data visualization.

Data science is a vast area. Besides visualization techniques and statistical analysis, it uses statistical programming language such as R programming, and a knowledge of databases (SQL or MySQL) or other data base management system.

One major application of data science is in the area of Machine Learning (ML) and Artificial Intelligence. The book provides a detailed overview of data science by defining and outlining the tools and techniques. As mentioned earlier, the book also explains the differences and similarities between data science and data analytics. The other concepts related to data science including analytics, business analytics, and business intelligence (BI) are discussed in detail. The field of data science is about processing, cleaning, and analyzing data. These concepts and topics are important to understand the field of data science and are discussed in this book. Data science is an emerging field in data analysis and decision making.

What Is Data Science?

Data science may be thought of as a data driven decision making approach that uses several different areas, methods, algorithms, models, and disciplines with a purpose of extracting insights and knowledge from structured and unstructured data. These insights are helpful in applying algorithms and models to make decisions. The models in data science are used in predictive analytics to predict future outcomes.

Data science, as a field, has much broader scope than analytics, business analytics, or business intelligence. It brings together and combines several disciplines and areas including statistics, data analysis[9], statistical modeling, data mining,[10,11,12,13,14] big data,[15] machine learning,[16] and artificial intelligence (AI), management science, optimization techniques, and related methods in order to "understand and analyze actual phenomena" from data.[17]

Data science employs techniques and methods from many other fields, such as mathematics, statistics, computer science, and information science. Besides the methods and theories drawn from several fields, data science also uses data visualization techniques using specially designed software—Tableau and other big data software. The concepts of relational data bases (such as SQL), R-statistical software, and programming language Python are all used in different applications to analyze, extract information, and draw conclusions from data. These are the tools of data science. These tools, techniques, and programming languages provide a unifying approach to explore, analyze, draw conclusions, and make decisions from massive amounts of data companies collect.

Data science employs the tools of information technology, management science (mathematical modeling, and simulation), along with data mining and fact-based data to measure past performance to guide an organization in planning and predicting future outcomes to aid in effective decision making.

Turing award[18] winner Jim Gray viewed data science as a "fourth paradigm" of science (empirical, theoretical, computational, and now data-driven) and asserted that "everything about science is changing because of the impact of information technology" and the data deluge. In 2015, the American Statistical Association identified database management, statistics and machine learning, distributed and parallel systems as the three emerging foundational professional communities.

Another Look at Data Science

Data science can be viewed as a multidisciplinary field focused on finding actionable insights from large sets of raw, structured, and unstructured data. The field primarily uses different tools and techniques in unearthing answers to the things we don't know. Data science experts use several different areas from data and statistical analysis, programming from varied areas of computer science, predictive analytics, statistics, and machine learning to parse through massive datasets in an effort to find solutions to problems that haven't been thought of yet.

Data scientists emphasis lies in asking the right questions with a goal to seek the right or acceptable solutions. The emphasis is asking the right questions and not seeking specific answers. This is done by predicting potential trends, exploring disparate and disconnected data sources, and finding better ways to analyze information. (https://sisense.com/blog/data-science-vs-data-analytics/)[19]

(Data Science: Wikipedia.org https://en.wikipedia.org/wiki/Data_science (From Wikipedia, the free encyclopedia))

Data Science and Statistics

Conflicting Definitions of Data Science and Its Relation to Statistics

Stanford professor David Donoho, in September 2015, rejected the three simplistic and misleading definitions of data science in lieu of criticisms.[20] (1) For Donoho, data science does not equate to big data, in that the size of the data set is not a criterion to distinguish data science and statistics.[20] (2) Data science is not defined by the computing skills of sorting big data sets, in that these skills are already generally used for analyses across all disciplines.[20] (3) Data science is a heavily applied field where academic programs right now do not sufficiently prepare data scientists for the jobs, in that many graduate programs misleadingly advertise their analytics and statistics training as the data science program.[20,21] As a statistician, Donoho, following many in his field, champions the broadening of learning scope in the form of data science.[20] John Chambers who urges statisticians to adopt an inclusive concept of learning from data.[22] Together, these statisticians envision an increasingly inclusive applied field that grows out of traditional statistics and beyond.

Role of Statistics in Data Science

Data science professionals and data scientists should have a strong background in statistics, mathematics, and computer applications. Good analytical and statistical skills are a prerequisite to successful application and implementation of data science tools. Besides the simple statistical tools, data science also uses visualization, statistical modeling including descriptive analytics, and predictive modeling for predicting future business outcomes. Thus, a combination of mathematical methods along with computational algorithms and statistical models is needed for generating successful data science solutions. Here are some key statistical concepts that every data scientist should know.

- Descriptive statistics and data visualization
- Inferential statistics concepts and tools of inferential statistics
- Concepts of probability and probability distributions
- Concepts of sampling and sampling distribution/ over and under-sampling
- Bayesian statistics
- Dimensionality reduction

Data Science: A Brief History

1997	In November 1997, C.F. Jeff Wu gave the inaugural lecture titled "Statistics = Data Science?"[28] for his appointment to the H. C. Carver Professorship at the University of Michigan. In this lecture, he characterized statistical work as a trilogy of data collection, data modeling and analysis, and decision making.
	In his conclusion, he initiated the modern, non-computer science, usage of the term "data science" and advocated that statistics be renamed data science and statisticians data scientists.[28] Later, he presented his lecture titled "Statistics = Data Science?" as the first of his 1998 P.C. Mahalanobis Memorial Lectures.

2001	William S. Cleveland introduced data science as an independent discipline, extending the field of statistics to incorporate "advances in computing with data" in his article "data science.
2002	In April 2002, the International Council for Science (ICSU): Committee on Data for Science and Technology (CODATA)[17] started the *Data Science Journal*, a publication focused on issues such as the description of data systems, their publication on the Internet, applications and legal issues.
2003	in January 2003, Columbia University began publishing *The Journal of Data Science*,[17] which provided a platform for all data workers to present their views and exchange ideas. The journal was largely devoted to the application of statistical methods and quantitative research.
2005	The National Science Board published "Long-lived Digital Data Collections: Enabling Research and Education in the 21st Century" defining data scientists as "the information and computer scientists, database and software and programmers, disciplinary experts, curators and expert annotators, librarians, archivists, and others, who are crucial to the successful management of a digital data collection" whose primary activity is to "conduct creative inquiry and analysis."[18]
2006/2007	Around 2007,Turing award winner Jim Gray envisioned "data-driven science" as a "fourth paradigm" of science that uses the computational analysis of large data as primary scientific method and "to have a world in which all of the science literature is online, all of the science data is online, and they interoperate with each other."
2012	In the 2012 *Harvard Business Review* article "Data Scientist: The Sexiest Job of the 21st Century",[24] DJ Patil claims to have coined this term in 2008 with Jeff Hammerbacher to define their jobs at LinkedIn and Facebook, respectively. He asserts that a data scientist is "a new breed" and that a "shortage of data scientists is becoming a serious constraint in some sectors" but describes a much more business-oriented role.
2014	The first international conference, IEEE International Conference on Data Science and Advanced Analytics, was launched in 2014.
	In 2014, the American Statistical Association (ASA) section on Statistical Learning and Data Mining renamed its journal to *Statistical Analysis and Data Mining: The ASA Data Science Journal*.
2015	In 2015, the *International Journal on Data Science and Analytics* was launched by Springer to publish original work on data science and big data analytics.
2016	In 2016, The ASA changed its section name to "Statistical Learning and Data Science."

Reference 17 cited above has excellent articles on Data Science.

Data Science and Data Analytics

(https://sisense.com/blog/data-science-vs-data-analytics/)

Data analytics focuses on processing and performing statistical analysis on existing datasets. Analysts apply different tools and methods to capture, process, organize, and perform data analysis to data in the data bases of companies to uncover actionable insights from data and find ways to present this data. More simply, the field of data and analytics is directed toward solving problems for questions we know we don't know the answers to. More importantly, it's based on producing results that can lead to immediate improvements.

Data analytics also encompasses a few different branches of broader statistics and analysis, which help combine diverse sources of data and locate connections while simplifying the results.

Difference Between Data Science and Data Analytics

While the terms data science and data analytics are used interchangeably, data science and big data analytics are unique fields with major difference being the scope. Data science is an umbrella term for a group of fields that are used to mine large datasets. Data science has much broader scope compared to data analytics, analytics, and business analytics. Data analytics is a more focused version of data science and focuses more on data analysis and statistics and can even be considered part of the larger process that uses simple to advanced statistical tools. Analytics is devoted to realizing actionable insights that can be applied immediately based on existing queries.

Another significant difference between the two fields is a question of exploration. Data science isn't concerned with answering specific queries, instead parsing through massive datasets in sometimes unstructured ways to expose insights. Data analysis works better when it is focused, having questions in mind that need answers based on existing data.

Data science produces broader insights that concentrate on which questions should be asked, while big data analytics emphasizes discovering answers to questions being asked.

More importantly, data science is more concerned about asking questions than finding specific answers. The field is focused on establishing potential trends based on existing data, as well as realizing better ways to analyze and model the data. Table 1.1 outlines the differences.

Table 1.1 Difference between data science and data analytics

	Data Science	Data Analytics
Scope	Macro	Micro
Goal	Ask the right questions	Find actionable data
Major fields	Machine learning, AI, search engine engineering, statistics, analytics	Healthcare, gaming, travel, industries with immediate data needs
Analysis of Data and Big Data	Yes	Yes

Some argue that the two fields—data science and data analytics—can be considered different sides of the same coin, and their functions are highly interconnected. Data science lays important foundations and parses big datasets to create initial observations, future trends, and potential insights that can be important. This information by itself is useful for some fields, especially modeling, improving machine learning, and enhancing AI algorithms as it can improve how information is sorted and understood. However, data science asks important questions that we were unaware of before while providing little in the way of answers. By combining data analytics with data science, we have additional insights, prediction capabilities, and tools to apply in practical applications.

When thinking of these two disciplines, it's important to forget about viewing them as data science versus data analytics. Instead, we should see them as parts of a whole that are vital to understanding not just the information we have, but how.

Knowledge and Skills for Data Science Professionals

The key function of the data science professional or a data scientist is to understand the data and identify the correct method or methods that will lead to desired solution. These methods are drawn from different fields including data and big data analysis (visualization techniques) statistics (statistical modeling) and probability, computer science and information systems, programming skills, and an understanding of data bases including querying and data base management.

Data science professionals should also have the knowledge of many of the software packages that can be used to solve different types of problems. Some of the commonly used programs are statistical packages (R statistical computing software), SAS, and other statistical packages, relational data base packages (SQL, MySQL, Oracle, and others), machine learning libraries (recently, many software to automate machine learning tasks are available from software vendors). The two known auto machine learning software are Azur by Microsoft and SAS auto ML. Figure 1.1 provides a broader view and the key areas of data science. Figure 1.2 outlines the body of knowledge a data science professional is expected to have.

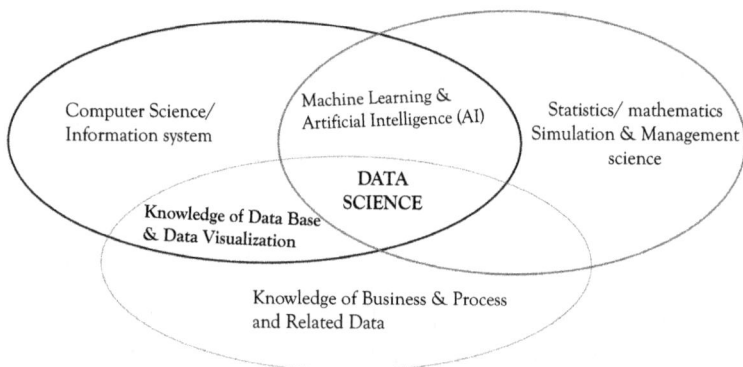

Figure 1.1 Broad view of data science with associated areas

There are a number of off-the-shelf data science software and platform in use. The use of these software requires significant knowledge and expertise. Without proper knowledge and background the off-the-shelf software may not be used relatively easily. (https://innoarchitech.com/blog/what-is-data-science-does-data-scientist-do)[23]

Some Technologies Used in Data Science

The following is a partial list of technologies used in solving data science problems. Note that the technologies are from different fields including statistics, data visualization, programming, machine learning, and big data.

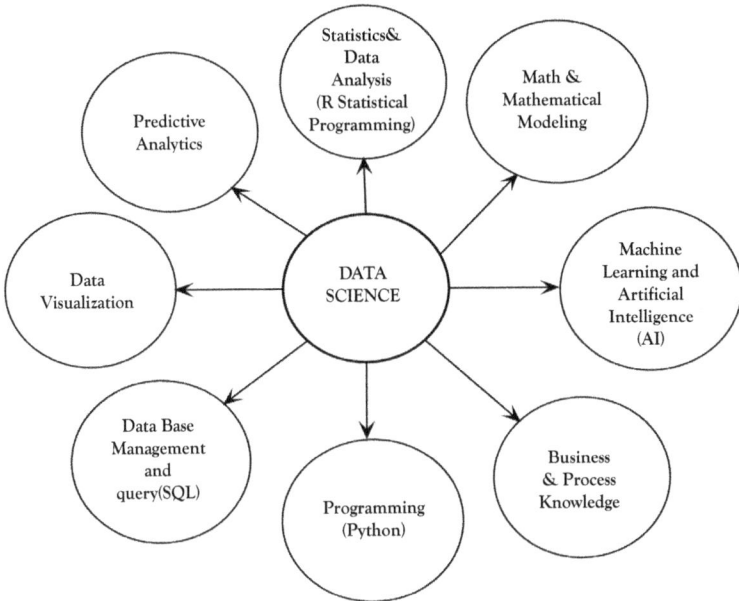

Figure 1.2 Data science body of knowledge

- Python is a programming language with simple syntax that is commonly used for data science.[34] There are a number of python libraries that are used in data science and machine learning applications including NumPy, pandas, Matplot, Scikit Learn, and others.
- R statistical analysis, a programming language that was designed for statistics and data mining[17,30] applications and is one of the popular application packages used by data scientists and analysts.
- TensorFlow is a framework for creating machine learning models developed by Google machine learning models and applications.
- Pytorch is another framework for machine learning developed by Facebook.
- Jupyter Notebook is an interactive web interface for Python that allows faster experimentation and is used in machine learning applications of data science.

- Tableau makes a variety of software that is used for data visualization.[32] It is a widely used software for big data applications and is used for descriptive analytics and data visualization.
- Apache Hadoop is a software framework that is used to process data over large distributed systems.

Career Path for Data Science Professional and Data Scientist

In order to pursue a carrier in data science, significant amount of education and experience is required. As evident from Figure 1.2, a data scientist requires knowledge and expertise from varied fields. The field of data science provides a unifying approach by combining varied areas ranging from statistics, mathematics, analytics, business intelligence, computer science, programming, and information systems. It is rare to find a data science professional with knowledge and background in all these areas. It is often the case that a data scientist has specialization in a subfield. The minimum education requirement for a data science professional is a bachelor's degree in mathematics, statistics, or computer science. A number of data scientists possess a master's or a PhD degree in data science with adequate experience in the field. The application of data science tools varies depending on the field it is applied to. Note that data science tools and applications when applied to engineering may be different from computer science or business. Therefore, successful application of tools of data science requires expertise and the knowledge of the process.

Future Outlook

Data science is a growing field. It continues to evolve as one of the most sought-after areas by companies. An excellent outlook is provided in reference[24]: *Davenport, T. H., and D.J. Patil (October 1, 2012). "Data Scientist: The Sexiest Job of the 21st Century". Harvard Business Review (October 2012). ISSN 0017-8012. Retrieved 3 April 2020.*

Data science is a growing field. It continues to evolve as one of the most sought-after areas by companies. An excellent outlook is provided in reference.[24]

A career in data science is ranked at the third best job in America for 2020 by Glassdoor, and was ranked the number one best job from 2016 to 2019.[29] Data scientists have a median salary of $118,370 per year or $56.91 per hour.[30] These are based on level of education and experience in the field. Job growth in this field is also above average, with a projected increase of 16 percent from 2018 to 2028.[30] The largest employer of data scientists in the United States is the federal government, employing 28 percent of the data science workforce.[30] Other large employers of data scientists are computer system design services, research and development laboratories, big technology companies, and colleges and universities. Typically, data scientists work full time, and some work more than 40 hours a week. See references[17,26,27] for the above paragraphs.

The outlook for data science field looks promising. It is estimated that 2 to 2.5 million jobs will be created in this area in the next ten years. The data science area is vast and requires the knowledge and training from different fields. It is one of the fastest growing areas. Data scientists can have a major positive impact on a business success.

Data science continues to evolve as one of the most promising and in-demand career paths for skilled professionals. Today, successful data professionals understand that they must advance past the traditional skills of analyzing large amounts of data, data mining, and programming skills. In order to uncover useful intelligence for their organizations, data scientists must master the full spectrum of the data science life cycle and possess a level of flexibility and understanding to maximize returns at each phase of the process.

Much of the data collected by companies underutilized. This data, through meaningful information extraction and discovery, can be used to make critical business decisions and drive significant business change. It can also be used to optimize customer success and subsequent acquisition, retention, and growth.

Business and research treat their data as an asset. The businesses, processes and companies are run using their data. The data and variables collected are highly dynamic and continuously change. Data science professionals are needed to process, analyze, and model the data, which is usually in the big data form to be able to visualize and help companies in making timely data-driven decision. "The data science professionals must be trained to understand, clean, process, and analyze the data to extract value from it. It is also important to be able to visualize the data using conventional and big data software in order to communicate data in a meaningful way. This will enable applying proper statistical, modeling, and programming techniques to be able to draw conclusions. All these require knowledge and skills from different areas and these are hugely important skills in the next decades," says Hal Varian, chief economist at Google and UC Berkeley professor of information sciences, business, and economics[3] The increase in demand for data science jobs is expected to grow by 28 percent by 2020 https://datascience.berkeley.edu/about/what-is-data-science/.

Summary

Data science is a data-driven decision-making approach that uses several different areas, methods, algorithms, models, and disciplines with a purpose of extracting insights and knowledge from structured and unstructured data. These insights are helpful in applying algorithms and models to make decisions. The models in data science are used in predictive analytics to predict future outcomes. Businesses collect massive amounts of data in different forms and by different means. With the continued advancement in technology and data science, it is now possible for businesses to store and process huge amounts of data in their data bases. At the core of data science is data. The field of data science is about using this data in creative and effective ways to help businesses in making data-driven business decisions.

Data science uses several disciplines and areas including, statistical modeling, data mining, big data, machine learning, and artificial intelligence (AI), management science, optimization techniques, and related methods in order to "understand and analyze actual phenomena" from data.[3]

Data science also employs techniques and methods from many other fields, such as mathematics, statistics, computer science, and information science. Besides the methods and theories drawn from several fields, data science uses visualization techniques using specially designed big data software and statistical programming language, such as R programming, and Python. Data science has wide applications in the areas of machine learning (ML) and artificial intelligence (AI). The chapter provided overview of data science by defining and outlining the tools and techniques and explained the differences and similarities between data science and data analytics. The other concepts related to data science including analytics, business analytics, and business intelligence (BI) were discussed. Data science continues to evolve as one of the most sought-after areas by companies. The chapter also outlined the career path and job-outlook for this area, which continues to be one of the highest of all field. The field is promising and is showing tremendous job growth.

CHAPTER 2

Data Science, Analytics, and Business Analytics (BA)

Chapter Highlights

- Data Science, Analytics, and Business Analytics
- Introduction to Business Analytics
- Analytics and Business Analytics
- Business Analytics and Its Importance in Data Science and in Decision Making
- Types of Business Analytics
  - Tools of Business Analytics
    1. Descriptive Analytics: Graphical and Numerical Methods in Business Analytics
       i. Tools of Descriptive Analytics
    2. Predictive Analytics
       i. Most Widely Used Predictive Analytics Models
       ii. Regression Models, Time Series Forecasting
       iii. Other Predictive Analytics Models
       iv. Recent Applications and Tools of Predictive Modeling
       v. Data Mining, Clustering, Classification Machine Learning, Neural Network, Deep Learning
    3. Prescriptive Analytics and Tools of Prescriptive Analytics
       i. Prescriptive analytics tools concerned with optimal allocation of resources in an organization.
- Applications and Implementation
- Summary and Application of Business Analytics (BA) Tools
- Analytical Models and Decision Making using Models
- Glossary of Terms Related to Analytics
- Summary

Data Science, Analytics, and Business Analytics

This chapter provides a comprehensive overview of the field of data science along with the tools and technologies used by data science professions. Data science is an emerging area in business decision making. From the past five years or so, it has been the fastest growing area with approximately 28 percent job growth. This is one of the most sought-after fields in demand and it is expected to grow in the coming years with one of the highest paying carriers in industry.

In Chapter 1, we provided a compressive overview and introduction of data science and discussed the broad areas of data science along with the body of knowledge for this area.

The field of data science is vast, and it requires the knowledge and expertise from diverse fields ranging from statistics, mathematics, data analysis, machine learning/artificial intelligence as well as computer programming and database management skills. One of the major areas of data science is analytics and business analytics. These terms are often used interchangeably with data science. Many analysts don't know the clear distinction between data science and analytics. In this chapter, we discuss the area of analytics and business analytics. We outline the differences between the two along with the explanation of different types of analytics and the tools used in each one. Data science is about extracting knowledge and useful information from the data and use different tools from different fields in order to draw conclusion(s) or make decisions. The decision-making process heavily makes use of analytics and business analytics tools. These are integral parts of data analysis. We therefore felt it necessary to explain and describe the role of analytics in data science.

Introduction to Business Analytics: What Is It?

This chapter provides an overview of analytics and business analytics (BA) as decision-making tools in businesses today. These terms are used interchangeably, but there are slight differences in the terms of tools and methods they use. Business analytics uses a number of tools and algorithms ranging from statistics and data analysis, management science, information systems, and computer science that are used in data-driven decision making in companies. This chapter discusses the broad meaning of the terms—analytics, business analytics, different types of analytics, the tools of analytics, and how they are used in business decision making. The companies now use massive amount of data referred to as *big data*. We discuss data mining and the techniques used in data mining to extract useful information from huge amounts of data. The emerging field of analytics and data science now use machine learning, artificial intelligence, neural networks, and deep learning techniques. These areas are becoming essential part of analytics and are extensively used in developing algorithms and models to draw conclusions from big data.

Analytics and Business Analytics

Analytics is the science of analysis—the processes by which we analyze data, draw conclusions, and make decisions.

Business analytics goes well beyond simply presenting data and creating visuals, crunching numbers, and computing statistics. The essence of analytics lies in the application—making sense from the data using prescribed methods of statistical analysis, mathematical and statistical models, and logic to draw meaningful conclusion from the data. It uses methods, logic, intelligence, algorithms, and models that enables us to reason, plan, organize, analyze, solve problems, understand, innovate, and make data-driven decisions including the decisions from dynamic real-time data.

Business analytics (BA) covers a vast area. It is a complex field that encompasses visualization, statistics and modeling, optimization, simulation-based modeling, and statistical analysis. It uses *descriptive*, *predictive*, and *prescriptive* analytics including text and speech analytics, web analytics, and other application-based analytics and much more.

Business analytics may be defined as the following:

Business analytics is a data-driven decision making approach that uses statistical and quantitative analysis, information technology, management science (mathematical modeling, simulation), along with data mining and fact-based data to measure past business performance to guide an organization in business planning and effective decision making.

Business analytics has three broad categories: (i) descriptive, (ii) predictive, and (iii) prescriptive analytics. Each type of analytics uses a number of tools that may overlap depending on the applications and problems being solved. The descriptive analytics tools are used to visualize and explore the patterns and trends in the data. Predictive analytics uses the information from descriptive analytics to model and predict future business outcomes with the help of regression, forecasting, and predictive modeling.

Successful companies use their data as an asset and use them for competitive advantage. Most businesses collect and analyze massive amounts of data referred to as *Big Data* using specially designed big data software and *data analytics*. Big data analysis is now becoming an integral part of business analytics. The organizations use business analytics as an organizational commitment to data-driven decision making. Business analytics helps businesses in making informed business decisions and in automating and optimizing business processes.

To understand business performance, business analytics makes extensive use of data and descriptive statistics, statistical analysis, mathematical and statistical modeling, and data mining to explore, investigate, draw conclusions, and predict and optimize business outcomes. Through data, business analytics helps to gain insight and drive business planning and decisions. The tools of business analytics focus on understanding business performance using data. It uses several models derived from statistics, management science, and operations research areas. Business analytics also uses statistical, mathematical, optimization, and quantitative tools for explanatory and predictive modeling.[15]

Predictive modeling uses different types of regression models to predict outcomes[1] and is synonymous with the field of data mining and machine learning. It is also referred to as predictive analytics. We will provide more details and tools of predictive analytics in subsequent sections.

Business Analytics and Its Importance in Data Science and in Decision Making

Business analytics helps to address, explore, and answer several questions that are critical in driving business decisions. It tries to answer the following questions:

- What is happening and why did something happen?
- Will it happen again?

- What will happen if we make changes to some of the inputs?
- What the data is telling us that we were not able to see before?

Business analytics (BA) uses statistical analysis and predictive modeling to establish trends, figuring out *why* things are happening, and making a prediction about how things will turn out in the future.

BA combines advanced statistical analysis and predictive modeling to give us an idea of what to expect so that one can anticipate developments or make changes now to improve outcomes.

Business analytics is more about anticipated future trends of the key performance indicators. This is about using the past data, models to learn from the existing data (descriptive analytics), and make predictions. It is different from reporting in business intelligence. Analytics models use the data with a view to draw out new, useful insights to improve business planning and boost future performance. Business analytics helps the company adapt to the changes and take advantage of future developments.

One of the major tools of analytics is *data mining*, which is a part of predictive analytics. In business, data mining is used to analyze huge amount of business data. Business transaction data along with other customer- and product-related data are continuously stored in the databases. The data mining software are used to analyze the vast amount of customer data to reveal hidden patterns, trends, and other customer behavior. Businesses use data mining to perform market analysis to identify and develop new products, analyze their supply chain, find the root cause of manufacturing problems, study the customer behavior for product promotion, improve sales by understanding the needs and requirements of their customer, prevent customer attrition, and acquire new customers. For example, Walmart collects and processes over 20 million point-of-sale transactions every day. These data are stored in a centralized database and are analyzed using data mining software to understand and determine customer behavior, needs, and requirements. The data are analyzed to determine sales trends and forecasts, develop marketing strategies, and predict customer-buying habits [http:// laits.utexas.edu/~anorman/BUS. FOR/course.mat/Alex/].

A large amount of data and information about products, companies, and individuals are available through Google, Facebook, Amazon, and several other sources. Data mining and analytics tools are used to extract meaningful information and pattern to learn customer behavior. Financial institutions analyze data of millions of customers to assess risk and customer behavior. Data mining techniques are also used widely in the areas of science and engineering, such as bioinformatics, genetics, medicine, education, and electrical power engineering.

Business analytics, data analytics, and advanced analytics are growing areas. They all come under the broad umbrella of *Business Intelligence (BI)*. There is going to be an increasing demand of professionals trained in these areas. Many of the tools of data analysis and statistics discussed here are prerequisite to understanding data mining and business analytics. We will describe the analytics tools including data analytics, and advanced analytics later in this chapter.

Types of Business Analytics

The business analytics area is divided into different categories depending upon the types of analytics and tools being used. The major categories of business analytics are:

- Descriptive analytics
- Predictive analytics
- Prescriptive analytics

Each of the above categories uses different tools and the use of these analytics depends on the type of business and the operations a company is involved in. For example, an organization may only use descriptive analytics tools, whereas another company may use a combination of descriptive and predictive modeling and analytics to predict future business performance to drive business decisions. Other companies may use prescriptive analytics to optimize business processes.

Tools of Business Analytics

The different types of analytics and the tools used are as follows:.

Descriptive Analytics: Graphical, Numerical Methods and Tools in Business Analytics

Descriptive analytics involves the use of descriptive statistics including the graphical and numerical methods to describe the data.

Descriptive analytics tools are used to understand the occurrence of certain business phenomenon or outcomes and explain these outcomes through graphical, quantitative, and numerical analysis. Through the visual and simple analysis, using the collected data we can visualize and explore what has been happening and the possible reasons for the occurrence of certain phenomenon. Many of the hidden patterns and features not apparent through mere examination of data can be exposed through graphical and numerical analysis. Descriptive analytics uses simple tools to uncover many of the problems quickly and easily. The results enable us question many of the outcomes so that corrective actions can be taken.

The successful use and implementation of descriptive analytics requires the understanding of types of data (structured vs. unstructured data), graphical/visual representation of data, and graphical techniques using specialized computer software capable of handling *big data*. Big data analysis is an integral part of business analytics. Businesses now collect and analyze massive amounts of data referred to as *big data*. Recently, interconnections of the devices in IoT (Internet of Things) generate huge amounts of data providing opportunities for big data applications. An overview of graphical and visual techniques is discussed in Chapter 3. The descriptive analytics tools include the commonly used graphs and charts along with some newly developed graphical tools such as bullet graphs, tree maps, and data dashboards. Dashboards are now becoming very popular with big data. They are used to display the multiple views of the business data graphically.

The other aspect of descriptive analytics is an understanding of numerical methods including the measures of central tendency, measures of position, measures of variation, measures of shape, and how different measures and statistics are used to draw conclusions and make decision from the data. Some other topics of interest are the understanding of empirical rule and the relationship between two variables—the covariance and correlation coefficient. The tools of descriptive analytics are helpful in understanding the data, identifying the trend or patterns in the data, and making sense from the data contained in the databases of companies. The understanding of databases, data warehouse, web search and query, and big data concepts are important for extracting and applying descriptive analytics tools. A number of statistical software are used for statistical analysis. Widely used software are SAS, MINITAB, and R programming language for statistical computing. Volume I of this book presents descriptive analytics that deals with a number of applications and a detailed case to explain and implement the applications.

Tools of Descriptive Analytics

Figure 2.1 outlines the tools and methods used in descriptive analytics. These tools are explained in subsequent chapters.

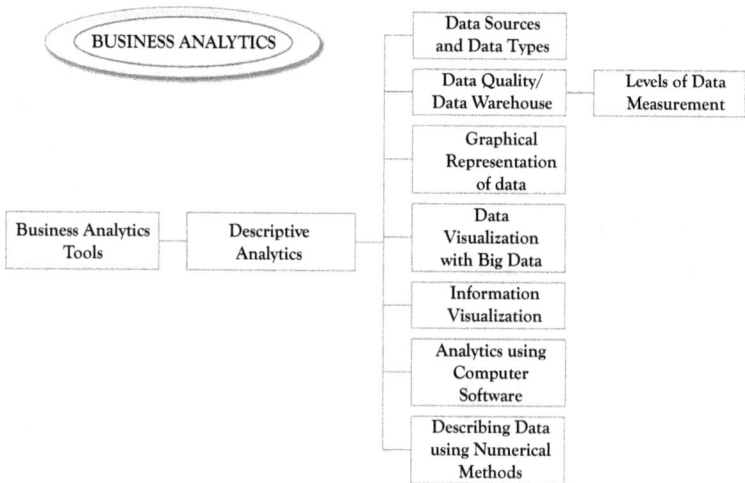

Figure 2.1 Tools of descriptive analytics

Predictive Analytics

As the name suggests, predictive analytics is the application of predictive models to predict future business outcomes and trends.

Most Widely Used Predictive Analytics Models

The most widely used predictive analytics models are regression, forecasting, and data mining techniques. These are briefly explained below.

Data mining techniques are used to extract useful information from huge amounts of data using predictive analytics, computer algorithms, software, mathematical, and statistical tools.

Regression models are used for predicting the future outcomes. Variations of regression models include: (a) simple regression models, (b) multiple regression models, (c) nonlinear regression models including the quadratic or second-order models, and polynomial regression models, (d) regression models with indicator or qualitative independent variables, and (e) regression models with interaction terms or interaction models. Regression models are one of the most widely used models in various types of applications. These models explain the relationship between a response variable and one or more independent variables. The relationship may be linear or curvilinear. The objective of these regression models is to predict the response variable using one or more independent variables or predictors.

Time series forecasting is widely used predictive models that involve a class of *time series analysis and forecasting models*. The commonly used forecasting models are regression-based models that uses regression analysis to forecast future trend. Other time series forecasting models are simple moving average, moving average with trend, exponential smoothing, exponential smoothing with trend, and forecasting seasonal data. All these predictive models are used to forecast the future trend. Figure 2.2 shows the widely used tools of predictive analytics.

Background and Prerequisites to Predictive Analytics Tools

Besides the tools described in Figure 2.2, an understanding of a number of other analytics tools is critical for describing and drawing meaningful conclusions from the data. These include: (a) probability theory, probability distributions and their role in decision making, (b) sampling and inference procedures, (c) estimation and confidence intervals, (d) hypothesis testing/inference procedures for one and two population parameters, and (e) analysis of variance (ANOVA) and experimental designs. The

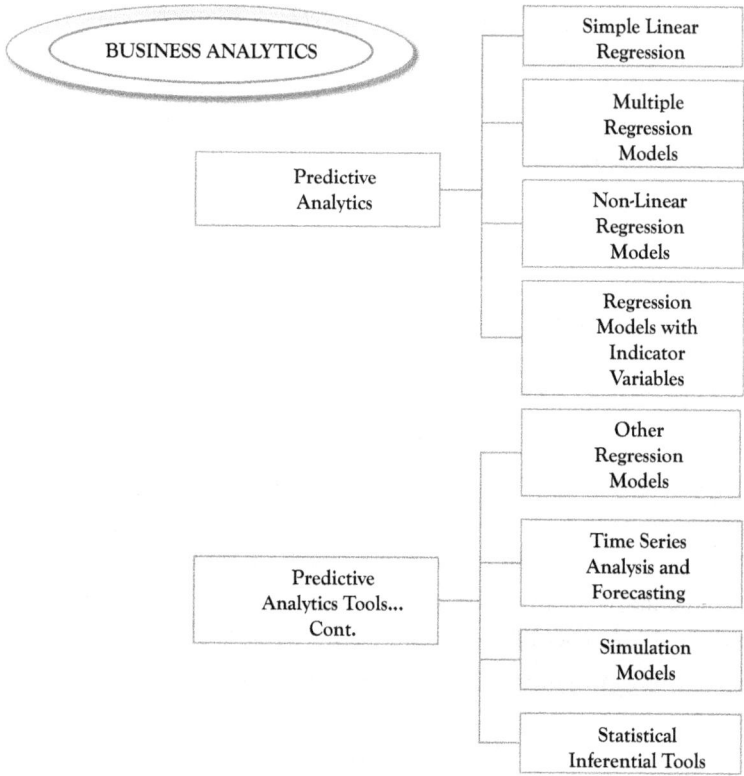

Figure 2.2 Tools of predictive analytics

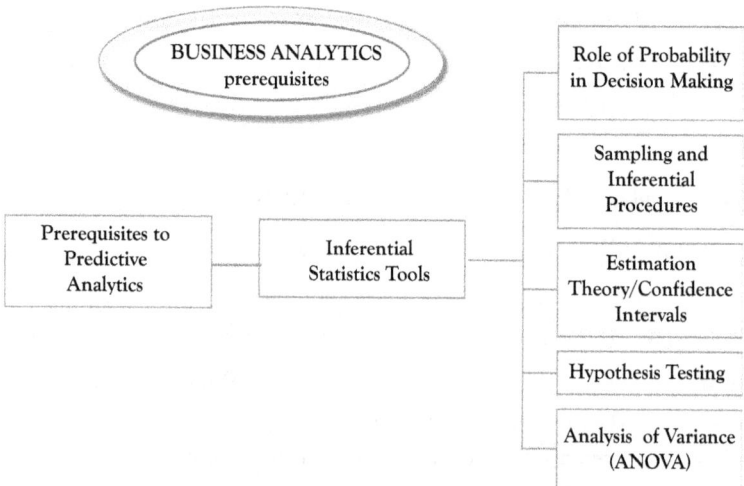

Figure 2.3 Prerequisite to predictive analytics

understanding of these tools is critical in understanding and applying inferential statistics tools in business analytics. They play an important role in data analysis and decision making. These tools are outlined in Figure 2.3.

Recent Applications and Tools of Predictive Analytics

Figure 2.4 outlines recent applications and tools of predictive analytics and modeling. The tools outlined in Figure 2.4 are briefly explained below. Extensive applications have emerged in recent years using these methods which are hot topics of research. A number of applications in business, engineering, manufacturing, medicine, signal processing, and computer engineering using machine learning, neural networks, and deep learning are being reported.

Prescriptive Analytics and Tools of Prescriptive Analytics

Prescriptive analytics tools are used to optimize business processes. It uses several different tools that depend on specific application area. Some of these tools are explained here.

Prescriptive analytics is concerned with optimal allocation of resources in an organization. Operations research and management science tools are applied for allocating the limited resources in the most effective way. The operations management tools that are derived from management science

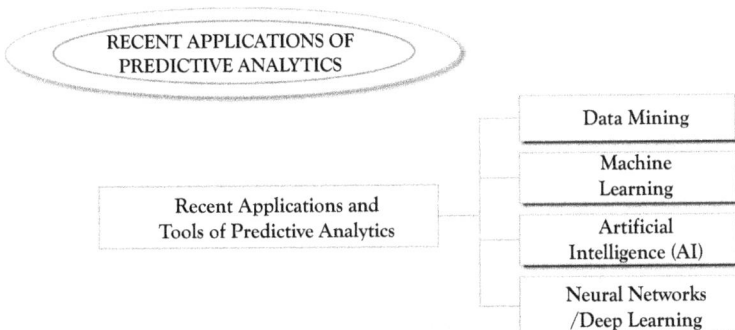

Figure 2.4 Recent applications and tools of predictive modeling

and industrial engineering including the simulation tools have also been used to study different types of manufacturing and service organizations. These are proven tools and techniques in studying and understanding the operations and processes of organizations. In addition, operations management has wide applications in analytics. The tools of operations management can be divided into three areas: (a) planning, (b) analysis, and (c) control tools. The analysis part is the prescriptive analysis part that uses the operations research, management science, and simulation. The control part is used to monitor and control the product and service quality. The prescriptive analytics models are shown in Figure 2.5.

Figure 2.6 outlines the tools of descriptive, predictive, and prescriptive analytics tools together.

This flowchart in Figure 2.6 is helpful in outlining the difference and details of the tools for each type of analytics. The flow chart shows the vast areas of business analytics (BA) that come under the umbrella of business intelligence (BI).

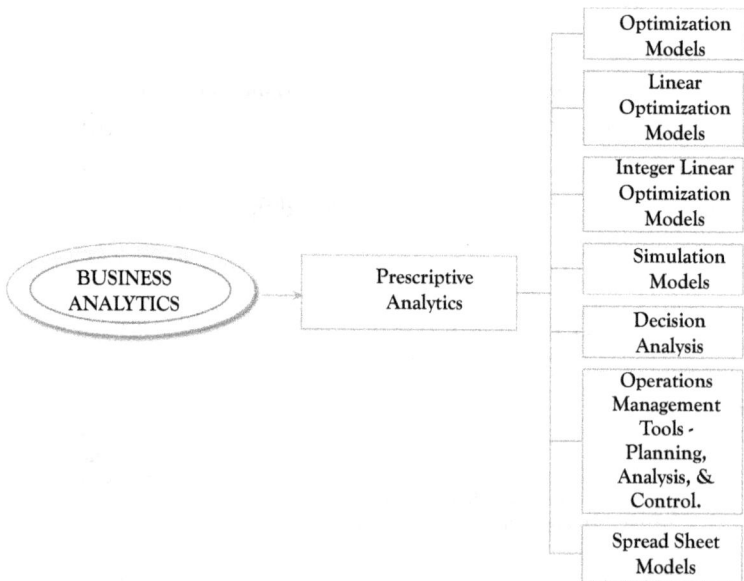

Figure 2.5 Prescriptive analytics tools

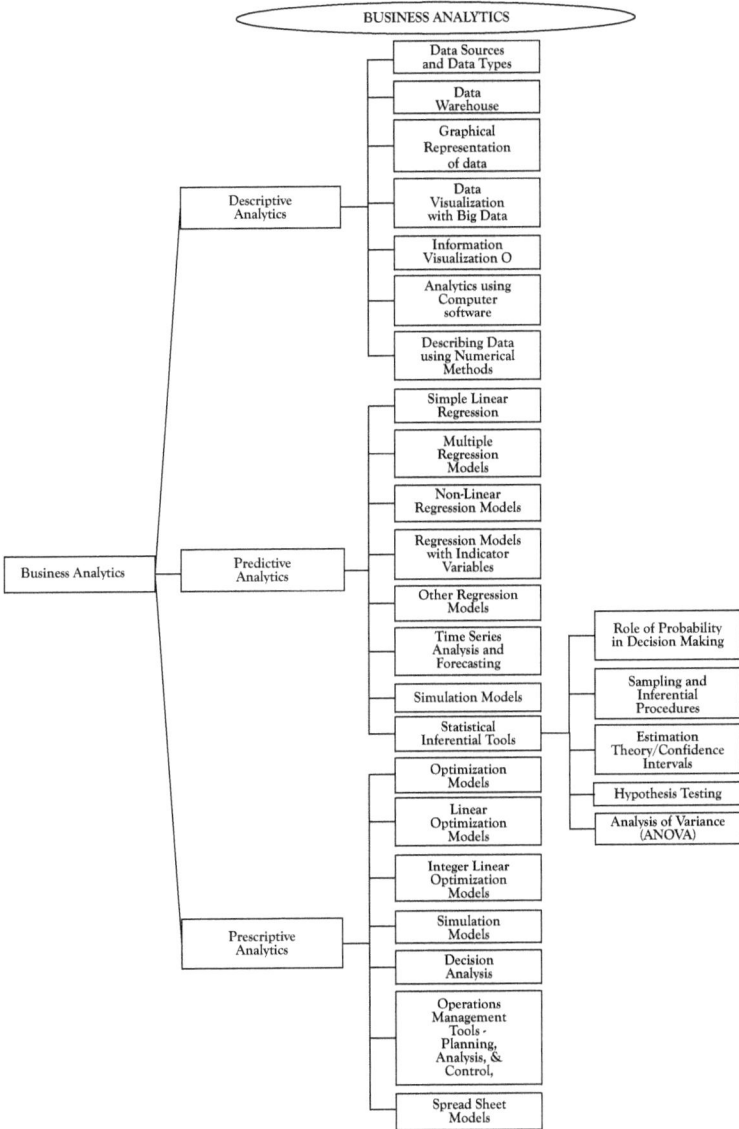

Figure 2.6 Descriptive, predictive, and prescriptive analytics tools

Applications and Implementation

Business analytics (BA) practice deals with extraction, exploration, and analysis of a company's information in order to make effective and timely decisions. The information to make decisions is contained in the data. The companies collect enormous amounts of data that must be processed and analyzed using appropriate means to draw meaningful conclusions.

Much of the analysis using data and information can be attributed to statistical analysis. In addition to the statistical tools, BA uses predictive modeling tools. Predictive modeling uses data mining techniques including anomaly or outlier detection, techniques of classification, and clustering, and different types of regression and forecasting models to predict future business outcomes. Another set of powerful tools in analytics is prescriptive modeling tools. These include optimization and simulation tools to optimize business processes.

While the major objective of business analytics is to empower companies to make data-driven decisions, it also helps companies to automate and optimize business processes and operations.

Summary and Application of Business Analytics (BA) Tools

Descriptive analytics tools use statistical, graphical, and numerical methods to understand the occurrence of certain business phenomenon. These simple tools of descriptive analytics are very helpful in explaining the vast amount of data collected by businesses. The quantitative, graphical, and visual tools along with simple numerical methods provide insights that are very helpful in data driven fact-based decisions.

Predictive modeling or predictive analytics tools are used to predict future business phenomenon. Predictive models have many applications in business. Some examples include the spam detection in messages and fraud detection. It has been used in outlier detection in the data that can point toward fraud detection. Other areas were predictive modeling tools have been used or being used are customer relationship management (CRM) and predicting customer behavior and buying patterns.

Other applications are in the areas of engineering, management, capacity planning, change management, disaster recovery, digital security management, and city planning. One of the major applications of predictive modeling is data mining. Data mining involves exploring new patterns and relationships from the data.

Data mining is a part of predictive analytics. It involves analyzing massive amount of data. In this age of technology, businesses collect and store massive amount of data at enormous speed every day. It has become increasingly important to process and analyze the huge amount of data to extract useful information and patterns hidden in the data. The overall goal of data mining is knowledge discovery from the data. Data mining involves (i) extracting previously unknown and potential useful knowledge or patterns from massive amount of data collected and stored, and (ii) exploring and analyzing these large quantities of data to discover meaningful pattern and transforming data into an understandable structure for further use. The field of data mining is rapidly growing, and statistics plays a major role in it. Data mining is also known as knowledge discovery in databases (KDD), pattern analysis, information harvesting, business intelligence, and business analytics. Besides statistics, data mining uses artificial intelligence, machine learning, database systems and advanced statistical tools, and pattern recognition.

- *Prescriptive analytics* tools have applications in optimizing and automating business processes. Prescriptive analytics is concerned with optimal allocation of resources in an organization. A number of operations research and management science tools are used for allocating limited resources in the most effective way. The common prescriptive analytics tools are linear and nonlinear optimization model including linear programming, integer programming, transportation, assignment, scheduling problems, 0–1 programming, simulation problems, and many others. Many of the operations management tools that are derived from management science and industrial engineering including the simulation tools are also part of prescriptive analytics.

Descriptive, Predictive, and Prescriptive Modeling

The predictive analytics is about predicting the future business outcomes. This chapter provides the background and the models used in predictive modeling with applications and cases. We have explained the distinction between descriptive, predictive, and prescriptive analytics. Prescriptive analytics is about optimizing certain business activities.

Summary

Business Analytics (BA) uses data, statistical analysis, mathematical and statistical modeling, data mining, and advanced analytics tools including forecasting and simulation to explore, investigate, and understand the business performance. Through data, business analytics helps to gain insight and drive business planning and decisions. The tools of business analytics focus on understanding business performance based on the data and a number of models derived from statistics, management science, and different types of analytics tools.

BA helps companies to make informed business decisions and can be used to automate and optimize business processes. Data-driven companies treat their data as a corporate asset and leverage it for competitive advantage. Successful business analytics depends on *data quality* and skilled analysts who understand the technologies. BA is an organizational commitment to data-driven decision making.

This chapter provided an overview of the field of business analytics. The tools of business analytics including the descriptive, predictive, and prescriptive analytics along with advanced analytics tools were discussed. The chapter also introduced a number of terms related to and used in conjunction with business analytics. Flow diagrams outlining the tools of each of the descriptive, predictive, and prescriptive analytics were presented. The decision-making tools in analytics are part of data science.

A detailed treatment of predictive analytics is provided in the book by this author. The book is titled *Business Analytics: A Data Driven Decision Making Approach for Business: Volume II*, published by Business Expert Press (BEP), New York, 2019.

[https://amazon.com/Business-Analytics-II-Decision-Approach/dp/1
631574795/ref=sr_1_2?dchild=1&keywords=Amar+Sahay&qid=
1615264190&sr=8-2]

Glossary of Terms Related to Analytics

Big Data

Big data is a collection of data sets so large and complex that it becomes
difficult to process using on-hand database management tools or traditional data processing application [Wikipedia]. Most businesses collect
and analyze massive amounts of data referred to as *big data* using specially
designed big data software and *data analytics*. Big data analysis is integral
part of business analytics.

Big Data Definition (*as per O'Reilly media*)

Big data is data that exceeds the processing capacity of conventional database systems. The data is too big, moves too fast, or doesn't fit the structures of your database architectures. To gain value from this data, you
must choose an alternative way to process it.

Gartner was credited with the 3 "V"s of Big Data. Gartner's Big Data
is high-volume, high-velocity, and/or high-variety information assets that
demand cost-effective, innovative forms of information processing that
enable enhanced insight, decision making, and process automation.

Gartner is referring to the size of data (large volume), speed with
which the data is being generated (velocity), and the different types of
data (variety) and this seemed to align with the combined definition of
Wikipedia and O'Reilly media.

Mike Gualtieri of Forrester said that the 3 "V"s mentioned by Gartner
are just measures of data. He insisted that following definition is more
actionable and can be seen as:

*Big Data is the frontier of a firm's ability to store, process, and access (SPA)
all the data it needs to operate effectively, make decisions, reduce risks, and
serve customers.*

Algorithm: A mathematical formula or statistical process used to analyze data.

Analytics: Involves drawing insights from the data including big data. Analytics uses simple to advanced tools depending upon the objectives. Analytics may involve visual display of data (charts and graphs), descriptive statistics, making predictions, forecasting future outcomes, or optimizing business processes. The more recent terms is *Big Data Analytics* that involves making inferences using very large sets of data. Thus, analytics can take different form depending on the objectives and the decisions to be made. They may be descriptive, predictive, or prescriptive analytics.

Descriptive Analytics: If you are using charts and graphs or time series plots to study the demand or the sales patters, or the trend for the stock market you are using descriptive analytics. Also, calculating statistics from the data such as the mean, variance, median, or percentiles are all examples of descriptive analytics. Some of the recent software are designed to create dashboards that are useful in analyzing business outcomes. The dashboards are examples of descriptive analytics. Of course, a lot more details can be created from the data by plotting and performing simple analyses.

Predictive Analytics: As the name suggests, predictive analytics is about predicting the future outcomes. It also involves forecasting demand, sales, and profits for a company. The commonly used techniques for predictive analytics are different types of regression and forecasting models. Some advanced techniques are data mining, machine learning, neural networks, and advanced statistical models. We will discuss the regression and forecasting techniques as well as the terms later in this book.

Prescriptive Analytics: Prescriptive analytics involves analyzing the results of the predictive analytics and "prescribes" the best category to target and minimize or maximize the objective(s). It builds on predictive analytics and often suggests the best course of action. leading to best possible solution. It is about optimizing (maximizing or minimizing) an objective function. The tools of prescriptive analytics are now used with big data to make data-driven decisions by selecting the best course of actions involving multicriteria decision variables. Some examples of prescriptive analytics models are linear and nonlinear optimization models, different types of simulations, and others.

Data Mining

Data mining involves finding meaningful patterns and deriving insights from large data sets. It is closely related to analytics. Data mining uses statistics, machine learning, and artificial intelligence techniques to derive meaningful patterns.

Analytical Models

The most used models that are parts of descriptive, predictive, or prescriptive analytics are graphical models, quantitative models, algebraic models, spreadsheet models, simulation models, process models, and other predictive and prescriptive models.

A major part of analytics is about solving problems using different types of models. The following are the most used models and are parts of descriptive, predictive, or prescriptive analytics models. Some of these models are listed below and will be discussed later.

Types of Models: (i) Graphical models, (ii) quantitative models, (iii) algebraic models, (iv) spreadsheet model, (v) simulation models, (vi) process modeling, and (vii) other predictive and prescriptive models.

IoT stands for Internet of Things or IOT. It means the interconnection of computing devices in embedded objects (sensors, cars, fridges etc.) via internet with capabilities of sending/receiving data. The devices in IOT generate huge amounts of data providing opportunities for big data applications and data analytics opportunities.

Machine learning: Machine learning is a method of designing systems that can learn, adjust, and improve based on the data fed to them. Machine learning works based on predictive and statistical algorithms that are provided to these machines. The algorithms are designed to learn and improve as more data flows through the system. Fraud detection, e-mail spam, GPS systems are some examples of machine learning applications.

R: R is a programming language for statistical computing. It is one of the popular languages in data science.

Structured versus Unstructured Data: refer to the "volume" and "variety"—the "V"s of big data. Structured data is the data that can be stored in the relational databases. This type of data can be analyzed and organized in such a way that can be related to other data via tables. Unstructured data cannot be directly put in the databases or analyzed or organized directly. Some examples are e-mail/text messages, social media posts, and recorded human speech.

CHAPTER 3

Business Analytics, Business Intelligence, and Their Relation to Data Science

Chapter Highlights

- Business Analytics (BA) and Business Intelligence (BI)
- Types of Business Analytics and Their Objectives
- Input to Business Analytics, Types of Business Analytics and Their Purpose
- Business Intelligence (BI) and Business Analytics (BA): Differences
- Business Intelligence and Business Analytics: A Comparison
- Summary

Business Analytics (BA), Business Intelligence (BI), and Data Science: Overview

The terms analytics, analytics and business intelligence (BI) are used interchangeably in the literature and are related to each other. *Analytics* is a more general term and is about analyzing the data using data visualization and statistical modeling to help companies make effective business decisions. The overall analytics process involves descriptive analytics involving processing and analyzing big data, applying statistical techniques (numerical methods of describing data, such as measures of central tendency, measures of variation, etc.), and statistical tools to describe the data. Analytics also uses predictive analytics methods, such as regression, forecasting, data mining, and prescriptive analytics tools of management science and operations research. All these tools help businesses in making informed business decisions. The analytics tools are also critical in automating and optimizing business processes.

The types of analytics are divided into different categories. According to the Institute of Operations Research and Management Science (INFORMS) (www.informs.org) the field of analytics is divided into three broad categories—descriptive, predictive, and prescriptive. We discussed each of the three categories along with the tools used in each one. The tools used in analytics may overlap and the use of one or the other type of analytics depends on the applications. A firm may use only the descriptive analytics tools or a combination of descriptive and predictive analytics depending upon the types of applications, analyses and decisions they encounter.

Data science, as a field, has much broader scope than analytics, business analytics, or business intelligence. It brings together and combines several disciplines and areas including statistics, data analysis, statistical modeling, data mining, big data, machine learning & artificial intelligence (AI), management science, optimization techniques, and related methods in order to "understand and analyze actual phenomena" from data. In this chapter, we describe business analytics, and business intelligence (BI). It can be seen that Data Science goes beyond these and uses and extracts knowledge from various other disciplines as described in Chapter 1.

Types of Business Analytics and Their Objectives

We described different types of analytics in previous chapter. The term *business analytics* involves modeling and analysis of business data. Business analytics is a powerful and complex field that incorporates wide application areas such as descriptive analytics including data visualization, statistical analysis, and modeling; predictive analytics, text and speech analytics, web analytics, decision processes; and prescriptive analytics including optimization models, simulation, and much more. Table 3.1 briefly describes the objectives of each of the analytics.

Table 3.1 Objective of each of the analytics

Type of Analytics	Objectives
Descriptive	Use graphical and numerical methods to describe the data. The tools of descriptive analytics are helpful in understanding the data, identifying the trend or pattern in the data, and making sense from the data contained in the databases of companies
Predictive	Predictive analytics is the application of predictive models that are used to predict future trends.
Prescriptive	Prescriptive analytics is concerned with optimal allocation of resources in an organization using a number of operations research, management science, and simulation tools.

Business Intelligence (BI) and Business Analytics: Purpose and Comparison

The flow chart in Figure 3.1 shows the overall business analytics process. It shows the inputs to the process that mainly consist of

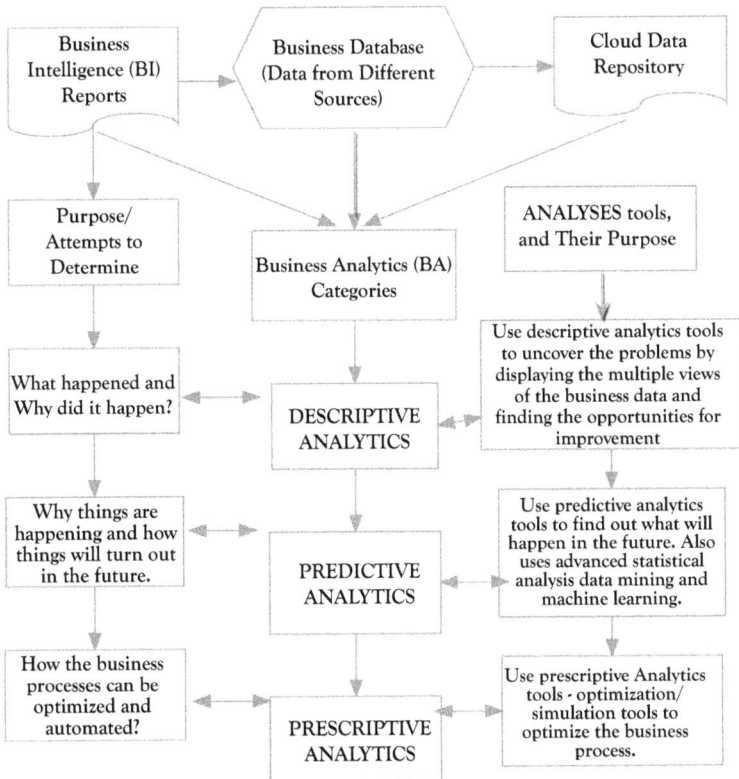

Figure 3.1 Input to the business analytics process, types of analytics, and description of tools in each type of analytics

business intelligence (BI) reports, business database, and Cloud data repository.

Figure 3.1 lists the purpose of each of the analytics—descriptive, predictive, and prescriptive. The problems they attempt to address are outlined below the top input row. For each type of business analytics, the analyses performed, and a brief description of the tools is also presented.

Tools and Objectives of Analytics

A summary of the tools of analytics with their objectives is listed in Tables 3.2, 3.3, and 3.4. The tables also outline the questions each of the analytics tries to answer.

Table 3.2 Descriptive analytics, questions they attempt to answer, and their tools

Analytics	Attempts to Answer	Tools
Descriptive	How can we understand the occurrence of certain business phenomenon or outcomes and explain: • Why did something happen? • Will it happen again? • What will happen if we make changes to some of the inputs? • What the data is telling us that we were not able to see before? • Using data, how can we visualize and explore what has been happening and the possible reasons for the occurrence of certain phenomenon.	• Concepts of data, types of data, data quality, measurement scales for data. • Data Visualization tools—graphs and charts along with some newly developed graphical tools such as bullet graphs, tree maps, and data dashboards. Dashboards are used to display the multiple views of the business data graphically. Big data visualization and analysis. • Descriptive statistics including the measures of central tendency, measures of position, measures of variation, and measures of shape. • Relationship between two variables—the covariance and correlation coefficient. • Other tools of descriptive analytics are helpful in understanding the data, identifying the trend or patterns in the data, and making sense from the data contained in the databases of companies. The understanding of databases, data warehouse, web search and query, and Big Data applications.

Table 3.3 Predictive analytics, questions they attempt to answer, and their tools

Analytics	Attempts to Answer	Tools
Predictive Analytics *Predictive Analytics*	• How the trends and patterns identified in the data can be used to predict the future business outcome(s)? • How can we identify appropriate prediction models? • How the models can be used in making prediction about how things will turn out in the future—what will happen in the future? • How can we predict the future trends of the key performance indicators using the past data and models and make predictions?	• Regression models including (a) simple regression models, (b) multiple regression models, (c) nonlinear regression models including the quadratic or second-order models, and polynomial regression models, (d) regression models with indicator or qualitative independent variables, and (e) regression models with interaction terms or interaction models. • Forecasting techniques. Widely used predictive models involve a class of *time series analysis and forecasting models*. The commonly used forecasting models are regression-based models that uses regression analysis to forecast future trend. Other time series forecasting models are simple moving average, moving average with trend, exponential smoothing, exponential smoothing with trend, and forecasting seasonal data. • Analysis of variance (ANOVA) and design of experimental techniques. • *Data mining* techniques—used to extract useful information from huge amounts of data known as knowledge discovery from data base (KDD) using predictive data mining algorithms, software, and mathematical and statistical tools. • *Prerequisite for Predictive Modeling:* (a) Probability and probability distributions and their role in decision making, (b) Sampling and inference procedures, (c) Estimation and confidence intervals, (d) hypothesis testing/inference procedures for one and two population parameters, and (e) chi-square and nonparametric Tests. • *Other tools of predictive analytics:* • Machine Learning, Artificial Intelligence, Neural Networks, Deep Learning (discussed later)

Table 3.4 Prescriptive analytics, questions they attempt to answer, and their tools

Analytics	Attempts To Answer	Tools
Prescriptive Analytics	• How can we optimally allocate resources in an organization? • How can the linear, nonlinear optimization, and simulation tools can be used for optimizing business processes and optimal allocation of resources?	A number of operations research and management science tools • Operations management tools derived from management science and industrial engineering including the simulation tools. • Linear and nonlinear optimization models • Linear programming, integer linear programming, simulation models, decision analysis models, spreadsheet models.

The three types of analytics are dependent and overlap in applications. The tools of analytics sometimes are used in combination. Figure 3.2 shows the interdependence of the tools used in analytics.

Tools used in Descriptive, Predictive, and Prescriptive Analytics

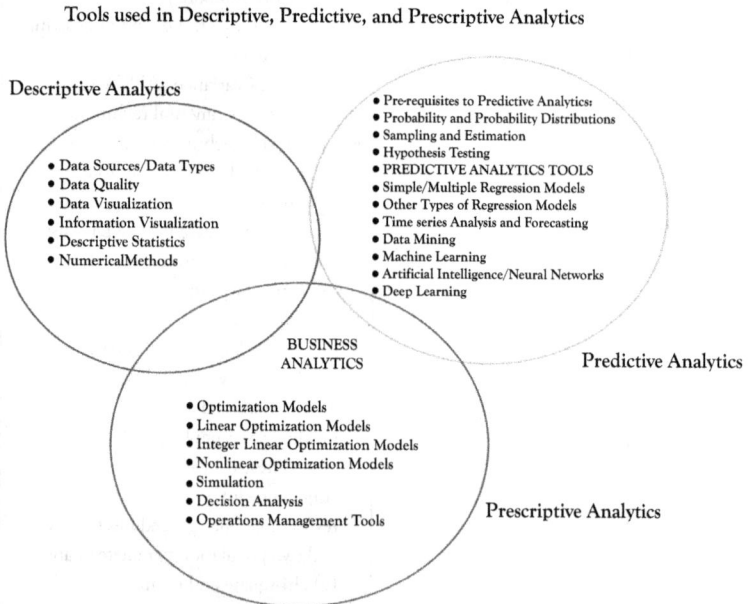

Descriptive Analytics

• Data Sources/Data Types
• Data Quality
• Data Visualization
• Information Visualization
• Descriptive Statistics
• NumericalMethods

• Pre-requisites to Predictive Analytics:
• Probability and Probability Distributions
• Sampling and Estimation
• Hypothesis Testing
• PREDICTIVE ANALYTICS TOOLS
• Simple/Multiple Regression Models
• Other Types of Regression Models
• Time series Analysis and Forecasting
• Data Mining
• Machine Learning
• Artificial Intelligence/Neural Networks
• Deep Learning

BUSINESS ANALYTICS

Predictive Analytics

• Optimization Models
• Linear Optimization Models
• Integer Linear Optimization Models
• Nonlinear Optimization Models
• Simulation
• Decision Analysis
• Operations Management Tools

Prescriptive Analytics

Figure 3.2 Interconnection between the tools of different types of analytics

Business Intelligence (BI) and Business Analytics (BA): Differences

Business intelligence and business analytics are sometimes used interchangeably, but there are alternate definitions. One definition contrasts the two, stating that the term "business intelligence" refers to collecting business data to find information primarily through asking questions, reporting, and online analytical processes (OLAP). Business analytics, on the other hand, uses statistical and quantitative tools and models for explanatory, predictive, and prescriptive modeling.[15]

BI programs can also incorporate forms of analytics, such as data mining, advanced predictive analytics, text mining, statistical analysis and big data analytics. In many cases, advanced analytics projects are conducted and managed by separate teams of data scientists, statisticians, predictive modelers, and other skilled analytics professionals, while BI teams oversee more straightforward querying and analysis of business data.

Thus, it can be argued that the business intelligence (BI) is the "descriptive" part of data analysis, whereas, business analytics (BA) means BI plus the predictive and prescriptive elements, and all the visualization tools and extra bits and pieces that make up the way we handle, interpret visualize, and analyze data. Figure 3.3 shows the broad area of BI that comprises business analytics, advanced analytics, and data analytics.

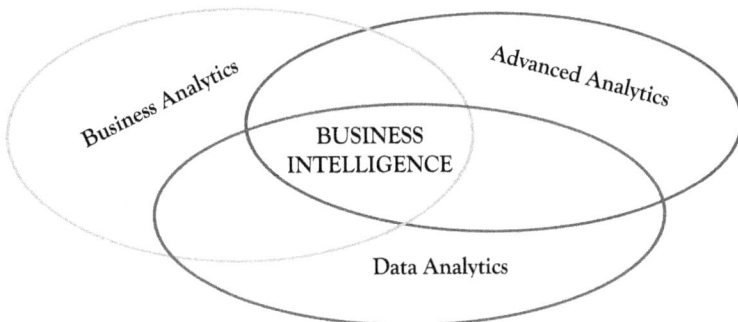

Figure 3.3 The broad area of business intelligence (BI)

Business Intelligence and Business Analytics:
A Comparison

The flow chart in Figure 3.4 compares the BI to business analytics (BA). The overall objectives and functions of a BI program are outlined. BI originated from reporting but later emerged as an overall business improvement process that provides the current state of the business. The information about what went wrong or what is happening in the business provides opportunities for improvement.

BI may be seen as the descriptive part of data analysis but when combined with other areas of analytics—predictive, advanced, and data analytics—provides a powerful combination of tools. These tools enable

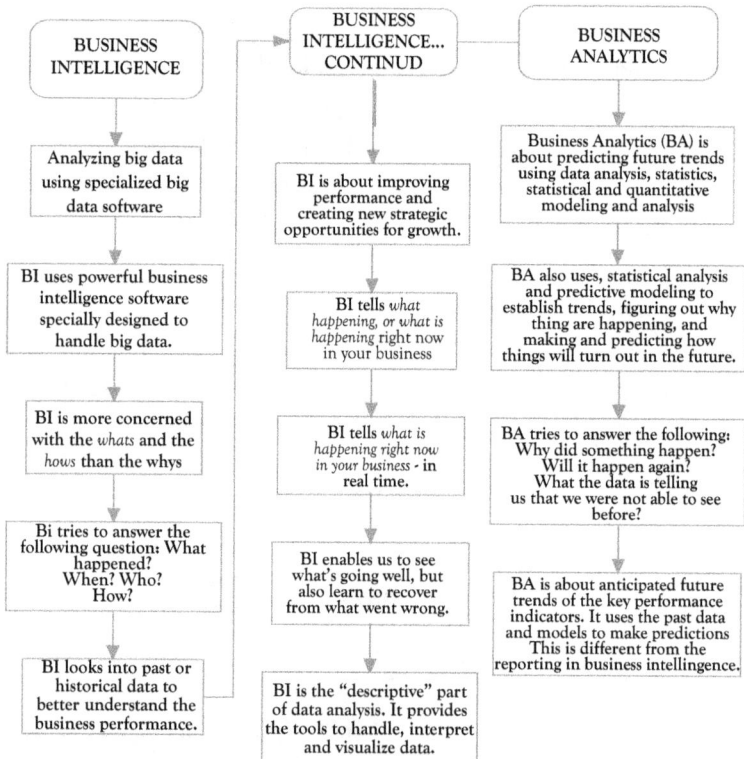

Figure 3.4 Comparing business intelligence (BI) and business analytics

BUSINESS ANALYTICS TOOLS

BUSINESS INTELLIGENCE TOOLS

DESCRIPTIVE ANALYTICS
• Data Visualization,
• Big Data Applications
• Describing data Numerically
PREDICTIVE ANALYTICS
Pre-requisite to Predictive Analytics:
• Probability and Probability Distributions
• Sampling and Estimation
• Hypothesis Testing
PREDICITVE ANALYTICS TOOLS
• Simple/Multiple Regression Models
• Other Types of Regression Models
• Time Series Analysis and Forecasting
• Data Mining
• Machine Learning
• Artificial Intelligence/Neural Networks
• Deep Learning
PRESCRIPTIVE ANALYTICS
• Linear and Non-linear Optimization Models
• Simulation models

• Querying, Reporting
• Online Analytical Processing (OLAP)
• Data Mining,
• Process Mining
• Business Performance Management
• Information Visualization
• Business Process Management
• Text mining

• All Descriptive, Predictive, and
  Prescriptive Analytics Tools

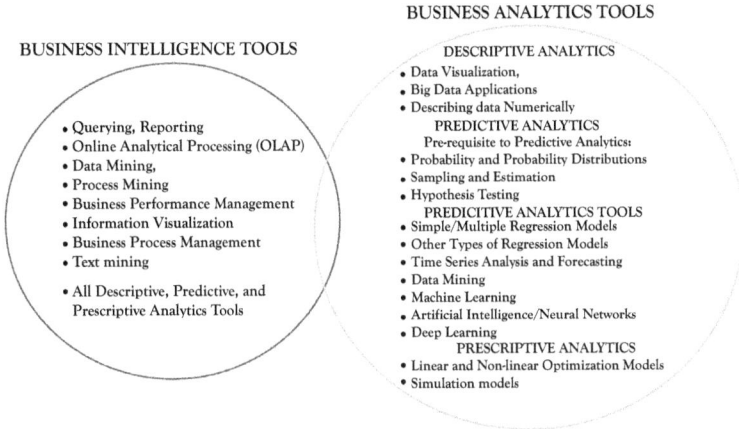

Figure 3.5 Business intelligence (BI) and business analytics (BA) tools

the analyst and data scientists to look into the business data, the current state of the business, and make use of predictive, prescriptive, data analytics tools as well as the powerful tools of data mining to guide an organization in business planning, predicting the future outcomes, and make effective data driven decisions.

The flow chart in Figure 3.4 also outlines the purpose of business analytics (BA) program and briefly mentions the tools and the objectives of BA. Different types of analytics and their tools were discussed earlier and are shown in Table 3.2.

The terms business analytics (BA) and business intelligence are used interchangeably and often the tools are combined and referred to as business analytics or business intelligence program. Figure 3.5 shows the tools of business intelligence and business analytics. Note that the tools overlap in the two areas. Some of these tools are common to both.

Summary

This chapter provided an overview of business analytics and business intelligence and outlined the similarities and differences between them. The business analytics, different types of analytics—descriptive, predictive, and prescriptive—and the overall analytics process were explained using a flow diagram. The input to the analytics process and the types of questions each analytics attempts to answer along with their tools were discussed in detail. The chapter also discussed business intelligence (BI) and a comparison between business analytics and business intelligence. Different tools used in each type of analytics and their relationship were described. The tools of analytics overlap in applications and in many cases a combination of these tools is used. The interconnection between different types of analytics tools were explained. Business analytics, data analytics, and advanced analytics fall under the broad area of business intelligence (BI). The broad scope of BI and the distinction between the BI and business analytics (BA) tools were outlined.

Data science, as a field, has much broader scope than analytics, business analytics, or business intelligence. It brings together and combines several disciplines and areas including statistics, data analysis, statistical modeling, data mining, big data, machine learning & artificial intelligence (AI), management science, optimization techniques, and related methods in order to "understand and analyze actual phenomena" from data.

PART II

Understanding Data and Data Analysis Applications

CHAPTER 4

Understanding Data, Data Types, and Data-Related Terms

Chapter Highlights

- Data and Data Analysis Concepts
- Making Sense from Data: Descriptive Statistics
    - A. Statistics and Data at a Glance: What You Need to Know
    - B. Current Developments in Data Analysis
- Preparing Data for Analysis
    - A. Data Cleansing and Data Transformation
    - B. Data Warehouse
- Data, Data Types, and Data Quality
- Data Types and Data Collection
    - A. Describing Data Using Levels of Measurement
    - B. Types of Measurement Scale
        - i. Nominal, Ordinal, Interval, and Ratio Scales
- Data Collection, Presentation, and Analysis
    - ○ How Data Are Collected: Sources of Data for Research and Analysis
    - A. Web as a Major Source of Data
- Analyzing Data Using Different Tools
- Data-Related Terms Applied to Analytics
    - ○ Big Data, Data Mining, Data Warehouse, Structured versus Unstructured Data, Data Quality

Making Sense From Data: Data and Data Analysis Concepts

Statistics and Data at a Glance

Statistics is the science and art of making decision using data. It is often called the science of data and is about analyzing and drawing meaningful conclusions from the data. Almost every field uses data and statistics to learn about systems and their processes. In fields such as business, research, health care, and engineering, a vast amount of raw data is collected and warehoused rapidly; this data must be analyzed to be meaningful. In this chapter, we will look at different types of data. It is important to note that data are not always numbers; they can be in form of pictures, voice or audio, and other categories. We will briefly explore how to make efficient decisions from data. Statistical tools will aid in gaining skills such as (i) collecting, describing, analyzing, and interpreting data for intelligent decision making, (ii) realizing that variation is an integral part of data, (iii) understanding the nature and pattern of variability of a phenomenon in the data, and (iv) being able to measure reliability of the population parameters from which the sample data are collected to draw valid inferences.

The applications of statistics can be found in a majority of issues that concern everyday life. Examples include surveys related to consumer opinions, marketing studies, and economic and political polls.

Current Developments in Data Analysis

Because of the advancement in technology, it is now possible to collect massive amounts of data. Lots of data, such as web data, e-commerce, purchase transactions at retail stores, and bank and credit card transaction data, among more, is collected and warehoused by businesses. There has been an increasing amount of pressure on businesses to provide high-quality products and services to improve their market share in this highly competitive market. Not only it is critical for businesses to meet and exceed customer needs and requirements, but it is also important for businesses to process and analyze a large amount of data efficiently in order to seek hidden patterns in the data. The processing and analysis of large data sets comes under the emerging field known as big data, data mining, and analytics.

To process these massive amounts of data, data analytics, and mining use statistical techniques and algorithms and extracts nontrivial, implicit, previously unknown, and potentially useful patterns. Because applications of data mining tools are growing, there will be more of a demand for professionals trained in data mining. The knowledge discovered from this data in order to make intelligent data-driven decisions is referred to as *business intelligence* and *business analytics*. Business intelligence (BI) is a hot topic in business and leadership circles today as it uses a set of techniques and processes which aid in fact-based decision making.

Preparing Data for Analysis

In statistical applications, data analysis may be viewed as the applications of descriptive statistics (descriptive analytics), data visualization, exploratory data analysis (EDA), and predictive and prescriptive analytics. Before data can be analyzed, data preparation is important. Since the data are collected and obtained from different sources, a number of steps are necessary to assure data quality. These include *data cleaning* or *data cleansing*, *data transformation*, *modeling*, *data warehousing*, and maintaining *data quality*. We provide an overview of these here.

Data cleansing or data cleaning is the process of detecting and correcting (or removing) corrupt or inaccurate records from a record set, table, or database and to identify incomplete, incorrect, inaccurate or irrelevant data and then replacing, modifying, or deleting the corrupt data.[1]

A scripting or script language is a programming language that supports scripts. Sometimes a script or scripting programs are used to automate or execute the tasks that could alternatively be executed one-by-one by a human operator. Scripting languages have applications in automating software applications, web pages in a web browser, operating systems (OS), embedded systems, and games. After cleansing, a data set should be consistent with other similar data sets in the system and suitable for further analysis (https://en.wikipedia.org/wiki/Data_cleansing).

Data transformation is the process of converting data from one format or structure into another format or structure. It is a fundamental aspect of most data integration and data management tasks such as *data warehousing** and *data integration* [https://en.wikipedia.org/wiki/Data_transformation].

Data warehouse: A data warehouse (DW or DWH), or enterprise data warehouse (EDW), is a system for storing, reporting, and analysis of huge amounts of data. The purpose of DW is creating reports and performing analytics which are core component of *business intelligence*. DWs are central repositories used to store and integrate current and historical data from one or many sources. Data are used for creating analytical and visual reports throughout the enterprise. The stored data in the warehouse are used for creating reports and performing analytics for the different operations and applications in an enterprise including sales, finance, marketing, engineering, and others. Before performing analyses on the data, cleansing, transformation, and data quality are critical issues.

It is also important to note that data may be both structured and unstructured. The distinction is explained here.

Structured versus unstructured data refer to the "volume" and "variety"—the "V"s of Big Data. Structured data is the data that can be stored in the relational databases. This type of data can be analyzed and organized in such a way that can be related to other data via tables. Unstructured data cannot be directly put in the databases or analyzed or organized directly. Some examples are e-mail/text messages, social media posts, and recorded human speech.

Data Types and Data Quality

In data analysis and analytics, data can be viewed as *information*. Data are also *measurements*. The purpose of data analysis is to make sense from data. Data when collected (in its raw form) is known as *raw data*. These are the data not processed.

In data analysis, data needs to be converted into a form suitable for reporting and analytics (http://searchdatamanagement.techtarget.com/definition/data). It is acceptable for data to be used as a singular subject or a plural subject. Data when collected is often referred to as raw data which is unprocessed data. Raw data is a term used to describe data in its most basic digital format.

Data Quality

Data quality is crucial to the reliability and success of business analytics (BA) and business intelligence (BI) programs. Both the analytics and business intelligence are data-driven programs. Analytics is about analyzing data to drive business decisions whereas, BI is about reporting.

Data quality is affected by the way data is collected, entered in the system, stored, and managed. Efficient and accurate storage (data warehouse), cleansing, and data transformation are critical for assuring data quality. The process of verifying the reliability and effectiveness of data is sometimes referred to as data quality assurance (DQA). The effectiveness, reliability, and success of business analytics (BA) and business intelligence (BI) depend on the acceptable data quality.

The following are important considerations in assuring data quality Aspects of data quality include (http://searchdatamanagement.techtarget.com/definition/data-quality):

(a) Accuracy
(b) completeness
(c) update status
(d) relevance
(e) Consistency across data sources
(f) reliability
(g) appropriate presentation
(h) Accessibility

Within an organization, acceptable data quality is crucial to operational and transactional processes. Maintaining data quality requires going through the data periodically and scrubbing it. Typically, this involves updating, standardizing, and de-duplicating records to create a single view of the data, even if it is stored in multiple disparate systems. There are many vendor applications on the market to make this job easier (http://searchdatamanagement.techtarget.com/definition/data-quality).

Much of the data analysis and statistical techniques discussed here are prerequisites to fully understanding data mining and business analytics. Besides statistics and data analysis, this book deals with several of the tools used in *data science*. Since statistics is at the core of data science and involves data analysis and modeling, we provide an introduction to statistics as a field before discussing applications.

Data and Classification of Data

Data are any number of related observations. We collect data to draw conclusions or to make decisions. Data often provide the *basis* for decision making.

A single data or observation is known as a *data point.* A collection of data is a *data set.* In statistics, reference to data means a collection of data or a data set.

Data can also be *qualitative* or *quantitative. Quantitative data* are numerical data that can be expressed in numbers. For example, data collected on temperature, sales and demand, length, height, and volume are all examples of quantitative data.

Qualitative data are data for which the measurement scale is categorical. Qualitative data are also known as *categorical data.* Examples of qualitative data include the color of your car, response to a yes/no question, or the product rating using a Likert scale of 1 to 5 where the numbers correspond to a category (excellent or good).

Data can also be classified as *time series data* or *cross-sectional data.* Time series data are the data recorded over time; for example, weekly sales, monthly demand for a product, or the number of orders received by an online shopping department of a department store.

Cross-sectional data are the values observed at the same point in time. For example, the closing value of the stock market on the 5th of each month for the past twelve months would be considered cross-sectional because all observations correspond to one point in time.

Statistical techniques are more suited to quantitative data. These techniques involve principles and methods used in collecting and analyzing data.

Data elements are the entities—the specific items—that we are collecting data about. For example, data collected on the stock price for the following companies (as of December 2, 2019):

Company	Stock price ($)
Amazon	1773.14
Pepsi	134.56
Microsoft	149.57
Google	1284.19
GE	12.21

Each company's stock price is an *element*. Thus, there are five elements in this data set.

Variable: In statistics, a variable can be thought of as an object upon which the data are collected. This object can be a person, entity, thing, or an event. The stock price of companies above is a *variable*. Note that stock values show variation. In case of stock prices for above companies, we can say that the stock price is a variable because the prices vary. If data are collected on daily temperature for a month, the temperature will show variation. Thus, the temperature is a *variable*. Similarly, data collected on sales, profit, the number of customers served by a bank, the diameter of a shaft produced by a manufacturing company, the number of housing starts; all show variation and therefore these are *variables*. Using statistics, we can study the variation. A variable is generally a characteristic of interest in the data. A data set may contain one or more variables of interest. For example, we showed the stock price of five companies in the above example. There is only one variable in the data: the stock price. If we also collected data on earnings and P/E (price to earnings) ratio of each company, we would have three variables.

Another Classification of Data

Data are also classified as discrete or continuous.

Discrete data are the result of a counting process. These are expressed as whole numbers or integers. Some examples of discrete data are cars sold by Toyota in the last quarter, the number of houses sold last year, or the number of defective parts produced by a company. All these are expressed in whole numbers and are examples of discrete data.

Continuous data can take any value within a given range. These are measured on a continuum or a scale that can be divided infinitely. More powerful statistical tools are available to deal with continuous data as compared to discrete data; therefore, continuous data are preferred wherever possible. Some examples of continuous data include measurements of length, height, diameter, temperature, stock value, sales, etc. Discrete and continuous data may also be referred as *discrete variable* and *continuous variables*.

Data Types and Data Collection

Data are often collected on a variable of interest. For example, we may collect data on the stock value of a particular technology stock, number of jobs created in a month, or diameters of a shaft manufactured by a manufacturing company. In all these cases, the data will vary, for example, the diameter measurement will vary from shaft to shaft. Data can also be collected using a survey where a questionnaire is designed for data collection purposes. The response in a survey generally varies from person to person. In other words, the response obtained is *random*.

In the data collection process, the response or the measurements may be *qualitative* or *quantitative, discrete* or *continuous*. If the data are quantitative, they can be either discrete or continuous. The quantitative data are also known as *numeric data*. Thus, the data can be classified as qualitative or quantitative data.

This classification of data is shown in Figure 4.1.

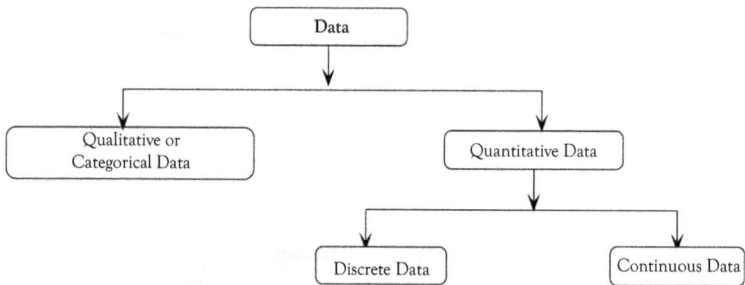

Figure 4.1 Classification of quantitative data

Describing Data Using Levels of Measurement

Data are also described according to the *levels of measurement* used. In the broadest sense, all collected data are *measured* in some form. Even the discrete quantitative data are nothing but *measurement through counting*. The type of data, and the way the data are measured, makes the weak or strong for analysis. The data measured at different levels and are classified into different measurement scales. These are discussed here.

Types of Measurement Scales

There are four levels or scales of measurements:

1. Nominal scale
2. Ordinal scale
3. Interval scale, and
4. Ratio scale.

The nominal is the weakest and ratio is the strongest form of measurement.

Nominal and Ordinal Scales

Data obtained from a qualitative variable are measured on a *nominal scale* or *ordinal scale*. If the observed data are classified into various distinct categories in which *no ordering* is implied, a *nominal level* of measurement is achieved. See the examples below.

Qualitative Variable Category

Marital status	Married/Single
Stock ownership	Yes/No
Political party affiliation	Democrat/Republican/Independent

If the observed data are classified into distinct categories in which ordering is implied, an *ordinal level* of measurement is obtained.

Qualitative variable Ordered categories

Student grades	A B C D F
Rank of employees	Senior engineer, Engineer, and Engineer trainee
Product quality	Excellent, good, poor (highest to lowest)

Nominal scale is the weakest form of measurement. Ordinal scale is also a weak form of measurement because no meaningful numerical statements can be made about the different categories. For example, the ordinal scale only tells which category is greater, but does not tell how much greater.

Interval and Ratio Scales

Interval Scale: These measurements are made on a quantitative scale. It is an ordered scale in which the difference between any two measurements is a meaningful quantity. For example, a person who is 70 inches tall is 2 inches taller than someone who is 68 inches tall. The difference of 2 inches would also be obtained if the heights of two persons were 78 and 76 inches. The difference has the same meaning anywhere on the scale. Some examples are:

- *Quantitative variable and levels of measurement*
  A. Temperature interval
  B. Time interval

Ratio scale: If in addition to the difference being meaningful and equal at all points on a scale, there is also a "true zero" point in which the ratio of measurements is sensible to consider, then the scale is a ratio scale. The measurements are made from the same reference point. For example, a measurement of 80 inches in length is twice as long as a measurement of 40 inches. Measurements of length are ratio scale. Examples of ratio scale are:

- *Quantitative variable: Level of measurements*
  o Height (in feet, inches) ratio
  o Weight (in pounds, or kilograms) ratio
  o Age (in years, days) ratio
  o Salary (in dollars) ratio

Data obtained from a quantitative variable are measured on an interval or a ratio scale. Ratio is the highest level of measurement. It tells which observed value is largest, and by how much. Figure 4.2 shows the classification of data according to the levels of measurements.

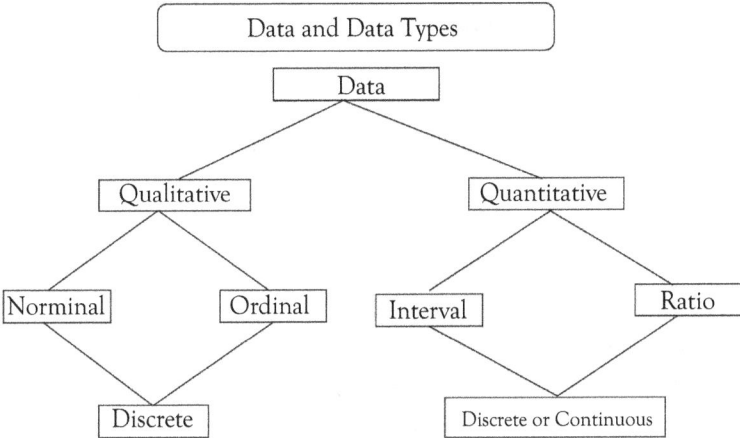

Figure 4.2 Classifications of data

Data Collection, Presentation, and Analysis

In this section we describe:

- How data are collected (obtained) and prepared for statistical analysis
- Tabular presentation of data
- Graphical presentation of data
- Analysis and interpretation of data

In statistical analysis, we always encounter situations where we need to draw conclusion from the data. Effective decision making requires information. For the statistician or researcher, the information needed to make effective decisions is in the data. For a statistical analysis to be useful, and to make an effective decision, the input data must be appropriate. If the data are insufficient, flawed, ambiguous, or have errors, even the most sophisticated statistical tools will not provide meaningful results.

How Data Are Collected: Sources of Data for Research and Analysis

Web as a Major Source of Data

Data can be obtained from industrial, individual, or government sources. The Internet is now one of the major sources of data. A number of websites can be accessed using search engines like Google to obtain data. There are several websites that collect data on employment, consumer price index, population, housing, and manufacturing. Law enforcement agencies collect data on crimes. A great deal of business and economic data can be obtained from the websites of Bureau of Economic Analysis (BEA), the Bureau of Labor Statistics (BLS), the U.S. Census Bureau, the Federal Reserve Economic Data (FRED), and the National Association of Manufacturers (NAM). Besides these, a vast amount of data on current issues, stock markets, economics, sports, and other areas of interest can be obtained from the websites of reputable publications including *USA Today*, *The Wall Street Journal*, the *Economist*, *New York Times*, to name a few.

Businesses collect massive amounts of data on a real-time basis and use big data software to perform analysis in real time. Imagine the volume of data collected and analyzed by Amazon, Walmart, banks, financial institutions, and online order services of businesses. The massive data collected are used for analysis and making quick decisions. The businesses are now run using data and major business decisions are data driven. The volume, variety, and speed with which data are now collected by different means are posing challenges in the storage, data preparation, data cleaning and analysis. To meet these challenging demand, different methods and software are being devised. The emergence of data science, data analytics, and business intelligence are the response to these challenges and needs. The techniques of machine learning and artificial intelligence that require large volumes of data are now becoming a necessity in this age of data. Data science and the different areas of data science are now one of the most sought-after skills in industries. We will explore several tools and technologies of data science in this book.

Some Other Sources of Data

- *Government agencies*: Government agencies, such as Bureau of Labor Statistics, collect data on travel, health care, economic measures, unemployment, interest rates, etc.

- *Experimental design*: An experiment is any process that generates data. Design of experiment involves changing the values of input variables and observing their effect on the output or response variable of interest. The process provides useful data that can be used to optimize or troubleshoot a system.
- *Telephone/mail surveys*: Data can be obtained using telephone or mail surveys. Telephone surveys are inexpensive and very commonly used data collection method. The drawback is that it may generate low response rate as people may refuse to take part in the survey. The data collection method using mail questionnaire usually has the lowest response rate.
- *Processes:* Data are also collected from processes including manufacturing and service systems and processes. Data may directly be obtained from the process or experiments may be designed to obtain the needed information.

Analyzing Data Using Different Tools

The data when collected are in usually referred to raw data. Raw data are the data that are not analyzed. There is always goal or objective behind collecting data. The raw data must be processed using different tools to make sense. The simple data analysis tools are the descriptive statistics that involves graphs and charts that provide visual representation of data. Among the data visualization tools, Excel is very widely used. The other simple set of techniques are the numerical methods. These methods consist of measures of central tendency, measures of position, measures of variation. In addition, covariance and coefficient of correlation are also simple but effective techniques of data analysis. Among other tools are the probability and probability distribution. The other set of tools widely used are the tools of inferential statistics. All these are discussed in subsequent chapters.

Data-Related Terms

Big Data: Big Data is a collection of data sets so large and complex that it becomes difficult to process using on-hand database management tools or traditional data processing application [Wikipedia].

As per O'Reilly media, big data is data that exceeds the processing capacity of conventional database systems. The data is too big, moves too fast, or doesn't fit the structures of your database architectures. To gain value from this data, you must choose an alternative way to process it. O'Reilly Media made Big Data popular.

Gartner who was credited with the 3 "V"s of Big Data classified the big data as *high-volume, high-velocity and/or high-variety information assets that demand cost-effective, innovative forms of information processing that enable enhanced insight, decision making, and process automation.*

Gartner is referring to the size of data (large volume), speed with which the data is being generated (velocity), and the different types of data (variety) and this seemed to align with the combined definition of Wikipedia and O'Reilly media.

According to Mike Gualtieri of Forrester, the three "V"s mentioned by Gartner are just measures of data. Mike insisted that Forrester's definition is more actionable. And that definition is: *Big Data is the frontier of a firm's ability to store, process, and access (SPA) all the data it needs to operate effectively, make decisions, reduce risks, and serve customers.*

Data mining: Data mining is about finding meaningful patterns and deriving insights in large sets of data using sophisticated pattern recognition techniques. It is closely related to Analytics that we discussed earlier. In data mining you mine the data to get analytics. To derive meaningful patterns, data miners use statistics and statistical modeling, machine learning algorithms, and artificial intelligence.

Data warehouse: A data warehouse (DW or DWH), or enterprise data warehouse (EDW), is a system for storing, reporting, and analysis of huge amounts of data. The purpose of DW is creating reports and performing analytics which are core component of *business intelligence*. DWs are central repositories used to store and integrate current and historical data from one or many sources. The data are readily available and are used for creating analytical and visual reports throughout the enterprise. The data stored in the warehouse may be used for creating reports and performing analytics for the different operations in an enterprise including, sales, finance, marketing, engineering, and others. Before performing analyses on the data; cleansing, transformation, and data quality are critical issues.

Structured versus Unstructured Data: are the "volume" and "variety"— the "V"s of big data. Structured data is the data that can be stored in the relational databases. This type of data can be analyzed and organized in such a way that can be related to other data via tables. Unstructured data cannot be directly put in the databases or analyzed or organized directly. Some examples are e-mail/text messages, social media posts and recorded human speech etc.

Data quality: Data quality is affected by the way data is collected, entered in the system, stored, and managed. Efficient and accurate storage (data warehouse), cleansing, and data transformation are critical for assuring data quality. The process of verifying the reliability and effectiveness of data is sometimes referred to as data quality assurance (DQA). The effectiveness, reliability, and success of business analytics (BA) and business intelligence (BI) depend on the acceptable data quality.

The following are important considerations in assuring data quality. Aspects of data quality includehttp://searchdatamanagement.techtarget.com/definition/data-quality):

(a) Accuracy

(b) Completeness

(c) Update status

(d) Relevance

(e) Consistency across data source

(f) Reliability

(g) Appropriate presentation

(h) Accessibility

Within an organization, acceptable data quality is crucial to operational and transactional processes.

Summary

Data science is about the study of data. Data are of various types and are collected using different means. Data are not only numbers but are classified as text data or qualitative or categorical data and also numerical or quantitative data. This chapter explained the types of data and their classification with examples. Data can also be collected through audio and video devices. Companies collect massive amounts of data. The volume of data collected and analyzed by businesses is so large that it is referred to as "Big Data." The volume, variety, and the speed (velocity) with which data are collected requires specialized tools and techniques including specially designed big data software for analysis. In many cases, the data must be analyzed in real time to make effective business decision. Data Science and associated analytical tools are being designed to meet these challenges.

CHAPTER 5

Data Analysis Tools for Data Science and Analytics: Data Analysis Using Excel

Chapter Highlights

- Introduction
- Getting Started with Excel
- Format Data as a Table, Filter and Sort, Perform Simple Calculations
  - ○ Data Manipulation
  - ○ Sorting and Filtering Data
  - ○ Derived Data
  - ○ Highlighting Data
  - ○ Aggregating Data: Count, Total Sum
  - ○ Basic Calculation using Excel
- Analyzing Data using Pivot Table/Pivot Chart
- Descriptive Statistics using Excel
- Visualizing Data using Excel Charts and Graphs
- Visualizing Categorical Data: Bar Charts, Pie Charts, Cross Tabulation
- Exploring the Relationship between Two and Three Variables: Scatter Plot Bubble Graph and Time-Series Plot

Introduction

In real world, companies use software programs to analyze data. Several excellent computer programs and software are available for this purpose. In this chapter we introduce Excel, a widely available and used software for data analysis. This software is mainly a spreadsheet program but also includes data manipulation, analysis, and visualization tools. There are several packages available as add-ins to this software to enhance its capabilities. The chapter presents the basic features of Excel as well as more involved features and capabilities. The chapter is divided into sections including "Getting Stated with Excel" followed by several applications. The examples provide downloadable data files and stepwise instructions.

Getting Started With Excel: Office 365

Excel Office 365 displays most of commands needed for a task at the top of Excel window. Opening Excel will show the basic features of Excel window are described below.

A brief description of buttons and tabs are as follows.

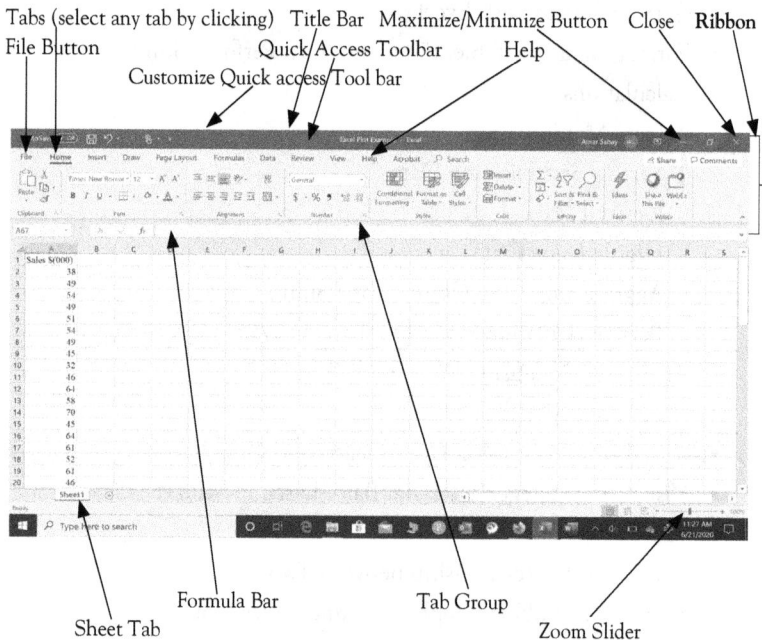

File Button: Clicking on this tab displays a drop-down menu with commonly used command: Open, Save, Print, Save as.

Tabs: Clicking on a tab the features, commands, and options related to a particular task to be performed. The figure above shows the home screen in excel. It shows the features, commands and options displayed. You should experiment with the Tabs to see the features, commands, and options related to the tab. For example, clicking the **Insert tab** will display tab groups like **Tables**, **Add-ins**, **Charts** with various options. This tab is used to create charts of various types. Similarly, other tabs provide different options.

Quick Access Toolbar: Provides commonly used commands. When Excel is launched, this toolbar shows Save, **Undo**, and **Redo** buttons. The toolbar can be customized by adding the shortcut buttons to other commands, for example, Open, print, and other buttons commonly used by the user. This can be done by clicking on the down arrow button on the right of quick access tool bar.

Title Bar: Shows the active Workbook. On the left of the title bar is the quick access toolbar and to the right is the maximize, minimize, and close buttons.

Help button: This tab includes help topics along with online help with search capability. To use the Help topics, click **Help** and then click on "Question Mark" from the screen that follows. On the left pane a search box will appear. Type the topic you need help with.

Ribbon: The ribbon displays a group of toolbars, tabs, commands, and features for performing a task or tasks. A task or feature on the ribbon is selected by selecting a tab. Initially the ribbon shows several features. The number of features on the ribbon can be minimized or customized by right clicking on the ribbon and selecting—Collapse or Customize the ribbon.

Sheet tabs show the name of each sheet in a workbook. Clicking on a particular sheet makes it active. The name of a sheet can be changed by double clicking on a sheet tab and entering a new name.

Formula bar: Clicking on any cell of the worksheet shows the content of that cell in the formula bar. If a cell contains a formula, such as Average, or Median, or any other function, that formula is displayed on the formula bar. The formula on the formula bar can be edited or modified to correct the error or change a formula.

Tab Group: This labeled on the Excel Workbook figure above. This contains a group of commands and features to perform a task.

Zoom slider: Moving the slider to the left or right results into expanding or reducing the size of the content in a workbook.

Once you are familiar with basic features of Excel and understand the task bar, tabs, ribbon, and other common features, you should be able to navigate through the program and perform many tasks and create applications. We assume that you are familiar with some common features, common to all windows program, such as opening an Excel workbook, entering data, saving, and printing your work, and so on.

An Example to Demonstrate the Basic Functions of Excel

Open Excel by clicking the Excel icon on your desktop or from the list of programs in your computer.

Entering Data

1. Click on cell *A1* of the workbook and type a label—Sales $(000). This is the name of the variable—sales in thousands of dollars. Note that Excel allows one variable per column.
2. Type the sales data from *Table 5.1 in column A*. You may read the data in any order (row-wise or column-wise), one value per cell but you must enter all the data in one column, A. The workbook in Figure 5.1 shows part of the data entered from Table 5.1. Enter all the values from Table 5.1 into *column A* of the Excel workbook.

Once the data is entered, we will create a simple time series plot to demonstrate the basic functions and a simple application of Excel.

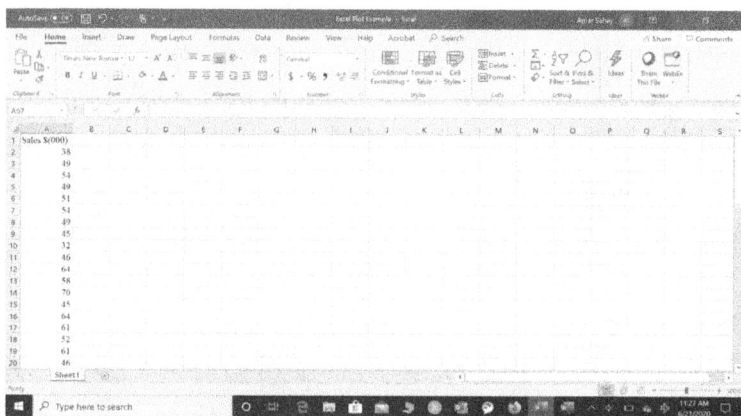

Figure 5.1 Excel workbook

Table 5.1 *Monthly sales of a company*

Sales $(000)								
38	49	54	49	51	54	49	45	32
46	6	58	70	45	64	61	52	61
46	54	63	61	49	57	54	69	67
56	75	67	57	64	80	75	70	70
67	57	86	70	69	79	82	98	77
86	73	73	79	66	81	66	67	79
85	86	73	93	85	77	82	82	80
87	77							

3. **Saving your data**. When all the data from Table 5.1 is entered, save your workbook by giving it a file name. To save your work:

   - Click on File tab or button and select "*Save as.*"
   - Select "Browse" from the options to save your file to the destination folder or the desktop. We selected "Desktop" to save the file.
   - Enter the desired File name in the window. We named the file "*Excel Example.*" Select Excel Workbook for "*Save as type.*"
   - Click the "Save" button in the "Save as" dialog box. Your file will be saved as **Excel Example** file.

4. **Retrieving a saved file**. To open a saved Excel Workbook, you can locate the file and click on the file icon or you can open excel and then use the command sequence

   File → Open → Browse then locate the file and click open.

5. **Creating a Time Series Plot of Sales data.** If the saved file "Excel Example" is not open, open this file. The sales data should be saved in column A of the workbook.

   - Select the range of data including the label. Click on cell A1 and drag your mouse pointer to the last value in column A. You can also select the data by typing the range, (A1:A67).
   - Select **Insert** → **Recommended Charts**. (Click on **Insert** from the main menu then select **Recommended Charts**).

- Selecting this option will display several charts for this data. The first one is a scatter plot with connected line. This is also a time series plot where the time scale is shown on the *x*-axis.
- Click on the first graph to select it. The graph with (Chart tools) or chart edits tools on the top right- hand corner will be displayed. See Figure 5.2.
- Click on Chat elements to provide a suitable chart and axis titles (the Chart title and axes title) and so on.
- Next, click on the Chart Styles and select the chart style you desire.

The edited chart will be like the one shown in Figure 5.3.

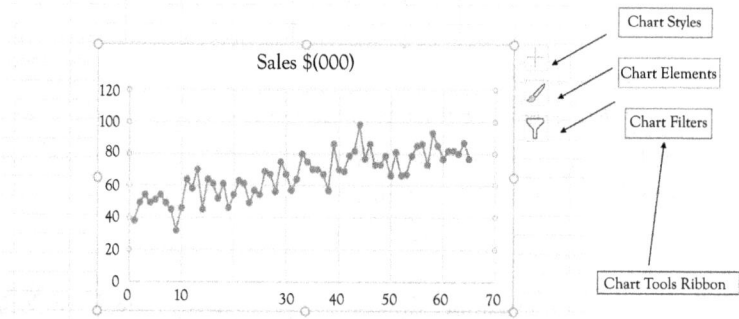

Figure 5.2 Time-series plot with chart tools

Figure 5.3 Edited time series plot from Figure 5.2

Alternate Way of Creating a Time Series Plot

The *Recommended Charts* option is a default option and is suggested by the program. To create a customize chart, follow the steps:

- Select the range of the data including the label. Click on cell A1 and drag your mouse pointer to the last value in column A.
- Once the data is selected, use the command sequence:
  Insert → Line Chart →: 2-D Line: Line with Markers
- When the above command sequence is executed, a gallery of line charts will be displayed below the menu bar and the *Design* tab on the main menu will be active. If the charts are not displayed, click on the Design tab on the main menu bar. From the gallery of charts, select the chart you desire.
- After selecting the chart, click on the chart anywhere to display the chart edit tools. Edit your chart to provide the chart title, axis title. The edited chart is shown in Figure 5.4.

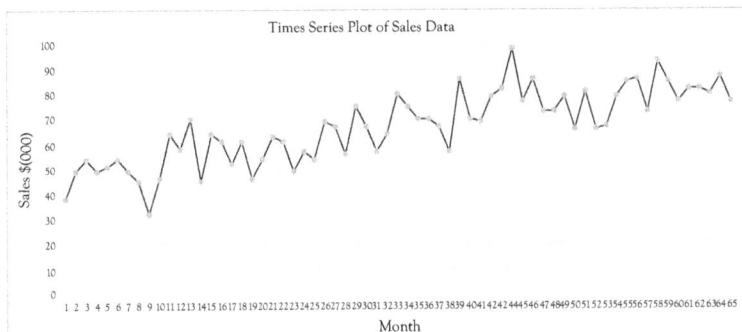

Figure 5.4 Alternate time series plot

Note: You can also edit the chart by moving the chart to a new worksheet called a chart sheet. To do this, click on the chart that you created to make it active. Then click on the *Design* tab on the main menu and select *Move Chart* as shown in the Figure 5.5a. Complete the Move Chart dialog box as shown in the figure then click *Ok*.

The chart will be moved to a new sheet called Chart Sheet with the chart edit tools ribbon. You can edit the chart using the Chart Elements

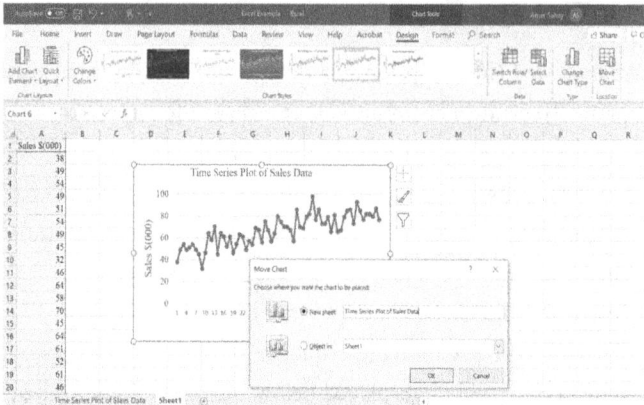

Figure 5.5a Move chart dialog box

tab (Figure 5.5b) to provide appropriate chart and axis titles and use the Chart Elements tab to select the design you prefer.

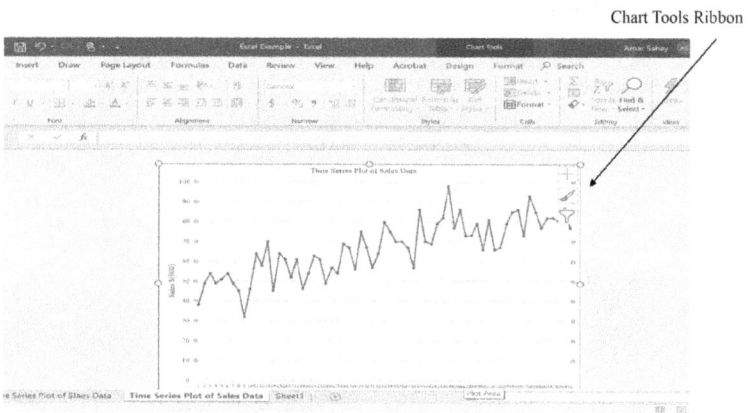

Figure 5.5b Plot with chart elements tab

Your edited chart will be like the one shown in Figure 5.6.

Alternate Ways of Editing a Chart

Once the chart is created, you can edit the portion of a chart. For example, you can right click on any of the points in the chart to show a menu box with several options. Select *Format Data Series*. This will provide many options to edit the plotted points and connected lines.

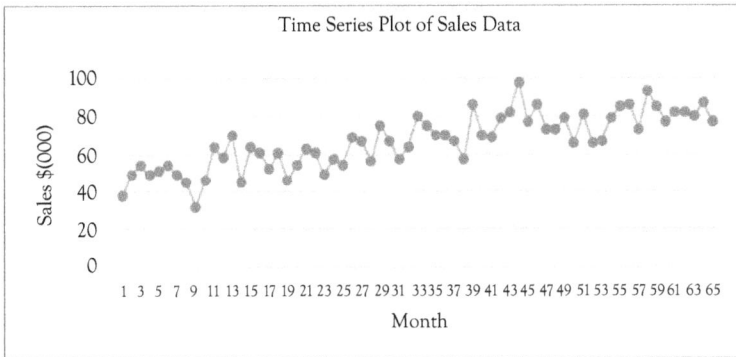

Figure 5.6 Edited chart with elements tab

Printing Your Graph

There are many options available to print the graph you created. One simple way to print the graph from the worksheet is by using the following command sequence:

File → Print

Select the printer, provide the print properties you desire and print your graph.

Printing Your Graph with the Worksheet Data

Figure 5.7 shows the worksheet content (data) and the graph next to it. To print the graph with spreadsheet, click outside the graph then follow the command sequence:

File → Print

Select the printer and edit the print properties you desire and print your graph.

Moving Your Charts and Table to a Word File

You can highlight the content (data and table) and the graph, copy them then paste to a word file if you want to include the tables and graphs to reports.

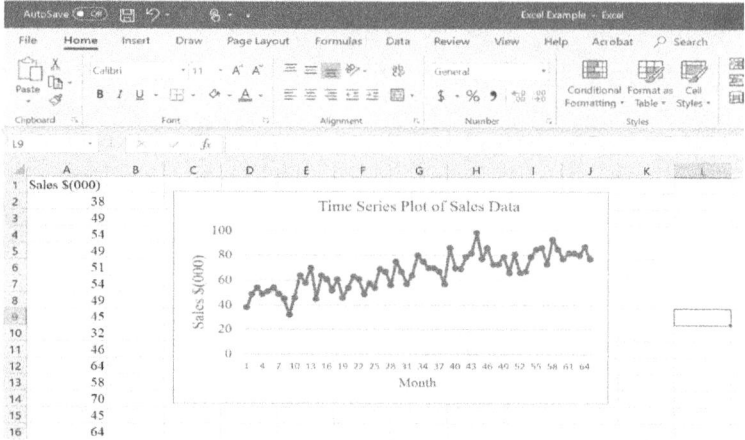

Figure 5.7 Edited chart with data

Format Data as a Table, Filter and Sort, Perform Simple Calculations

Open the Workbook or Data File. **Sales and Ad Data (ORIGINAL)**.

1. Click the *Sales and Ad Data (ORIGINAL).xlsx* file in your data file folder to open it in Excel. When opened, it should look like this (*note*: only a part of the file is shown here).

Day	Month	Advertisement $(000)	Sales $(000)	Profit ($000)	Revenue $(000)	Region
Mon	January	45	114	100	125	North
Tues	January	45	135	114	142.5	North
Sat	July	45	126	112	140	South
Fri	June	47.7	120	106	132.5	North
Sat	July	47.7	129	110	137.5	South
Fri	June	48.6	135	130	162.5	North
Sat	July	48.6	135	132	165	South
Tues	January	49.5	132	106	132.5	North
Thurs	June	49.5	135	136	170	North
Thurs	June	51.3	144	144	180	North
Tues	February	52.2	135	116	145	North
Thurs	June	52.2	129	120	150	North
Sun	November	54	163.8	162.4	182	North
Fri	June	56.7	156	138	172.5	North
Sat	July	56.7	198	174	217.5	South
Sat	October	57.24	156	153.7	172.25	MidWest
Sun	November	57.24	167.7	159.5	178.75	North
Sun	November	58.32	175.5	188.5	211.25	MidWest
Mon	November	58.32	175.5	191.4	214.5	North

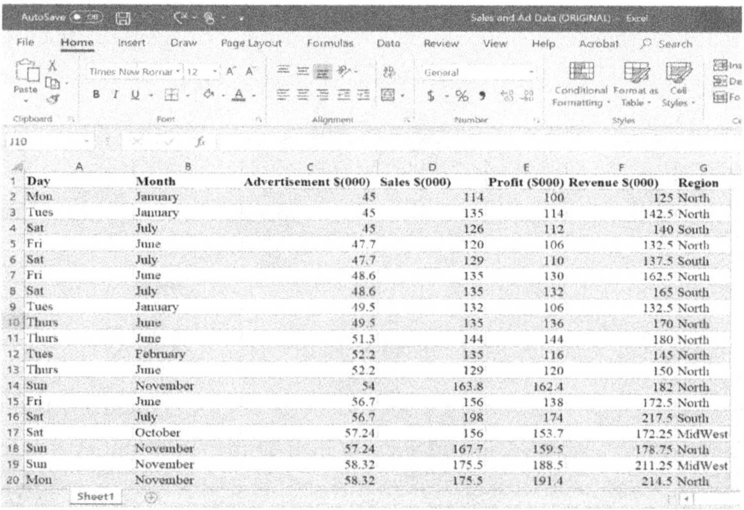

Figure 5.8 Sales and Ad Data (ORIGINAL)

Formatting Data as a Table

2. Select cell *A1*, then click the **Insert** tab of the ribbon above the worksheet. Then click on *Table. A Create Table* dialog box will appear. In this box, *your data range =$A$1:$G$151* should appear in the box. *If not, select the range of your data by clicking on cell A1* (where the data starts and drag down to the end of the table). Then check the box—*My table has headers* and click *OK*. Excel will automatically detect the data in the range *$A$1: $G$151*, and *My table has headers* checkbox is selected. Click *OK*. Excel will format the data as a table and adds drop-down buttons to the header row as shown in Figure 5.9.

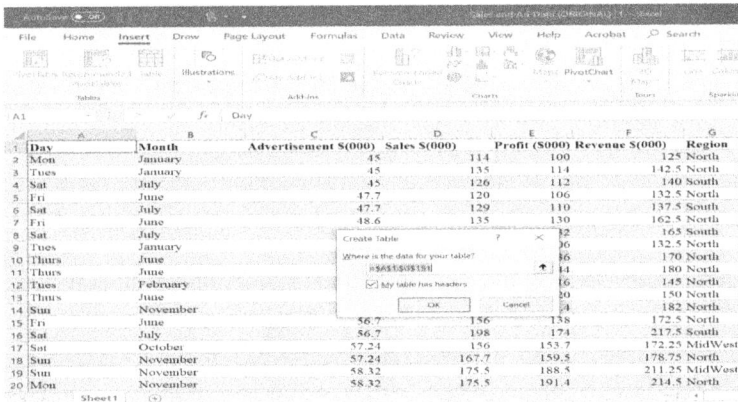

Figure 5.9 Formatting data as tables dialog box

Excel will format the data as a table and adds drop-down buttons to the header row as shown here. Your formatted data table will show like the one shown in Figure 5.10.

Filter and Sort the Data: Filter

If the data table is selected or highlighted, click any cell to deselect the table, and then click the drop-down button for the *Day* column. The *Sort and Filter* dialog box will be displayed.

In the *Filter* dialog box, clear the *(Select All)* checkbox, and then select only the *Saturday check box* as shown in Figure 5.11. Click *OK*.

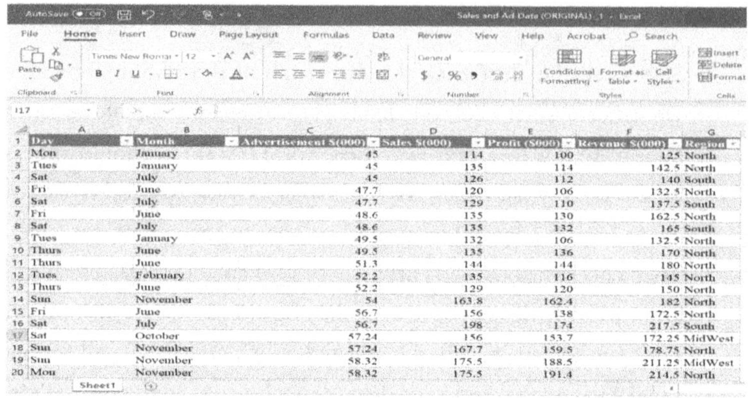

Figure 5.10 Data formatted as table

The data table is now filtered and shows the records only for Saturday. See Figure 5.12.

Next, click the drop-down button for the *Day* column and select "Clear Filter from Day" to restore the data table.

Self-Test: Find the Weekday With the Lowest Temperature

1. Using the filter and sort capabilities in Excel Online, filter the data so that only weekdays (Monday to Friday) are shown, and sort the data so that the first row contains data for the weekday with the lowest temperature.

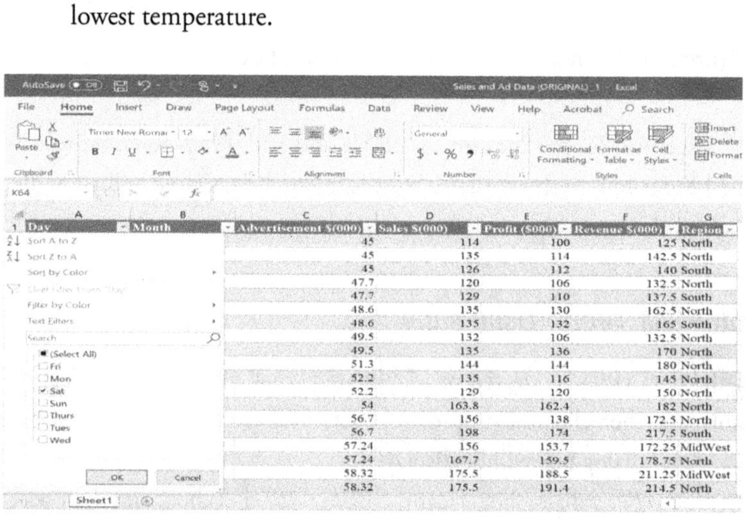

Figure 5.11 Filtering data

Day	Month	Advertisement $(000)	Sales $(000)	Profit ($000)	Revenue $(000)	Region
Sat	July	45	126	112	140	South
Sat	July	47.7	129	110	137.5	South
Sat	July	48.6	135	132	165	South
Sat	July	56.7	198	174	217.5	South
Sat	October	57.24	156	153.7	172.25	MidWest
Sat	June	58.5	165	140	175	North
Sat	July	59.4	162	150	187.5	North
Sat	October	59.4	175.5	197.2	221	MidWest
Sat	October	61.56	187.2	208.8	234	MidWest
Sat	October	62.64	167.7	174	195	MidWest
Sat	July	66.6	180	162	202.5	North
Sat	July	70.2	192	174	217.5	South
Sat	July	72	189	166	207.5	South
Sat	March	90	168	150	187.5	South
Sat	March	108	207	182	227.5	South
Sat	March	126	201	176	220	South
Sat	May	135	219	190	237.5	North
Sat	May	143.1	255	224	280	North
Sat	May	145.8	258	232	290	North

Figure 5.12 Filtered data

2. Make a note of the day and the temperature, and then clear the filter and re-sort the data back into chronological order.

Sort the Data

Click the drop-down arrow for the *Advertisement column* and select Sort *Largest to Smallest*. The table of data is sorted from largest to smallest order of Advertisement dollars, so the first row contains the data for the largest amount spent on advertisement. The table is shown in Figure 5.13.

Day	Month	Advertisement $(000)	Sales $(000)	Profit ($000)	Revenue $(000)	Region
Thurs	June	224.1	341.25	329.875	360.815	MidWest
Thurs	December	222.75	243.75	246.5	269.62	South
Thurs	December	216	219.375	239.25	261.69	South
Sun	January	216	277.875	275.5	301.34	South
Thurs		205.2	377	432.825	390.65	MidWest
Sun	December	202.5	263.25	257.375	281.515	South
Thurs	December	195.75	307.125	300.875	329.095	South
Sun	February	193.05	258.375	264.625	289.445	South
Sun	March	190.35	292.5	293.625	321.165	South
Wed	September	186.75	262.5	227.5	277.55	MidWest
Mon	August	185.625	187.5	170	207.4	South
Fri	October	183.6	362.7	365.4	409.5	South
Mon	August	180	168.75	165	201.3	South
Mon	August	180	213.75	190	231.8	South
Sun	April	179.55	326.625	315.375	344.955	West
Thurs	September	179.28	315.9	307.4	344.5	MidWest
Thurs	September	174.96	335.4	336.4	377	South
Sat	October	174.96	312	301.6	338	South
Fri	October	172.8	331.5	339.3	380.25	South

Figure 5.13 Data sorted in advertisement column

Restore the original data by sorting the Advertisement column "Sort Smallest to Largest." Open the Workbook Sales and AD_ PRODUCT 2 (ORIG.)

Column A of the worksheet shows the dates for the sale of a new product the company launched. The sales are recorded in column B labeled *Sales New ($000)*.

Format the data as a table that adds drop-down buttons to the header row as shown here (the steps are like that of the first data file). Your formatted data table will show like the one shown in Figure 5.14 (*note*: only part of the table is shown).

Insert a Blank Column

Insert a blank column between A and B. Click *column B* header to select the entire B column. Then right-click the column B and select *Insert* from the drop-down menu. This inserts a new blank Column B by shifting the original B column to the right which is now column C.

Name the blank column *Month* (type over Column heading that was given to the blank column). Now, column B is between the *Date* and *Sales_New* and is labeled *Month*. In cell B2, enter the following formula:

=TEXT (A2, "mmmm") and hit the enter key.

Date	Sales_New ($000)	Total Cost $(000)	Revenue_New $(000)	Profit_New $(000)	Store Size	Region
4/1/2019 $	41.80 $	60.20 $	72.24 $	12.04 M		North
4/2/2019 $	53.90 $	70.20 $	84.24 $	14.04 L		North
4/3/2019 $	59.40 $	76.20 $	91.44 $	15.24 S		South
4/4/2019 $	53.90 $	75.00 $	90.00 $	15.00 L		North
4/5/2019 $	56.10 $	76.30 $	91.56 $	15.26 L		South
4/6/2019 $	59.40 $	78.40 $	94.08 $	15.68 L		North
4/7/2019 $	53.90 $	72.90 $	87.48 $	14.58 M		South
4/8/2019 $	49.50 $	77.30 $	92.76 $	15.46 M		North
4/9/2019 $	48.40 $	70.00 $	84.00 $	14.00 M		North
4/10/2019 $	50.60 $	72.20 $	86.64 $	14.44 S		North
4/11/2019 $	70.40 $	88.50 $	106.20 $	17.70 M		North
4/12/2019 $	63.80 $	82.40 $	98.88 $	16.48 M		North
4/13/2019 $	77.00 $	95.50 $	114.60 $	19.10 L		North
4/14/2019 $	49.50 $	74.20 $	89.04 $	14.84 S		North
4/15/2019 $	70.40 $	90.30 $	108.36 $	18.06 L		South
4/16/2019 $	67.10 $	88.30 $	105.96 $	17.66 M		MidWest
4/17/2019 $	57.20 $	80.50 $	96.60 $	16.10 S		North
4/18/2019 $	67.10 $	86.50 $	103.80 $	17.30 M		MidWest
5/19/2019 $	50.60 $	72.30 $	86.76 $	14.46 S		North

Figure 5.14 Data columns formatted as table

After you enter the formula, it should show the month for the date in column H2. Copy the value in the cell to show the *Month* for each record in the date column (if it is not done automatically). The data table with months in column is shown in Figure 5.15.

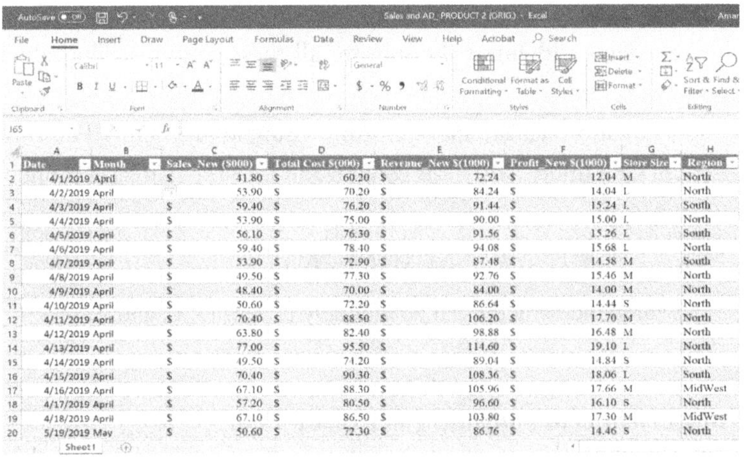

Figure 5.15 *Formatting date column to month*

Formatting data as Currency (U.S. dollars)

Columns C, D, E, and F show *Sales*, *Total Cost*, *Revenue*, and *Profits* for the new product. These columns are identified with *_New* label. The values in these columns are in thousands of dollars.

We want to formulate these columns are "$." To do this, select the column headers C, D, E, and F to select the entire columns, and then on the *Home* tab of the ribbon, in the *Number* section, Click the ($) sign. This formats these columns as dollars ($).

Calculating the Profit Using a Simple Formula

The profit in column F is calculated using the following formula:

$$\text{Profit} = \text{Revenue} - \text{Total Cost}$$

To calculate the profit, select cell F2 and type the formula: =E2 – D2 in cell F2. Hit enter and copy the formula down to the remaining cells. The values are shown in column F.

Calculating the sum of the values in columns C, D, E, and F. - Sales, *Total Cost, Revenue,* and *Profits.*

Scroll down to the bottom of the table of data, select cell *C63* and drag the cursor to F63 (under the *Sales, Total Cost, Revenue,* and *Profits* columns). Then on the *Home* tab of the ribbon, click the *Formulas* tab and from the *Auto Sum* drop-down menu, select Σ *Sum.* This calculates and enters the sum for all these columns. The values are shown in red.

You can also calculate the sum using a simple function. To do this, select cell C63 under *Sales_New* column and type the following formula in the cell C63:

=SUM (C2:C61)

Hit enter and copy the cell horizontally to cells D, E, and F.

Using Conditional Formatting to Explore Data

In this exercise, you will apply conditional formatting to the data to highlight key values of interest.

Highlighting Extremes and Outliers

1. Click on cell C2. With your mouse drag the pointer down to the last value in column C. This will select all the values in the *Sales_New column.*

2. Click on the *Home* tab of the ribbon. From the *Conditional Formatting* drop-down list, point to *Color Scales,* and select the *White-Red Color Scale* (with white at the top and red at the bottom). The *values in the Sales_New column* are reformatted so that the higher sales values are colored an intense red, and the lower sale are much lighter in color intensity. Scrolling through the data now, it is easier to find days that have high and low sales.

Repeat the above steps with column F but select Yellow-Green Color scales. The resulting spreadsheet in Figure 5.16.

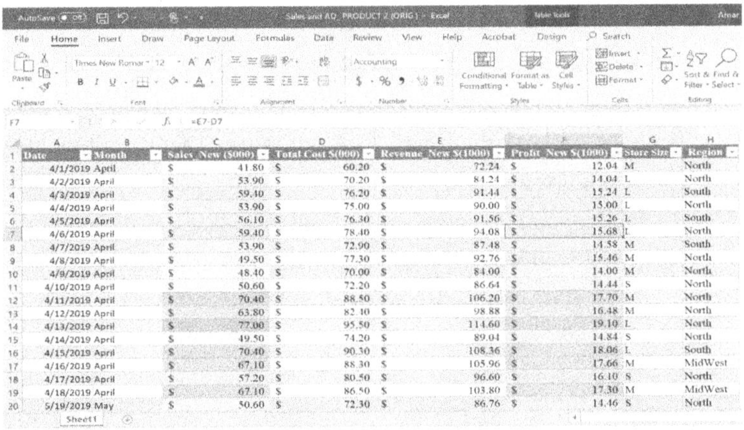

Figure 5.16 Applying conditional formatting

Analyzing Data Using PivotTable/Pivot Chart

Exercise: Analyzing Data with a PivotTable

1. Open the Workbook **Sales and Ad Data (ORIGINAL)**.
2. Select any cell in the table of data. Click *Insert* tab of the ribbon and select *PivotTable*.

   A create PivotTable dialog box will appear.
3. Click on Select a table or range. Put the cursor in the Table/Range box, then select cell A1 and drag down with your mouse pointer to the last value in the data. This will select and print the data range in the box.
4. Check the circle next to *New worksheet*. Excel adds a new worksheet with a PivotTable that looks Figure 5.17.

Figure 5.17 Pivot table example

5. In the *PivotTable Fields* pane, select *Month*. Excel automatically adds *Month* to the *Rows* area of the PivotTable and displays the month names in chronological order. If a row with a label (blank) appears, click on the Row Labels drop-down menu and uncheck the blank box and click OK.

6. In the *PivotTable Fields* pane, select *Sales ($000)*. Excel automatically adds *Sales* to the *Values* area of the PivotTable and displays the sum or the total of sales for each month as in Figure 5.18.

Figure 5.18 *Pivot table showing the months and sales values*

Change the Aggregation Changing sum of the Sales to Average

1. In the *PivotTable Fields* pane, in the *Values* area, click the drop-down arrow next to *Sum of Sales*, and then click *Value Field Settings*.

2. In the *Value Field Settings* dialog box, select *Average*.

3. The table of data now shows the average number of sales for each month (Figure 5.19).

Adding a Second Dimension

In the *PivotTable Fields* pane, check the box next to *Zone*. Excel will add *Zones* to the *Rows* area of the PivotTable and will show the total or sum of sales for each Zone within each month. The resulting spreadsheet is shown Figure 5.20.

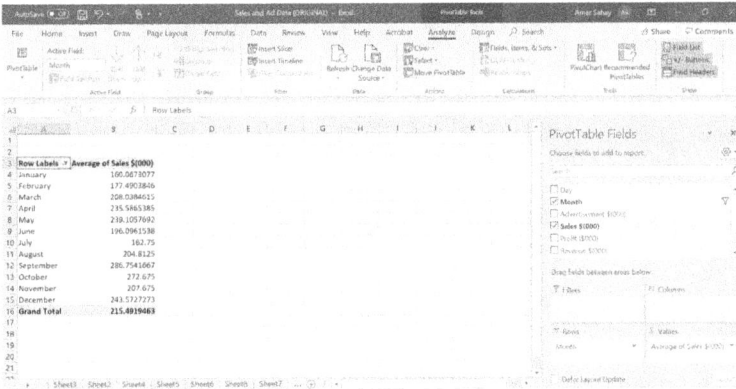

Figure 5.19 Pivot table showing the months and average sales values

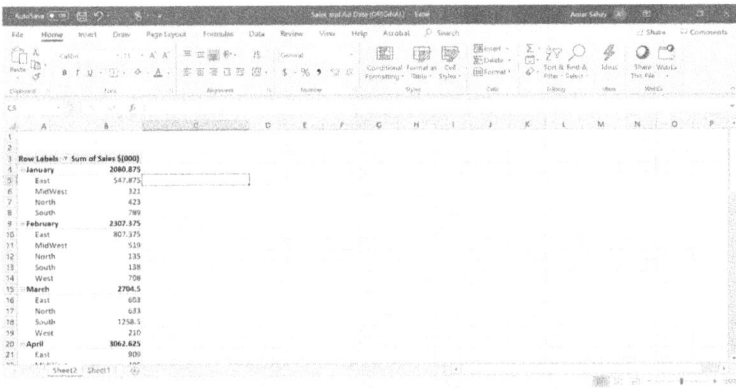

Figure 5.20 Adding another dimension to a pivot table

In the *PivotTable Fields* pane, check the boxes *Month, Sales* and drag the *Zone* to the column area. Excel will add *Zones* to the *Column* area of the PivotTable and will show the total or sum of sales of each Zone for each month. The resulting spreadsheet is shown in Figure 5.21.

Using Pivot Chat and Pivot Table

The first column of the data file **Sales and Ad Data (ORIGINAL)** lists the Day the sales were recorded in a random order. It will be beneficial to create a table and a bar chart that shows the number of sales for each

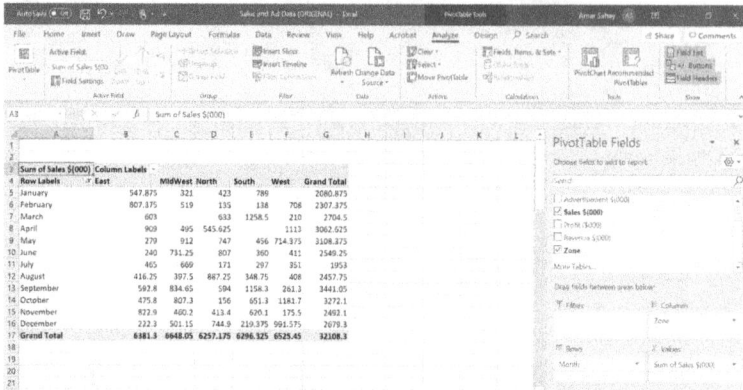

Figure 5.21 Sales for different zones in the pivot table

day of the week. This can be done using the *Pivot Chat & Pivot Table* *option*.

1. Open the Workbook **Sales and Ad Data (ORIGINAL)**.
2. Select any cell in the table of data. Click *Insert* tab of the ribbon and select *Pivot Chart &Table* option from the Pivot Chart drop-down menu selection. A create PivotTable dialog box will appear.
3. Click on *Select a Table or Range*. Put the cursor in the Table/Range box, then select cell A1 and drag down with your mouse pointer to the last value in the data. This will select and print the data range in the box. (Note: You may select only the Day column in the data file if you want a summary table and graph of this column only.)
4. Check the circle next to *New worksheet*. Excel adds a new worksheet with a PivotTable that looks like Figure 5.22.

In the PivotChart fields, drag the *Day* field to Access (Categories). Next, drag the *Day* field to ∑ Values area. The work sheet with a table and graph of number of sales records for each day will be displayed as shown Figure 5.23. If the table displays the "Sum of Sales" instead of Count, change it to count. Edit the graph by typing a title and printing

Figure 5.22 Pivot chart and pivot table

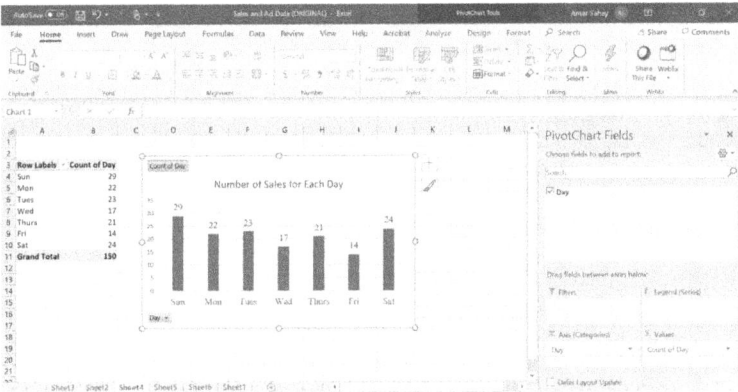

Figure 5.23 Pivot chart and pivot table for each day of the week

the numbers on the top of each bar by right clicking any bar and selecting Add Data Labels. You may also change the color of the bars.

Plotting Monthly Revenue

Follow the steps 1 to 4 in the previous section (*Using Pivot Chat & Pivot Table*).

Drag the Month field under Axis (Categories)

Drag the Revenue field under Values field

A table with Month and Sum of Revenue and a graph of average revenue will be displayed as in Figure 5.24a.

Plotting Sum of Revenue and Profit

Follow the steps 1 to 4 in the previous section (*Using Pivot Chat & Pivot Table*):

Drag the Month field under Axis (Categories)
Drag the Revenue field under Values field

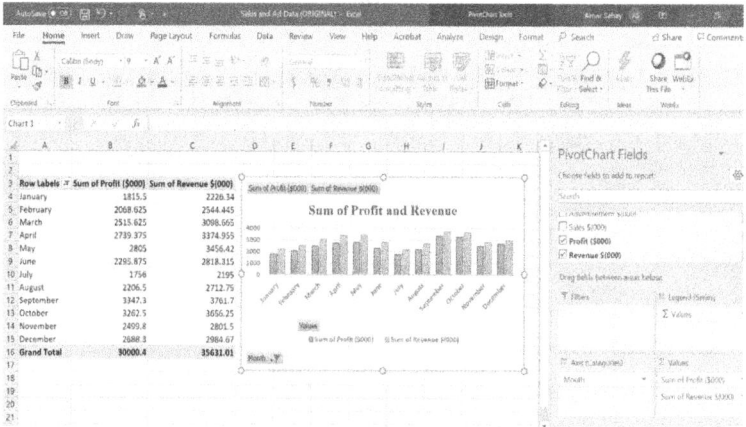

Figure 5.24a Pivot table and chart showing monthly revenue

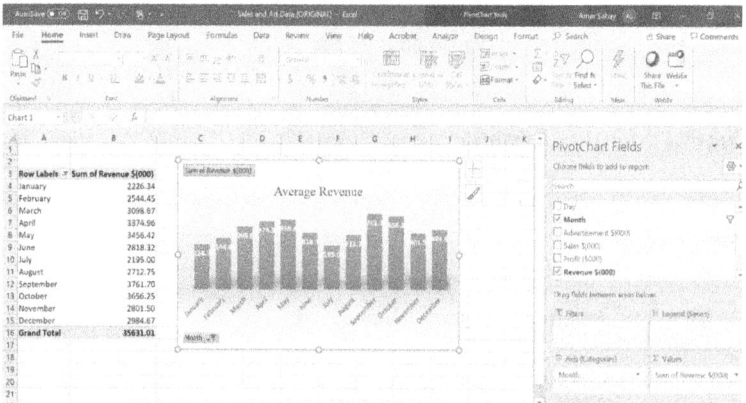

Figure 5.24b Pivot table and chart showing sum of profit and revenue

A table with Month, Sum of Revenue and a graph of average revenue will be displayed.

Plotting Sum of Profit and Sum of Revenue Using Pivot Chat & Pivot Table

Follow the instructions of previous graph. Drag the Data Fields to the areas shown on the right side of the figure below. Your resulting graph will be as shown in Figure 5.25. Note that you can edit the graph to change the titles, fonts, and colors.

Pivot Tables: Applications in Descriptive Statistics and Data Analysis

The pivot table is one of the most powerful and easy to use tools in Excel. This application is particularly helpful in extracting large amount of useful information from a data set. Using Excel's pivot table you can do the following:

- Create cross tabulation or break the data down by categories so that you can see the customer rating by gender, or see the total dollars spent on online orders by the day of the week, region of the country, time of the day, or a combination of these.
- Create tables of counts to display the sale of a product by brand name, or number of customers by region. You can create cross tabulation or contingency tables to display the counts only. The pivot tables provide more flexibility compared to cross tables. The pivot tables can be used to display counts, sums, averages, and other summary measures of the data.

Use Pivot Chart to Summarize Qualitative or Categorical Data

Problem: Develop a frequency distribution and graphical display (a bar chart and a pie chart) for the categorical data in the data file PivotTable3. xlsx. This data file contains the name brand television sets sold by an electronic retailer over a period of two months. The management would like to know how many televisions of each brand was sold. Follow the steps below.

Steps:

1. Open the worksheet **PivotTable3.xlsx**. This file contains different brands of televisions sold over a period of two months.
2. Click the *Insert* tab on the Excel main menu.
3. In the *Charts* group, click the downward pointing arrow and select *Pivot Chart & Pivot Table.*
4. *Create PivotTable* dialog box will be displayed. In this dialog box,

   Click on circle to the left of *Select a table or range.*

   Click on the *Table/Range* box and select the range by clicking on cell A1 and dragging down the cursor to the last value which is A151.
5. Click on the circle to the left of *Existing Worksheet* (to display the *Pivot Table* and *PivotChart* on the existing work sheet).

   Click in the Location box then click on cell C4 (or any blank cell) of the worksheet).

   Click OK. You will see boxes entitled Pivot Table 3 and Chart displayed. On the right pane PivotTable Fields will be displayed (if you don't see Pivot Table Fields on the right side, click on Pivot Table box).
6. In the *PivotTable Field List* go to *Choose Fields to add to report.*

   Click on TV Brands Sold and drag this field to the ROWS box. Next, drag the TV Brands sold field to the VALUES box. The PivotTable and the Bar Chart will be displayed.
7. Click on the displayed bar chart, select *Design* from the main menu and choose the desired design from the options.
8. From the top right of the displayed bar chart, click the box with + sign. If the box is not displayed, click on the chart and the tab will appear.
9. Check the *Axes, Axis Title, Chart Title,* and *Data Labels.* Type the axes titles and the chart Title. Figure 5.25. Selecting *Data Labels*

will put the values of each category on the top of the bar (some designs will automatically print the values on the top of each bar).

10. Right click on any bar of the displayed chart. Select *Fill* to change the color and the type of fill of the bars.

11. Repeat step 10 and select *Outline* to change the outline or the color of the outline of the bars of the histogram.

12. **Create a pie chart of the data:** To create a pie chart select the two columns of the PivotTable (the brands under *Row Labels* and *Count of TV Brands Sold*).

13. From the main menu, click on *Insert* and from the charts group click on *Pie* and select the first option under *2-D Pie*.

14. A *Pie chart* of the PivotTable data will be displayed. Click on the pie chart then select *Design* from the main menu and select the design of your choice.

15. From the top right of the displayed pie chart, click the box with + sign. If the box is not displayed, click on the chart and the tab will appear.

16. Edit your histogram by selecting appropriate boxes.

On the top left of the chart a button *Count of TV Brand Sold* is displayed. To hide this, right click on it and select *Hide all Field Buttons on Chart*.

Table 5.2 shows the PivotTable. The bar chart and the pie chart are shown in Figures 5.25 and 5.26. Note that your charts may look different depending on the designs you selected.

Table 5.2 PivotTable

Row Labels	Count of TV Brands Sold
Mitsubishi	18
Panasonic	45
RCA	8
Sanyo	13
Sharp	19
Sony	47
Grand Total	150

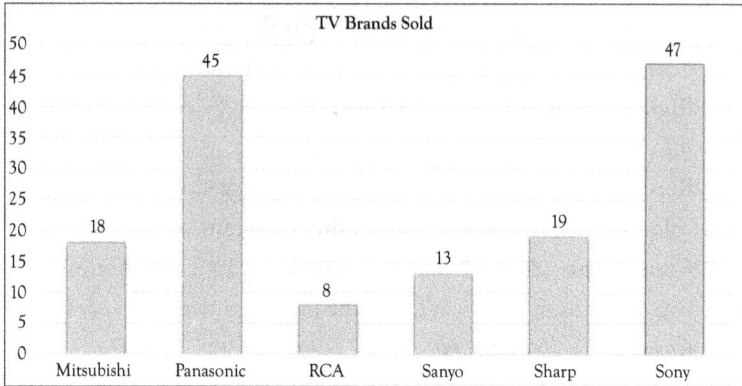

Figure 5.25 Bar chart of categorical

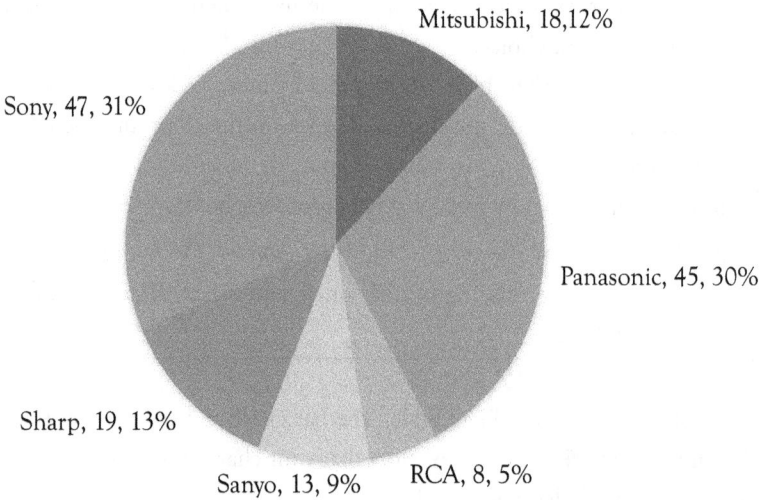

Figure 5.26 Pie Chart of categorical data

Cross Tabulation With Two and Three Qualitative or Categorical Data

The PivotTable can also be used to summarize the data for two or more variables simultaneously. This exercise will enable you develop a cross tabulation of the data provided in the data file **Pivot Table2.xlsx**. This file contains data on student major by gender and employment status.

Problem: Develop a cross tabulation to summarize the data by gender and student major, that is, create a PivotTable that will have gender as the row variable and student major as the column variable. Create a chart of your table. Follow the steps below to create such a table.

Steps:

1. Open the worksheet *PivotTable2.xlsx.*
2. Click the *Insert* tab on the EXCEL main menu.
3. In the *Charts* group, click the downward pointing arrow and select *Pivot Chart & Pivot Table.*
4. *Create PivotTable* dialog box will be displayed. In this dialog box

   Click the on circle to the left of *Select a table or range.*

   Click on the *Table/Range* box and select the range by clicking on cell A1 and dragging down the cursor to the last value which is C201.

5. Click on the circle to the left of *Existing Worksheet* (to display the *Pivot Table* and *PivotChart on* the existing work sheet).

   Click in the *Location* box then click on cell *E5* (or any blank cell) of the worksheet.

   Click *OK.* You will see boxes titled *Pivot Table # and Chart #* displayed. On the right pane *PivotTable Fields* will be displayed (if you don't see *Pivot Table Fields* on the right side, click on *Pivot Table* box.

6. In the *PivotTable Field List* go to *Choose Fields to add to report.*

   Click on *Gender* and drag this field to the *ROWS* box.

   > Next, drag the *Major* field to the *COLUMNS* box
   > Next, drag the *Major* to the *VALUES* box.

   In the Values box, click on the downward pointing arrow and select *Value Field Setting.*

7. In the *Value Field Setting* box, select *Count.*

   The PivotTable of student major and gender along with the bar chart will be displayed.

8. Click on the displayed bar chart, select *Design* from the main menu and choose the desired design (we selected the last one).

9. From the top right of the displayed bar chart, click the box with + sign. If the box is not displayed, click on the chart and the tab will appear.

10. Check the *Axes*, *Axis Title*, *Chart Title*, and *Data Labels*. Type the axes titles and the chart title if needed. Selecting *Data Labels* will put the values of each category on the top of the bar (some designs will automatically print the values on the top of the bars).

Figure 5.27 shows the Cross Tabulation and Bar Chat of this Categorical Data.

Note: On the top left of the chart three buttons—*Count of Major, Major,* and Gender—are displayed. To hide these, right click on any button and select *Hide all Field Buttons on Chart.*

Descriptive Statistics Using Excel

Most of the numerical measures we have discussed in this chapter can be calculated using Excel. In this section, we explain how Excel can be used to calculate several measures including the measures of central tendency, measures of variation, measures of position, and measures of shape. In

Count of Major	Column Labels					
Row Labels	1	2	3	4	5	Grand Total
Female	6	11	34	32	19	102
Male	12	28	11	31	16	98
Grand Total	18	39	45	63	35	200

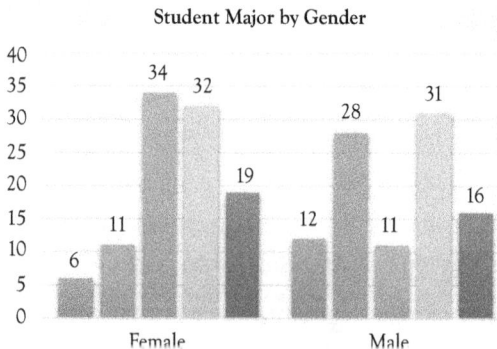

Figure 5.27 Cross tabulation and bar chat of categorical data

addition, we will also provide the functions that can be used to compute the covariance and coefficient of correlation.

(1) Using Excel Functions

The descriptive statistics measured can be calculated using the built-in Excel functions. Table 5.3 explains the numerical measures, their explanation and the Excel functions used to calculate them. The use of all these functions are demonstrated using an example.

Table 5.3 Excel functions to calculate descriptive statistics individually

Numerical Measure	Explanation	Excel Function
Mean Sample Mean: $\bar{x}$ Population Mean: μ	The average of observations	=AVERAGE (range) (range is the range of values for which statistic is to be calculated, e.g. A1:A30)
Median (No specific symbols for sample or population data)	Middle value in the sorted data (data sorted from low to high)	=MEDIAN (range)
Mode	The value that occurs most frequently in the data set	=MODE (range)
Percentile	Value such that a specified percentage of observations lie below it	=PERCENTILE (range, pct) where pct is a decimal value between 0 and 1
Quartile	Q1: First quartile or 25th percentile Q2: Second quartile or 50th percentile or the median Q3: Third quartile or 75th percentile	=QUARTILE (range, n) where n is 1, 2, or 3
Interquartile range (IQR)	IQR = Q3 – Q1 (the difference between the third and the first quartile)	=QUARTILE (range,3) – QUARTILE (range,1)
Minimum	Smallest value	=MIN (range)
Maximum	Largest value	=MAX (range)
Range	Difference between largest and smallest value	=MAX (range) – MIN (range)
Variance s^2 : Sample variance σ^2 : Population variance	Measure of variation: it is the average of squared distances from the mean	Sample variance =VAR (range) Population variance =VARP (range)

Table 5.3 **(Continued)**

Numerical Measure	Explanation	Excel Function
Standard deviation s : Sample standard deviation σ : Population standard deviation	Measure of variation or measure of deviation from the mean. It is measured in the same unit as the data.	Sample standard deviation =STDEV (range) Population standard deviation =STDEVP (range)
Covariance	Measure of association between two quantitative variables. It is affected by units of measurement.	=COVAR (range1,range2)
Coefficient of correlation r: Sample correlation ρ : Population correlation	Measure of association between two quantitative variables; not affected by unit of measurement. The value is always between −1 and +2.	= CORREL (range1,range2)

(2) Computing Descriptive Statistics using Excel

An example is provided below to demonstrate the calculation of the statistics.

Steps: As you follow the steps below, refer to Table 5.3 above for the functions to be typed in.

1. Enter the data from Table 5.4 in column A of Excel worksheet. The data range will be A1:A22. The statistics will be calculated for this range.
2. Type the statistics to be calculated in a blank column such as, column C.
3. Type the function for the statistics to be calculated in the next column such as, column D.
4. As you type the function and hit the enter key, the values will be calculated and stored in the cell where the function was typed.

Figure 5.28 shows the screen shot of the functions as they should be typed in. Do not forget to type an equal to ("=") sign before typing the function. Figure 5.29 shows the results.

Table 5.4 **Home heating cost ($)**

Home Heating Cost ($)
82 145   95 130 102 108 109 111 114 116 119 123 127 128 129 130 130   82 137 139

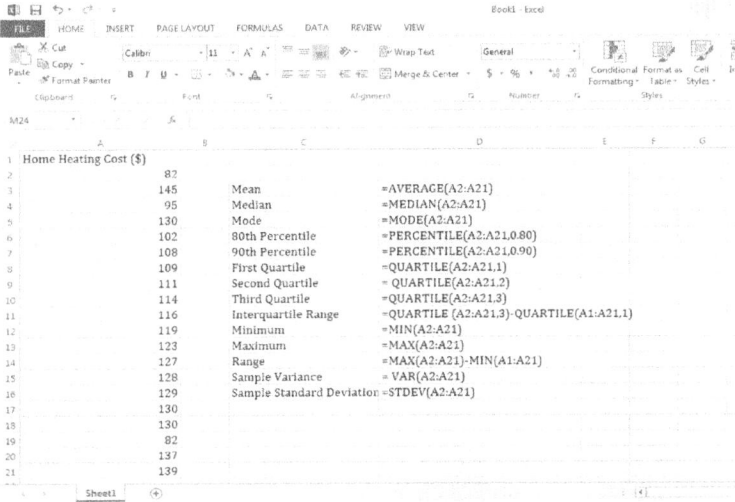

Figure 5.28 Excel functions to calculate the statistics individually

(3) Excel's Descriptive Statistics Tool

In the previous section, we explained the functions that Excel uses to compute the numerical measures. These functions are used to compute one measure or one statistic at a time. For example, using the functions in Table 3B.1, we can compute the mean, median, and standard deviation individually. Excel also provides another option to calculate several

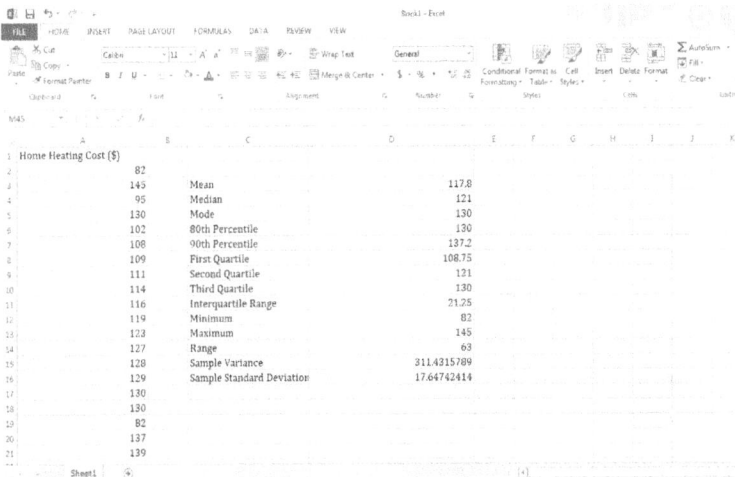

Figure 5.29 Results of functions entered in Figure 5.28

statistics at the same time. These are included in the *Descriptive Statistics* option under the *Data Analysis Tools*. The steps to calculate the descriptive statistics are explained below with an example. We will demonstrate how to calculate the descriptive statistics for home heating cost data in Table 3B.2. This data was used to calculate the statistics individually in the previous section. The steps are outlined below.

1. Label column A of Excel: Home Heating Cost ($) and enter the data in Table 5.4 in the Excel worksheet.
   (Note: You must enter all the data of a variable in a single column. In our example, Home Heating Cost is a variable and it must be entered in a single column for Excel to identify this data as one variable. See the screen shot in Figure 5.30 for the entered data).

2. Select *Data* from the Excel main menu option.
   (*Note*: If you don't see the Data Analysis tab after clicking the Data tab, you will need to install it using steps below. You must have Data Analysis installed to calculate many of the statistics)

3. Choose *Data Analysis* (extreme right of the menu option).

4. When the Data Analysis dialog box appears:
   Select *Descriptive Statistics* by clicking on it then click *OK*.

5. The *Descriptive Statistics* dialog box will be displayed.
   Type *A1:A21* in the *Input Range* box or, click in the Input Range box for the cursor to appear in that box then click in cell A1 and drag the flashing box down to the last data value in that column to select the range.

6. Check the box *Labels in first row*.

7. Click the circle to the left of *Output Range*.
   Type C1 in the *Output Range* box. This will identify the column where the results of the calculated descriptive statistics will be stored.
   You may also click the Output Range box for the cursor to appear in the box and then click column C1 or any blank column to identify that column as the starting column for the results to be stored.

8. Check the box to the left of *Summary Statistics*.

9. Click *OK*.

The summary statistics will be calculated and stored starting from the column you specified in the output range box. The results are shown in Figure 5.30.

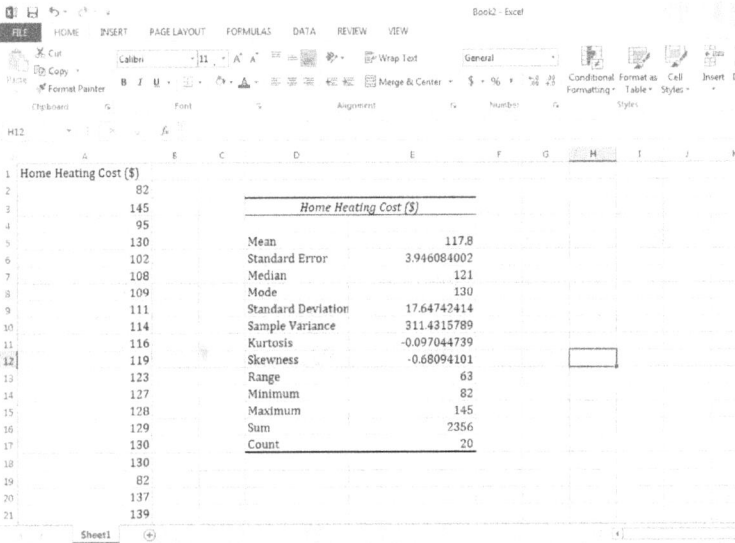

Figure 5.30 Descriptive statistics using Excel.

(4) Computing Z-score using Excel

Excel uses the *STANDARDIZE* function to compute Z scores. Note that the Z formula is given by

$$Z = \frac{x - \mu}{\sigma} \text{ or } Z = \frac{x - \bar{x}}{s}$$

where Z is the distance from the mean to the point of interest, x in standard deviations, x is the point of interest; μ, $\sigma / \bar{x}$, s are the mean and standard deviation for population and sample respectively.

The *STANDARDIZE* function to calculate the Z score has the following form:

STANDARDIZE (value, mean, standard deviation)

In this function, x is the value for which the Z score is to be calculated. The mean and the standard deviation are the parameters of Z score formula.

Example: Computing Z-Score using Excel

The data in Table 5.5 shows the price of a small flat screen TV. The mean price, $\bar{x} = 203.65$ and the standard deviation, $S = 92.09$. Calculate the Z-score for the TV price data.

Steps

1. Label column A as TV Price and enter the data of Table 5.5 in column A of Excel.
2. Calculate the mean and standard deviation of the data using the instructions described above.
3. In cell B2, type the function
   = STANDARDIZE(A2,203.7,92.1) check these values and hit enter. Note that 203.7 and 92.1 are the mean and standard deviation of the data in Table 5.5.

Table 5.5 Price of TV ($)

270 217 131 138 145 161 166 218 95 131 216 219 263 163 207 376 402 98 101 356

4. The Z-score for the value in cell A2 will be calculated and displayed in cell B2.
5. Click on the calculated value with your mouse, hold the square at the right bottom corner of the rectangle with the + and drag it down to calculate the Z-value for the rest of the values in column A.
6. Round the values of Z-score to two decimal places and label column B as Z-score.
7. The calculated Z-scores are shown in Table 5.6. Note that the table shows the values rounded to two decimal places.

(5) Calculating the Covariance and the Coefficient of Correlation

We will calculate the covariance and the coefficient of correlation between Advertising (x) and Sales (y) using Excel. The steps are explained below.

Table 5.6 Calculated Z-value

	A	B
1	Price of TV	Z-score
2	270	0.73
3	217	0.14
4	131	-0.80
5	138	-0.72
6	145	-0.65
7	161	-0.47
8	166	-0.41
9	218	0.15
10	95	-1.19
11	131	-0.80
12	216	0.14
13	219	0.17
14	263	0.65
15	163	-0.45
16	207	0.04
17	376	1.89
18	402	2.18
19	98	-1.16
20	101	-1.13
21	356	1.67

Steps:

1. Enter the advertising and sales data in columns A and B of Excel worksheet as shown in Table 5.7.
2. In cells D2, D3, and D7 type Population Covariance, Coefficient of Correlation, and Sample Covariance. These are the statistics we want to calculate. See Table 5.7.
3. In cell E2, type the following function:
   =COVAR (A2:A13, B2, B13)
   Hit enter. The covariance will be calculated and stored in cell E2.
4. In cell E3, type the following function
   =CORREL (A2:A13, B2, B13)
   Hit the enter key. The coefficient of correlation will be calculated and stored in cell E3.
5. The covariance calculated in cell E2 is the population covariance. Excel does not automatically calculate the sample covariance. To calculate the sample covariance, the covariance function entered in cell E2 should be modified by multiplying the covariance function

in E2 by $n/(n-1)$ where n is the number of observations. In our case, $n=12$. Therefore, the sample covariance,

$$s_{xy} = \frac{n}{(n-1)} * E2 = \frac{12}{11} * 30.42 = 33.18$$

where E2 is the value of population covariance calculated and stored in cell E2. Based on the above modification in cell E7, type

$$=(12/11*E2)$$

to calculate the sample covariance. The result in cell E7 shows the sample covariance.

(6) Generating Random Numbers from Normal Distribution and Verifying the Empirical Rule Using Excel

In this exercise, we will generate random numbers from a normal or bell-shaped distribution. Since the normal distribution is symmetrical, the empirical rule will apply. Recall that the empirical rule states that whenever the data are symmetrical or bell-shaped (normally distributed),

- approximately 68 percent of all observations will lie between the mean and ± 1 Standard Deviation
- approximately 95 percent of all observations will lie between the mean and ± 2 Standard Deviation

	A	B	C	D	E
1	Advertising (x)	Sales (y))			
2	1	2		Population Covariance	30.42
3	2	6		Coefficient of Correlation	0.959
4	11	25			
5	9	18			
6	7	13			
7	6	12		Sample Covariance	33.18
8	15	28			
9	3	9			
10	13	20			
11	5	12			
12	4	6			
13	8	17			

Table 5.7 Covariance and coefficient of correlation using excel

- approximately 99.7 percent of all observations will lie between the mean and ± 3 Standard Deviation

We will check to see if the empirical rule holds for the normal or symmetrical distribution by generating 1,000 random numbers from a normal distribution.

Generating Random Numbers From a Normal Distribution

To generate 1,000 random numbers from a normal or symmetrical distribution, follow the steps below.

Steps:

1. From the Excel main menu select

   Data → Data Analysis → Random Number Generation

   Complete the Random Number Generation dialog as shown below:

Number of variables	1
Number of Random Numbers	1000
Distribution	Normal (select from the drop-down menu)
Mean =	80
Standard deviation =	5
Output Range	$A$2 or click on cell A2
Click OK.	

   This will generate 1,000 random numbers from a Normal distribution with mean equal to 80 and standard deviation equal to 5.

2. Label Colum A as Random Numbers.

3. Round the random numbers generated to two decimal places (for ease of calculations).

4. Construct a histogram of the random numbers to verify that the shape is symmetrical (this step is optional). The histogram, of course, will display a symmetrical shape as the random numbers were generated using a normal or bell-shaped distribution. The histogram constructed from the random numbers is shown in Figure 5.31.

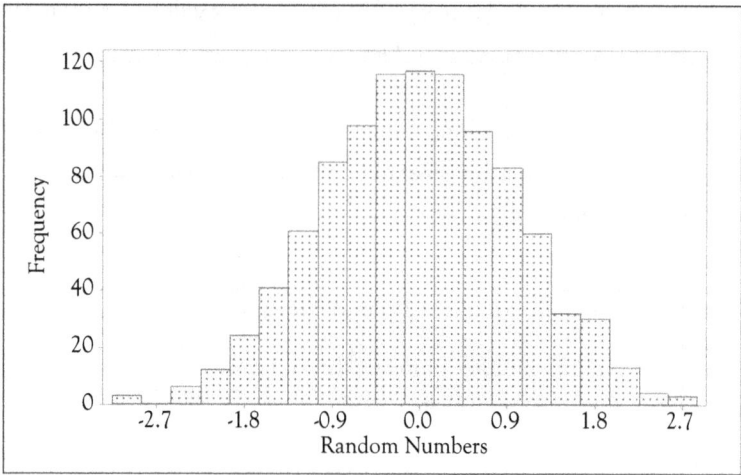

Figure 5.31 Histogram of 1,000 random numbers from a normal distribution

Next, we will use the random numbers generated to verify the empirical rule.

(7) Verifying the empirical rule

In this section, we will use the 1,000 random numbers generated to verify the empirical rule. If the empirical rule holds, approximately 68 percent or 680 of the 1,000 random numbers will fall within ±1 standard deviation of mean, approximately 95 percent or 950 of the 1,000 random numbers generated will fall within ±2 standard deviation of the mean, and approximately all of the 1,000 random numbers will be within ±3 standard deviation of the mean. Follow the steps below to verify the empirical rule.

Steps:

1. ***Name the range:*** Naming the range is a very convenient way of addressing the range of values in a column while writing the functions. Once the range of values in a column is named, it is not necessary to drag the cursor from the first to the last value in the cell to specify the range. The range can simply be addressed by selecting

its name. This is particularly desirable if a cell has hundreds or even thousands of numbers. To name the range of the values in a cell,

- Right click the label of the column you want to name and select *Define Name* (in our case, the column A should have Random Number as the label)
- In the *New Name* dialog box that is displayed, Random Numbers should be displayed in *Name* box.
- Select *Sheet1* from the drop-down menu for *Scope*.
- In the *Refers to:* box, select the range A2: A1001 by clicking the button at the end of the box then placing the cursor on the first value in cell A2 and dragging it down to A1001

Click *OK.*

The above steps will name the column A. The range in this column can now be referenced by Random Numbers.

For the steps below, refer to Figure 5.32.

2. Label columns B, C, and D as shown in Figure 5.32. These columns are named as Mean & 1 StdDev, Mean & 2 StdDev, and Mean & 3 StdDev. The columns will store the number of values

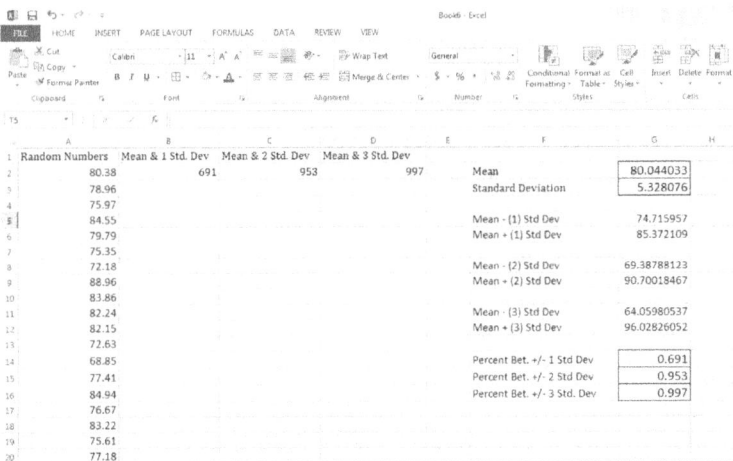

Figure 5.32 Verifying the empirical rule

within 1, 2, and 3 standard deviations (from the 1,000 random numbers generated and stored in column A).

3. Name the cells F2 and F3 as mean and standard deviation. In cell G2, type the functions

=AVERAGE (Random Numbers)

In cell G3, type the function

=STDEV (Random Numbers)

This will calculate the mean and standard deviation of the random numbers in column A. Note that the range in column A has been named Random Number. As you start typing the name of this range, type the first word of the range name and it will allow you to select it from the drop-down menu where the range name is stored.

4. Label column F5, F6, F8, F9, F11, F12, and F14 through F16 as shown in Figure 5.32.

5. Calculate the values within 1, 2, and 3 standard deviations of the mean using the calculated mean and standard deviation in the previous step. To do this, type the following functions in cells indicated below:

In cells G5 and G6, type

$$=G2 - G3$$

$$=G2 + G3$$

Note that in cells G2 and G3, the mean and standard deviation are stored. The above formulas will calculate the values between the mean and ± one standard deviation and store them in the cells G5 and G6.

To calculate the values within the mean and ± 2 and 3 standard deviations, type the following formulas in the cells indicated:

In cells G8 and G9, type

$$=G2 - 2*G3$$

$$=G2 + 2*G3$$

In cells G11 and G12, type

$$=G2 - 3*G3$$
$$=G2 + 3*G3$$

6. Next, we will write the function to count the number of values between the mean and ± 1, 2, and 3 standard deviations in column A where 1,000 random numbers are stored. To do this, type the following functions in the cells indicated:

In cell B2, type the function

=SUMPRODUCT
((Random_Numbers>=G5)*(Random_Numbers<=G6))

This will count the number of values between the mean and ± one standard deviation from the random numbers in Column A and store the number in cell B2. Note that your numbers will be different from what is shown in cell B2 of Figure 5.32 example, as your random numbers will be different. However, the result should be close to 68 percent.

To calculate the number of values between the mean and ±2 and 3 standard deviations, type the functions below.

In cell C2 type

=SUMPRODUCT
((Random_Numbers>=G8)*(Random_Numbers<=G9))

In cell D2 type

=SUMPRODUCT
((Random_Numbers>=G11)*(Random_Numbers<=G12))

The above functions will count the number of values between ±2 and 3 standard deviation of the mean and store them in cells C2 and D2. Refer to cells B2, C2, and C3 for the values. Note that your numbers will be different than what is shown in cells C2 and C3 because your random numbers will be different.

7. Finally, we calculate the percent of observations within ±1, 2, and 3 standard deviations of the mean. To do this, divide the numbers in cells B2, C2, and D2 by the total number of random

numbers generated (in our case, it is 1,000). The percentages are calculated and stored in cells G14, G15, and G16. To calculate the percentages, type the following formulas:

In cell G14 type, =B2/1000

In cell G15 type, =C2/1000

In cell G16 type, =D2/1000

The percentages are 69.1, 95.3, and 99.7 percent (0.691, 0.953, and 0.997). These values agree with the empirical rule.

Visualizing Data Using Excel Charts and Graphs

Visualize the Distribution of Home Sales with a Histogram

1. Open the Worksheet *Home Sales* ($000).
2. Select all the data in the *Home Sales* column including the header. Click on the *Insert* tab of the ribbon and select *Recommended Charts*. A few possible charts for the data you selected will be displayed. Click the *Histogram* by double clicking on it (this should be the third one under recommended charts). A histogram is a plot of frequency distribution and is constructed by dividing the data into groups or class intervals also known as Bins) and counting the

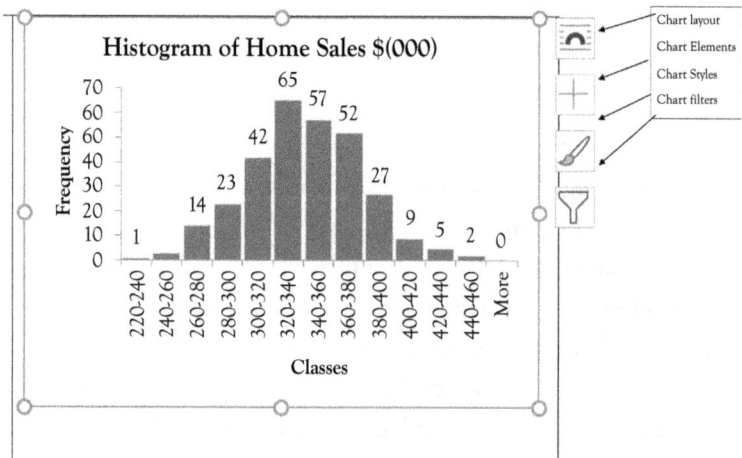

Figure 5.33 Distribution of home sales data

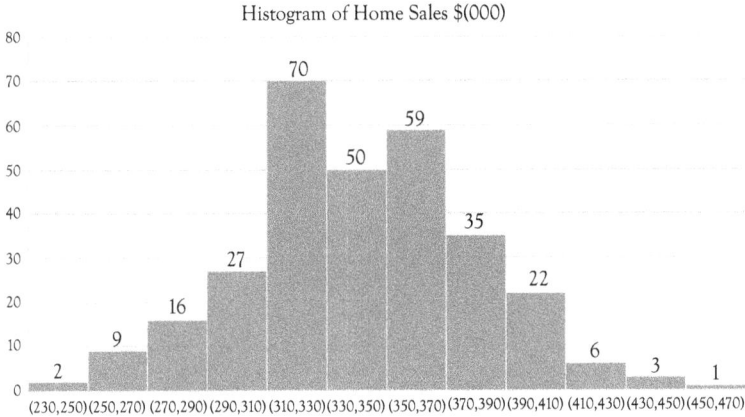

Figure 5.34 A default histogram of home sales data

number of occurrences in each group. It shows a pattern from the data and is excellent way of summarizing large data sets.

3. Click on the default title on the chart and provide a suitable title as shown. The histogram is shown in Figure 5.33. Right-click on any bar of the histogram to select all the bard and then select *Add Data Labels* to add the frequency or the count on the top of each bar.

(*Note*: You can also move the chart next to the original data in the data file so that it is to the right of the original data in column A.)

A Pareto Chart of Home Sales Data

In step 2 above, a *Pareto Chart* will also be displayed under. A Preto Chart plots the distribution of data in decreasing order. The chart also plots a cumulative line on the *y*-axis, which shows the percentage of the total. This line is shown in a red color.

Edit the Pareto chart to provide a suitable title. The chart is shown in Figure 5.35 and also in the data file below the histogram.

Alternate Way of Creating a Histogram

The histogram in the previous section is a default histogram where the class intervals or the bins are selected by the software. Excel has an option

A Preto Chart of the Home Sales

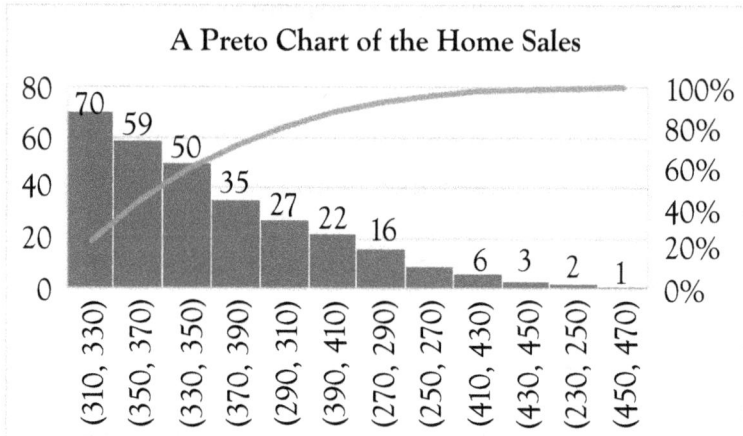

Figure 5.35 A pareto chart of home sales data

to create a custom histogram with user-specified class intervals. Excel calls the class intervals Bins. We will create a custom histogram for the Home Sales data here. To divide the data into specific classes or Bins, it is important to know the range of the data. This can be achieved by sorting the data.

Refer to Worksheet with *Home Sales* ($000) data.

1. Sort the data in column A. The sorted data is shown in column B. The home sales data has a minimum value of 230 and maximum value of 452.

2. Using the rules for forming frequency distribution, the data was divided into the classes and that such that the first group or the class contains the minimum value and the last class has the maximum values. One possible grouping is shown in column C of the data file.

3. Label column D as Bins and type the upper limit of each class in the Bins column. When creating a histogram with a user-specified classes, Excel requires the Bins vale, which are the upper limit of each class.

4. With your actual or ungrouped data in column A and Bins in column D, follow the instructions below.

5. Click the Data tab on the main menu and select the command sequence shown

Data → Data Analysis → Histogram
OK

A Histogram dialog box will be displayed. In this box,
For Input Range, select column A including the label
For Bins, select column D including the labels
Check the Labels box
Select New Worksheet Ply to put your histogram and table on a separate sheet
Check the Chart Output box
Click OK.

A frequency table and a histogram will be displayed on a new sheet. Edit the histogram to show an appropriate title and other details.

i. Put your cursor in the Bins column and type the lower limit of each class, for example, in the first cell under bins, type 220 and hit enter. It will show the class interval as 220–240 and will also modify your graph. Do the same for each cell as shown in the table below with the histogram.

ii. Double click on any bar of the histogram and from the right-side edit options, close the gap width by dragging the cursor to the left.

iii. Double click again on any bar and select add data labels to put the frequencies on the top of each bar.

iv. Edit the Chart and axes title by clicking on the existing titles and typing appropriate titles.

The histogram with frequency table should look as shown in Figure 5.36 (also shown in the data worksheet).

A histogram not only provides a compact representation of data but also displays the shape or the distribution. The plot in Figure 5.37

Bins	Frequency
220-240	1
240-260	3
260-280	14
280-300	23
300-320	42
320-340	65
340-360	57
360-380	52
380-400	27
400-420	9
420-440	5
440-460	2
More	0

Histogram of Home Sales $(000)

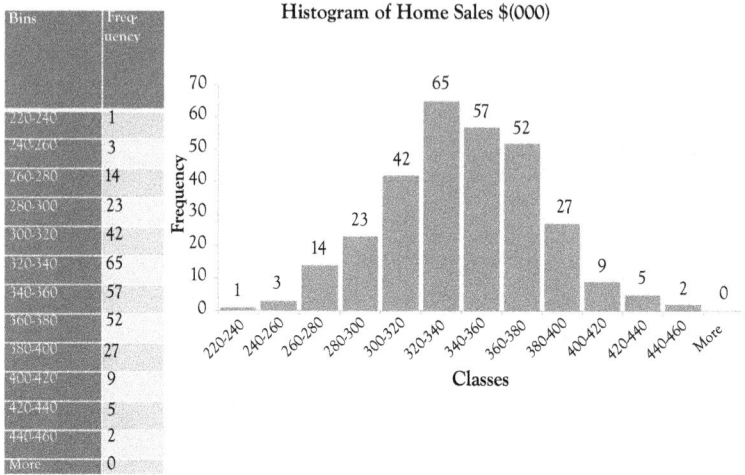

Figure 5.36 A Histogram of Home Sales data) with user-specified bins

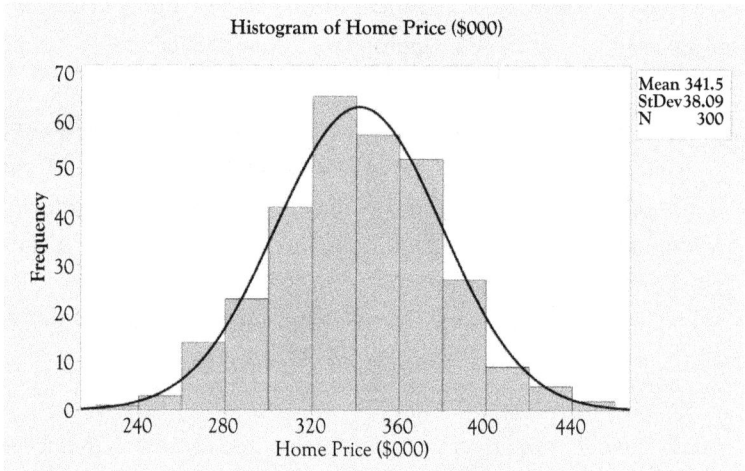

Histogram of Home Price ($000)

Mean 341.5
StDev 38.09
N   300

Home Price ($000)

Figure 5.37 A histogram of home sales data approximating the shape

shows a symmetrical or bell-shaped data that is characterized by a normal distribution.

(*Note:* This histogram is done using MINITAB statistical software and is for illustration purposes.)

Interpreting the Histogram

1. Refer to the histogram of Home Sales $(000) in Figure 5.36. It shows the frequency of different values for *Home Sales* values grouped into Class intervals or ranges, or *bins*. For example, there are around 65 homes sold between $320,000 and $340,000 with a and 13.8; and there are around nine homes sold between $400,000 and $420,000.

2. The maximum frequency is 65 that indicates that the most frequently occurring *Sales* values are between $320,000 and $340,000. This range includes the mean, median, and mode you calculated previously.

3. The distribution is approximately symmetrical around the middle values, forming a "bell-shaped curve" with few occurrences of extreme values of *Sales*. This bell-shaped pattern (see Figure 5.36) is referred by statisticians as a *symmetrical* or *normal distribution*.

4. The standard deviation of home sales data is 38.09 (see Figure 5.37; top right box). This value is 38.09*1000 = $38,090 This statistic provides a standard unit of variance (or deviation) around the mean where the mean or average home price is $342.5 thousands (or, $ 341,500). For symmetrical, bell-shaped or normal data, the mean and standard deviation are combined to provide specific conclusions. This is rule is known as the

5. *Empirical Rule.*

   In a normal distribution, around 68.26 percent of the data falls within a single standard deviation; so in this case, approximately 68 percent of home prices are between $341,500 ± 38,090); approximately 95.45 percent of values fall within 2 standard deviations within the mean in a normal distribution or between [$341,500 ± (2) 38,090)] and approximately 99.73 percent of the home values fall between fall within 3 standard deviations of the mean which is [$341,500 ± (3) 38,090)] so there were between 12.5 and 39.1 sales on 95.4 percent of days.

Creating a Histogram Using Pivot Chart and Pivot Table Option

You may use the Pivot Chart and Pivot Table option to create a frequency distribution table and a histogram.

6. Open the Workbook Home Sales ($000) (A).

7. Select any cell in the data column. Click *Insert* tab of the ribbon and select *Pivot Chart & Pivot Table* option from the Pivot Chart drop-down menu selection, A create PivotTable dialog box will appear.

8. Click on Select a table or range. Put the cursor in the Table/Range box, then select cell A1 and drag down with your mouse pointer to the last value in the data. This will select and print the data range in the box.

9. Check the circle next to *New worksheet.* Excel adds a new worksheet with a PivotTable that looks like Figure 5.38.

10. In the PivotChart fields (on the right), drag the *Home Sales $(000)* field to Access (Categories). Next, drag the *Home Sales $(000)* field to ∑ Values area. The work sheet with a table and graph with the sum of home sales will be displayed. The sum of home sales values needs to be changed to numbers. To change this, we need to change the aggregation.

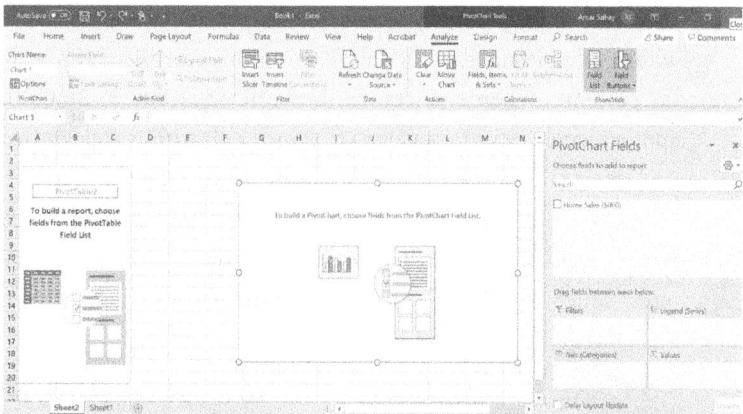

Figure 5.38a Creating a Histogram using Pivot chart, Pivot table Option.

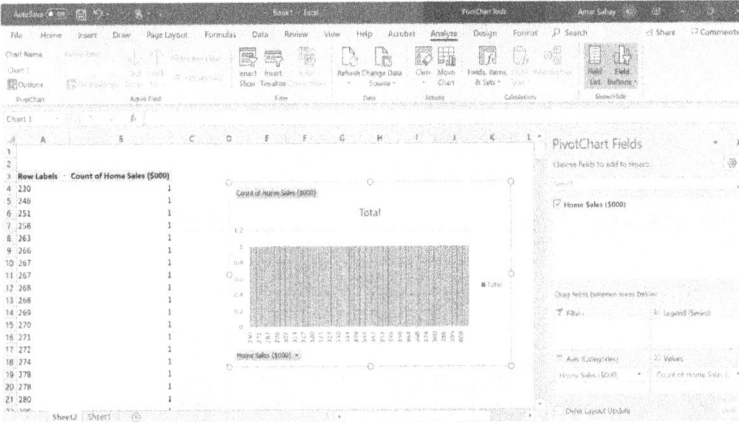

Figure 5.38b *Changing the aggregation in a pivot chart, pivot table*

Change the Aggregation (or the Sum of Home Sales to Count)

11. In the *PivotTable Fields* pane, in the *Values* area, click the drop-down arrow next to *Sum of Home Sales $ (000)* and click *Value Field Settings*.

12. In the *Value Field Settings* dialog box, select *Count*. The table and the graph area will now display *Count of Home Sales*. Your worksheet should look like the one in Figure 5.38b. Note that the Table on the left now shows the count or number of home sales individual home values. of sum. We need to group the values for the histogram.

Grouping the Row labels

Under the Row Labels in the Table above, right click with your mouse and select *Group*. A *Grouping* table will be displayed asking for starting, ending values for the group and the steps. Type the following values:

Starting at	220
Ending at	460
By	20
Click OK.	

13. A frequency table and a histogram of Home Sales will be displayed as in the worksheet below (Figure 5.39). Note that you can click on the default title and provide a suitable title, add the data labels, and close the gap width by clicking on any bar of the histogram.

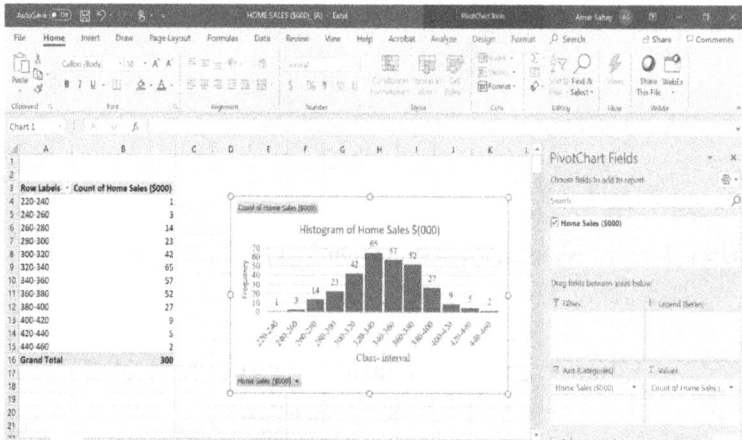

Figure 5.39 Histogram with frequency table

A Box and Whisker Plot of Home Sales Data

1. Refer to Worksheet with *Home Sales ($000)* data or open the worksheet.

2. Select all the data in the *Home Sales* column or column A including the header. Then click the *Insert* tab of the ribbon under chart group click *Insert Statistic Chart* and select Box and Whisker Plot.in the *Other Charts* drop-down list, click the *Box A Box and Whisker* chart (which is the third one in the group).

A *Box and Whisker* Plot similar to Figure 5.40 will be displayed.

3. Select the chart and edit the chart using the edit buttons to change the title to *Box Plot of Home Sales $(000)*.

Interpreting the Plot

1. A Box and Whisker plot is a plot of five statistics calculated from the data. These are the minimum, maximum, Q1—the

Box Plot of Home Sales $(000)

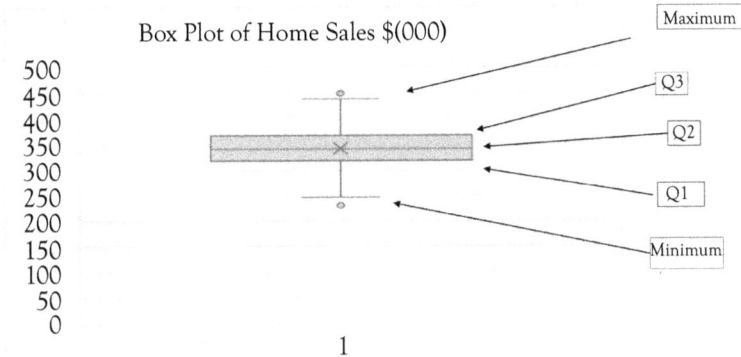

Figure 5.40 A box plot of home sales data

Table 5.8 Descriptive statistics of home sales

Home Sales ($000)	
Mean	342.49
Standard Error	2.20
Median	342.07
Mode	#N/A
Standard Deviation	38.09
Sample Variance	1450.77
Kurtosis	0.03
Skewness	0.02
Range	222.23
Minimum	230.00
Maximum	452.23
Sum	102448
Count	300

first quartile or 25th percentile, Q2—the second quartile (50th percentile or the median), Q3—third quartile (or 75th percentile), and the maximum. All these values are obtained by calculating the descriptive statistics shown in Table 5.8.

2. The above five measures are plotted. The box like shape in the middle shows the values of Q1, Q2, and Q3. The horizontal line in the middle of the box indicates the *median* value for home sales. This is also the 50% *percentile*. This means that 50 percent of the values

are higher than this, and 50 percent are lower. From Table 5.8, The median home price is 342.07 (or, 342.07 * 1000 = $341,070). Half of the home values are above this and the other half below this median value.

3. For our home sales data, the mean or the average home price is 342.49 (or, 342.49 * 1000 = $341,490). This is slightly higher the median. When the mean and median are equal or approximately equal, it indicates that the distribution or the shape of Home Sales data is symmetrical, bell shaped or normal. Our data is approximately symmetrical.

4. The filled box indicates the range of values in the first and third *quartiles (Q1 and Q3)*—or, from the 25th percentile to the 75th percentile.

5. The lines extending from the box are known as *whiskers*.

Create a Histogram of Income Data and Analyze the Graph

1. Open the Workbook **Income Data.**
2. The data shows the annual income of 1,000 wage earners. The data values are in thousands of dollars.
3. Create a histogram of *Income data* by *Selecting* all the data in the Income $(000) column including the header. Click on the *Insert* tab of the ribbon and select *Recommended Charts*. A few possible charts for the data you selected will be displayed. Click the *Histogram* by double clicking on it (this should be the third one under recommended charts). The histogram created is a default one.
4. Add an appropriate chart title and move the chart to the right of Income Data column. The histogram Figure 5.41. Also select the pareto chart from the recommended charts (shown in the Income worksheet and below the histogram). The Pareto chart is shown in Figure 5.42.

Interpreting the Histogram

From the histogram, it is evident that the distribution of the income data is not *normal or symmetrical.* This type of shape is characterized by a right skewed or positively skewed. The statistics of the income data are:

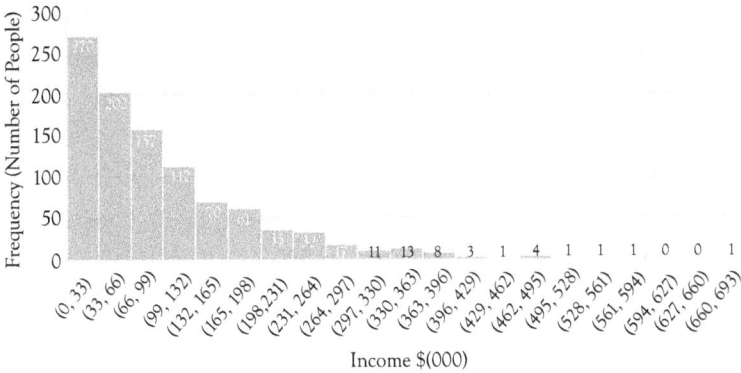

Figure 5.41 Histogram of income data

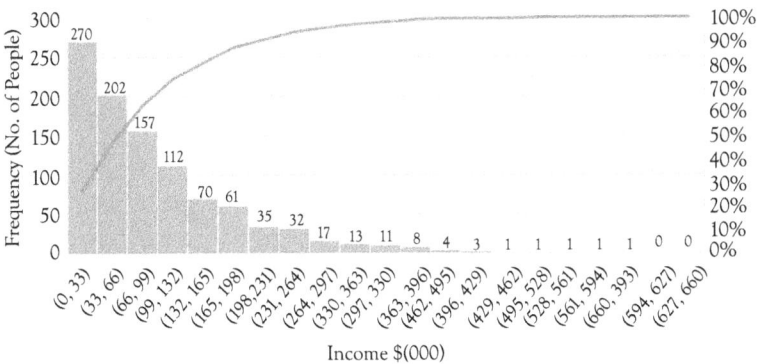

Figure 5.42 Pareto chart of income data

Mean	98.294
Median	72
Standard Deviation	93.1831

In a positively skewed data, the mean is greater than the median. It seems obvious that the number wage earners in the higher range have less occurrence. These infrequent numbers of high incomes have less frequency and are *skewing* the distribution by "pulling" the mean to the right. This results in a long tail of infrequently occurring values that extends toward the right. The distribution is therefore referred to as a *right-skewed or positively skewed* distribution.

In some other data, the mean is pulled to the left resulting into infrequent values tapered to the left of the distribution resulting into a *left-skewed or negatively skewed* distribution or a negatively skewed distribution.

A Pareto chart of the data is also shown that plots the data in decreasing order of frequency. In the income data, the range with lower annual income is higher than the less occurring value of high wage earners.

Create a Box and Whisker Chart of Income

Follow the instructions provided earlier and create the chart. The box and whisker plot are shown in Figure 5.43. and in the Income Data worksheet. Provide an appropriate title and interpret the graph.

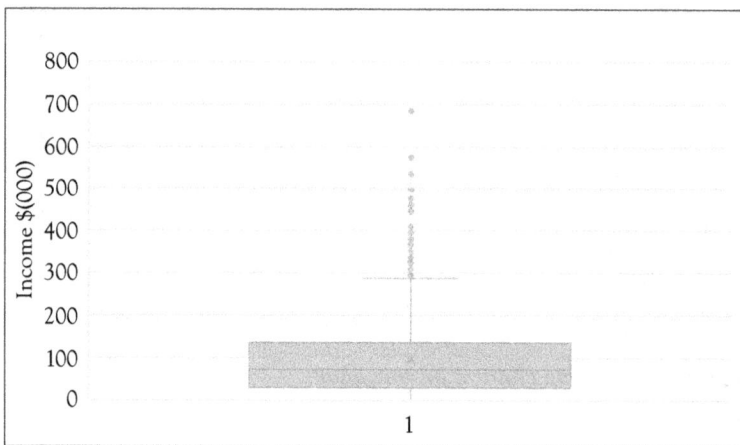

Figure 5.43 Box and Whisker plot of income data.

From the box and whisker plot above, we can draw the following conclusions:

1. The length of the whiskers is not equal—it is much longer from the Q3 to the maximum value. This is an indication that the income data is skewed to the right. For a symmetrical data, the median line (in the box) divides the data in approximately equal half.
2. The line indicating the median (50th percentile) in the box is noticeably lower than the mean (indicated by an X).

3. The dots indicate *outliers*; or extreme values that are considered extreme compared to the typical range of values, which lies within the whiskers.

(Note: this plot is useful in visualizing the distribution.)

Visualizing Categorical Data: Bar Charts, Pie Charts, Cross Tabulation

Bar Charts

1. Open the Workbook **Categorical Data.**
2. The data shows the revenue of top Internet companies as of April 2020. The data values are in billions of dollars.
3. Create different variations of bar chart by *Selecting* all the data in columns A and B including the header. Click on the *Insert* tab of the ribbon and select *Recommended Charts*. A few possible charts for the data you selected will be displayed. Click the first bar chart from the list by double clicking on it. Click on the plot and select the edit tools to provide appropriate chart and axes titles and to change the color. The variations of bar charts by selecting the recommended charts option are shown in Figures 5.44, 5.45, and 5.46 and on the data worksheet.

(*Note*: These charts can also be created individually by selecting the *Data → Insert → 2-D bar or column charts.*)

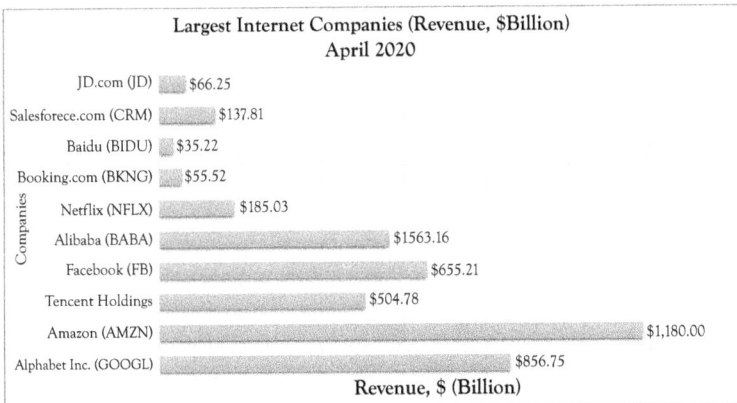

Figure 5.44 shows a horizontal bar chart titled "Largest Internet Companies (Revenue, $Billion) April 2020" with the y-axis labeled "Companies" and x-axis labeled "Revenue, $ (Billion)":

Company	Revenue ($ Billion)
JD.com (JD)	$66.25
Salesforece.com (CRM)	$137.81
Baidu (BIDU)	$35.22
Booking.com (BKNG)	$55.52
Netflix (NFLX)	$185.03
Alibaba (BABA)	$1563.16
Facebook (FB)	$655.21
Tencent Holdings	$504.78
Amazon (AMZN)	$1,180.00
Alphabet Inc. (GOOGL)	$856.75

Figure 5.44 Bar Chart—largest Internet companies (April 2020)

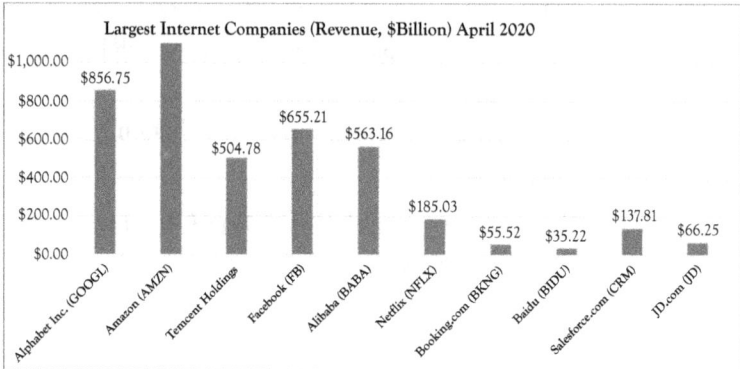

Figure 5.45 *A vertical bar chart—largest Internet companies (April 2020)*

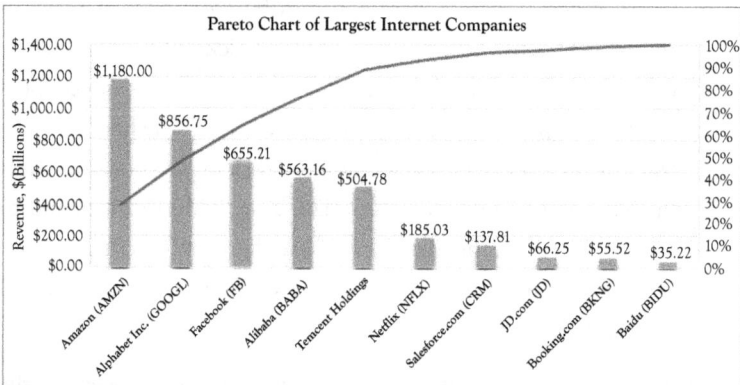

Figure 5.46 *Pareto Chart—largest Internet companies (April 2020)*

Variations of Bar Chart

In the Workbook select **Categorical Data**, select columns U,V,W,X, and Y.

1. The data shows the quarterly sales (in millions of dollars) of a company that markets its product in their different zones.

2. Create different variations of bar chart by **Selecting** all the data in columns U through Y including the header. Click on the **Insert** tab of the ribbon and select **Recommended Charts. A few possible charts for the data you selected will be displayed.** The four possible charts explained below can be used to display this data. These charts are variations of bar graph that can be used to

describe the sales activities. You can choose the most appropriate chart for the purpose. When the charts are displayed, click the **first bar chart from the list** by double clicking on it. Click on the plot and select the edit tools (on the right top corner of the chart with a + sign) to provide appropriate chart and axes titles and change the colors as desired. The variations of bar charts by selecting the recommended charts option are shown in Figures 5.47, 5.48, and 5.49 and on the data worksheet. These charts are explained here. (*Note*: These charts can also be created individually by selecting the Data → Insert → 2-D bar or column charts).

i. **A Clustered Column Chart**

A clustered column chart is useful in comparing values across a few categories when the order of categories is not important.

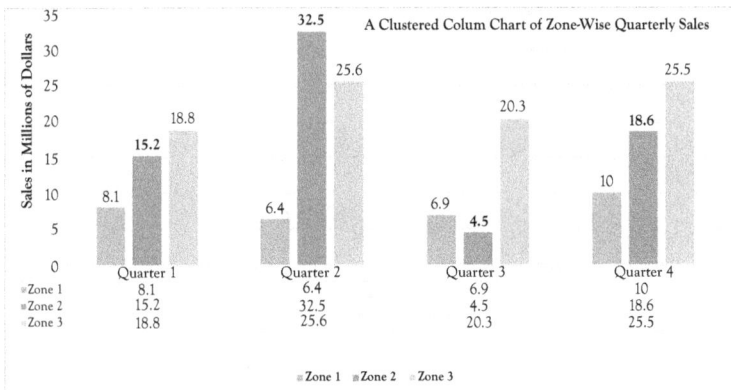

	Quarter 1	Quarter 2	Quarter 3	Quarter 4
Zone 1	8.1	6.4	6.9	10
Zone 2	15.2	32.5	4.5	18.6
Zone 3	18.8	25.6	20.3	25.5

Figure 5.47 A clustered column chart of quarterly sales

ii. **A Stacked Column Chart**

A stacked column or chart shown below is used to compare parts of a whole. The chart is used to show how the parts of a whole change over some period. The plot below shows the change is sales for three zones over four quarters.

iii. **Clustered Bar Column Chart**

This chart is used to compare the values in a variable (sales) across different categories.

STACKED COLUMN CHART
Zone 1 Zone 2 Zone 3

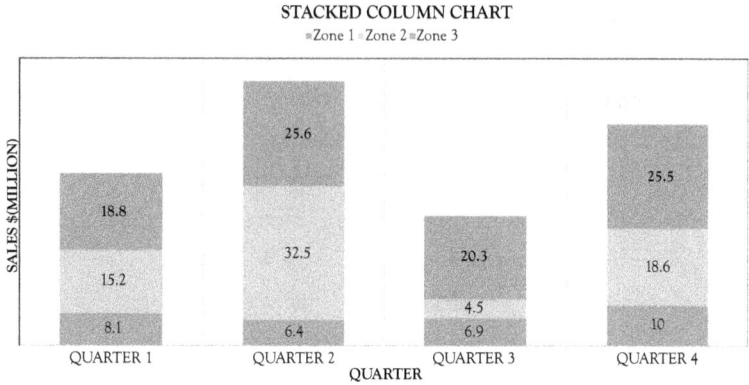

Figure 5.48 A Stacked column chart of quarterly sales

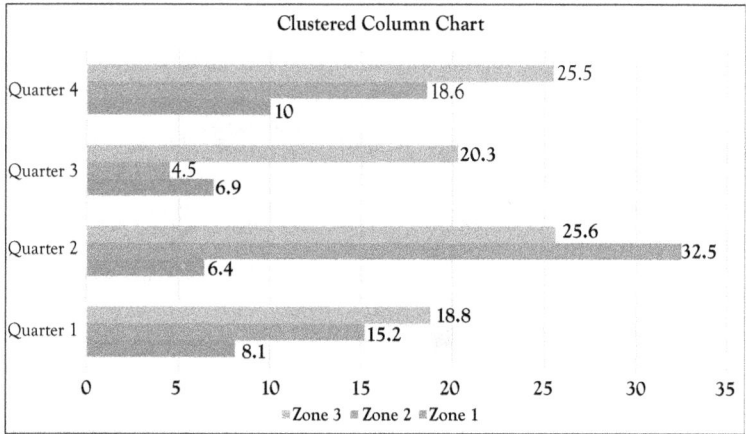

Figure 5.49 A variation of Clustered column chart of quarterly sales

iv. **Stacked Area Chart**

A stacked area chart is used to show the relationship of parts to whole over time or different categories. The chart is used to display the magnitude of change in a variable or variables over time or in different categories (Figure 5.50).

v. **Stacked Area Chart: Another Example**

The chart in Figure 5.51 shows another example of a stacked area chart of U.S. primary energy consumption by major sources from 1950 to 2019. The data is in the worksheet **Historical Energy Consumption 1950–2019.**

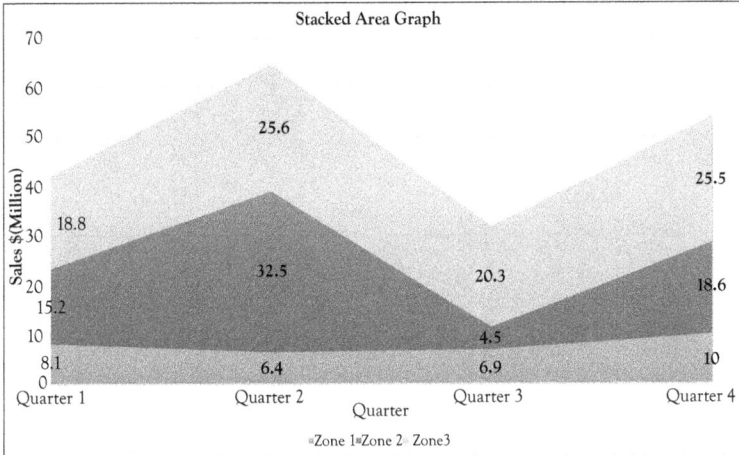

Figure 5.50 A stacked Area chart of quarterly sales

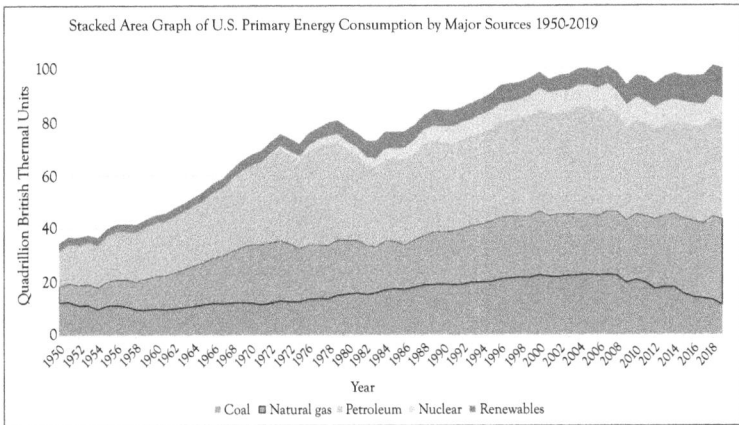

Figure 5.51 A stacked area graph of energy consumption

Line Chart

Open the worksheet **Historical Energy Consumption 1950–2019** and construct a line chart.

Line Chart of U.S. primary energy consumption by major sources from 1950 to 2019. This chart shows the trends over time (days, months, years, etc.) or categories when the order is important. The chart can be used for large data sets when the order of data is important as in time-series. An example is shown in Figure 5.52.

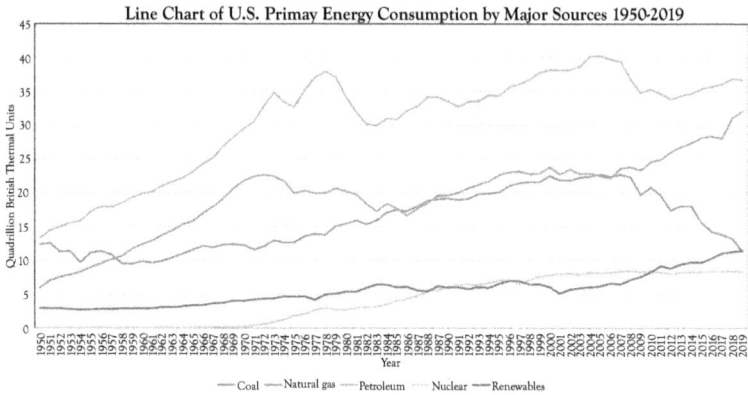

Figure 5.52 A line chart of energy consumption

A Bar or a Column Chart

Create a bar or a column chart *Selecting* all the data in columns AD and AE of the worksheet **Categorical Data**, the data shows the revenue of amazon from 2005 to 2019 in millions of U.S. dollars. Edit the chart and provide appropriate chart and axes titles. The chart is in Figure 5.53.

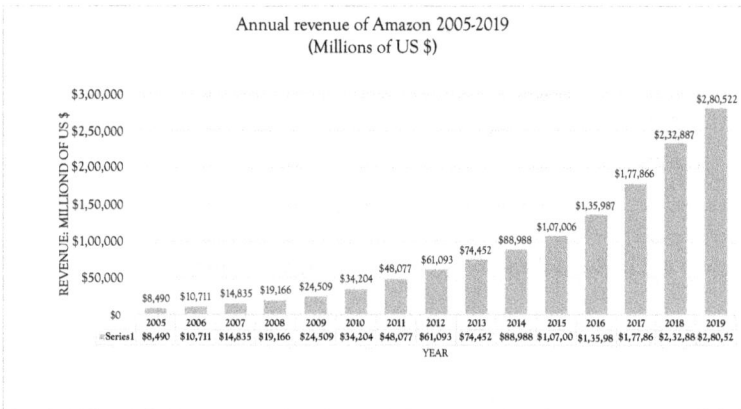

Figure 5.53 A bar chart of categorical variable showing revenue of Amazon

Pie Chart

Create a pie chart by *Selecting* all the data in columns AG and AH of the worksheet *Categorical Data*. The data shows U.S. auto market share of selected auto makers for the year 2018. To construct the chart, select the data in columns AG and AH. Click on Recommended charts or click insert and select Pie Chart option. Edit the chart and provide appropriate chart and axes titles. The chart is shown Figure 5.54. Two versions of pie chart (a 3-D and a 2-D) are shown in Figures 5.54 and 5.55. Feel free to experiment with design options once your chart is created.

Bar of a Pie Chart

This chart is useful in displaying the categories with small percentages as a separate bar or a pie chart that is created as an extension of the main chart of Excel has two options. Open the worksheet Bar of a Pie chart. The data shows U.S. primary energy production by major sources, 2019. The data is shown in columns B9 to C17. The data contains three categories with small percentage (Wind, Hydro, and other). These are less than 6 percent. The smaller categories may be displayed as a bar chart or a pie chart to make them more visible. Excel provides the *Pie of Pie* and *Bar of Pie* (see Figures 5.55 and 5.56) chart subtypes to achieve this.

Bar of a Pie Chart

To construct the bar of the Pie, follow the instructions below.

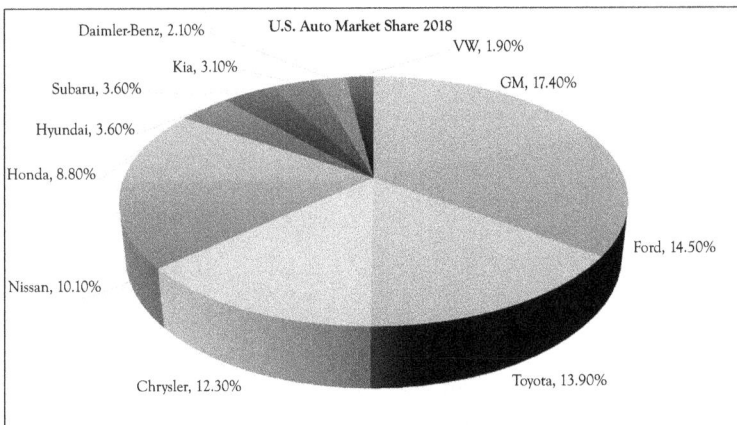

Figure 5.54 A Pie Chart of U.S. market share for 2018

1. Open worksheet **Bar of a Pie chart**.
2. Select the data in cells B9 to C17.
3. On the *Insert* tab, in the *Charts* group, choose the *Pie* button and select Bar of Pie chart.
4. A pie chart with an extended bar chart will be displayed.
5. Pie of Pie Chart in Excel 2016.
6. Right-click in the chart area. In the popup menu, select *Format Data Series*.
7. In the Format Data Series task pane, on the *Series Options* tab, select which data to display in the bar chart (in this example, the bar chart shows all values less than 5 percent) by selecting:

   Split Series by   *Percentage Value*
   Values less than   5%

8. Click on the graph then select *Design* from the main menu and select the design that displays the categories name and percentage or
9. Click of the graph and provide appropriate titles by clicking *Chart Elements*—the (+) edit button box on the top right of the graph then click on *Chart Style* below the chart element and select the slice labels and percentage labels.

A bar of a pie chart as shown in Figure 5.55 will be displayed.

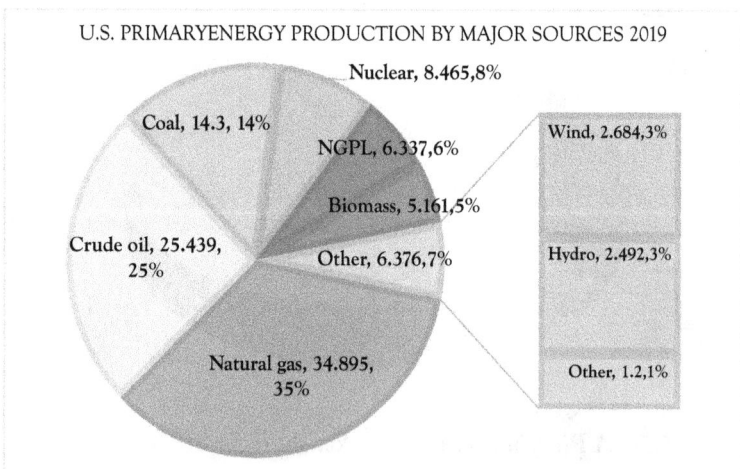

U.S. PRIMARYENERGY PRODUCTION BY MAJOR SOURCES 2019

Nuclear, 8.465,8%
Coal, 14.3, 14%
NGPL, 6.337,6%
Biomass, 5.161,5%
Crude oil, 25.439, 25%
Other, 6.376,7%
Natural gas, 34.895, 35%

Wind, 2.684,3%
Hydro, 2.492,3%
Other, 1.2,1%

Figure 5.55 A Bar of a pie chart of U.S. market share for 2018

A pie of pie chart shown in Figure 5.56 will be displayed.

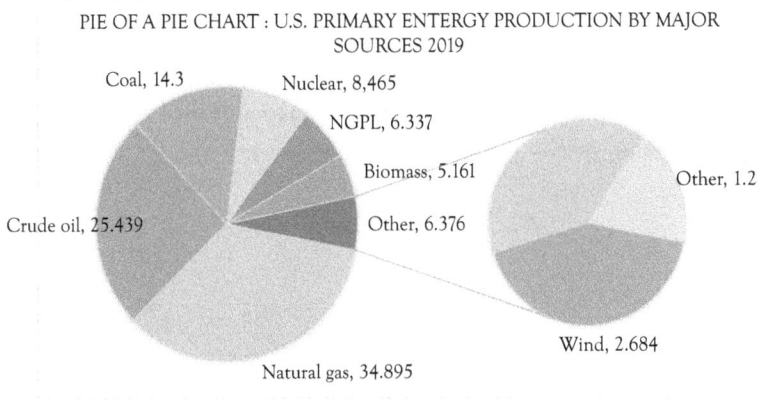

PIE OF A PIE CHART : U.S. PRIMARY ENTERGY PRODUCTION BY MAJOR
SOURCES 2019

Coal, 14.3   Nuclear, 8,465

NGPL, 6.337

Biomass, 5.161   Other, 1.2

Crude oil, 25.439   Other, 6.376

Wind, 2.684

Natural gas, 34.895

Figure 5.56 A pie of pie chart

Relationship Between Two and Three Variables: Scatter Plot Bubble Graph and Time-Series Plot

Scatter Plot

Open the Work Sheet **Scatter Plot and Bubble Graph**.

Columns B and C of data shows the sales and profit (in thousands of dollars) of a company.

Select all the data in columns B and C including the header. Click on the *Insert* tab of the ribbon and select *Recommended Charts*. A few possible charts for the data you selected will be displayed. The first plot of interest is the *scatter plot,* which is the most appropriate chart for the purpose. When the charts are displayed click on the first plot (scatter plot) and select the edit tools (on the right top corner of the chart with a + sign) to provide appropriate chart and axes titles and change the colors as desired. This plot can also be done by selecting the data in columns B and C, clicking on the *Insert* tab, and selecting *scatter plot.*

The scatter plot of sales and profit is shown in Figure 5.57. The plot is used to explain the relationship between two variables. The scatter plot shows an increasing or a positive relationship between sales and profit. It means that as the sale is increasing so is the profit. The relationship between the two variables may be linear, or quadratic (nonlinear).

Scatter Plot With Line of Best-Fitted (Fitted Line Plot)

The scatter plot above shows a linear relationship. A trend line can be fitted to the data which will show a line of best fit. Such a plot with a trend line and the equation of the trend line can be constructed. This line is also known as a regression line and the equation is used to forecast (in this case, sales, y).

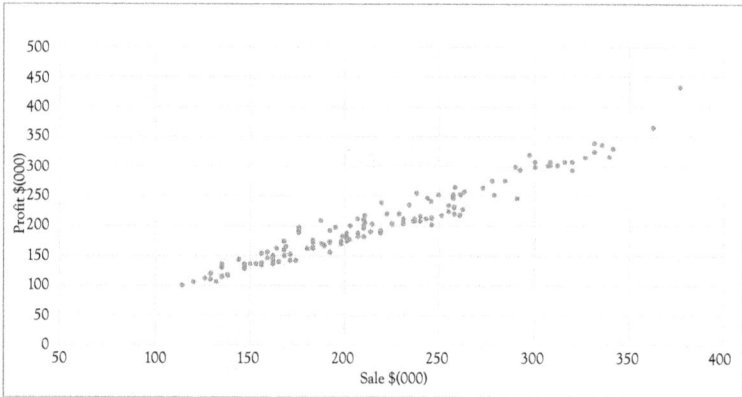

Figure 5.57 Scatter plot of sales and profit

When the scatter plot is completed right-click on any of the plotted point on the graph. and select *Add Trend line*. A trend line will be displayed on the plot and a *Trend line Options* dialog box will appear on the right pane. Scroll down and from the available options, check the boxes *Display Equation on chart* and *Display R-squared value on chart* (optional). You may move the equation to the other side of the graph.

Your chart will be similar Figure 5.58.

Bubble Chart

The bubble graph or chart is like the scatter plot but instead of two variables, it shows the relationship between three variables. The value of the third variable is determined by the relative size of the bubble. The chart below shows two different variations of the bubble plot for the same data. To construct the plot:

In the *Workbook Scatter Plot and Bubble Graph*, select columns O, P, and Q. These columns show the data for advertisement, sales for different

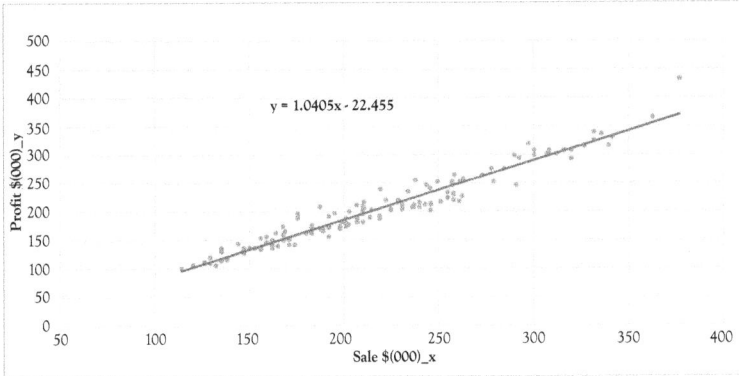

Figure 5.58 Fitted line plot of sales and profit

store sizes (small, medium, large labeled 3,2, and 1 respectively). Click on the *Insert* tab of the ribbon and select *Recommended Charts*. A few charts for the data you selected will be displayed. The plot of interest is the *Bubble Graph*, which should be the fourth one on the list. The chart shows advertisement on the *x*-axis, sales on the *y*-axis and the store size is depicted by the relative size of the bubbles. When the charts are displayed click on the plot and select the edit tools (on the right top corner of the chart with a + sign) to provide appropriate chart and axes titles and change the colors as desired. This can also be done by selecting the data in columns O, P, and Q, clicking on the *Insert* tab, and selecting *scatter plot* from the charts group. The drop-down menu in this group contains the bubble graph. The graphs are shown in Figures 5.59 and 5.60.

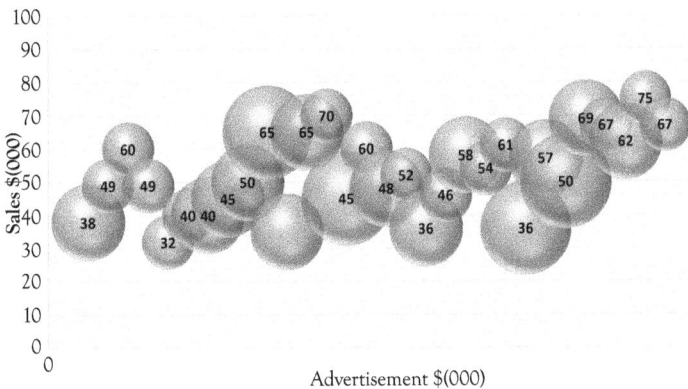

Figure 5.59 Bubble chart of advertisement, sales, and store size

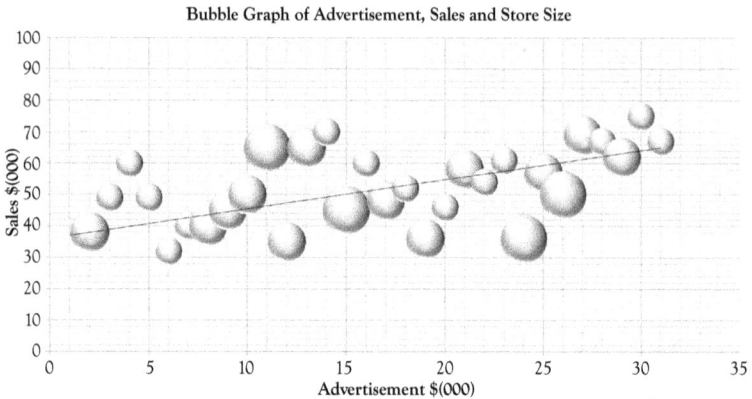

Figure 5.60 A Variation of bubble chart of advertisement, sales, and store size

Time Series Plot

In the **Workbook Scatter Plot and Bubble Graph**, select columns *AD* and *AE*. These columns show the weekly demand data for a cell phone of a retailer. Click on the *Insert* tab of the ribbon and select *Recommended Charts*. A few charts for the data you selected will be displayed. The first plot displayed should be a scatter plot with connected line and the second one a line chart. Both charts show the time or the week on the *x*-axis and demand on *y*-axis. Since the data is plotted over time, it is a time series plot. Click on the first plot to select it. Click on the plot and select the edit tools (on the right top corner of the chart with a + sign) to provide appropriate chart and axes titles and change the colors as desired. This plot also can also be done by selecting the data in columns AD and AE, clicking on the Insert tab, an selecting the appropriate chart from the group *2-D line* group or from *scatter plot* from the plot group. The edited *Time Series Plot of Demand of Cell Phone Data* is shown in Figure 5.61.

Sales and Forecast: In the *Workbook Scatter Plot and Bubble Graph*, select columns A0, AP, and AQ. These columns show the weekly sales and forecast data for a cell phone of a retailer. Follow the instructions for the time series plot in the previous graph and construct a connected

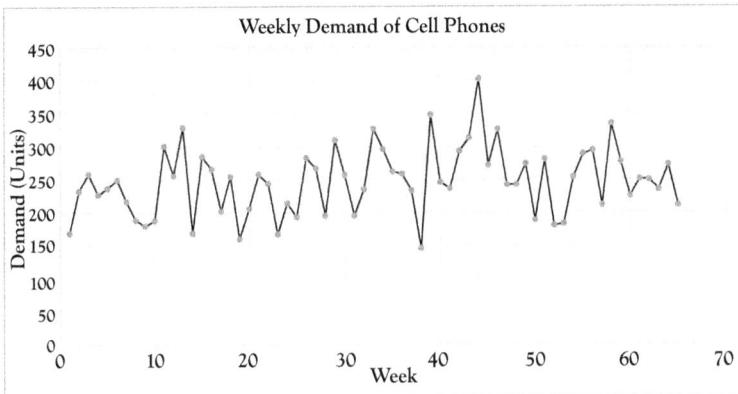

Figure 5.61 Time series plot of demand data

Figure 5.62 Time series plot of sales and forecast demand data

line graph to show both the sales and forecast on the same plot. Edit the graph to provide the chart and axes titles and choose different colors for the sales and the forecast data. Your chart should be like the one shown in Figure 5.62.

Summary

This chapter introduced Excel using Office 365, a widely available and used software for data science and analysis. This software contains data manipulation, analysis, and visualization tools along with advanced data analysis capabilities. There are several packages available as add-ins to this software to enhance its capabilities. In this chapter, we presented basic to more involved features and capabilities. The chapter is divided into sections including "Getting Stated with Excel" followed by several applications and graphics using recent data and applications. The examples provide downloadable data files and stepwise instructions.

(*Note:* The data files in this chapter will be made available as a downloadable folder.)

PART III

Data Visualization and Statistics for Data Science

CHAPTER 6

Basic Statistical Concepts for Data Science

Chapter Highlights

The concepts of statistics are essential in solving data science related problems.

The major topics in this chapter are:

- Applications and importance of Statistics in Data Science
- Statistics as a Science of Variation
- Concepts of Variation, Variables, and Statistical Thinking
- Basic Vocabulary of Statistics and Different Ways of Defining Statistics
- Identify Data and Different Classifications of Data
- Two Broad Categories of Statistics: Descriptive and Inferential Statistics
- Define and Understand Basic Statistical Terms Including Population, Sample, Parameters, and Statistics
- Tools of Descriptive and Inferential Statistics
- Current Trends in the Ever-Growing Area of Statistics and Data Analysis

Statistics at a Glance

Statistics is the science and art of making decision using data. It is often called the science of data and is about analyzing and drawing meaningful conclusions from the data. Almost every field uses data and statistics to learn about systems and their processes. In fields such as marketing, business, research, health care, and engineering, a vast amount of raw data is collected and warehoused rapidly. This data must be analyzed to be meaningful. Statistics and statistical tools enable us to make efficient decisions from data. Statistical methods aid in gaining skills such as (i) collecting, describing, analyzing, and interpreting data for intelligent decision making, (ii) realizing that variation is an integral part of data, (iii) understanding the nature and pattern of variability of a phenomenon in the data, and (iv) being able to measure reliability of the population parameters from which the sample data are collected to draw valid inferences.

The applications of statistics can be found in a majority of issues that concern everyday life. Examples include surveys related to consumer opinions, marketing studies, and economic and political polls.

Some Applications: Statistics from Some Areas of Interest

Student Loan Debt in the United States

The CNBC financial news channel reported in October 2019 that U.S. student loan debt exceeded $2.6 trillion. *The Economist* reported in June 2014 the total student debt in the United States exceeded $2.2 trillion with over 7 million debtors in default. Public universities increased their fees by a total of 27 percent over the past five years (20 percent when adjusted for inflation). Public university students paid an average of almost $8,400 annually for in-state tuition, with out-of-state students paying more than $19,000. In each year of the past two decades, college costs rose 2.6 percent above the inflation rate. Government funding per student fell 27 percent between 2007 and 2012. Student enrollment rose from 15.2 million in 1999 to 20.4 million in 2011 but fell 2 percent in 2012 (*Source: The Economist*, Creative destruction, June 28, 2014).

Manufacturing: Here are some statistics regarding the state of manufacturing in the United States.

Manufacturers in the United States account for 12.69 percent of the total output in the economy. Total output from manufacturing was $2,334.60 billion in 2018. In addition, there were an average of 12.8 million manufacturing employees in the United States in 2018, with an average annual compensation of $84,832.13 in 2017. Some other manufacturing statistics:

Total Manufacturing Output ($billions, 2018)	$2,334.60
(Percent share of total gross domestic product)	11.39
Manufacturing Firms in the United States (2016)	249,962
Manufacturing Employment (2018)	12.69
(Percent share of nonfarm employment)	8.51%
Average Annual Compensation (Manufacturing, 2017)	$84,832.13
(Nonfarm Businesses, 2017)	$66,538.49

Sources: U.S. Bureau of Economic Analysis and the U.S. Census Bureau

Manufacturers in the United States perform more than three-quarters of all private-sector research and development (R&D) in the nation, driving more innovation than any other sector. (*Source:* National Association of Manufacturer Report, www.nam.org.)

Current Developments in Data Analytics

Because of the advancement in technology, it is now possible to collect massive amounts of data. Lots of data, such as web data, e-commerce, purchase transactions at retail stores, and bank and credit card transaction data, among more, is collected and warehoused by businesses. There has been an increasing amount of pressure on businesses to provide high-quality products and services to improve their market share in this highly competitive market. Not only it is critical for businesses to meet and exceed customer needs and requirements, but it is also important for businesses to process and analyze a large amount of data efficiently in order to seek hidden patterns in the data. The processing and analysis of large data sets comes under the emerging field known as big data, data mining, and analytics.

To process these massive amounts of data, data mining uses statistical techniques and algorithms and extracts nontrivial, implicit, previously unknown, and potentially useful patterns. Because applications of data mining tools are growing, there will be more of a demand for professionals trained in data science and analytics. The knowledge discovered from this data in order to make intelligent data-driven decisions is referred to as business intelligence (BI) and business analytics. These are hot topics in business and leadership circles today as it uses a set of techniques and processes which aid in fact-based decision making.

Much of the data analysis and statistical techniques we discuss in this and coming chapters are prerequisites to fully understanding data science and business analytics. In this text, we provide an overview of data science techniques. These are at the core of data science.

What Is Statistics?

The study of statistics involves making sense from the data by extracting useful information from the collected data and drawing meaningful conclusions. The science of statistics enables us to find patterns in the random data and describe this randomness using mathematical and statistical methods that have been developed over the years. These methods are useful in the decision-making process. To draw meaningful conclusion, it is important to collect the right and sufficient amount of data and be able to apply correct statistical tools.

We find statistics and data in day to day applications for example, stock market activities, unemployment rates, medical research findings, opinion poll results, weather forecasts, sports data, business transaction data all use some form of statistics. Today, businesses are run using data.

To learn about a process or a business, we often collect data. Also, to learn about the present state of the economy, the opinion of voters in the presidential election, the average life of a light bulb, the effectiveness of a new drug, or to understand the variation in a process, we often collect and analyze data. This chapter reviews the statistical methods used in collecting, presenting, and analyzing data.

Statistics and Variation

Statistics deals with *variation*. All data show variation and statistics is the tool that deals with the variation in data. Statistical tools and techniques allow us to study the variation in the data. Variation is a part of any process or system, and it must be kept within certain limit for any process to work efficiently. Analyzing and reducing variation is the major goal of many companies using quality control programs such as Six Sigma and lean Six Sigma. The topics in this course will help you understand the concepts of statistics and data analysis, variation, and introduce you to the tools and techniques used in analyzing data from businesses and other processes. Use of computer software in analyzing data is emphasized throughout the text.

The basic concepts presented in this chapter are important in understanding the uses and importance of statistics in data science.

Definitions of Statistics

Some definitions of statistics are given below:

1. Statistics is about making decisions from data.
2. Statistics is a science that deals with collection, tabulation, analysis, interpretation, and presentation of data (in order to make decisions).
3. Statistics is the science concerned with problems involving chance variations that result from many small and independent influences operating on each measured result.
4. Statistics is concerned with making decisions from data involving chance variations.
5. Statistics deals with making inferences or predictions about a population based on sample data.

Why Study Statistics?

There are two main characteristics that make the study of statistics important.

1. Statistics is the branch of mathematics that deals with *variation* and is often called mathematics of variation. Most data we collect show variation and an element (such as, a person, thing, or event) upon which we collect data can be seen as a *variable. A variable*

is a characteristic of interest that differs among observations or measurements. We can study the variation in data using statistics. Statistical thinking and variation reduction are major goals in data analysis, decision making, and quality improvement programs such as Six Sigma.

2. Statistical methods enable us to draw conclusions using limited data, or they enable us to draw conclusion about a *population* using the *sample* data. For example, we can predict an election outcome without seeking the opinion of the entire population of voters who are eligible to vote. We rely on a small sample to draw conclusion about the entire population.

Statistical tools and methods are used to describe, organize, and interpret information and data. The data contains information that help us understand the world around us and provide a better understanding of the systems and processes from which data are collected. It enables us to make better decisions with the information we have available. By analyzing the data and applying the statistical tools, we can learn about what happened in the past and predict the future outcomes. With the advancement in technology, the data collection process is now mostly automatic. Businesses are now able to collect massive amounts of data and are able to process and analyze the data in real time to learn and make quick and effective decisions about their businesses.

Uses and Application Areas of Statistics

Statistics are used in nearly every profession. Businesses use statistics in analyzing operations, cost accounting, financial analysis, marketing, and other management courses. A quality engineer will use statistics and data for processes that will improve product quality. Because of the continued advancement in technology and data storage capability, businesses are now run using data. The emerging fields of data science and analytics big data are now making possible to make critical business decisions using real time. The algorithms and models used in machine learning and artificial intelligence (AI) use huge amounts of data. The areas of machine learning and AI are emerging fields of research and application development.

They use statistics and statistical modeling in different forms among other areas of computer science and programming.

Subdivisions of Statistics

Statistics is studied under two broad categories: *descriptive statistics* and *inferential statistics*. *Descriptive statistics* uses graphical and numerical methods to describe and analyze data. *Inferential statistics or inference procedures* are part of statistics concerned with drawing conclusions about the *population* using *sample data*. The details of these subdivisions of statistics are provided later in this chapter. The chapters in this book cover both descriptive and inferential statistics tools in detail. To understand inferential statistics, the understanding of probability theory, probability distributions, sampling and sampling techniques are a prerequisite. These topics are discussed in subsequent chapters.

Descriptive Statistics

Descriptive statistics is defined as the methods involving the collection, presentation, and characterization of a set of data in order to properly describe the various features of that set of data. Descriptive statistics is important in presenting and characterizing information. In other words, the tools of descriptive statistics are used to describe the data. There are two ways we can describe the collected data: (1) through charts and graphs and (2) using numerical methods. Charts and graphs fall under the category of graphical methods. Graphical techniques include charts and graphs including bar charts, pie charts, histograms, polygons, and scatter diagrams. The details of graphical techniques are presented in Chapter 7.

Descriptive statistics can be used to display graphically the profits, revenues, or sales of a company or the change in sales and demand of a product over time using time series plots. Several charts and graphs such as the pie chart, bar charts, scatter plots, and others are excellent ways of describing data visually. The numerical methods of descriptive statistics are used to study the variation in data. Several measures or statistics including the mean or average, median, variance, standard deviation, or percentiles calculated from a set of data help us learn a great deal about the data. For example, suppose we calculate the average grade for a class. This tells us about the performance of the class. Statistics calculated from the data help us summarize and describe the data.

Inferential Statistics

Inferential statistics is the process of using *sample* statistics to draw conclusions about the *population* parameters. Inference procedures make generalizations about the population, which is usually a larger data set compared to the sample data.

Population denotes the entire measurements that are theoretically possible. It is also known as the universe and is the totality of items or things under consideration. For example, total number of light bulbs manufactured by a company in a given period of time, or number of people who can vote in a country, and so on.

Sample is the portion of the population that is selected for analysis (a subset of population).

A population is described by its *parameter* whereas a sample is described by its *statistics*.

A *parameter* is a summary measure that is computed to describe the characteristic of a population. A *statistic* is a summary measure that is computed to describe the characteristic of a sample. Table 6.1 summarizes the population parameters and the sample statistics, and the symbols used to describe them.

Table 6.1 Population parameters and sample statistics

Population parameters:
μ: *the population mean*; σ^2: *the population variance*
σ: *the population standard deviation*; p: *the population proportion*
N: *the population size*
Sample statistics
The corresponding sample statistics are denoted using the symbols below.
$\bar{x}$: *the sample mean* s^2: *the sample variance*
s: *the sample standard deviation* $\bar{p}$: *the sample proportion*
n: *the sample size*

The population mean is denoted using the Greek symbol μ (read as "mu"), population variance by σ^2 (read as sigma-squared), the population standard deviation is denoted using another Greek symbol σ (read as "sigma"), and the population proportion is denoted by "p". Note that each parameter is denoted using a specific symbol.

The sample statistics are the *sample mean*, $\bar{x}$ (read as "x-bar"), *sample variance (s^2), sample standard deviation, (s), sample median*, and sample proportion,

$\bar{p}$ (read as p-bar). It is important to know the distinction between the population parameters and the sample statistics and the way they are described. We will describe these symbols and their meaning in the chapters that follow.

Interference problems are those that involve inductive generalizations. For example, we use the *statistics* of the sample to draw conclusions about the *parameters* of the population from which the sample was taken. An example would be to use the average grade achieved by one class to estimate the average grade achieved in all ten sections of the same course.

The process of estimating this average grade would be a problem of inferential statistics. In this case, any conclusion made about the ten sections would be a generalization, which may not be completely valid so it must be stated how likely it is to be true.

Statistical inference involves generalization and a statement about the reliability or probability of its validity. For example, an engineer or a scientist can make inferences about a population by analyzing the samples. Decisions can then be made based on the sample results. Making decisions or drawing conclusions using sample data raises question about the likelihood of the decisions being correct. This helps us understand why probability theory is used in statistical analysis.

Using probability models, we can apply the probability approach to estimate the population parameters. The choice of the proper probability distribution to represent any given data comes with experience and knowledge of statistical theory. By using certain statistical hypothesis, we test the correctness of the probability distribution.

The Importance and Overall Idea Behind Statistics

Using statistical methods, we can make inferences or make decisions because the methods utilize certain orderliness (pattern) which exists in statistical measurements (data). The wide application of statistics is because of the development of inferential statistics methods, which is an outgrowth of probability theory. Probability theory came from the investigation of games of chance.

We also use the concept of *frequency* (number of occurrences of a given value) and *frequency distribution*. A pattern is often derived from the frequency distribution, which may be related to a mathematically derived distribution or a probability distribution. These distributions are used to draw conclusions and make decisions from the data.

Graphs, charts, and tables that display data are all examples of descriptive statistics and are helpful in drawing conclusions from the data. Estimation and hypothesis testing are major tools of inferential statistics that use the sample data to estimate the unknown population parameters or make decisions about the population parameter based on the information contained in the sample data.

Role of Computers in Statistics

Advancement in the computing technology has led to widespread use of statistics in real-world applications. Excellent software programs are available for analyzing data. In recent years, the volume, variety, and the velocity (speed) of data has increase manifolds. The volume of collected data by big companies and organizations is so massive that traditional statistical methods and software are not capable of handling the volume. The massive volume of data in the databases of companies are so large that they are often referred to as Big Data. Several big data and analytics software are now developed that combine the traditional as well as newly developed methods of statistics and data analysis. Applications in machine learning (ML) and artificial intelligence (AI) require enormous data storage and computing capabilities. It is not possible to process and analyze the massive volumes of data without interfacing different software. Some of the newly developed applications and software are Tableau, SAS, and

Microsoft machine learning software that are used to automate machine learning applications. The new applications are continuously improving as the computing and storage capacity (memory) is increasing. There has been tremendous growth and improvement in the technology through research. All this is making big data analysis, modeling, and automating the applications using massive volume of data.

Statistical Thinking

The concept of *statistical thinking* is critical in statistics and data analysis. It is a thought process that focuses on ways to reduce variability. In the study of statistics, it is important to understand that almost all measurements show variation. Statistical thinking is an overall approach to improving any process or product. According to the *Glossary and Tables for Statistical Quality Control* (Quality Press), statistical thinking is the philosophy of learning and action based on the following fundamental principles:

1. All work occurs in a system of interconnected *processes* where a process can be seen as a series of activities or operations that turns inputs into outputs;
2. Variation—all processes and data exhibit variation which gives rise to uncertainty; and
3. Understanding and reducing variation.

These are the major objectives of data and process analysis and are keys to success. The definition of statistical thinking emphasizes several key components including processes that transforms inputs into outputs; variation—understanding, quantifying, and reducing variability in the processes and products; understanding and managing uncertainty; and using data to make decisions—data-driven decision making.

Statistical thinking is a philosophy and a mindset. It is an *overall approach to understanding and improving processes* and has much broader scope than just using the statistical methods. The concepts of process focus, and variation reduction concepts of statistical thinking provide the basis for broader and more effective use of statistical methods. Two very important concepts in statistics are sampling and estimation. These are described in coming chapters.

Recent Trend: Data Science, Analytics, Business Intelligence, and Data Mining

A recent trend in data analysis is the emerging field of data science. Other areas have evolved with different names. These are data mining, business analytics, and business intelligence (BI). All these areas have common tools and techniques and they overlap as far as the applications are concerned. All these areas come under the broad scope of data science.

Data mining involves analyzing massive amount of data. In this age of technology, massive amount of data is collected and stored at enormous speed every day by businesses and other entities. It has become increasingly important to process and analyze the huge amount of data to extract useful information and patterns hidden in the data. The overall goal of data mining is knowledge discovery from the data. Data mining involves (i) extracting previously unknown and potential useful knowledge or patterns from massive amount of data collected and stored and (ii) exploring and analyzing these large quantities of data to discover meaningful patterns and transforming data into an understandable structure for further use. The field of data mining is a rapidly growing and statistics plays a major role in it. Data mining is also known as knowledge discovery in databases (KDD), pattern analysis, information harvesting, business intelligence, and business analytics. Besides statistics, data mining uses artificial intelligence, machine learning, database systems and advanced statistical tools, and pattern recognition.

Business analytics makes extensive use of data, statistical analysis, mathematical and statistical modeling, and data mining to explore, investigate, and understand the business performance. Through data, business analytics helps to gain insight and drive business planning and decisions. The tools of business analytics focus on understanding business performance using data, statistical models, and management science tools.

Business intelligence (BI) is another hot topic in business today. It uses a set of techniques, algorithms, and tools in data analysis that enables managers to make fact-based decisions.

All these areas were described in Chapters 1 through 3.

The goal of this text is to provide a comprehensive overview of data science. Statistics is at the core of data science; therefore, we devote several chapters describing tools and methods of statistics. A good background and understanding of statistics are critical to understanding and applying data science. The tools of statistics help us realize the similarities and differences between data science, analytics, data mining, and business intelligence—rapidly growing fields involving statistics and data analysis. The following examples emphasize the importance of data mining, and data science applications in different fields.

Data in Retail Business: In today's businesses, raw data are being collected by companies at an enormous rate. For example, Walmart collects and processes over 20 million point-of-sale transactions every day. These data are stored in a centralized database and are analyzed using data mining software to understand and determine customer behavior, needs, and requirements. The data must be analyzed to determine sales trends and forecasts, develop marketing strategies, and predict customer buying habits.

[http://laits.utexas.edu/~anorman/BUS.FOR/course.mat/Alex/].

Data Mining in Finance: A major financial application is the collection and analysis of customer transaction data. Every time a customer uses a credit or debit card, places online order, or uses a store card, data are being collected about the customer. A large amount of data and information about products, companies and individuals are available through Google, Facebook, Amazon, and several other sources. Data mining and analytics tools are used to extract meaningful information and pattern to learn customer behavior. Financial institutions analyze data of millions of customers to assess risk and customer behavior. Data mining techniques are also used widely in the areas of science and engineering, such as bioinformatics, genetics, medicine, education, and electrical power engineering.

Data science is one of the fastest growing areas. There is and will be an increasing demand of professionals trained in this area. Many of the tools of data analysis and statistics you will learn in this course are prerequisite to understanding data science and business analytics.

Summary

Statistics, data analysis, and analytics are at the core of data science applications. Statistics involves making decisions from the data. Making effective decisions using statistical methods and data require the understanding of three areas of statistics: (1) descriptive statistics, (2) probability and probability distributions, and (3) inferential statistics. Descriptive statistics involves describing the data using graphical and numerical methods. The descriptive statistics problems involve a population of interest from which a sample or samples are drawn. These samples usually represent one or more variables of interest. Graphical and numerical methods are used to create visual representation of the variables or data and to calculate various statistics to describe the data. Graphical tools are also helpful in identifying the patterns in the data.

In statistical analysis, probability plays an important role in decision making. Probability distributions are essential part of drawing conclusion from the data and these distributions are used in problems involving inferential statistics.

Statistical inference involves generalization about a population based on the information contained in the sample data. The process of inferential statistics involves a population of interest from which sample or samples are taken. These samples may contain one or more variables of interest. Statistical tools are used to draw inference about the population based on sample data. The wide application of statistics is due to the development of inferential statistical methods, which is an outgrowth of probability theory and probability distributions.

Some Important Concepts: Questions and Answer

1. **Describe your understanding of statistics, its uses, applications, and importance.**

   Statistics is the science and art of making decision using data. It is often called the science of data. Almost every field uses data and statistics to learn about their systems and processes. In fields such as business, research, health care, and engineering, a vast amount of raw data are collected and warehoused rapidly. The data must be analyzed to be meaningful. We now live in the age of data. A knowledge and understanding of statistics provide necessary tools to make intelligent data-driven decisions.

2. **How would you define the field of statistics?**

The field of statistics is described as:

- Statistics is about making decisions from data.
  Statistics is a science that deals with collection, tabulation, analysis, interpretation, and presentation of data (in order to make decisions).
- Statistics is concerned with making decisions from data influencing chance variations.
- Statistics deals with making inferences or predictions about a population based on sample data.

3. **What are the two main reasons behind the study of statistics?**

(1) Statistics is the branch of mathematics that deals with variation. It is mathematics of variation and allows us to study the variation in data. Statistical methods enable us to draw conclusions using limited data, or it enables us to draw conclusion about a population using the sample data. For example, we can estimate the average height of women in a county without actually measuring the height of all of them.

4. **Explain what is meant by a variable.**

Most of the data we collect show variation and the element such as, a person, thing, or event upon which we collect data can be seen as a *variable*. *A variable is a characteristic of interest that differs among observations or measurements.* We can study the variation in data using statistics. Statistical thinking and variation reduction are major goals in data analysis, decision making, and quality improvement programs, such as Six Sigma.

5. **Describe the two broad categories under which statistics is studied.**

Statistics is studied under two broad categories: *descriptive statistics* and *inferential statistics*. *Descriptive statistics* uses graphical and numerical methods to describe and analyze data. *Inferential statistics or inference procedures* are part of statistics concerned with drawing conclusions about the *population* using *sample data*.

6. **What are data? Explain different classifications of data**

   Data are any number of related observations. Data are also measurements.

   Data can also be *qualitative* or *quantitative*. *Quantitative data* are numerical data that can be expressed in numbers. For example, data collected on temperature, height, and stock values of companies are all examples of quantitative data.

   Qualitative data are data for which the measurement scale is categorical. Qualitative data are also known as *categorical data*. Examples of qualitative data include the color of your car, response to a yes/no question, and so on.

   Data can also be classified as *time series data* or *cross-sectional data*. Time series data are data recorded over time; for example, weekly sales, monthly demand for a product, or the number of orders received by an online shopping department of a department store. *Cross-sectional data* are the values observed at the same point in time. Data are also classified as discrete and continuous. *Discrete data* are the result of a counting process. These are expressed as whole numbers or integers. *Continuous data* can take any value within a given range. These are measured on a continuum or a scale. Discrete and continuous data are also referred to as *discrete variable* and *continuous variables*.

7. **Explain the terms: population, sample, parameters, and statistics.**

   Population denotes the entire measurements that are theoretically possible. It is also known as the universe and is the totality of items or things under consideration. For example, total number of light bulbs manufactured by a company in a given period of time, or number of people who can vote in a country, and so on.

   Sample is the portion of the population that is selected for analysis (a subset of population).

A *parameter* is a summary measure that is computed to describe the characteristic of a population. A *statistic* is a summary measure that is computed to describe the characteristic of a sample.

8. **Explain Descriptive, Inferential Statistics and their tools.**

Descriptive statistics is defined as the methods involving the collection, presentation, and characterization of a set of data. The major tools of descriptive statistics are graphs, charts, and visual tools. *Inferential statistics* is the branch of statistics concerned with drawing conclusions about the *population* using *sample data*. The major tools of inferential statistics are estimation and hypothesis testing.

CHAPTER 7

Descriptive Analytics_ Visualizing Data Using Graphs and Charts

Chapter Highlights

- Introduction
- Grouping and Summarizing Data
- Visualizing Data
- Basic Concepts in Data Visualization
- Presenting Data: Collection and Presentation of Data
    - Organizing Data: An Example
- Summarizing Quantitative Data: Frequency Distribution
    - Histogram: A Graph of Frequency Distribution
    - Example: Histogram: Summarizing Data and Examining the Distribution
- Graphical Summary of Data
- Graphical Display of Variation
- Data visualization: Conventional and Simple Techniques
    - Stem-and-Leaf Plot
    - Box Plots
    - Dot Plots
    - Bar Charts, a Cluster Bar Chart, Stacked Bar Chart
- Describing, Summarizing, and Graphing Categorical Variables
    - Creating Bar Chart from a Simple Talley
- Example: Cross Tabulation with Two and Three Categorical Variables

- Pie Charts
- Interval Plots
- Time Series Plots
- Sequence Plot: Plot of Process Data
  - Example: Sequence Plot
- Connected Line Plot
- Area Graph
- Summary of Widely Used Charts and Graphs

Introduction

Data visualization means presenting the data visually or graphically. The graphical displays are extremely helpful in detecting the patterns, trends, and correlations that are not usually apparent from the raw data. The trends and the patterns in the data cannot be recognized and they go undetected if not in the visual form.

Data visualization is an integral part of business intelligence (BI). Most of the BI application software heavily emphasize on data visualization and have strong data visualization capabilities. One of the reasons for the popularity of visualization tools is that they are easier to use and comprehend and do not require extensive training as in the case of statistical software. Several statistical software are available that heavily emphasize on analysis and modeling along with graphing capabilities. They are typically easier to operate than traditional statistical analysis software or earlier versions of BI software. This has led to a rise in lines of business implementing data visualization tools on their own without support from IT.

The data visualization tools and software now have advanced capabilities. They go beyond the standard charts and graphs used in Microsoft Excel and other standard statistical software. Current data visualization software can display data in form of graphs and charts contained in dashboards that display multiple views of data. These dashboards are extremely helpful decision-making tools. A number of specialized graphs including infographics, heat maps, geographic maps, detailed bar, and pie charts can be created using visualization software. In many cases, the visuals created may have interactive capabilities that allow for manipulating data, querying, and analysis.

Data visualization software plays an important role in big data and advanced analytics projects. Massive amounts of data are now collected by businesses. The visualization and analysis of this data is referred to as *big data* analysis. Visualization of big data requires specially designed software to quickly and easily get an overview through data dashboards.

The success of the two leading software vendors—Tableau and Qlik—has moved other vendors toward a more visual approach in their software. Virtually all big data software in the BI space has strong data visualization functionality. It does not mean that only the software designed for big data, such as Tableau and Olick (the two leading vendors in the BI space) can only be used for data visualization. A number of standard statistical software including MINITAB, SAS, STATS PRO, SPSS, and others along with widely used spreadsheet program Excel are widely used for data visualization. The basics and fundamentals of visuals and graphics created using the standard statistical software or big data software are the same. The difference lies in their capabilities. Big data visualization software has capabilities of handling massive amounts of data. They are capable of creating *dashboards* that can provide multiple views of data on one plot. In this chapter, we provide the fundamentals of data visualization along with several examples of visuals that can be created from the data. We also provide the applications and interpretation of these visuals.

Graphical Presentation of Data: Some Examples

Data are often presented using tables, charts, and graphs. Graphical or visual representation of data is an effective way of describing data. Many of these charts and graphs are very commonly used in trade journals, company and business reports. Examples of some commonly used charts and graphs are shown in Figure 7.1. These charts can be produced easily using statistical software. In Chapter 5, we provided details on creating these charts and graphs using Excel. The graphs shown in figure are histogram, bar charts, and a pie chart. These are examples of descriptive statistics and are used in presenting and describing data. Data are also analyzed by calculating summary statistics including the mean, median, mode, percentile and several other measures called statistics.

Basic Concepts in Data Visualization

One of the major functions of data analysis is to describe the data in a way that is easy to comprehend and communicate. This can be done both by presenting the data in graphical form and by calculating various summary statistics such as the measures of central tendency and the measures of variability.

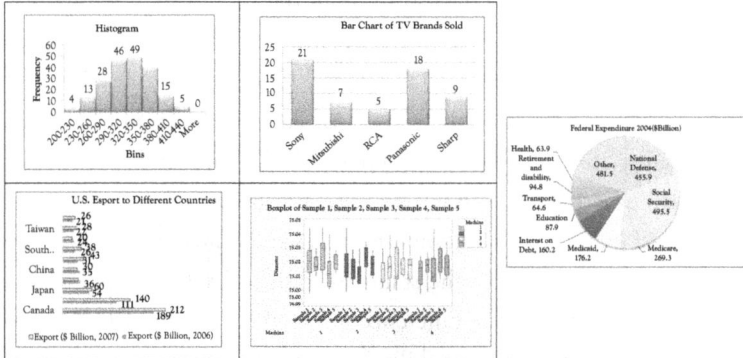

Figure 7.1 Examples of commonly used charts and graphs

The graphical techniques enable the analyst to describe a data set that is more concise than the original data. These techniques help reveal the essential characteristics of the data so that effective decisions can be made.

In this chapter, we have presented numerous graphical techniques using standard computer software. You may be familiar with many of the commonly used charts and graph. We will explain the charts with their applications without going into theoretical details.

Presenting Data: Collection and Presentation of Data

In the previous chapter, we discussed the concepts and types of data. This chapter deals with applications. The following two methods are commonly used for describing data:

- Tables
- Graphs

The purpose of collecting data is to draw conclusions or to make decisions. To draw meaningful conclusion, the data are organized, grouped, plotted, and analyzed. Organizing data into groups is known as frequency *distribution. The data should represent all relevant groups.* Suppose a market survey is conducted to forecast the demand for a product in a particular area and 200 consumers are surveyed. It is important that this group contains a variety of consumers representing variables such as income level, education, gender, and race.

Data can be collected through actual measurements or observations or can be obtained from government or company records. This information can be organized in a way that can be used to make decisions or draw conclusions. When data are arranged in a compact, usable form, decision makers can obtain reliable information and use it to make decisions.

Arrangement and display of data are important elements of descriptive statistics. Without some arranging, shifting, sorting, and grouping of the original data, we would not be able to arrive at a conclusion. Also, we need enough data to draw valid and meaningful conclusions. Decisions made from insufficient data may be misleading and incorrect.

Before analyzing the data, it should be tested by answering the following questions:

- Are the data biased? That is, will the data lead to different conclusions?
- How many observations do we have—do we have sufficient data?
- Do they represent all the groups we wish to study?
- Is the evidence missing that might cause us to come to a different conclusion?
- Is the conclusion drawn from data valid?

A Look at Data: frequency Tables—Grouping and Summarizing Data

Organizing Data: An Example

Initially when the data are collected, they are unorganized and in raw form that do not convey much meaning. The raw data must be organized in certain ways to be meaningful. Here we provide an example on how data can be arranged and organized before analysis can be performed.

Table 7.1 shows the speed of 100 cars in miles per hour (mph) passing through a highway intersection with a 60-mph speed limit. These cars were randomly selected and represent a sample of $n=100$.

The data of Table 7.1 are called *raw data* (data which are not arranged and analyzed). The speeds of the cars were recorded in the order in which they occurred. This is *ungrouped data*. Ungrouped data enable us to study the sequence of values, for example, "low" or "high" values. The data may also be helpful in determining some causes of variation. However, for a large data set, the ungrouped data do not provide much information.

Table 7.2 shows the data of Table 7.1 ranked in increasing order of magnitude; that is, in *rank order*. This is also known as *data array* or *ordered array*. A data array arranges the values in increasing or decreasing order.

Table 7.1 Driving speed (mph)

51	46	62	70	54	59	59	57	61	66	49	57	57	65	61	62	51	63	62	65	55	55	65
64	60	55	70	61	63	55	70	65	51	53	49	62	56	61	64	54	60	63	69	72	69	60
57	63	60	56	60	61	57	57	61	54	58	55	69	63	55	58	58	62	59	59	62	53	69
56	59	57	60	63	60	56	52	65	58	60	62	54	57	60	53	56	60	71	59	64	58	71
68	62	61	61	67	59	58	49															

Table 7.2 Driving speed (mph) - (Sorted Data)

46	49	49	49	51	51	51	52	53	53	53	54	54	54	54	55	55	55	55	55	55	56	56
56	56	56	57	57	57	57	57	57	57	57	58	58	58	58	58	58	59	59	59	59	59	59
59	60	60	60	60	60	60	60	60	60	60	61	61	61	61	61	61	61	61	62	62	62	62
62	62	62	63	63	63	63	63	63	64	64	64	65	65	65	65	65	66	67	68	69	69
69	69	70	70	70	71	71	72															

Summarizing Quantitative Data: Frequency Distribution

A *frequency distribution* provides a compact representation of data. This is also known as grouping. Compact representation is obtained by arranging the data into groups or *class intervals* usually of *equal width* and then recording or counting the number of observations in each interval. Counting the number of observations in each group is called the *class frequency*. For example, examine the data in Table 7.2. We can divide this data into 10 class intervals with a width of 3 and tabulate the results as shown below.

Class-interval Frequency

45–48 1

48–51 4

51–54 9

….. and so on.

The above class frequency is an example of a frequency distribution. The class interval of 45–48 means that this interval contains all the values from 45 to 48 (not including 48). If we count the number of observations between 45 and 48 in Table 4.2; we will find there is one observation in this group. The count of 1 is known as the frequency. The class interval can also be written in a formal way as:

$$45 \leq X < 48$$

This means that the values in this class interval include the value 45 but not 48. The value 45 is known as the *lower-class boundary or lower-class limit* and the value 48 is known as the *upper-class boundary or upper-class limit.*

There are several other possibilities of grouping or constructing frequency distributions using the information in Table 7.2. The following information is helpful while grouping or forming a frequency distribution:

- When dividing the data into class intervals, 5–15 class intervals are recommended. If there are *too many class intervals*, the class frequency (count) is low and the savings in computational effort is small. If there are too few class intervals, the true characteristic of the distribution may be obscured, and some information may be lost.
- The *number of class intervals* should be governed by the *amount* and *scatter* of data present.
- For large number of observations, the *width* of the class interval can be decreased as there will be more observations in any interval.

Forming *Frequency Distribution or Grouping* the data in Table 4.2.

- For the data in Table 7.2, approximate number of classes can be found using the formula: $K = 1 + 3.33 \log_{10} n$ where K is the number of classes and n is the number of observations. Using this formula, the number of class-intervals was found to be 7.66 or 8. Note that the value obtained using this formula is approximate. We may decide to divide the data into 10 class intervals. The next step is to find the *width* of the class or *class-width*.
- Note that the number of observations in Table 4.2 is $n = 100$ and we decide to divide the data into $K =$ number of classes $= 10$. Using these values, the class width using the following equation:

$$Class\ width = \frac{72 - 46}{10} = 2.6$$

This width is also approximate. We may choose to have a width of 3.0 rather than 2.6. From the data in Table 7.2, suppose we decided to divide the data into 10 class intervals with a class-width of 3.0. Using a class width of 3.0, the frequency distribution is shown in Table 7.3.

Table 7.3 Frequency distribution of 100 drivers with 60 miles per hour (mph) speed limit

Class-interval (mph)	Frequency (f)
45–48	1
48–51	3
51–54	7
54–57	15
57–60	21
60–63	26
63–66	14
66–69	3
69–72	9
72–75	1
Total	$\Sigma f_i = 100$

The second column contains the frequency or the number of observations in each class. This is obtained by sorting the data from the lowest to the highest number (as seen in Table 7.2) and counting the number of observations in each class. The interval 45– 48 is read as 45 but less than 48. This means that the upper-class boundary is exclusive. The class boundaries can also be formed with the upper boundary *inclusive*. In that case the class interval would be 45–47. In general, there should be *no gap* and *no overlap* between the class intervals. *Note:* For a given set of data, there is no one unique frequency distribution. Several frequency distributions are possible for the same set of data.

Visualizing Data: Histogram: A Graph of Frequency Distribution

A *histogram* is a graph used to illustrate the frequency distribution in a graphical form as shown in Figure 7.1a. This graph is useful because it shows the pattern that is not so obvious when the data are in a table form. The histogram is also useful as it summarizes a large set of data. It is also useful in the study of probability distributions.

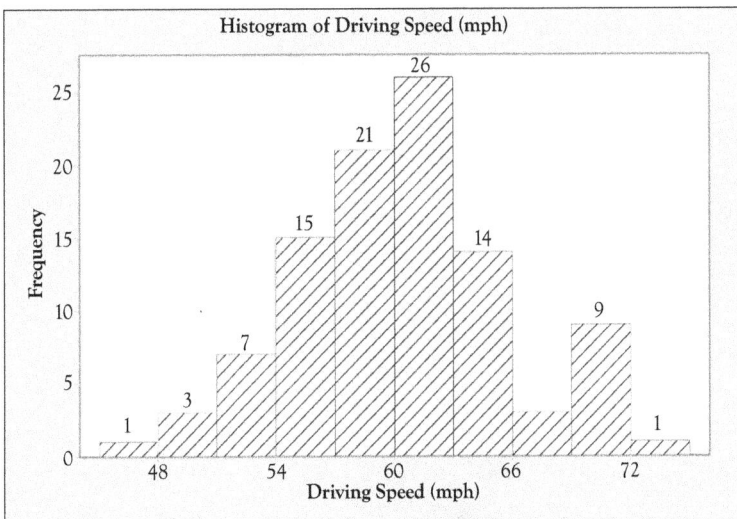

Figure 7.1a Histogram of driving speed (mph) (10 class-intervals).

In a histogram, the class intervals are plotted on the horizontal axis and the frequencies are plotted on the vertical axis. The histogram is a series of rectangles, each proportional in width to the range of values within each class and is also proportional in height to the number of observations falling within each class.

Example: Histogram—Summarizing the Data and Examining Distribution

The selling price of 300 homes for the past six months in a certain city is summarized in Figure 7.2 in form of a histogram. The bars show the intervals of $20,000. The first class-interval of 220–240 indicates the selling price of home between $220,000 but less than $240,000 and so on. From the figure we can see that 14 houses were sold between $260,000 and $280,000 (not including $280,000 dollars). The histogram is a plot of frequency distribution and is an excellent way of summarizing data sets. Figure 7.3 shows the percent for each category. Figure 7.4 shows a histogram with a normal curve superimposed. The graph shows that the home price data has a symmetrical shape, which is characterized by the normal distribution.

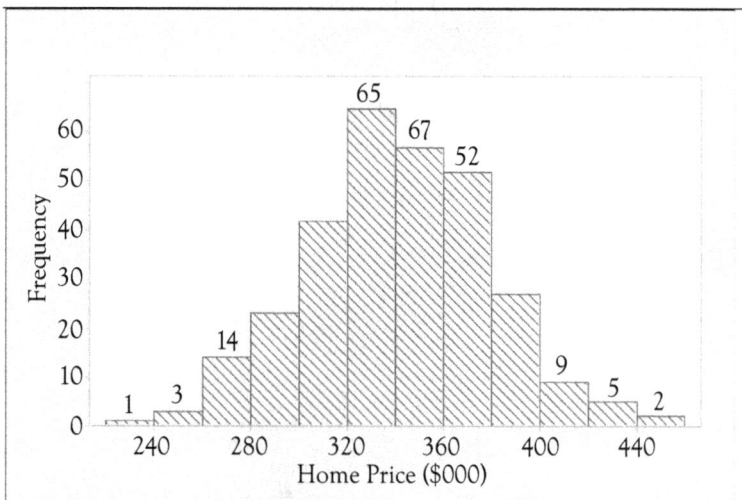

Figure 7.2 Histogram of home price ($000)

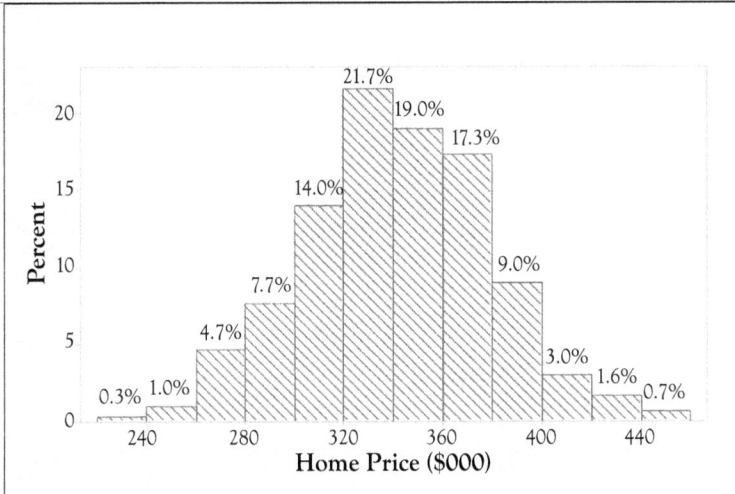

Figure 7.3 Percent histogram of home price

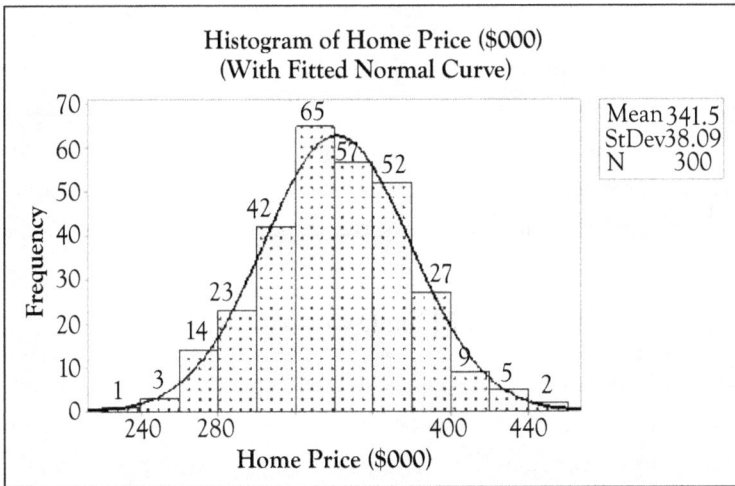

Figure 7.4 Histogram of home price ($000) with a normal curve

Graphical Summary of Data

This option provides useful statistics of the data along with graphs. The graphical summary of 300 home prices is shown in Figure 7.5. The summary report provides the plot of the data in form of a histogram with a normal curve superimposed. A boxplot of the data is shown below the

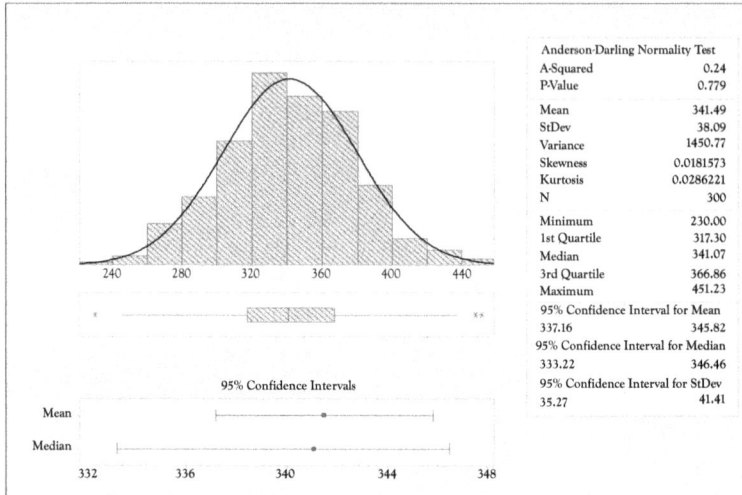

Anderson-Darling Normality Test	
A-Squared	0.24
P-Value	0.779
Mean	341.49
StDev	38.09
Variance	1450.77
Skewness	0.0181573
Kurtosis	0.0286221
N	300
Minimum	230.00
1st Quartile	317.30
Median	341.07
3rd Quartile	366.86
Maximum	451.23
95% Confidence Interval for Mean	
337.16	345.82
95% Confidence Interval for Median	
333.22	346.46
95% Confidence Interval for StDev	
35.27	41.41

Figure 7.5 Summary report of home price ($000)

histogram. Both plots—histogram and the box—plot summarize the data and provide information about the distribution of home price. On the right-hand side, the calculated statistics are displayed. These statistics give us an idea about the average and the median house price along with the minimum, maximum, and the standard deviation. Several other statistics are calculated which are extremely useful in analyzing the data.

Graphical Display of Variation

Variation is one of the most important aspects of statistical analysis. Statistics is the science of variation and allows us to study variation. Almost all data show variation. The measurement and reduction of variation is one of the major objectives of quality programs. Figures 7.6 and 7.7 below give us an idea about the variation in the data visually.

Data Visualization: Conventional and Simple Techniques

In this section, we discuss the most widely used data visualization techniques. These graphical displays are most effective and useful in displaying the main features and drawing conclusions and making decisions from the data.

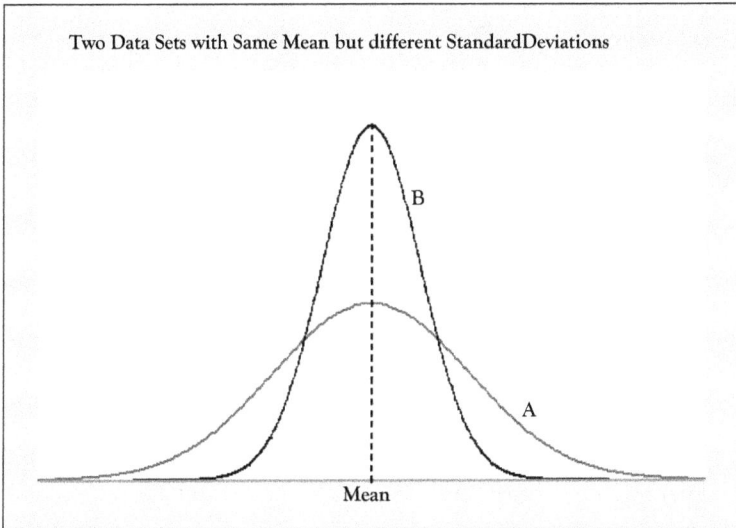

Two Data Sets with Same Mean but different StandardDeviations

Figure 7.6 Data sets A and B with same mean but different variations

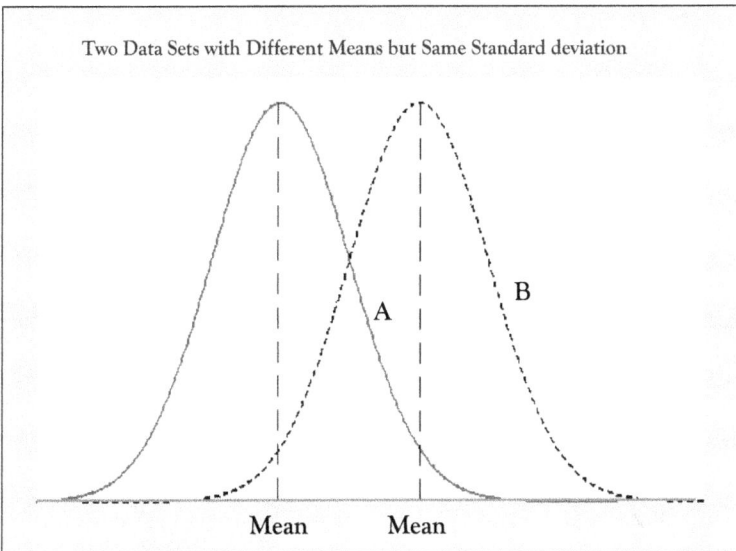

Two Data Sets with Different Means but Same Standard deviation

Figure 7.7 Data sets A and B with same variation but different means

Stem-and-Leaf Plot

Stem-and-leaf plot is a very efficient way of displaying data and checking the variation and shape of the distribution. This plot is obtained by dividing each data value into two parts; stem and leaf. For example, if the data are two-digit numbers (e.g., 34, 56, 67, etc.), then the first number (the tens digit) is considered the stem value, and the second number (the ones digit) is considered the leaf value. Thus, in data value 56, 5 is the stem and 6 is the leaf. In a three-digit data value, the first two digits are considered the stem and the third digit as the leaf.

Example

The stem-and leaf plot in Figure 7.8 shows the number of orders received per day by a company. It is convenient to construct the plot using sorted data. There are three columns in the plot. The first column (labeled: 1) shows the cumulative count of the number of observations, the second (middle) column (labeled: 2) shows the stem values and the numbers following the second column (labeled: 3) represent the leaves. The first row has the following values:

1   92

This means that there is one observation in this row, the stem value is 9, and the leaf value is 2. Thus, first value is 92. The second row also has one value in this row with a stem-value of 10 and the leaf value of 3 shown as:

2   10 3

The first column in the second row shows the cumulative count of observations up to this point. This value is 2. This means that there are two observations up to this row (1 in the first row and 1 value in the second row); the stem is 10 and leaf value is 3, making the value in the second row 103.

Refer to Figure 7.8, column 1 again. The values from the top are 1, 2, 5, 7, 8, 11, 15, 22, and 27. This means that there are 27 observations up to row 9. The next number is 11, which is enclosed in a parenthesis: (11). This indicates that there are 11 observations in this row and this row contains the *median value* of the data. Once the median is determined, the count begins starting from the bottom row. Look into the bottom row that shows 2 23 18. This indicates there are two observations in this row, which are 231 and 238. The next to the last row shows

4   22 45

1	2	3
1	9	2
2	10	3
5	11	245
7	12	78
8	13	2
11	14	137
15	15	1229
22	16	2266778
27	17	01599
(11)	18	0013346799
17	19	03346
12	20	4679
8	21	0177
4	22	45
2	23	18

[a] How many days were studied? **55** *(obtained by adding the numbers above and below the row median row that is, 27+11+17)*

[b] How many observations are in the fourth class? **2**

[c] What are the smallest and largest orders? **92, 238**

[d] List the actual values in the sixth class? **141, 142, 147**

[e] How many days did the firm receive less than 140 orders? **8**

[f] How many days did the firm receive 200 or more orders? **12**

[g] How many days did the firm receive 180 orders? **3**

[h] What is the middle value? **180**

[i] What can you say about the shape of the data? **Left or negatively skewed**

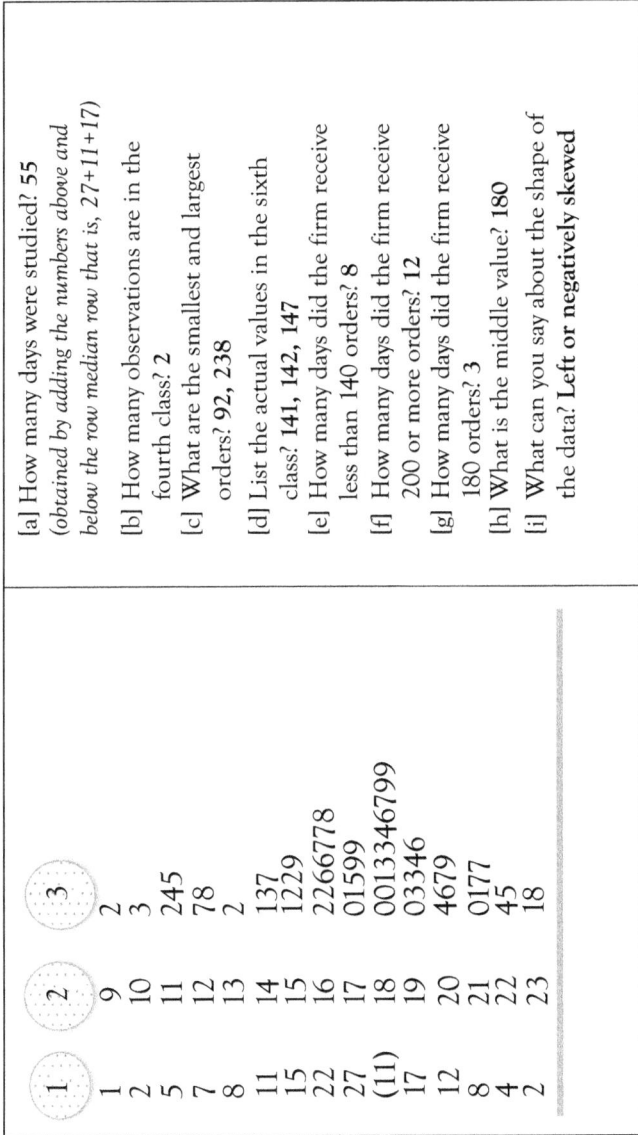

Figure 7.8 Stem-and-leaf of orders received

This means that the values in this row are 224 and 225. The value "4" in this row means that there are four observations up to this row (from the bottom). The cumulative count continues upward until the median row (not including the median row).

You can see from the above figure that the shape of the data is left skewed or negatively skewed, the minimum value is 92—the first value in the first row and the maximum value is 238, the last value. To find the total number of observations, add the observations in the median row, which is (11) and the observations above and below the median row; that is, 27+11+17 = 55. The stem-and-leaf can be used to obtain the following information (see second column in Figure 7.8). The answers are shown in bold.

Box Plots

The boxplot displays the smallest and the largest values in the data along with the three quartiles: Q_1, Q_2, and Q_3. The display of these five numbers (known as five measure summary) may be used to study the shape of the distribution and draw conclusion from the data. Different types of box plots can be created from the data. Some of these plots are shown below.

Example of Box Plots

The waiting times for 50 patients in an outpatient hospital clinic are shown in Table 7.4. The descriptive statistics of the waiting time is shown in Table 7.5

Table 7.4 Waiting Time Data

Waiting Time(min.)
6.8 9.9 12.0 12.8 12.6 14.0 16.0 8.0 10.1 12.1 12.8 12.6 14.0 16.6 8.2
10.2 12.3 12.9 12.6 14.0 8.8 10.4 12.4 12.0 12.7 14.2 9.0 10.5 12.5 12.0
13.0 14.3 9.1 10.7 12.6 12.1 13.1 14.4 9.3 10.8 12.7 12.2 13.1 14.5 9.5
10.8 12.7 12.5 13.3 14.5

Table 7.5 Descriptive statistics of waiting time

Descriptive Statistics of Waiting Time								
Variable	N	N*	Mean	SE Mean	StDev	**Minimum**	Q1	**Median**	Q3
Waiting Time	50	0	12.784	0.289	2.045	6.800	10.475	12.800	13.100
Maximum								
16.600								

The descriptive statistics showing the five-measure summary of the data was calculated using MINITAB. The results are shown in Table 4.5.

From the above table, the five-measure summary calculated is:

Minimum value = 6.8 min., Q1 = 10.48 min., Q2 = 12.80 min., Q3 = 13.10 min., and Maximum value = 16.6 min.

The box plot shown in Figure 7.9 displays these five measures. This box plot shows that the minimum and maximum waiting times are 6.8 and 16.6 minutes. For 25 percent of the patients, the waiting time is less than 10.48 minutes, whereas 75 percent of the patients wait more than 10.48 minutes. The median waiting time is 12.8 minutes, which means that for 50 percent of the patients the waiting time is less than 12.8 minutes. while for the other 50 percent, the waiting time is more than 12.8 minutes. The distribution of waiting time is approximately symmetrical.

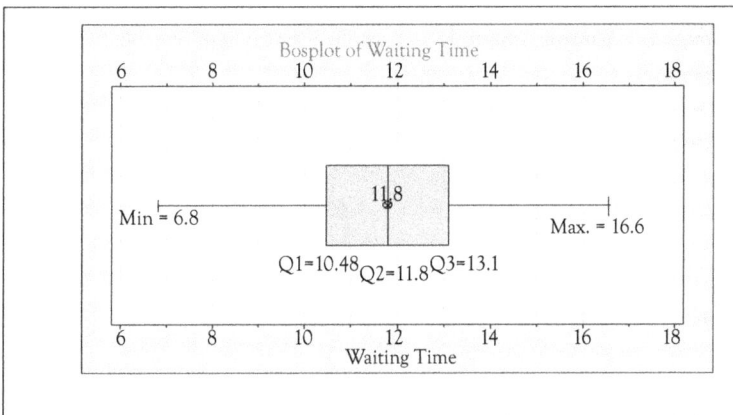

Figure 7.9 Box plot of waiting time data

More Applications of Box Plot

The box plot in Figure 7.10 is useful in monitoring one variable of interest (shaft diameter in this case) over several days or shifts. The box plots for each day of production are plotted. These plots are useful in monitoring the variation and shift in the process over time. Figure 7.11 shows the box plots of five samples each of size 36 from a shaft manufacturing process. Four machines were used in the production of these shafts. The plot can be used to check the consistency and distribution of the diameters with respect to the machines.

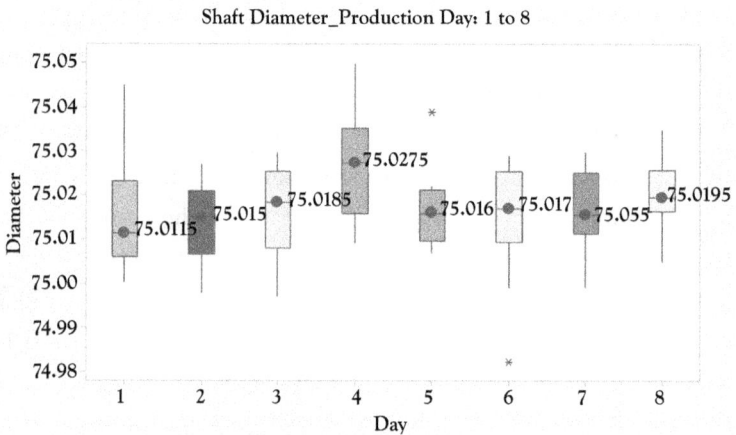

Figure 7.10 Box plots of shaft diameter over a period of 8 days

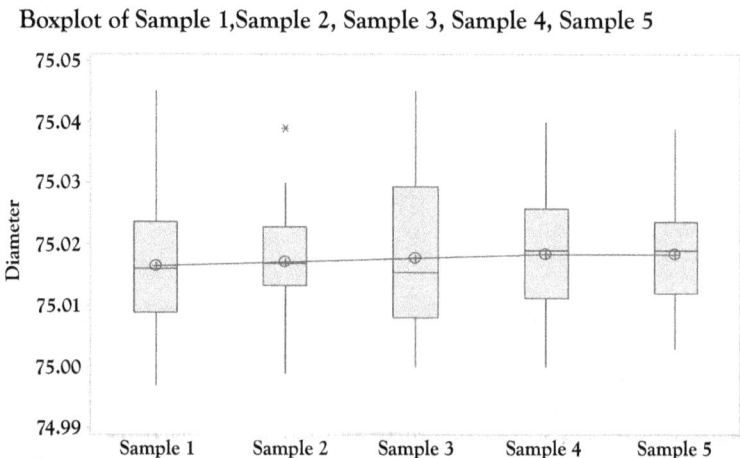

Figure 7.11   Box plots for five samples of same

Figure 7.12 shows the variation of the box plots where samples from each of the four machines in production are plotted separately. These plots can be used to check the consistency and distribution of the diameter with respect to each machine. Figure 7.13 shows the box plot of operators versus the samples produced by them.

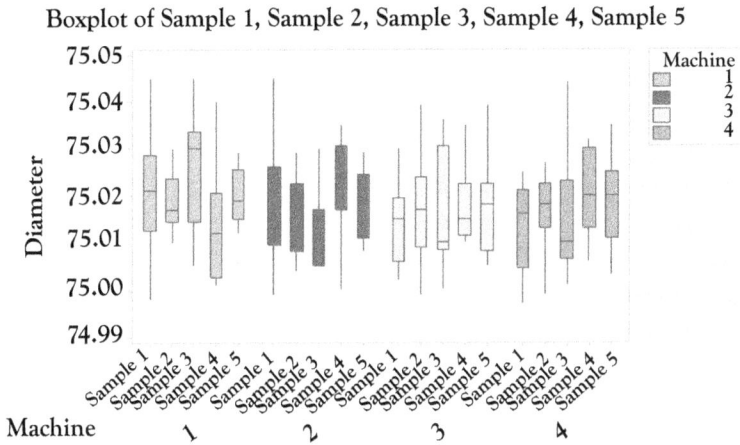

Figure 7.12 Box plots of samples vs. machines

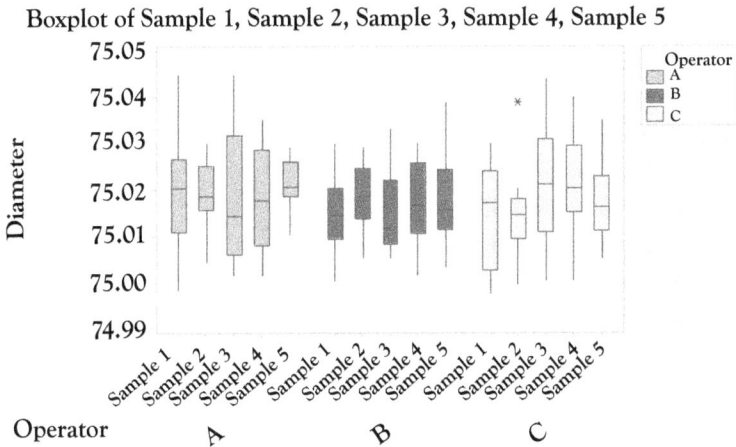

Figure 7.13 Box plots of samples vs. operators

Bar Charts

Bar charts are one of the widely used charts to display categorical data. These charts can be used to display monthly or quarterly sales, revenue, and profits for a company. Figure 7.14 shows the monthly sales of a company. Figure 7.15 shows a variation of the bar chart.

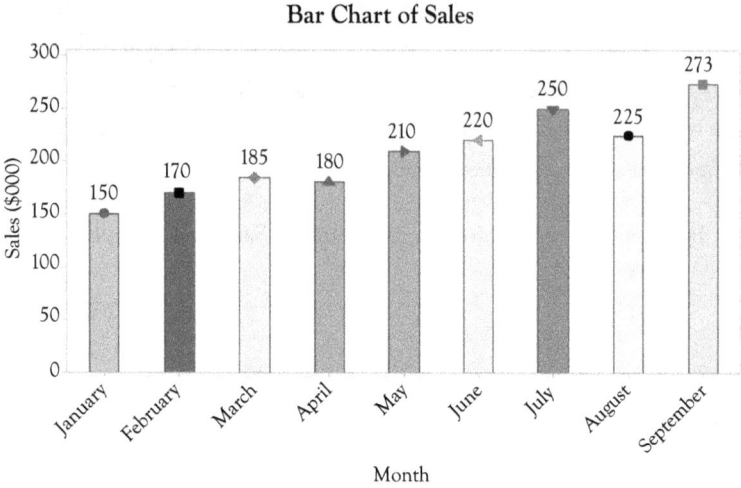

Figure 7.14 *A bar chart of monthly sales*

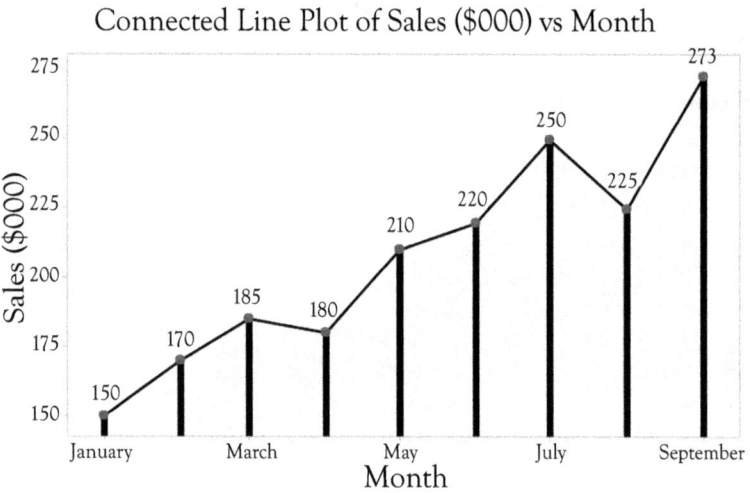

Figure 7.15 *Connected line over the bars*

Example: More Examples of Bar Chart_ Categorical Data

A Vertical Bar Chart. Figure 7.16 shows a vertical bar chart showing the gold price from 1975 to 2011. The chart is useful in visualizing the trend and the percent increase and decrease in the value over the years. For example: Percent increase in the price of gold (per ounce) between 1980 and 2011 can be determined as:

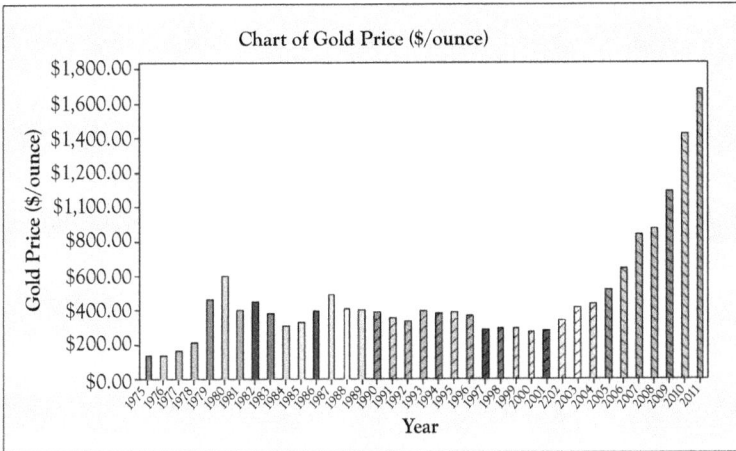

Figure 7.16 A vertical bar chart of gold price

The price in 1980 = $594.90 per ounce and the price in 2011 = $1680.0

Therefore, the percent increase = (1680 − 594.90)/594.90*100 = 182.4%.

Example of Cluster Bar Chart

An example of a cluster bar chart is to compare the quarterly sales for the past four years. A good way is to plot the sales of each quarter using a bar chart. We can use the cluster option to group the four quarters of each of the four years. Figure 7.17 shows a cluster bar chart.

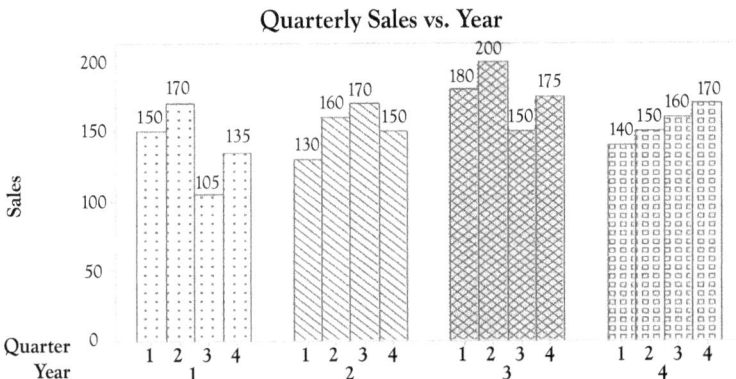

Figure 7.17 Quarterly sales for four years

(a)   Stacked Bar Chart

Stacked bar charts are used to compare different measure of data categories. In the most common form, a stacked bar chart displays a count of a category. These charts can also be created to represent a function of a category (such as the mean, or sum) or the summary values. Figure 7.18 shows an example of a stacked bar chart. This chart shows carbon dioxide emissions by different sectors—residential, commercial, industrial, and transportation. Each of these sectors is categorized by year and is displayed as a stacked chart.

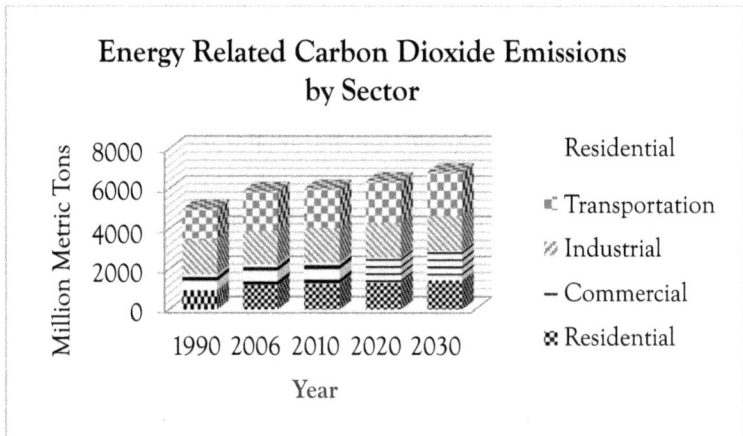

Figure 7.18 A stacked bar chart of carbon dioxide emissions by sector

Describing, Summarizing, and Graphing Categorical Variables

Categorical data are the data arranged in classes or categories. In many practical applications, counts provide important statistics. Some examples of categorical data are the number of orders received by a company per day, the number of companies belonging to a certain industrial classification, or people from a certain region responding to a product promotion questionnaire. Categorical data also result from the classification of elements into groups based on some common attribute. For example, we can group the companies into "small," "medium," or "large," based on the number of employees. We can also group people based on their annual income and their occupation. In this section, we will provide several examples of bar charts describing categorical variables.

Example: Creating a Bar Chart From a Simple Tally

A tally is a count or percentage of number of cases in a category. Table 7.6 shows the ratings for Product 1 for a sample of 200 product users. The variable Product Rating is a categorical variable where the responds were asked to rate the product as unacceptable, fair, poor, satisfactory, good, and excellent. These categories were coded in a scale ranging from 0 to 5 (0= Unacceptable, 1=Fair, 2=Poor, 3=Satisfactory, 4=Good, 5=Excellent). A tally was created before plotting the data.

Table 7.6 Rating for product 1 provided by 200 customers using a scale of 0 to 5

Product 1 Rating
0 1 3 3 4 5 1 4 3 3 4 5 1 0 3 4 5 3 4 3 5 0 1
3 4 5 4 3 2 1 4 3 0 0 0 3 3 1 1 1 1 4 4 4 5 4
5 5 3 2 3 3 4 4 4 4 4 5 3 2 4 5 3 1 4 5 5 0 0
0 0 3 3 4 2 1 5 2 2 4 4 1 1 4 4 2 2 4 4 5 5 5
3 3 1 1 0 0 4 5 4 4 5 5 5 3 3 1 5 3 4 4 3 3 4
2 3 5 4 0 0 0 3 4 3 2 4 4 4 4 4 5 3 3 0 4 4 3
3 5 4 4 5 3 3 2 2 5 4 3 2 1 1 2 3 4 5 4 3 2 1
0 5 4 2 3 1 0 0 4 4 4 4 5 4 3 2 1 5 4 3 2 2 1
0 3 3 4 5 4 2 4 4 5 3 4 4 3 2 1

Table 7.7 provides the ratings for Product 2. Unlike Table 7.6, the data is not coded for Product 2. Table 7.7 also shows the ratings in categorical form.

The data in Tables 7.6 and 7.7 convey very little meaning. To make the ratings data more meaningful, we prepare a simple tally for Product 1 and 2 and present the information in a graphical form using bar charts. The tables and graphs of the product ratings will immediately tell us how these products were rated by the customers.

Table 7.7 Rating for product 2 provided by 200 customers (Not Coded)

Product 2 Rating (partial data)					
Poor	Fair	Satisfacory	Good	Very Good	Excellent
Poor	Fair	Satisfacory	Good	Satisfacory	Good
Very Good					
Excellent	Poor	Satisfacory	Good	Very Good	
:					
:					
Excellent	Poor	Fair	Satisfacory	Good	Satisfacory

Before plotting the ratings data, we create a tally shown in Table 7.8.

The bar charts of the tallies created from Tables 7.8 and 7.9 are shown in Figures 7.19 (a), (b), 7.20 (a) and (b).

Tallies and Graphical Displays of Product 1 Rating:

Table 7.8 Tally for product 1 rating

1 Rating	Count	Percent	CumCnt	CumPct
Tally for Discrete Variables: Product 1 Rating: Product				
0	20	10.00	20	10.00
1	23	12.50	43	22.50
2	21	10.50	64	32.00
3	45	22.50	109	54.50
4	59	29.50	168	84.00
5	32	16.00	200	100.00
N=	200			

Figures 7.19a and b show the bar charts of Product 1 rating. The figure on the left clearly shows that 59 of the 200 or 29.5 percent users rated the product as "good."

Tallies and Graphical Displays of Product 2 Rating:

The tally and bar chart for Product 2 ratings are shown in Table 7.9 and Figures 7.20a and b. Note that the ratings were not coded for this product.

Table 7.9 *Tally for product 2 rating*

Tally for Discrete Variables: Product 2 Rating				
Rating	Count	Percent	CumCnt	CumPct
Excellent	30	13.64	30	13.64
Fair	18	8.18	48	22.82
Good	57	25.91	105	47.73
Poor	25	12.36	130	59.09
Satisfactory	49	22.27	179	82.36
Very Good	41	18.64	220	100.00
N=	220			

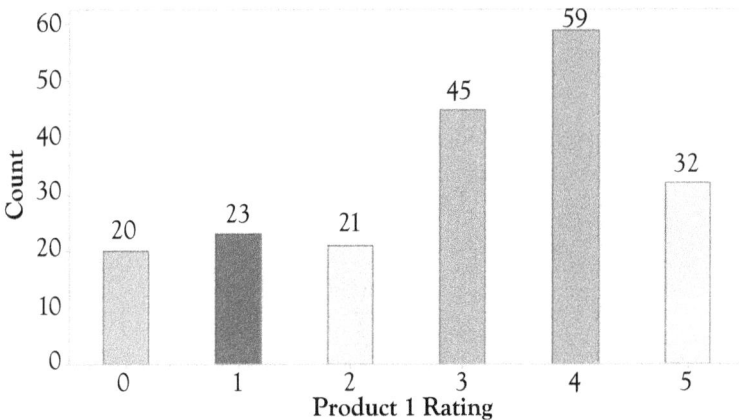

Figure 7.19a Bar chart of product 1 rating.

Example: Cross Tabulation with Two and Three Categorical Variables

The data for variables: Gender (male, female); degree major (1=computer science, 2=engineering, 3=social science, 4=business, 5=other); and employment status (employed, self-employed) are summarized in Table 7.10. Using cross tabulation, we construct bar charts to show the employment status and degree major for the male and female respondents. The bar charts from the Table 7.10 are shown in Figures 7.21 and 7.22. The figures are self-explanatory. These visual displays clearly

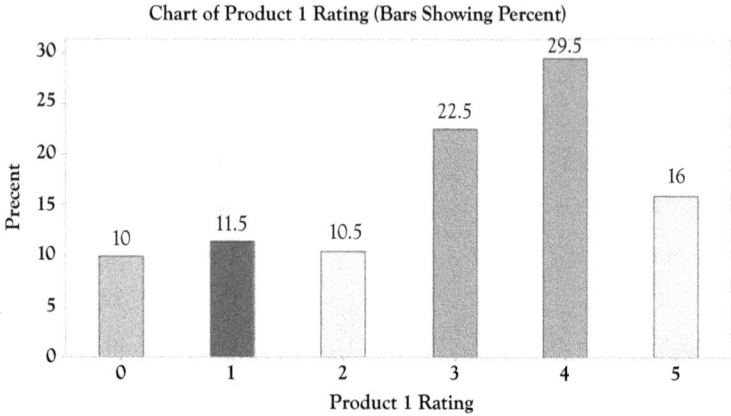

Chart of Product 1 Rating (Bars Showing Percent)

Percent within all data.

Figure 7.19b Bar chart of product 1 rating (bars showing percent)

summarize the data and reveal important features that are not apparent from the raw data or the tables created.

Table 7.10 Cross-table_ Employment Status, Degree Major and Gender

Tabulated statistics: Employment Status, Major, Gender

Results for Gender = Female

Rows: Employment Status   Columns: Major

	1	2	3	4	5	All
Employed	5	7	26	26	16	80
Self-employed	1	4	8	6	3	22
All	6	11	34	32	19	102

Cell Contents: Count

Results for Gender =   Male

Rows: Employment Status   Columns: Major

	1	2	3	4	5	All
Employed	9	22	9	20	15	75
Self-employed	3	6	2	11	1	23
All	12	28	11	31	16	98

Cell Contents: Count

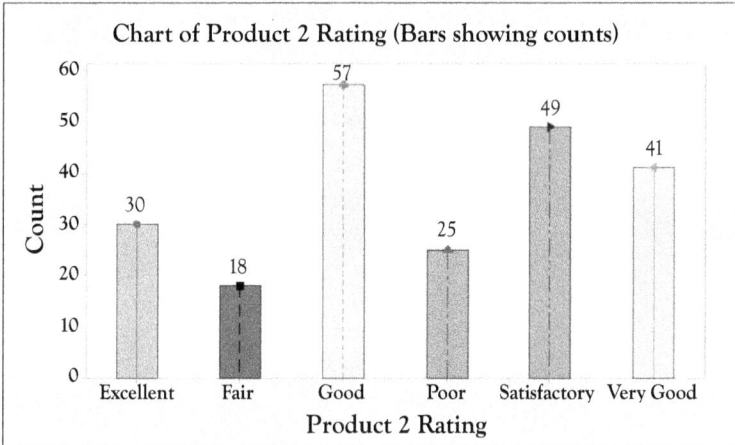

Figure 7.20a Bar chart of product 2 rating

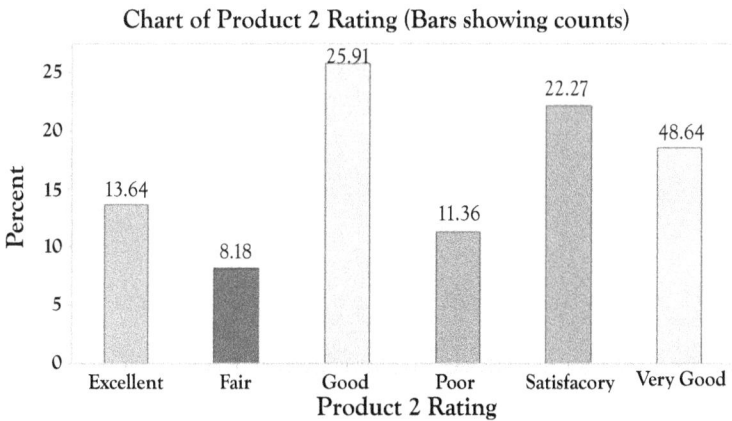

Percent within all data.

Figure 7.20b Bar chart of product 2 rating (bars showing percent).

Pie Charts

A pie chart is used to show the relative magnitudes of parts to a whole. In this chart relative frequencies of each group of data are plotted. A circle is constructed and is divided into distinct sections. Each section represents one group of data. The area of each section is determined by multiplying the relative frequency of each section by the angle of a circle or 360°.

Cluster Bar Chart of Gender and Major Field of Study

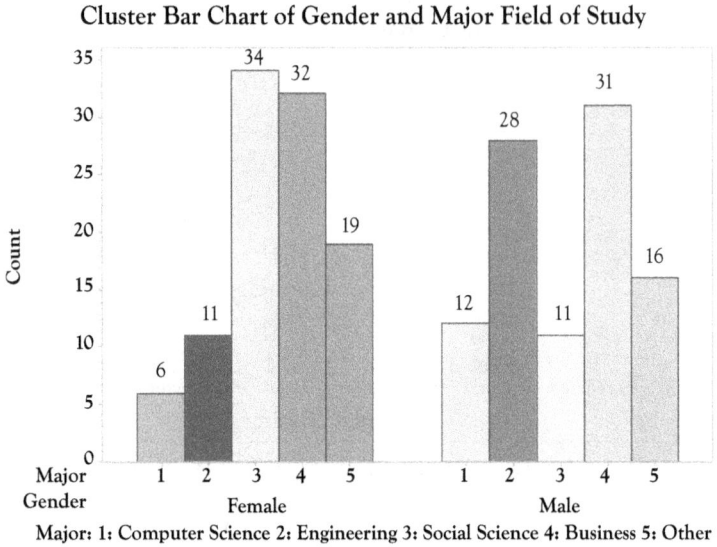

Major: 1: Computer Science 2: Engineering 3: Social Science 4: Business 5: Other

Figure 7.21 A bar chart of gender and major

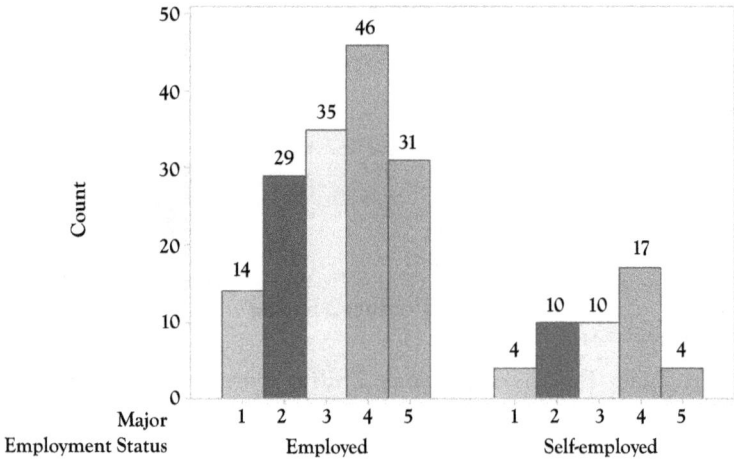

Figure 7.22 A bar chart of employment status and major

Example: A Simple Pie Chart

Figure 7.23 shows a simple pie chart of U.S. federal budget expenditures. The chart clearly shows the major categories along with the dollar values and the percentages. Several variations of this chart can be created.

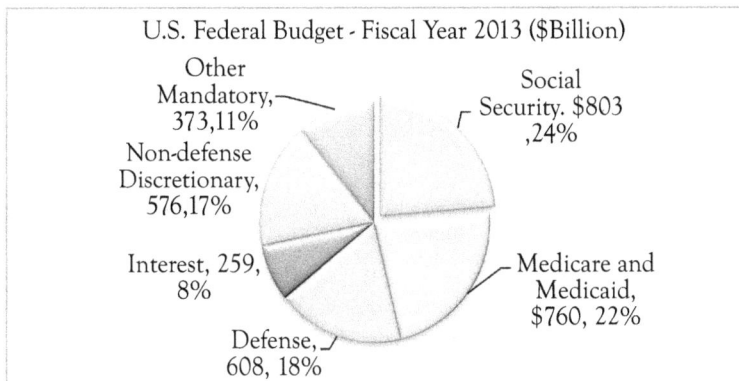

U.S. Federal Budget - Fiscal Year 2013 ($Billion)

Other Mandatory,— 373,11%

Social Security. $803 ,24%

Non-defense Discretionary, 576,17%

Interest, 259, 8%

Medicare and Medicaid, $760, 22%

Defense, 608, 18%

Figure 7.23 U.S. federal budget

Example: Variations of Pie Chart: Bar of a Pie Chart

Figure 7.24 shows a variation of the pie chart. This chart is commonly known as bar of pie. A bar chart is created that is an extension of the pie chart. The purpose of the bar chart is to show the important features of one of the main categories. The pie chart shows the energy consumption for 2014 by different energy sources. The renewable energy usage is 10 percent of the total and this category comprises of different categories, the percentages of which are shown using a bar chart.

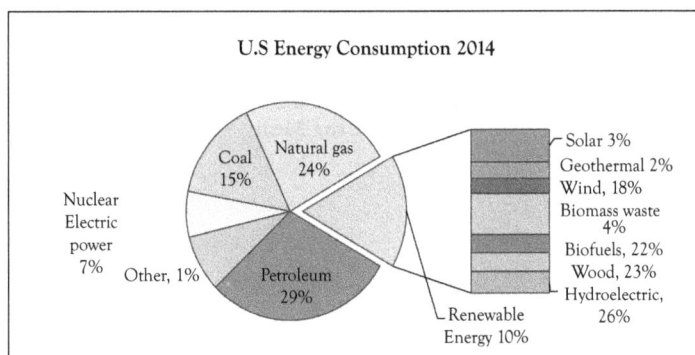

U.S Energy Consumption 2014

Coal 15%

Natural gas 24%

Nuclear Electric power 7%

Other, 1%

Petroleum 29%

Renewable Energy 10%

Solar 3%
Geothermal 2%
Wind, 18%
Biomass waste 4%
Biofuels, 22%
Wood, 23%
Hydroelectric, 26%

Figure 7.24 Bar of pie chart

Example: Another Variation of Pie Chart—Pie of a Pie chart

Figure 7.25 displays a *pie of pie* chart. In this chart, the bar is replaced with a pie chart to show the proportions of a category of interest.

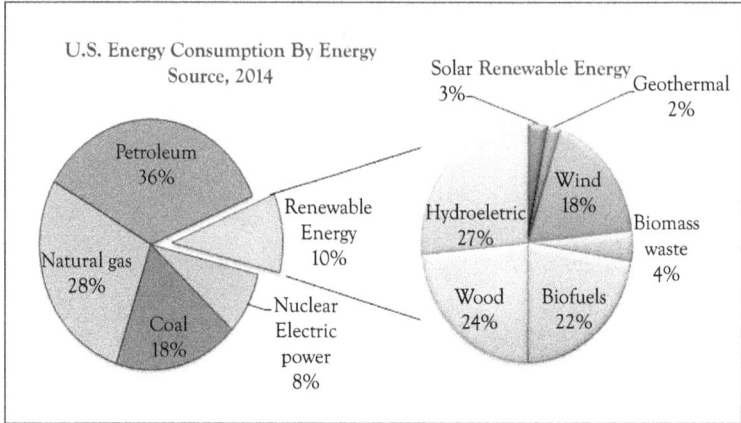

Figure 7.25 Pie of pie chart

Interval Plots

The interval plot displays mean and/or confidence interval for one or more variables. This plot is useful for assessing the measure of central tendency and variability of data. The plot in Figure 7.26 shows the amount of beverage in 16 oz. cans from five different production lines. The operations manager suspects that the mean content of the cans differs from line to line. He randomly selected five cans from each line and measured the content. The interval plot from five different production lines is plotted in Figure 7.26.

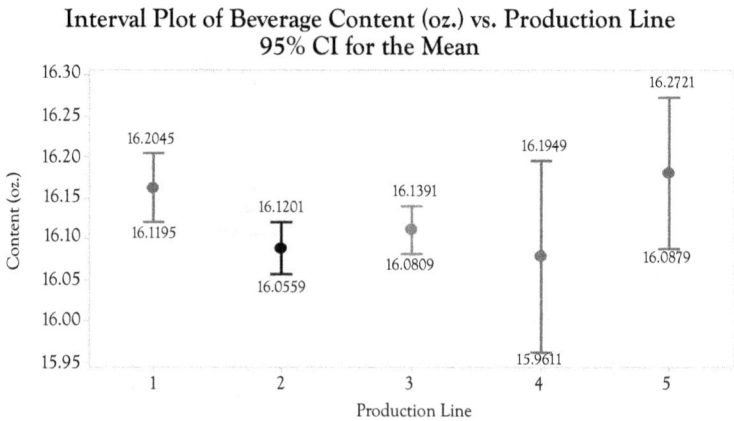

Individual standard deviations were used to calculate the intervals.

Figure 7.26 Interval plot of beverage content from five production lines

Example: Interval Plot Showing the Variation in Sample Data

Interval plot is also useful in visualizing the variation in samples. The data plotted in Figure 7.27 shows 20 samples each of size 10 of finished inside diameter of piston ring (in mm). The variation from sample to sample and the mean for each sample is plotted using an interval plot in Figure 7.27.

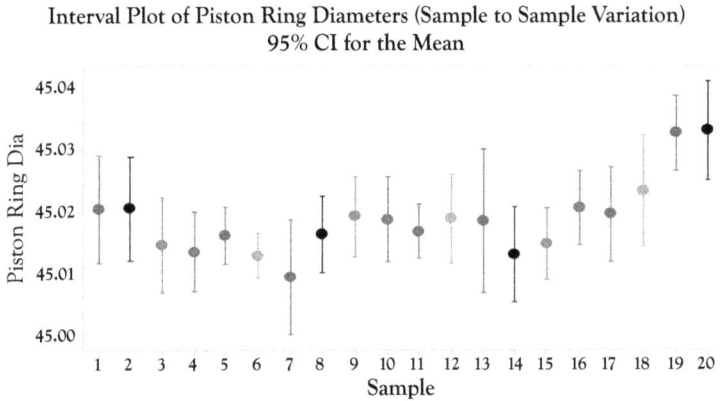

Interval Plot of Piston Ring Diameters (Sample to Sample Variation)
95% CI for the Mean

Individual standard deviations were used to calculate the intervals.

Figure 7.27 Interval plot of piston ring diameter

Time Series Plots

A time series plots the data over time. The graph plots the (x_i, y_i) pairs of points and connects these plots using straight lines where the x values are time. The plot is helpful in visualizing a trend or pattern in a data set. Figure 7.28 shows a time series plot of demand data over time. The plot shows the sales over time for a company. The data plotted shows weekly demand data for the past 60 weeks. Figure 7.29 is a plot of sales. This plot shows an increasing trend. Figure 7.30 shows the sales and short term forecast over a period of 60 weeks. The forecast is plotted using a dotted line. Notice how the forecast follows the trend in the sales. Figure 7.31 shows a seasonal pattern for the furnace filter demand and Figure 7.32 shows an increasing trend in sales over time.

In the above time series plots, the trends and patterns cannot be seen without plotting the data.

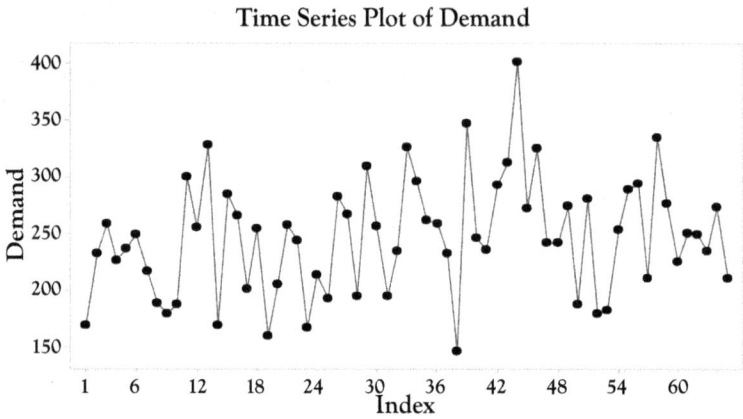

Figure 7.28 *A simple time series plot of demand*

Figure 7.29 *A simple time series plot of sales*

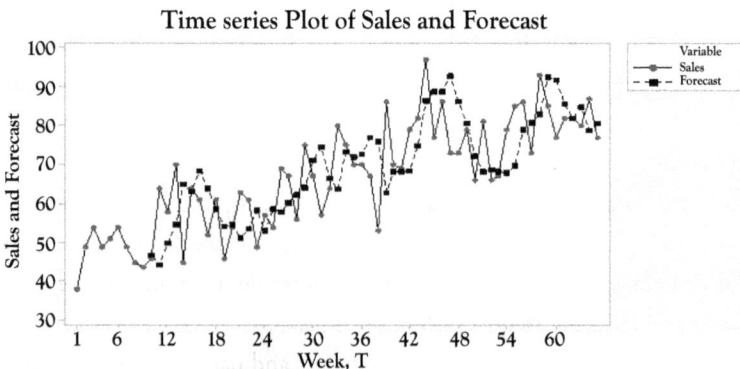

Figure 7.30 *A multiple time series plot showing sales and forecast*

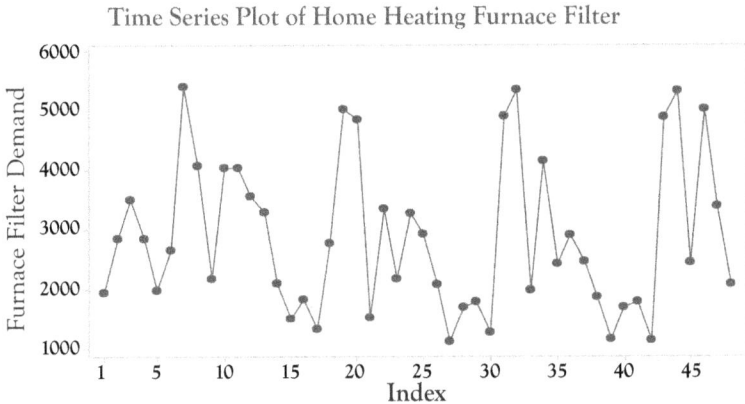

Figure 7.31 A time series plot showing a seasonal pattern

Figure 7.32 A time series plot showing a trend

Sequence Plot: Plot of Process Data

A sequence plot is used to show the evolution of a measured characteristic over time. This plot is like a time-series plot, with the time plotted on the horizontal axis and the corresponding process characteristic on the vertical axis. The sequence plot is a simple plot showing the behavior of the process over time. The variation or the trend in the process can be seen easily from this plot. The plot can also be used to see the deviation of a process from a specified target value.

Example

The data in Table 7.11 list the deviation (in 0.00025-inch units) of the diameter of 90 machined shafts from the target value. In the data; 0 means that the measured diameter was right on target, 2 means that the measured diameter was 0.0005 inch above the target value; whereas, a 3 means that the measured diameter was 0.00075 above the target value. We constructed a sequence plot of the data and interpret the results.

Table 7.11 Measured Diameter of a Machined Part

Diameter Deviation from Target [Coded in 0.00025 inch deviation from target]												
-4	-1	1	-5	6	-1	6	0	2	-2	-2	4	-5
0	-4	1	-4	0	-3	-4	-5	-3	2	0	-3	2
17	1	6	-8	2	1	2	-1	4	-1	2	-4	2
0	3	1	2	12	-8	2	2	1	2	1	2	7
-1	-5	-1	-1	0	1	1	-1	9	-1	0	-3	-4
3	-1	3	-2	-2	0	-12	2	0	2	0	-1	-2
-5	-2	-2	2	0	2	4	6	-3	0	7	-6	

Figures 7.33 and 7.34 show two variations of the sequence plot. Figure 7.33 shows large deviation for part numbers 27, 30, 44, 45, and 72. The rest of the measurements do not show large deviation. To see if

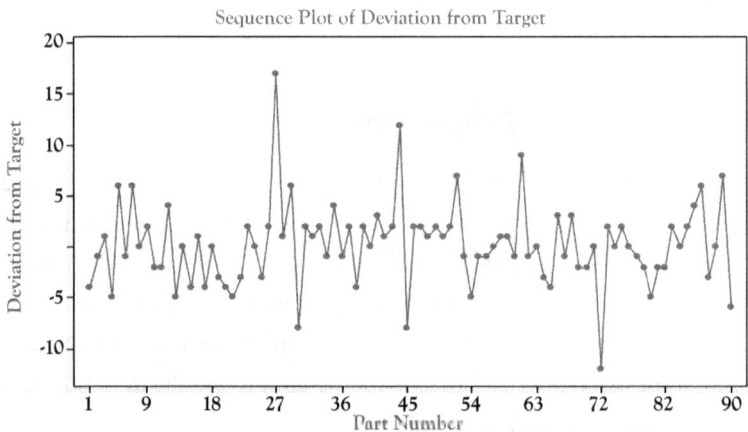

Figure 7.33 Sequence plot of the measurements on machined parts

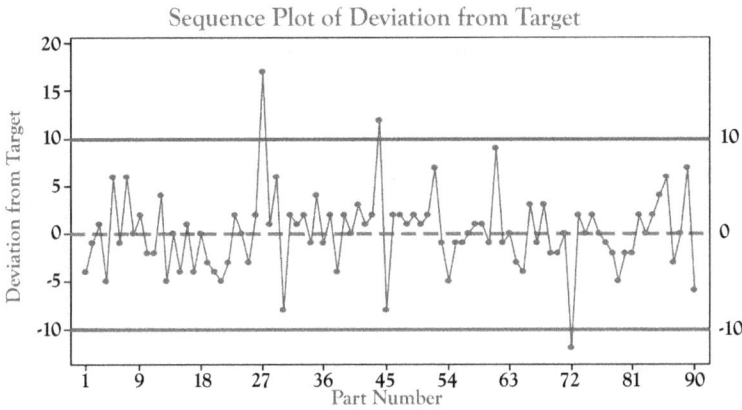

Figure 7.34 Sequence plot with specification limits

all the measurements are within the specified limits, we can also plot the specification limits on the plot (see Figure 7.34).

Suppose that the specification limits on the shaft diameter are 2±0.0025 inch. This means that in Figure 7.34 the target value coded 0 is 2, the upper limit is 10 (which is 0.00025*10 =0.0025), and the lower limit is -10. Figure 7.34 shows the sequence plot with specification limits. From this plot, you can see that part numbers 27, 44, and 72 are outside of the specification limits. At this stage, identifying the problems and taking corrective actions will bring the products under control.

Example: Sequence Plot

Because of increased competition, a large pizza chain is going to launch a new marketing campaign. The chain would like to advertise that they will make the delivery in 15 minutes or less; otherwise, the pizza is free. Before they launch the campaign, the pizza chain would like to study the current delivery process. If the current process indicates large variations in the delivery time, the causes of variation will be studied, and corrective actions will be taken to meet the target delivery time of 15 minutes or less. The data for the delivery time (in minutes) of 120 deliveries by different carriers were collected. A sequence plot of the delivery time data is shown in Figure 7.35. We would like to analyze the graph to get an idea of the variation in the current delivery process. The plot will also tell us whether the current process is meeting the target time of 15 minutes or less.

From Figure 7.35, we see that the delivery times vary considerably A line is drawn at 15 minutes to show the target value. The values above this line indicate delivery exceeding 15 minutes. There are 13 or 10.8 percent (13/120=0.108*100) or, 11 percent deliveries exceeding 15 minutes. This amounts to 108,000 missed deliveries in a million deliveries. The pizza chain needs to study the causes of variation to stabilize this process and meet the target delivery.

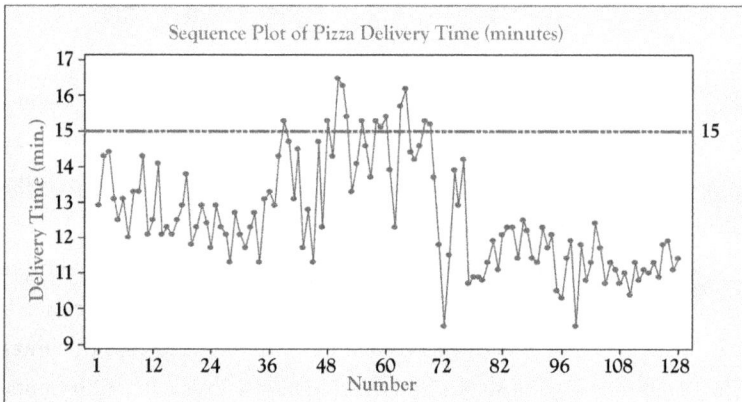

Figure 7.35 Sequence plot of pizza delivery time

Summary and Applications of Widely Used Charts and Graphs

Type of Chart/Graph	Applications
Histogram 	A *histogram* summarizes a large set of data. It is a plot of frequency distribution. Displays the pattern that is not so obvious when the data are in a table form. Useful in the study of variability in the data and the probability distributions. In a histogram, the class intervals are plotted on the horizontal axis and the frequencies are plotted on the vertical axis.

Histogram with Fitted Distribution 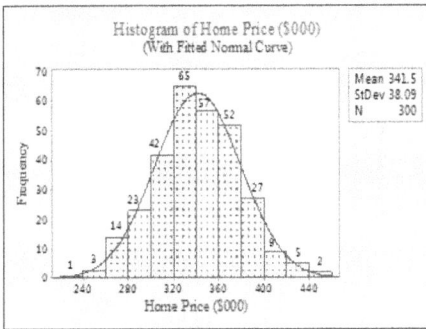	Histogram with a normal curve superimposed. The graph shows whether the plotted data can be approximated by a symmetrical (normal distribution) or some other distribution. The distribution is used in drawing conclusion and making decision about the process from which the data were extracted.
Graphical summary of data 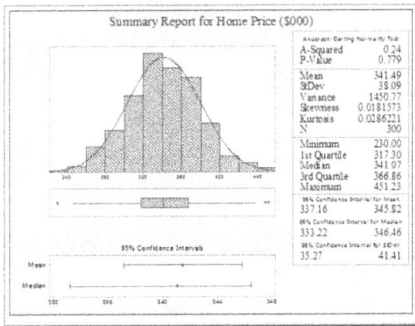	Graphical summary report provides the plot of the data in form of a histogram with a normal curve superimposed. A boxplot of the data is shown below the histogram. Both of these plots—histogram and the box plot—summarize the data and provide information about the distribution. On the right-hand side, the calculated statistics are displayed.
Graphs Displaying Variation 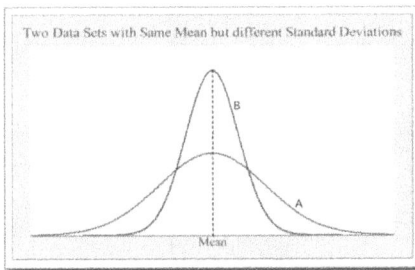	Data sets A and B with the same mean but different variations. The plot can be used to study the variation in different data sets
Plot of Cumulative Frequency:Ogive 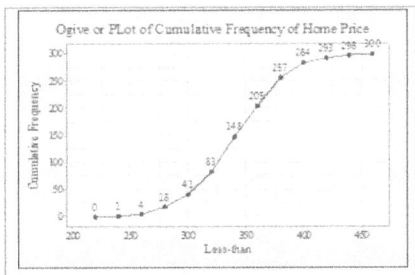	The plots of the cumulative frequency or relative cumulative frequency (also known as the ogive) are created from the frequency distribution. These plots are useful in estimating the values that cannot be read from the frequency distribution. The plot of relative cumulative frequency can be used to determine the median value, percentiles, or values at certain percentile value.

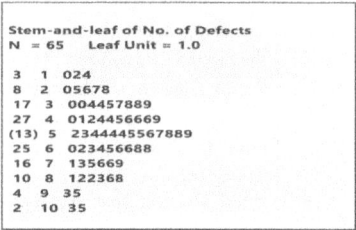

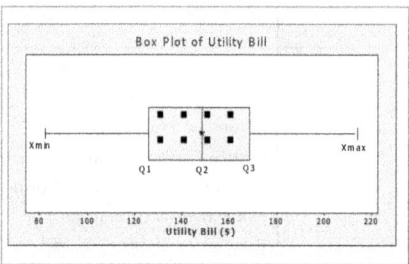

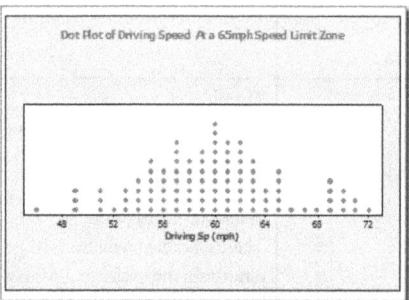

Stem-and Leaf Plot	Stem-and-leaf plot is a very efficient way of displaying data and checking the variation and shape of the distribution.
Stem-and-leaf of No. of Defects N = 65 Leaf Unit = 1.0 3 1 024 8 2 05678 17 3 004457889 27 4 0124456669 (13) 5 2344445567889 25 6 023456688 16 7 135669 10 8 122368 4 9 35 2 10 35	
Box Plot	The box-plot displays the smallest and the largest values in the data along with the three quartiles: Q_1, Q_2, and Q_3. The display of these five numbers (known as five measure summary) is used to study the shape of the distribution and draw conclusion from the data. Different types of box plots can be created from the data. Some of these plots are shown here.
Box Plot of Utility Bill	
Variations of Box Plot	Box plots can be grouped to show variations from different groups. for example, comparing production from different machines.
Boxplot of Sample 1, Sample 2, Sample 3, Sample 4, Sample 5	
Dot Plot:	A *dot plot* is used to study the shape of the distribution or to compare two or more than two sets of data. In a dot plot, the horizontal axis shows the range of values in the data. Each observation is represented by a dot placed above the axis. If the data value repeats, the dots are piled up at that location, showing a dot for each repeated value. The plot is effective in displaying the graphical summary of the data of small data sets.
Dot Plot of Driving Speed At a 65mph Speed Limit Zone	

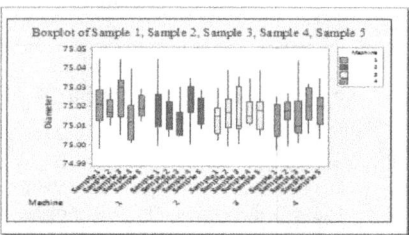

Bar Chart	Bar charts are one of the widely used charts to display categorical data. These charts can be used to display monthly or quarterly sales, revenue, and profits for a company. Usually there are two columns of data; the first column is the categorical variable (e.g., month) and the second column contains the numerical values (e.g., sales in dollars).
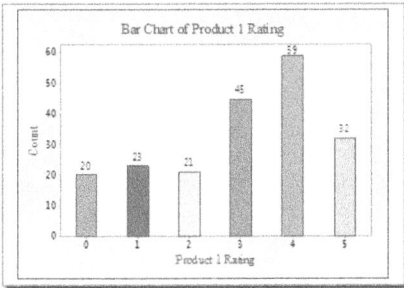 Bar Chart of Product 1 Rating	
Variation of Bar Chart	A vertical bar chart shows the values and the pattern in the data. The visual displays make the pattern visible.
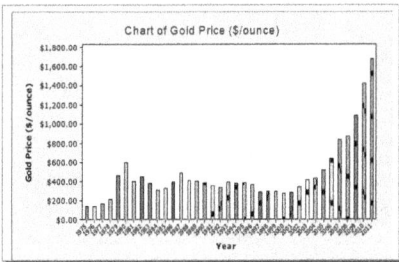 Chart of Gold Price ($/ounce)	
Variation of Bar Chart	A horizontal bar chart shows the values of each category. Simple and very effective way of visualizing and comparing groups or categories.
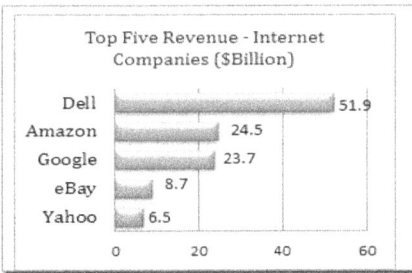 Top Five Revenue - Internet Companies ($Billion)	
A Cluster Bar Chart	A cluster bar chart can be used to compare data categories.
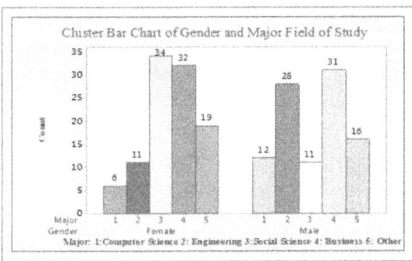 Cluster Bar Chart of Gender and Major Field of Study	

A Variation of a Cluster Bar Chart  Quarterly Sales vs. Year	A cluster bar chart can be used to compare data categories. For example, the quarterly sales for the past four years. A good way is to plot the sales of each quarter using a bar chart. We can use the cluster option to group the four quarters of each of the four years.
Stacked Bar Chart 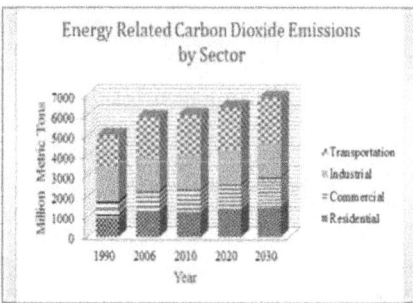 Energy Related Carbon Dioxide Emissions by Sector	Stacked bar charts are used to compare different measure of data categories. In the most common form, a stacked bar chart displays a count of a category. The stacked bar chart on the left shows carbon dioxide emissions by different sectors—residential, commercial, industrial, and transportation. Each of these sectors is categorized by year and is displayed as a stacked chart.
Connected Line Graph  Gold Price per Ounce (1975-2011)	The connected line plot connects each of the data values using a line. The graph is very useful in visualizing the trend in the plot. This is also called the line graph.
Variation of Line Graph 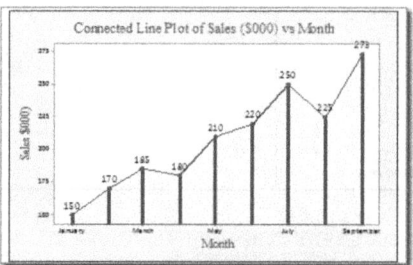 Connected Line Plot of Sales ($000) vs Month	Line chart superimposed over the bar chart can provide more clarity. It is helpful in visualizing the trend.

Pie Chart	A pie chart is used to show the relative magnitudes of parts to a whole. In this chart relative frequencies of each group of data are plotted. A circle is constructed and is divided into distinct sections. Each section represents one group of data. The area of each section is determined by multiplying the relative frequency of each section by the angle of a circle.

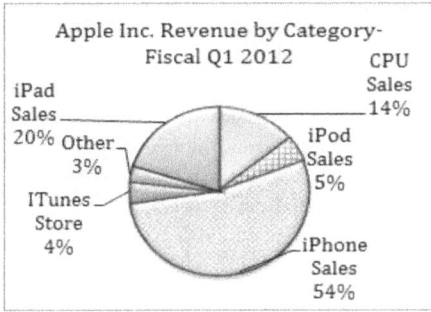

Apple Inc. Revenue by Category- Fiscal Q1 2012

iPad Sales 20%
Other 3%
ITunes Store 4%
CPU Sales 14%
iPod Sales 5%
iPhone Sales 54%

Variation of Pie Chart: 3-D Pie	A 3-D view of the pie chart. One or more section can be exploded to show the relative importance of that category.

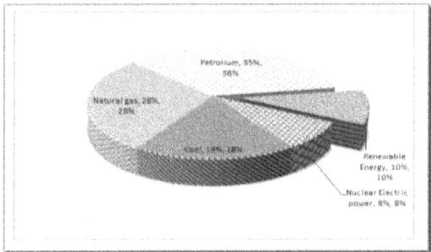

Bar of a Pie Chart	Bar of pie chart is an extension of the pie chart. The purpose of the bar chart is to show the important features of one of the main categories.

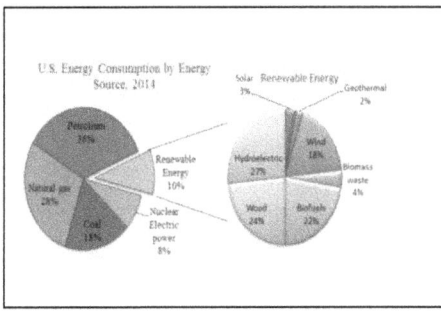

Pie of a Pie Chart	In this chart, the bars in the bar chart are replaced with a pie chart to show the proportions of a category of interest.

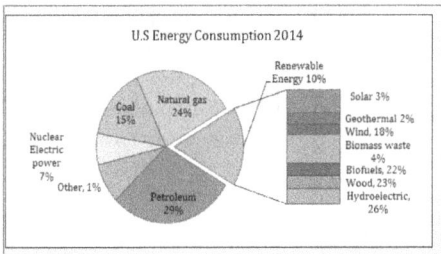

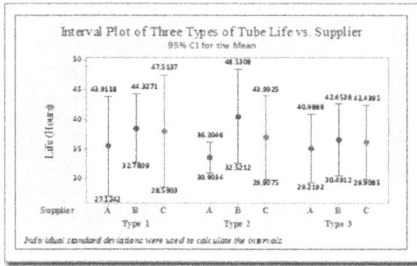

Interval Plot	The interval plot displays the means and/or confidence intervals for one or more variables. This plot is useful for assessing the measure of central tendency and variability of data. The default confidence interval is 95%; however this can be changed.
Variation of Interval Plot	Interval plot is also useful in visualizing the variation in samples. The plot shows sample to sample variation and the mean for each sample using an interval plot.
Time Series Plot	A time series plots the data over time. The graph plots the (x_i, y_i) pairs of points and connects these plots using straight lines where the x values are time. The plot is helpful in visualizing a trend or pattern in a data set. The time series plot of demand data over time is shown.
Variation of Time Series Plot	Time series plot showing the actual sales and the forecast of the sales on the same plot. The plot is useful in comparing two variables for example, the sales and forecast using the same plot.

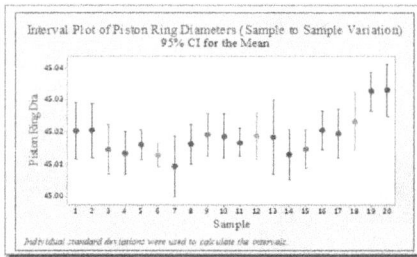

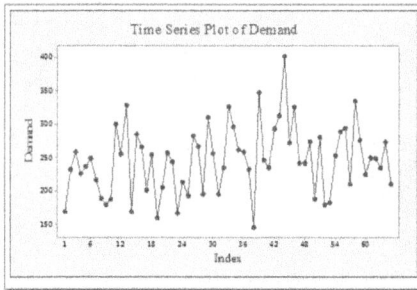

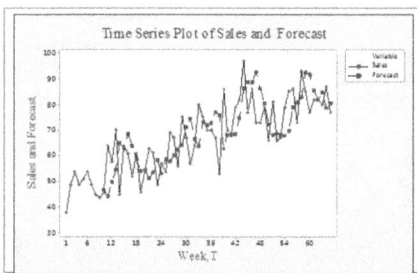

Variation of Time Series Plot	A time-series plot showing the sales over time for a company. The plot shows an increasing trend. These patterns cannot be seen from the data alone.

Sequence Plot	The sequence plot is a simple plot showing the behavior of the process over time. The variation or the trend in the process can be seen easily from this plot. The plot can also be used to see the deviation of a process from a specified target value.
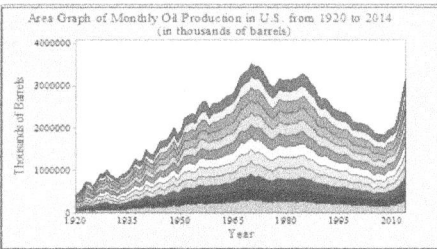	
Area Plot	The area graph is used to examine trends in multiple time series as well as each series' contribution to the sum.
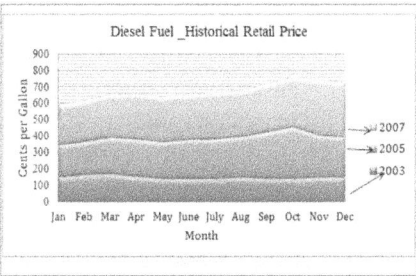	
Variation of Area Plot	In this plot, the area below each line represents the cumulative total.
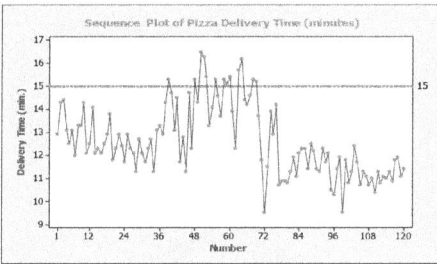	

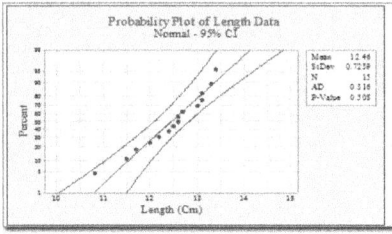

Probability Plot	The probability plots are a good way of determining graphically whether the given data follow a normal or any other assumed distribution. In statistical analysis, often conclusions are drawn based on using one or more distributions. A probability plot is of great value because of its usefulness in verifying one of the major assumptions underlying the analysis of variance and regression analysis.
Probability Plot and Histogram	Histograms and probability plots together can show how well the data fits a distribution. The first two graphs on the left shows how well the data fits a normal distribution. The bottom two graphs show deviation from normality.
Symmetry Plot	This plot provides a quick and easy way to check if the data are from a symmetrical distribution. In many statistical analyses, the underlying assumption is that the data are from a normal distribution which can be verified using this plot.
Another Example of a Symmetry Plot	The plot is useful in determining the shape and location of data measured on one characteristic. Also used for detecting process problems, evaluating process capability (ability of the process to be within its specification limits), and determining the process variation.

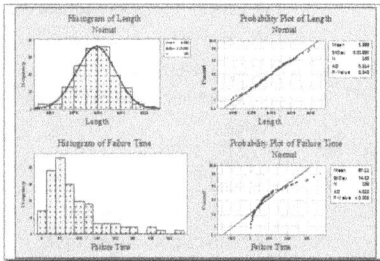

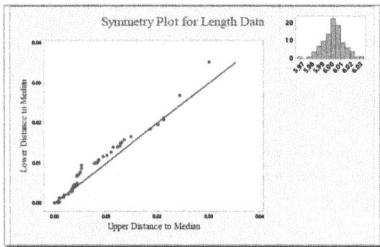

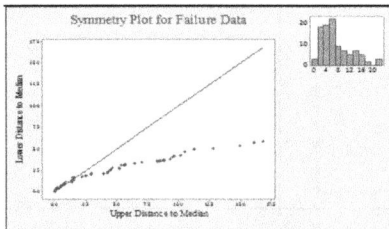

CHAPTER 8

Numerical Methods for Data Science Applications

Chapter Highlights

Explain the techniques of describing data using numerical methods and use these methods to compare and draw meaningful conclusions from data. This chapter explains how to:

- Calculate and apply the *measures of central tendency* including the mean, median, mode.
- Calculate the measures of position—percentiles, quartiles, and interpret their meaning.
- Calculate and apply various *measures of variation*—range, interquartile range, variance, and standard deviation for both grouped and ungrouped data.
- Compare the mean, median, mode, and standard deviation to draw meaningful conclusions from the data.
- Relate the mean and standard deviation using the Chebyshev's and empirical rules and understand the importance of empirical rule in statistics and data analysis.
- Calculate and apply the *measures of shape* to learn about the data.
- Explain the *relationship between two variables*—covariance and coefficient of correlation.

Statistics at a Glance

The previous chapter focused on describing data using charts and graphs. We explored a number of charts and graphs that were used to present and summarize data. Several graphs including histograms, bar charts, pie charts, and stem-and-leaf plots were introduced. These graphs are widely used in the real world. Charts and graphs are an integral part of data analysis and are used widely to illustrate several of the key features of the data.

When graphical tools are combined with numerical measures, they provide more insight and meaning to the data. In this chapter, we discuss several numerical measures to describe data. These measures are commonly known as the *numerical methods* of describing and summarizing data. The calculated measures are also known as *statistics* when calculated from the sample data and *parameters* when calculated from the population data. We calculate the *measures of central tendency*, which are the *mean*, *median*, and *mode*. These statistics measure the central value of the data set. When these measures are calculated and compared, they tell us about the shape or the distribution of data and are helpful in drawing appropriate conclusion about the data set under study. We also discuss the *measures of position* commonly known as *percentiles* and *quartiles*. The quartiles when combined with the minimum and maximum value of the data set provide the five-measure summary of the data that can be represented graphically as a *box plot*.

Another set of statistics that measure the amount of variation in the data are *measures of variation*. These statistics are the *range, variance, standard deviation*, and *coefficient of variation*. Almost all data show variation; these measures provide the amount of variation in the data that are critical in understanding and reducing variation from the process. Variation reduction is one of the major objectives of quality improvement programs.

In this chapter, we will also study empirical rules that relate the mean and standard deviation and aid in understanding what it means for a data set to be normal. Finally, we study the statistics that measure the association between two variables—*covariance* and *correlation coefficient*. To describe the data, we need more than just a visual picture in the form of a graph or chart. For example, Figure 8.1 shows the annual household income in the United States.

According to a report, the median household income in the United States was $50,502. This is based on the survey of 114 million U.S. households. In reporting the income data, the *average* U.S. income is a less useful measure because it is skewed by high income households and a

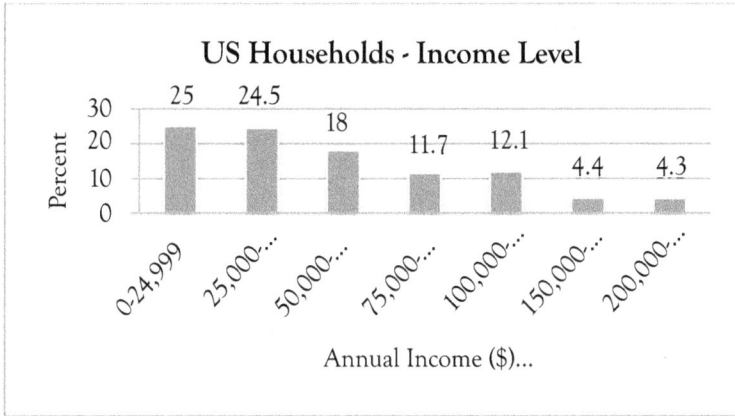

US Households - Income Level

Figure 8.1 Annual household income of the United States for 2012

very small percentage of extremely high-income earners. This pushes the average household income to $72,000.

According to a more recent census bureau report, the median household income in the United States was $68,703 in 2019, an increase of 6.8 percent from the 2018 median of $64,324 (September 15, 2020). Figure 8.1 provides the range and percentage of the household income, the shape, and the distribution of the income data. This graph alone does not provide complete information. It is also critical to know several other numerical measures from the data. For example, we may be interested in the median household income and other statistics such as the mean, variance, standard deviation, and the percentiles. These measures—when combined with appropriate visual pictures—provide a more comprehensive analysis and description of the data. Figure 8.2 shows the graph of the income data along with several important statistics. Combining the graphs and charts with the calculated statistics adds depth to the analysis.

Descriptive Statistics: Numerical Methods

The numerical methods of describing data can be divided into following categories: (1) measures of central tendency or measures of location, (2) measures of position, (3) measures of variation or dispersion, and (4) the measures of shape.

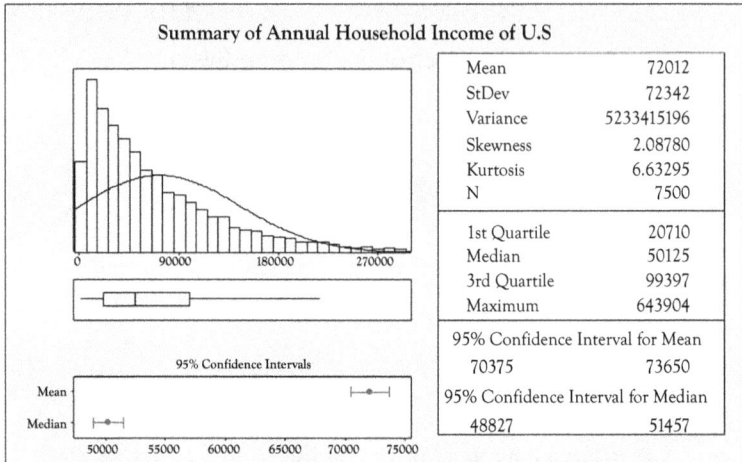

Summary of Annual Household Income of U.S	
Mean	72012
StDev	72342
Variance	5233415196
Skewness	2.08780
Kurtosis	6.63295
N	7500
1st Quartile	20710
Median	50125
3rd Quartile	99397
Maximum	643904
95% Confidence Interval for Mean	
70375	73650
95% Confidence Interval for Median	
48827	51457

Figure 8.2 Annual household income and related statistics

Symbols Used to Describe the Population Parameters and Sample Statistics

The statistical measures can be calculated from population or sample data. In most cases, we deal with sample data. A *population* is described by its *parameters*, whereas a sample is described by its *statistics*. These are described below.

Symbols Used for Population Parameters

μ: *the population mean* σ^2: *the population variance*
σ: *the population standard deviation* p: *the population proportion*
N: *the population size*

The symbol μ is read as "mu" and the symbol σ is read as "sigma." A *sample* is described by its *statistics*. The corresponding sample statistics are:

$\bar{x}$: sample mean

s^2: sample variance

s: sample standard deviation

$\bar{p}$: sample proportion

n: sample size

(x is read as "x-bar")

Measures of Central Tendency or Measures of Location

Central tendency is described by the "average" and is also called the measure of location. The central tendency of a data set is the tendency of the data to cluster about certain numerical values, such as the mean or median. If the shape of the data (distribution) is symmetrical, the mean, median, and mode are all centrally located. If the shape is not symmetrical (skewed), then the mean, median, and mode are in different places. Figure 8.3 shows the shape or the distribution of a set of data.

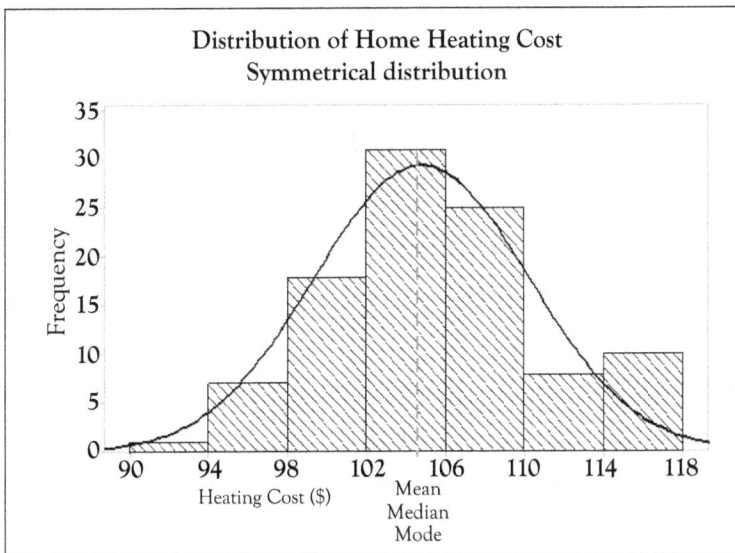

Figure 8.3 A symmetrical distribution

In the above figure, the data represents the home heating cost for 100 households during winter months. The pattern emerging from the data can be described by a distribution. This shape is known as a symmetrical distribution as seen by the smooth curve in the figure.

The *mean* or the average is a statistical constant which enable us to comprehend the significance of the whole. It provides an idea about the concentration of the data in the central part of the distribution. The requirements for the ideal measures of central tendency are that they should be (1) uniquely defined, (2) based on all observations, (3) affected as little as possible by fluctuations in sampling, and (4) suitable for further mathematical treatment.

The median is the value of the variable that divides the data into two equal parts, such that half of the value lies above the median and the other half below it.

The mode is the value of the variable, which occurs most frequently or repeated the maximum number of times in a data set. We will discuss these in more detail in sections that follow.

The common measures of central tendency are:

(1) Mean, (2) Median, and (3) Mode.

The above measures of central tendency can be calculated from either sample data or from population data. If the measures are computed using the population data, they are called *population parameters* and are described using the symbols of *population parameters*. On the other hand, if the measures are computed using the sample data, they are called *sample statistics*, which use different symbols to describe them. These parameters and statistics were described earlier.

Mean or the Average

The mean or the average is commonly used to obtain a typical representation of a group. When we refer to the "average" of something, we are talking about the arithmetic mean. For example, the average grade of students in a statistics course, average life of a car battery, and so on.

The mean of a data set is sum of the values divided by the number of observations. The mean of n observations $x_1, x_2, \ldots, x_n$ is given by

$$Mean = \frac{\sum all\ values}{n} = \frac{\sum x}{n}$$

In the above formula x_1 is the first value of the variable, x_2 is the second value and so on. The total number of observations is n and the symbol "Σ" Σ is the summation sign. Suppose we collected data on the hourly wages for five employees of a company. Then the wage is a *variable*. If the wages are \$12, \$13, \$10, \$15, and \$10 per hour then x_1 is 12, which is the first data point or the first value of variable; and x_1 is 13 or the second value of the variable and so on. To calculate the average wage, we would sum all the values and divide the sum by 5, the total number of observations. Thus, the mean or the average wage would be

$$Mean = \frac{12 + 13 + 10 + 15 + 10}{5} = \frac{60}{5} = 12$$

In the above example, we collected data on only five employees. We call this a sample data. If we collected data on all the employees in that company, such data would be called population data.

A sample is part of a population and statistical analysis mostly relies on taking samples. The reason for taking the samples and not studying the entire population is that the population may be infinitely large in many cases. It is important to distinguish whether the summary statistics, such as the mean is being calculated from sample or population data. The formulas for the sample and population mean are given below.

Sample Mean	Population Mean
$\bar{x} = \dfrac{\sum x_i}{n}$ (8.1)	$\mu = \dfrac{\sum x_i}{N}$ (8.2)

Example 1

The number of accidents per month for the past 6 months on a highway is given below.

| 5 | 8 | 10 | 7 | 10 | 14 |

The sample mean $\bar{x}$ can be calculated as

$$\bar{x} = \frac{\sum x}{n} = \frac{5 + 8 + 10 + 7 + 10 + 14}{6} = 9$$

The above calculation shows that the average number of accidents was 9. The mean can be interpreted in the following ways:

- It provides a single number presenting the whole data set.
- It gives us the significance of the whole.
- It is unique because a given data set has only one mean.
- It is useful for comparing different data sets in terms of average.

Disadvantages of Mean

The mean can be affected by *outliers or extreme* values (extreme values are very high or very low values in a data set that may be difficult to detect in a large data set).

Weighted Mean

While discussing the measures of central tendency, we described the sample mean using Equation 8.1.

In calculating the mean using the above formula, each observation in the data has equal weight. In some cases, each observation in the data may not be given the same weight and therefore the mean cannot be calculated by taking the simple average as shown above by the sample mean formula. When the data values cannot be weighted equally, we calculate a weighted mean of the data by providing different weight or importance to different data values. The weighted mean is calculated using the following formula:

$$\bar{x} = \frac{\sum w_i x_i}{\sum w_i} \tag{8.3}$$

where x_i is the ith observation and w_i is the weight given to the i-th observation.

Example 2

One of the common applications of weighted average is the calculation of the grade point average (GPA) where each letter grade is given a different value. For most colleges and universities, the letter grades usually are based on similar data values. Suppose your college uses the following values for the letter grades:

A (4), A– (3.7), B+ (3.3), B (3.0), B– (2.7), C (2.0), D (1), F (0)

Suppose you have completed 75 credit hours of course work and earned an A grade for 18 credit hours, A– for 21 credit hours, B+ for 28 credit hours, and a B for 3 credit hours. What is your grade point average?

Solution: The grade point average can be calculated using the weighted average.

Grade, x_i	A (4)	A– (3.7)	B+ (3.3)	B (3.0)	Total
Weight, w_i	18	21	28	3	70 Credits

The weighted average,

$$\bar{x} = \frac{\sum w_i x_i}{\sum w_i} = \frac{18(4) + 21(3.7) + 28(3.3) + 3(3)}{18 + 21 + 28 + 3} = 3.587 \approx 3.6$$

Median

The *median* is another measure of central tendency. The median is the middle value of a data set when the data are arranged in increasing (or decreasing) order. The median divides the data into two equal parts, such that half of the values lie above the median and the other half below it. The median is the value that measures the central item in the data. For the ungrouped data (data not grouped into a frequency distribution) the median is calculated based on whether the number of observations is odd or even.

Calculating Median When the Number of Observations is Odd

If the number of observations is odd, the median can be calculated by

- Arranging the data in increasing order.
- Locating the middle value after the values have been arranged in ascending order of magnitude.

Note that there is a distinct median when the number of observations is odd. Unlike the mean, the median is not affected by extreme values.

Median When the Number of Observations Is Even

When the number of observations is even, there are two middle values, and the median is obtained by taking the arithmetic mean of the middle terms.

Example 3

Suppose we have the following observations arranged in increasing order.

1	2	3	4	5	6	7
8.2	8.3	8.9	9.6	9.8	10.2	12.0

The number of observations is seven ($n = 7$), which is odd. Therefore, the middle value or the median is 9.6.

The data below are the annual incomes in thousands of dollars for a sample of eight employees of a manufacturing company for the past year. Find the median.

1	2	3	4	5	6	7	8
70	62	60	45	40	56	38	35

The number of observations is $n = 8$ (even). To find the median,

- Arrange the data in increasing order:

1	2	3	4	5	6	7	8
35	38	40	45	56	60	62	70

- Next, find the location of the median. The location of the median for the data set with even number of observations is given by

$$\frac{n+1}{2} = \frac{8+1}{2} = 4.5 \qquad (8.4)$$

Therefore, in this case, the median is the average of 4th and 5th values

$$Median = \frac{45+56}{2} = 50.5$$

This means that 50.5 is the median income. Note that the number of observations is even; therefore, there is no distinct median. One advantage of the median over the mean is that it is not affected by extreme values in a data set and is easy to understand and calculate. The disadvantage is that in case of even number of observations, the median cannot be calculated exactly. It can only be estimated by taking the mean of two middle terms.

Mode

The mode is the value that occurs most frequently in a set. In other words, it is the value that is repeated most often in a data set. Sometimes chance causes a single often-repeated value to be the most frequent value in the data set.

Example 4

The following data represent the number of hours of use of personal computer per day by a sample of 20 employees at work:

3	2	3	4	3	0	1	3	5
2	3	4	3	1	1	3	2	1
3	3							

The mode for this data is 3 hours because this value is repeated the maximum number of times. Therefore,

$$\text{Mode} = 3 \text{ hours}$$

If you calculate the average for the data, you will find,

$$\bar{x} = \frac{\sum x}{n} = \frac{50}{20} = 2.5 hours$$

The mode of 3 hours tells us that the usage is higher than the average of 2.5 hours. It also tells us that 3 is the most frequent number of hours of usage, but it fails to tell us what values are above or below this value.

- It is easy to calculate. In some cases, it can be located by inspection.
- It is not affected by extreme values.
- It is not always possible to find a unique mode in a data set.

Comparing Mean, Median, and Mode

The mean, median, mode, and other statistics are calculated from the data in order to characterize and describe the data. Mean, median, and mode are some of the simple statistics we calculate to draw meaningful conclusions from the data. Since we use these measures to describe the data, it is important to know which measure of central tendency best describes the data (the mean, median, or mode).

If the values of the mean, median and mode are equal or approximately equal, the shape or the distribution of the data is *symmetrical*. A symmetrical distribution is also known as a bell-shaped or normal distribution. If the data are symmetrical, the mean, median, and mode are all centrally located, and they have the same value (see Figure 8.1).

In case of skewed data, the mean, median, and mode are not located at the same place. Skewness means the lack of symmetry. A distribution (shape) can be right skewed or left skewed. *The right skewed distribution* is tailed to the right and is also known as *positively skewed*. A *left skewed distribution* is tailed to the left and is also known as *negatively skewed*. In a right skewed or positively skewed data set:

Mean > Median, and

Mean > Mode

Figures 8.4a and b show a right skewed or positively skewed and a left or negatively skewed distribution. In a left skewed or negatively skewed data set,

Mean < Median, and

Mean < Mode

Note that when the distribution is skewed—negatively or positively—the *median* is always midway between the mean and the mode. Therefore, median is often used to describe a skewed data and is the best measure for central tendency whenever data are skewed.

Comparing the mean, median, and mode we can determine whether the shape of the data is symmetrical or skewed. Some data such as age or income are often skewed. Therefore, when drawing conclusion from such skewed data, we compare the median age or the median income.

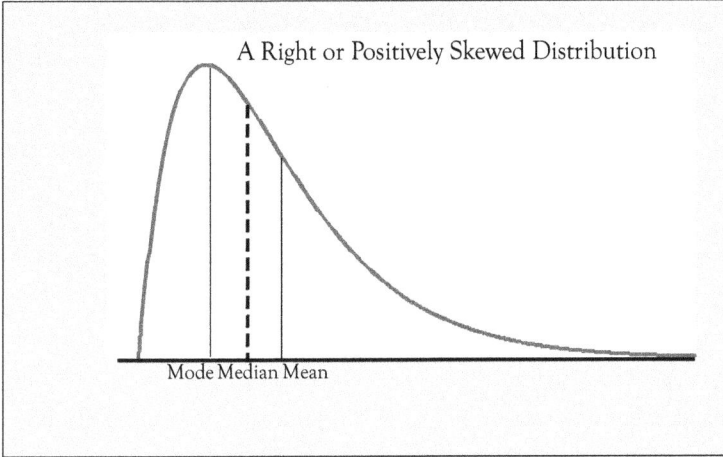

Figure 8.4a A right or positively skewed

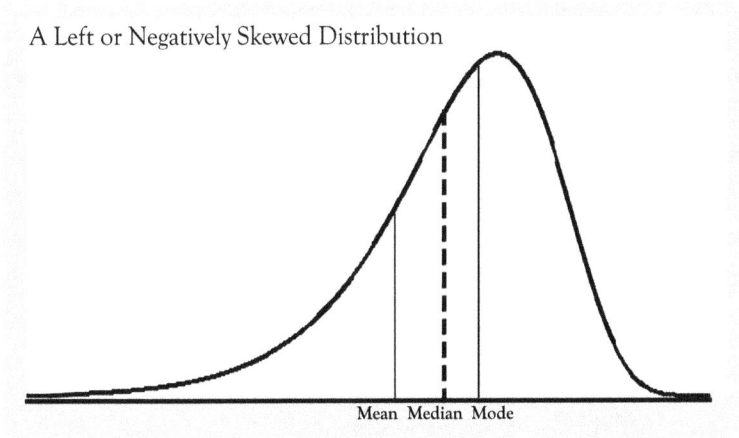

Figure 8.4b A left or negatively skewed

Measures of Position

Other important measures in describing the data are percentile and quartiles. These are known as *measures of position* and are described below.

Percentiles and Quartiles

Quantitative data are sometimes summarized in terms of percentiles. A percentile is a point below which a stated percentage or proportion of observations lie. Quartiles are special percentiles, which divide the observations into groups of successive size, each containing 25 percent of the data points. The quartiles are denoted by Q_1: the first quartile or 25th percentile; Q_2: the second quartile or 50th percentile (which is also the median); and Q_3: the third quartile or 75th percentile. Another measure calculated using the quartiles is *interquartile range*. It is the difference between the third quartile and the first quartile and encompasses the middle 50 percent of the values. One very useful data summary called *the five-measure summary* provides a visual display of the data in form of a plot known as the *box plot*. This is a plot of the minimum, maximum and three quartiles, Q_1, Q_2, and Q_3. The box plot shows the data extremes, the range, the median, the quartiles, and the interquartile range. A percentile tells us how the data values are spread out over the interval from the smallest value to the largest value.

If a score on a SAT test states that a student is at 85th percentile, it means that 85 percent who took the test had scores at or below this value and 15 percent of those who took the test scored higher than this value. The percentile value provides us with a comparison in relation to other values.

The quartiles divide the data into four parts. For a large data set, it is often desirable to divide the data into four parts. This can be done by calculating the quartile. Note that

Q_1 = first quartile or 25th percentile
Q_2 = second quartile or 50th percentile or the median
Q_3 = third quartile or 75th percentile

The first quartile or Q_1 is the value such that 25 percent of the observations are below Q_1 and 75 percent of the values are above Q_2. The other quartiles can be interpreted in a similar way. Using the formula below, we can determine the percentile and quartile for any data set.

Calculating Percentiles and Quartiles

The pth percentile of a data set is a value, such that at least p percent of the values are less than or equal to this value, and at least (100 − p) percent of the values are greater than or equal to this value.

To find a percentile or quartile

- Arrange the data in increasing order
- Find the location of the percentile using the following formula:

$$L_p = (n+1)\frac{P}{100} \tag{8.5}$$

where L_p = location of the percentile.
n = total number of observations and P = desired percentile.

Example 5

Find the median, the first quartile, and the third quartile for the data in Table 8.1.

Table 8.1 Data for calculating quartiles

2038 1758 1721 1637 2097 2047 2205 1787 2287 1940 2311 2054
2406 1471 1460

Solution: Note that the number of observations is 15 (n = 15). First, arrange the data in increasing order. The sorted values are shown in Table 8.2.

Table 8.2 Sorted data

Sorted data
1460 1471 1637 1721 1758 1787 1940 2038 2047 2054 2097 2205 2287
2311 2406

Table 8.3 shows the descriptive statistics of the data in Table 8.1 calculated using MINITAB. MINITAB calculates the median, the first quartile Q1, and the third quartile Q3, among other statistics. We have verified the results of the median or the 50th percentile (also known as Q2), Q1, and Q3 as reported by MINITAB using manual calculations.

Table 8.3 Descriptive Statistics using MINITAB

Descriptive Statistics Calculations using MINITAB					
Variable	N	Mean	Median	TrMean	StDev	SE Mean
Data	15	1947.9	2038.0	1950.2	298.8	77.1
Variable		Minimum	Maximum	Q1	Q3	
Data		1460.0	2406.0	1722.0	2205.0	

(a) Calculate the median or Q2 (50th percentile) using equation (8.4) and compare it to the median calculated by MINITAB in Table 8.3.

First, calculate the position of the median or Q2 using equation (8.5) as shown below.

$$L_p = (n+1)\frac{P}{100} = 16\left(\frac{50}{100}\right) = 8$$

Therefore, the 8th value in the sorted data (Table 8.2) is the median or Q2. This value is 2038. Therefore,

$$\text{Median} = 2038$$

This result is same as the value of the median calculated using MINITAB in Table 8.3.

Calculate the first quartile or Q1 (25th percentile) using equation (8.4) and compare it to the Q1 value calculated by MINITAB in Table 8.3.

Calculate the position of Q1 using equation (8.5) as shown below.

$$L_P = (n+1)\frac{P}{100} = 16\left(\frac{25}{100}\right) = 4$$

The 4th value in the sorted data (Table 8.2) is Q2. This value is 1722. Therefore,

$$Q1 = 1721$$

Calculate the third quartile or Q3 (75th percentile) using equation (8.5) and compare it to the Q3 value calculated by MINITAB in Table 8.3.

$$L_p = (n+1)\frac{P}{100} = 16\left(\frac{75}{100}\right) = 12$$

The 12th value in the sorted data is Q3. This value is 2205. Therefore,

$$Q3 = 2205$$

The values of Q1, Q2 (the median), and Q3 calculated using equation (8.5) agree with the computer result in Table 8.3.

Example 6

The data in Table 8.4 show the monthly income of 20 part-time employees of a company. Find the median, the first quartile, and the third quartile values of the income data. Table 8.5 shows the sorted values from Table 8.4.

Table 8.4 Monthly income

Monthly Income							
2038	1758	1721	1637	2097	2047	2205	1787
2287	1940	2311	2054	2406	1471	1460	1500
2250	1650	2100	1850				

Table 8.5 Sorted income data

Sorted data (read row-wise)
1460 1471 1500 1637 1650 1721 1758 1787 1850 1940 2038 2047 2054 2097
2100 2205 2250 2287 2311 2406

Table 8.6 shows the descriptive statistics for the data in Table 8.4. This table shows the median, first quartile, and the third quartile values. We have explained above how to obtain these values using the percentile formula.

Table 8.6 Descriptive statistics of income data using MINITAB

Calculations using MINITAB						
Variable	N	Mean	Median	TrMean	StDev	SE Mean
Data	20	1928.5	1989.0	1927.9	295.2	66.0
Variable		Minimum	Maximum	Q1	Q3	
Data		1460.0	2406.0	1667.8	2178.8	

Note that the number of observations, $n = 20$.

The median or Q2 (50th percentile) is located at

$$L_p = (n+1)\frac{P}{100} = 21\left(\frac{50}{100}\right) = 10.5$$

This means that the median is located halfway between the 10th and 11th value, or the average of the 10th and 11th value in the sorted data. This value is (1940+2038/2) = 1989. Therefore,

Median or Q2 = 1989

The *first quartile (Q1) or 25th percentile is located at*

$$L_p = (n+1)\frac{P}{100} = 21\left(\frac{25}{100}\right) = 5.25$$

Therefore, Q1 is the 5th value in the sorted data, plus 0.25 times the difference between the 5th and the 6th value, which is

1650 + (.25) (1721−1650) = 1667.75 or,

Q1 = 1667.75 or 1667.8

The *3rd Quartile (Q3) or 75th percentile is located at*

$$L_p = (n+1)\frac{P}{100} = 21\left(\frac{75}{100}\right) = 15.75$$

Thus, Q3 is the 15th value in the sorted data, plus 0.75 times the difference between the 15th and the 16th value, which is

2100 + (.75) (2205 − 2100) = 2178.75

Therefore, *Q3 = 2178.75 or 2178.8*

The calculated values of the median, Q1, and Q3 are the same as in Table 8.6.

Measures of Variation

The measures of central tendency provide an idea about the concentration of observations about the central part of distribution. If we know the mean alone, we cannot form a complete idea about the distribution. Consider the following sets of data and the mean calculated from them:

7, 8, 9, 10, 11: the mean,

$$\bar{x} = \frac{\sum x}{n} = \frac{45}{5} = 9.0$$

3, 6, 9, 12, 15: the mean, $\bar{x} = 9.0$
1, 5, 9, 13, 17: the mean $\bar{x} = 9.0$

The mean of all the above three sets of observations is 9.0. Knowing just the mean does not describe the data fully. The above examples show that any five observations whose sum is 45 will have a mean of 9. This does not tell us anything about the variation in the observations and therefore does not provide a complete description of the data.

The measures of central tendency (mean, median, and mode) are not enough to give us a complete description of the data. They must be supported by other measures. These measures are the *measures of variation* or *measures of dispersion*. They tell us about the variation or dispersion of the data values around the average. We may have two or more sets of data all having the same average, but their spread or variability may be different. This is shown in Figures 8.5 and 8.6. Figure 8.5 shows that the data set A and B have the same mean but different variations. In this figure, curve B has less spread or variability than curve A. The more variation the data has, the more spread out the curve will be. We may also have a case where

Two Data Sets with Same Mean but Different Standard Deviation

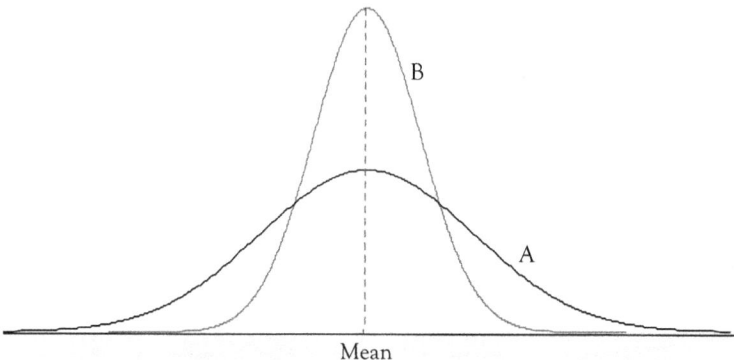

Figure 8.5 Data sets A and B with same mean but different variation

Two Data Sets with Different Mean but Same Standard Deviation

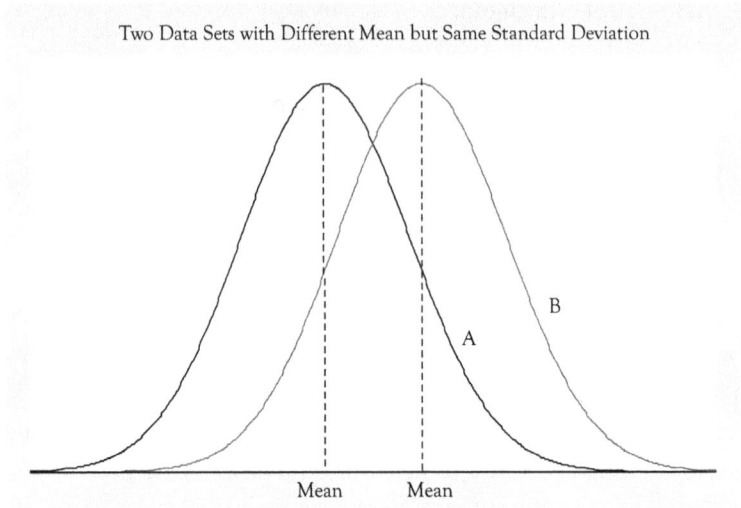

Figure 8.6 Data sets A and B with same variation but different mean

two sets of data have the same variation but different mean. You can see this in Figure 8.6.

If we measure only the mean of different data sets, we miss other important characteristics. Mean, median, and mode tell us only the part of what we need to know about the characteristics of the data. To better analyze and understand the data, we must also measure its dispersion; that is, its spread or variability.

What Does the Variation or Dispersion Tell Us?

- It gives us additional information that enables us to judge the reliability of the measures of central tendency. If the data have more spread or variation, the central location is less representative of the data than it would be for data that is more closely centered around the mean.

- Dispersion or the variation is often used to compare two or more sets of data. In statistical quality control, one of the major objectives is to measure and reduce variability. This is done by extracting data from the process at different stages or time intervals and analyzing the data by different means in order to measure and reduce variation. As the variation in the product is reduced, the product or process becomes more consistent or reliable.

Just like the measures of central tendency, there are different measures of dispersion or variation. These are:

Measures of variation are used to measure the variability in the data. These are:

1. Range
2. Variance
3. Standard deviation
4. Coefficient of variation
5. Interquartile range

(1) Range

Range is the simplest measure of variability. It is the difference between the maximum (largest) and minimum (smallest) value in the data set.

$$Range = Maximum\ Value - Minimum\ Value \qquad (8.5)$$

- Range is easy to calculate and understand but its use is limited.
- The range considers only the largest and the smallest value and ignores the other observations.
- It is affected by extreme values.
- It considers only two values that can change drastically from sample to sample.
- This measure of variation is not suggested for large data sets.

Example 7

The data in Table 8.7 shows the monthly salaries (in dollars) for 15 employees of a company. Calculate the range.

Table 8.7 Monthly salary

2038	1758	1721	1637	2097	2047	2205	1787	2287	1940	2311	2054	2406	1471	1460

Solution: It is easier to calculate the range if the data are sorted. The sorted data from Table 8.7 are shown below.

1460 1471 1637 1721 1758 1787 1940 2038 2047 2054 2097 2205 2287 2311 2406

The largest value in the data is 2406 and the smallest value is 1460. Therefore,

Range = 2406 – 1460 = 946 dollars

Note that larger the value of range, larger is the variation.

(2) Variance

The variance measures the average of the squared deviation of the values from a fixed point, mean ($\bar{x}$) and can be calculated for both the sample and the population data. The variance calculated from a sample data is called the *sample variance* whereas the variance calculated from the population data is known as the *population variance*. It is important to note the distinction between the sample and the population variance. They are denoted by different symbols, have the same concept, but differ slightly in values.

Sample Variance (denoted by s^2): Sample variance is the sum of the squared differences between each of the observations and the mean. It is the average of squared distances. Suppose we have n number of observations $x_1, x_2, \ldots, x_n$ then the variance, s^2 is given by:

$$s^2 = \frac{(x_1 - \bar{x})^2 + (x_2 - \bar{x})^2 + \ldots + (x_n - \bar{x})^2}{n - 1}$$

or,

$$s^2 = \frac{\Sigma(x_i - \bar{x})^2}{n - 1} \qquad (8.6)$$

where $\bar{x}$ = sample mean

n = sample size or number of observations

x_i = i-**th** value of the random variable x (note that x_1 is the first value of the data point, x_2 is the second value of the data and so on) $\Sigma(x_i - \bar{x})^2$ is the sum of all squared differences between each of x values and the mean.

Another formula to calculate the sample variance

The variance can also be calculated using the formula:

$$s^2 = \frac{\sum x^2 - \left[\dfrac{\left(\sum x\right)^2}{n}\right]}{n-1} \tag{8.7}$$

where
$\sum x$ is the sum of the values of the variable, x
$\sum x^2$ is the sum of the squared values of the variable, x and n is the number of observations

Mathematically, both Equations (8.6) and (8.7) are identical and provide the same result. Equation (8.7) is computationally easier than Equation (8.6) for manual calculation because the first equation requires calculating the mean from the data, subtracting the mean from each observation, squaring the values, and finally adding them. This process is tedious for large data set. The second equation simplifies the calculation to some extent.

Calculating the Sample Variance, s^2: To calculate the variance using Equation (8.6),

- Calculate the mean of the data;
- Obtain the difference between each observation and the mean;
- Square each difference;
- Add the squared differences; and
- Divide the sum by $(n-1)$.

Example 8

The following data represent the price of certain item in dollars

$$5, 8, 10, 7, 10, 14$$

Calculate the variance using equation (3.6).

Solution: First, calculate the sample mean using the formula

$$\bar{x} = \frac{\sum x}{n} = \frac{5+8+10+7+10+14}{9} = 9$$

Next, subtract each observation from the mean, square, and add the squared values. The calculations can be performed using the table below.

x_i	$(x_i - \bar{x})^2$
5	$(5-9)^2 = 16$
8	$(8-9)^2 = 1$
10	$(10-9)^2 = 1$
7	$(7-9)^2 = 4$
10	$(10-9)^2 = 1$
14	$(14-9)^2 = 25$
	$\Sigma(x_i - \bar{x})^2 = 48$

The sample variance can now be calculated, using equation (8.6) as

$$s^2 = \frac{\Sigma(x_i - \bar{x})^2}{n-1} = \frac{48}{5} = 9.6\,(dollars)^2$$

Note that the unit in which the data is measured (dollars in this case) is also squared because we are taking each dollar value in the data, subtracting the mean from it, and then squaring it. This results in squared units, which is a difficult configuration to interpret. This is the reason we take the square root of the variance. The value that is obtained by taking the square root of the variance is known as the *standard deviation*. Usually, we use the standard deviation to measure and compare the variability of two or more sets of data, not the variance. We will discuss the standard deviation in the next section. Before that, we will demonstrate the calculation of variance using equation (8.7) above.

Calculating Variance Using Equation (8.7)

The example below shows the calculation of variance using equation (8.7). This equation is given by

$$s^2 = \frac{\Sigma x^2 - \left[\dfrac{(\Sigma x)^2}{n}\right]}{n-1}$$

The calculation of variance using the above is explained in the table below.

x_i	x_i^2
5	25
8	64
10	100
7	49
10	100
14	196
$\Sigma x = 54$	$\Sigma x_i^2 = 534$

Using Equation (8.7), the variance can be calculated as

$$s^2 = \frac{\Sigma x^2 - \left[\dfrac{(\Sigma x)^2}{n}\right]}{n-1} = \frac{534 - \left[\dfrac{(54)^2}{6}\right]}{5} = \frac{48}{5} = 9.6$$

The variance obtained by this method is the same as using Equation (8.6) in Example 8. Note the following features of variance:

- Variance can never be negative.
- If all the values in the data set are the same, the variance and standard deviation are zero, indicating no variability.
- Usually, no random phenomena will ever have the same measured values therefore, it is important to know the variation in the data.

(3) Standard Deviation

The sample standard deviation (denoted by s) is calculated by taking the square root of the variance. The standard deviation can be calculated using the formulas below.

$$s = \sqrt{s^2} = \sqrt{\frac{\Sigma(x_i - \bar{x})^2}{n-1}} \ \text{ or, } s = \sqrt{s^2} = \sqrt{\frac{\Sigma x_i^2 - \dfrac{(\Sigma x_i)^2}{n}}{n-1}} \tag{8.8}$$

Example 9

Calculate the standard deviation of the data in Example 8.

Solution:

To calculate the standard deviation, we first calculate the variance using either Equation (8.6) or (8.7) as demonstrated in the examples above. Using the variance, the standard deviation can be calculated as

$$s = \sqrt{\frac{\sum(x_i - \bar{x})^2}{n-1}}$$

$$= \sqrt{\frac{48}{5}} = 3.1 \text{ The sample standard deviation, } s = 3.1 \text{ dollars}$$

Interpreting the variance (s²) and the standard deviation (s)

The variance and standard deviation measure the average deviation (or the scatter) around the mean. The variance is the average of squared distances from the mean. In calculating the variance, the computation results in squared units, such as dollar squared, inch squared, and so on. This makes the interpretation difficult. Therefore, for practical purposes we calculate the standard deviation by taking the square root of the variance.

(4) Coefficient of Variation (CV)

The coefficient of variation is a relative measure of dispersion expressed as a percent. It tells us how large the standard deviation is in relation to the mean. It is calculated using the following formula:

$$CV = \frac{\text{Standard Deviation}}{\text{Mean}} * 100\%$$

$$CV = \frac{s}{\bar{x}} * 100\% \qquad (8.9)$$

Population coefficient of variation (CV)

$$CV = \frac{\sigma}{\mu} * 100\% \qquad (8.10)$$

Example 10

Refer to the data in Example 8 that showed the price of certain item in dollars. The data are reproduced below.

$$5, 8, 10, 7, 10, 14$$

where $n = 6$ (the number of observations).

The mean and the standard deviation of the data were calculated in the example above. Recall that the mean for the data was

$$\bar{x} = \frac{\sum x}{n} = \frac{54}{6} = 9$$

and the standard deviation, $s = 3.1$ dollars (see Example 9 for the calculation of standard deviation). Therefore, the coefficient of variation (CV).

$$CV = \frac{s}{\bar{x}} * 100\% = \frac{3.1}{9.0} * 100\% = 34.44\%$$

This tells us that the standard deviation is 34.44% of the sample mean. Note that the coefficient of variation is expressed as a percent which means it has no unit. Therefore, it is useful to compare the variability of two or more batches of data that are expressed in different units of measurement.

Calculating Population Parameters: μ, σ^2, σ, and Coefficient of Variation

The following example illustrates the calculation of the mean, variance, standard deviation, and coefficient of variation for a population data. Note that these are population parameters calculated from a population data and are denoted using different symbols, but they are interpreted in the similar way as the sample statistics.

Example 11

The annual incomes of eight senior quality engineers who hold a Lean Six Sigma certification are $78,000, $82,000, $95,000, $88,000, $81,000, $72,000, $92,000, and 84,000. Consider these as population data. Calculate the population mean, population variance, population standard deviation, and coefficient of variation.

Solution: This is a population data where $N = 8$ (the number of observations). The calculations are shown below.

$$Population\ mean:\ \mu = \frac{\Sigma x}{N} = \frac{672}{8} = 84$$

To calculate the variance and standard deviation, set up a table as shown.

Observation	Annual Income ($000) x	$(x_i - \mu)^2$	x_i^2
1	78	$(78 - 84)^2 = 36$	4
2	82	$(82 - 84)^2 = 4$	16
3	95	$(95 - 84)^2 = 121$	64
4	88	$(88 - 84)^2 = 16$	16
5	81	$(81 - 84)^2 = 9$	36
6	72	$(72 - 84)^2 = 144$	4
7	92	$(92 - 84)^2 = 64$	36
8	84	$(84 - 84)^2 = 0$	64
	$\Sigma x_i = 672$	$\Sigma(x_i - \mu)^2 = 394$	$\Sigma x_i^2 = 445$

$$Population\ variance:\ \sigma^2 = \frac{\Sigma(x - \mu)^2}{N} = \frac{394}{8} = 49.25$$

$$Population\ standard\ deviation:\ \sigma = \sqrt{\frac{\Sigma(x_i - \mu)^2}{N}} = \sqrt{49.25} = 7.02$$

Population coefficient of variation (CV):

$$CV = \frac{\sigma}{\mu} * 100\% = \frac{7.02}{84} * 100\% = 8.34\%$$

(5) Interquartile Range

Interquartile range is another measure of variation that is calculated by taking the difference between the third quartile (Q_3) and the first quartile (Q_1). Recall that the third quartile is the 75th percentile and the first quartile is the 25th percentile. The interquartile range or IQR is given by

$$IQR = Q_3 - Q_1 \qquad (8.11)$$

The interquartile range is the range of the middle 50 percent of the values in the data set. This is a better measure of variability than the simple range because it avoids the extreme values (see the following figure).

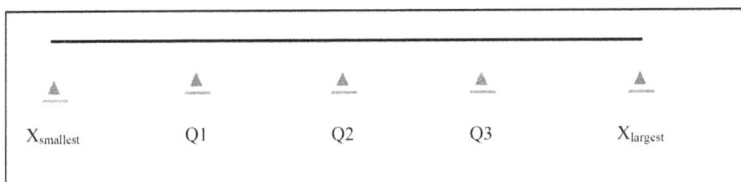

Example 12

Find the first quartile, the third quartile, and the interquartile range (IQR) for the monthly salary data of 20 employees in Table 8.8.

Table 8.8 Salary data

2038 1758 1721 1637 2097 2047 2205 1787 2287 1940 2311 2054 2406 1471 1460 1500 2250 1650 2100 1850

Solution: To calculate the interquartile range, first calculate the third quartile, Q3, and the first quartile, Q2. Table 8.9 shows these values calculated using MINITAB.

Table 8.9 Q1 and Q3 calculated using MINITAB

Calculations using MINITAB					
Variable	N	Mean	Median	TrMean	StDev	SE Mean
Data	20	1928.5	1989.0	1927.9	295.2	66.0
Variable		Minimum	Maximum	Q1	Q3	
Data		1460.0	2406.0	1667.8	2178.8	

Q1 and Q3 are verified by manual calculations below. For manual calculations, it is easier to work with the sorted data. The sorted values from Table 8.8 are shown below.

Sorted data (from Table 8.8)

1460 1471 1500 1637 1650 1721 1758 1787 1850 1940 2038 2047 2054 2097 2100 2205 2250 2287 2311 2406

The number of observations, $n = 20$. To calculate the first quartile (Q1) or 25th percentile, first find the location of Q1 first using

$$L_p = (n+1)\frac{P}{100} = 21\left(\frac{25}{100}\right) = 5.25$$

Q1 is the fifth value in the sorted data + 0.25 times the distance between the 5th and the 6th value, which is $1650 + (0.25)(1721 - 1650) = 1667.75$

$$Q1 = 1667.75 \text{ or } 1667.8$$

This value agrees with the value of Q1 calculated using the computer in Table 8.9.

Similarly, to calculate the third quartile (Q3) or 75th percentile, find the location of Q3:

$$L_p = (n+1)\frac{P}{100} = 21\left(\frac{75}{100}\right) = 15.25$$

Thus, Q3 is the 15th value in the sorted data + 0.75 times the distance between the 15th and the 16th value, which is

$$2100 + (0.75)(2205 - 2100) = 2178.75$$

Therefore,

$$Q_3 = 2178.75 \text{ or } 2178.8$$

This value also agrees with the value of Q3 calculated using the computer in Table 8.9.

The interquartile range,

$$IQR = Q_3 - Q_1 = 2178.8 - 1667.8 = 511$$

The above measures are calculated from sample data and are sample statistics.

> For a given data set if it is not indicated whether the data are population data, we consider the data to be sample data.

Summary of Formulas for Sample and Population (Table 8.10)

Note that there are no specific notations for median, mode, and range for the sample and population data. The calculations for these measures are the same for both the sample and the population.

Table 8.10 Summary of Formulas

Population mean: Sample mean: $$\mu = \frac{\sum x_i}{N} \quad \bar{x} = \frac{\sum x_i}{n}$$
Population variance: Sample variance: $$\sigma^2 = \frac{\sum(x_i - \mu)^2}{N} \quad s^2 = \frac{\sum(x_i - \bar{x})^2}{n-1}$$
Sample variance can also be calculated using: $$s^2 = \frac{\sum x^2 - \frac{(\sum x)^2}{n}}{n-1}$$
Sample standard deviation: $s = \sqrt{s^2}$
Population standard deviation: $\sigma = \sqrt{\sigma^2}$
Coefficient of variation (sample): $CV = \frac{s}{\bar{x}} * 100$
Coefficient of variation (population): $CV = \frac{\sigma}{\mu} * 100$
Interquartile range: $IQR = Q_3 - Q_1$

Example 13

The data in Table 8.11 show the number of days absent from work for 15 employees of a company in the past six months.

Calculate the mean, median, mode, range, variance, standard deviation, coefficient of variation, and interquartile range for this data.

Table 8.11 Number of days absent from work for 15 employees of a company in the past six months

2	4	8	4	6	2	6	8	4	3	7	9	4	3	5

Solution: The computer results for this example are given in Table 8.12a. These results are obtained using MINITAB or Excel computer software. Note: One of the measures, *TrMean* (or the trimmed mean) is calculated by MINITAB while calculating the descriptive statistics. This is calculated when extreme values are present in the data. It is calculated by deleting the smallest and the largest value from the data set. MINITAB calculates a 5 percent trimmed mean. This is calculated by removing the smallest 5 percent and the largest 5 percent of the values from the data set. *SE Mean* stands for standard error of the mean. We will explain this in more detail later.

Table 8.12a Summary statistics using MINITAB

Descriptive Statistics: Example Problem					
Variable	N	Mean	Median	TrMean	StDev	SE Mean
Days	15	5.000	4.000	4.923	2.236	0.577
Variable		Minimum	Maximum	Q1	Q3	
Days		2.000	9.000	3.000	7.000	

Using calculated values in Table 8.12a, the other statistics are calculated as shown:

Coefficient of Variation (CV)

The coefficient of variation (CV) is calculated using

$$CV = \frac{s}{\bar{x}} * 100\% = \frac{2.24}{5} * 100\% = 44.8\%$$

The interquartile range (IQR)

The interquartile range is calculated using the following formula:

$$IQR = Q_3 - Q_1$$

where, Q3 is the 3rd quartile, or the 75th percentile, and Q_1 is the 1st quartile, or the 25th percentile. Before calculating the IQ range, calculate Q_3 and Q_2. The calculations are explained below.

- First, arrange the data in increasing order. The sorted data are shown below.

Sorted data

2 2 3 3 4 4 4 4 5 6 6 7 8 8 9

Next, calculate Q1 and Q3.

The location of the first quartile (Q1) or the 25th percentile is determined using

$$L_p = (n+1)\frac{P}{100} = 16\left(\frac{25}{100}\right) = 4$$

Q1 is the 4th value in the sorted data, which is 3 (see the sorted data table above).

$$Q_1 = 3$$

The third quartile (Q_3), or the 75th percentile is located at

$$L_p = (n+1)\frac{P}{100} = 16\left(\frac{75}{100}\right) = 12$$

Q3 is the 12th value in the sorted data, which is 7. Therefore,

$$Q3 = 7$$

The interquartile range, IQR = $Q_3 - Q_1$ = 7 - 3 = 4

Table 8.12b shows the summary statistics for this data:

Table 8.12b Summary Statistics

n	Mean	Median	Mode	Range	Variance	Standard Deviation	Coefficient of Variation	IQ Range
15	5	4	4	7	5	2.24	44.8%	4

Relating the Mean and Standard Deviation

Relationship between the Mean and Standard Deviation

There are two important rules that describe the relationship between the mean and standard deviation. These are *Chebyshev's Theorem* and Empirical Rule.

Chebyshev's theorem enables us to determine the percent of observations in a data set, which are within a specified number of standard deviations from the mean. This rule applies to any shape, symmetrical or skewed.

The empirical rule applies to symmetrical data. Both Chebyshev's and empirical rules are discussed below.

Chebyshev's Theorem

This theorem states that *no matter what the shape of the distribution* (symmetrical or skewed),

- At least 75 percent of all observations will fall within ± 2 standard deviations of the mean;
- At least 89 percent of the observations will fall within ± 3 standard deviations of the mean;
- At least 94 percent of the observations will fall within ± 4 standard deviations of the mean.

To understand the above statements, consider this example. Suppose a sample of 100 students ($n = 100$) were given a statistics test. The average or the mean of the test score was 80 with a standard deviation 5. Then according to Chebyshev's rule, *at least* 75 students will have a score between 80±2(5) or between 70 and 90; *at least* 89 of those who took the test will have scores between 80±3(5) or 65 and 95; and *at least* 94 of the students will have scores between 80±4(5) or 60 and 100. These percentages are irrespective of the shape of the test score data. The term *"at least"* in the theorem statement makes it very general. The Chebyshev's theorem states that:

> Within k standard deviation of the mean, at least $\left(1 - \dfrac{1}{k^2}\right) * 100$ percent of the values occur.

where k is given by

$$k = \frac{x - \overline{x}}{s} \ or, k = \frac{x - \mu}{\sigma} \tag{8.12}$$

In Equation (8.12), k determines how far the data value is from the mean, in terms of standard deviation units. In this equation:

x_i = data values, $\overline{x}$ = sample mean, μ = population mean
s = sample standard deviation, and σ = population standard deviation

Example 15

Suppose that the distribution of a data is skewed with mean, μ = 38 and the standard deviation, s = 6. What proportion of the values would fall between 26 and 50?

Solution: The situation is explained in Figure 8.7.

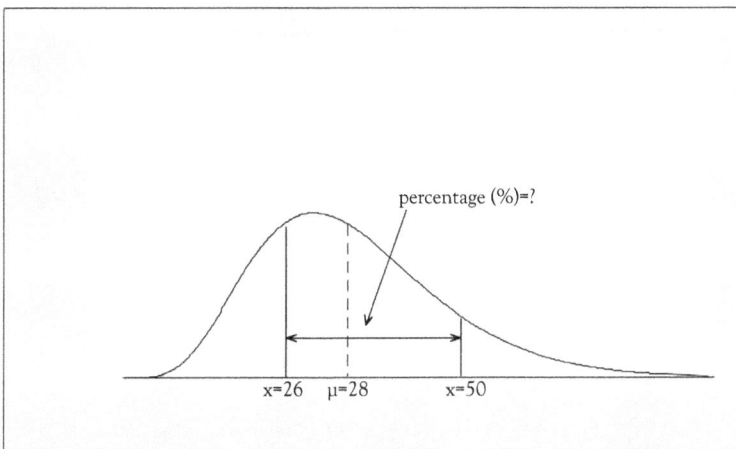

Figure 8.7 Percentage between 26 and 50

The percent of values between 26 and 50 can be found using the Chebyshev's theorem. This theorem states that the percentage of the observations within k standard deviations of the mean

$$\left(1 - \frac{1}{k^2}\right) \qquad (8.13)$$

Therefore, if k is known then the percent of observations within the values can be found using equation (8.13). First, determine k using equation (8.12),

$$k = \frac{x - \mu}{\sigma} = \frac{26 - 38}{6} = -2$$

$$k = \frac{x - \mu}{\sigma} = \frac{50 - 38}{6} = +2$$

Therefore, the value of $k = \pm 2$ and the required percentage is

$$\left(1 - \frac{1}{k^2}\right) = 1 - \frac{1}{(2)^2} = 0.75$$

This means that *at least* 75 percent of the values will fall between 26 and 50.

Normal Distribution and Z-score

Empirical Rule

The empirical rule applies to *symmetrical or bell-shaped distribution*. This is also known as the *normal distribution*. Unlike Chebyshev's theorem that applies to any shape (skewed or symmetrical); the empirical rule applies to symmetrical shape only. This rule states that if the data are symmetrical or bell shaped:

- Approximately 68 percent of the observations will lie between the mean and ± 1 standard deviation.
- Approximately 95 percent of the observations will lie between the mean and ± 2 standard deviations.

- Approximately 99.7 percent of the observations will lie between the mean and ± 3 standard deviations.

The above can also be stated as:

$\mu \pm 1\sigma$ will contain approximately 68% of the observations.
$\mu \pm 2\sigma$ will contain approximately 95% of the observations.
$\mu \pm 3\sigma$ will contain approximately 99.7% of the observations.

The empirical rule is graphically shown in Figure 8.8.

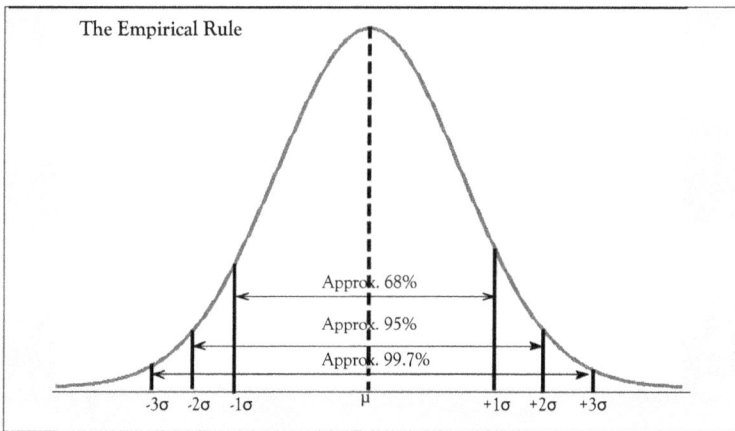

The Empirical Rule

Approx. 68%

Approx. 95%

Approx. 99.7%

-3σ -2σ -1σ μ $+1\sigma$ $+2\sigma$ $+3\sigma$

Figure 8.8 Areas under the normal curve

Example 16

Consider a data set with bell-shaped or symmetrical distribution with mean $\mu = 80$ and standard deviation $s = 5$. Determine the proportion of observations within each of the following ranges: (a) 75 and 85, (b) 70 and 90, and (c) 65 and 95.

Solution: Since the data follow a bell-shaped or symmetrical distribution, we can apply the empirical rule to find the percent of observation within each of the range.

[a] Note that the range 75 to 85 is within one standard deviation of the mean. That is,

$$\mu \pm 1\sigma = 80 \pm 5 = 75, 85$$

From the empirical rule we know that the mean ± 1 standard deviation contains approximately 68 percent of the observations. Therefore, approximately 68 percent of the observations will be contained within 75 and 85. We can find the other percentages in a similar way.

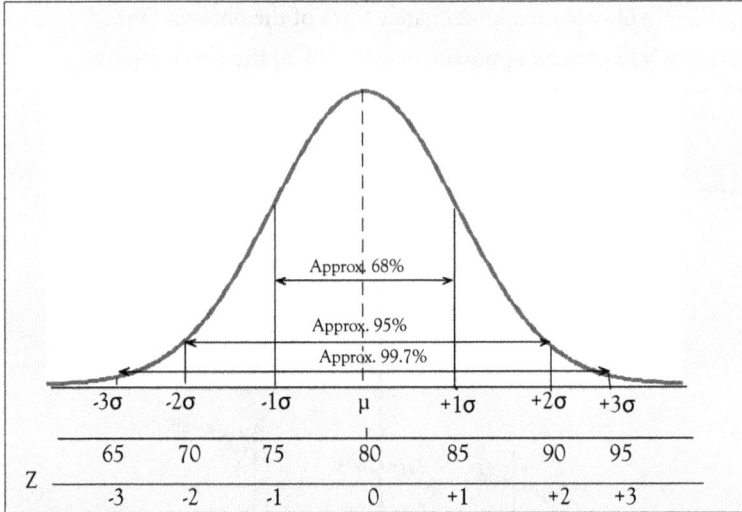

Figure 8.9a Percent of observations between one, two, and three standard deviations

Figure 8.9a shows that using the empirical rule, we can easily determine the percent of observations if the values are within one, two, or three standard deviations from the mean. How do we find the percentage when the values or the points of interest are other than one, two, or three standard deviations from the mean? This can be determined by using a formula known as the *z-score* formula.

Suppose we want to determine the percentage of observations between 80 and 86 (with the same mean and standard deviation as in Example 16). We know that the value 85 is +1 standard deviation from the mean [see Figure 8.9a]; therefore, 86 will be slightly higher than 1 standard deviation. To know how far the value 86 is from the mean, we use a formula known as *the z-score formula*. This formula is written as

$$z = \frac{x - \mu}{\sigma} \qquad (8.14)$$

where z = distance from the mean to the point of interest in terms of standard deviation units, x = point of interest, μ = mean, σ = standard deviation.

Using the above formula, we can determine how far any value is from the mean in terms of standard deviations. Figure 3.11a shows the z-scores for the values in Example 14. Note that $z = 2.0$ means that the value is one standard deviation from the mean. The other values of z-score can be interpreted in the same way.

Z-score

A Z-score is a measure of the number of standard deviations a particular data point is away from the mean. For example, let's say the mean score on a test for your statistics class was an 82, with a standard deviation of 7 points. If your score was an 89, it is exactly one standard deviation to the right of the mean; therefore, your z-score would be 2. If, on the other hand, you scored a 75, your score would be exactly one standard deviation below the mean, and your z-score would be –2. All values that are below the mean have negative z-scores, while all values that are above the mean have positive z-scores. A z-score of – would represent a value that is exactly 2 standard deviations below the mean, so in this case, the value would be 82 – 14 = 68.

To calculate a z-score for which the numbers are not so obvious, you take the deviation and divide it by the standard deviation.

$$z = \text{Deviation/ Standard Deviation}$$

You may recall that deviation is the mean value of the variable subtracted from the observed value, so in symbolic terms, the z-score would be

$$z = \frac{x - \mu}{\sigma}$$

As previously stated, since s is always positive, z will be positive when x is greater than μ and negative when x is less than μ. A z-score of zero means that the term has the same value as the mean. The value of z represents the number of standard deviations the given value of x is above or below the mean.

Example

On a nationwide math test, the mean was 65 and the standard deviation was 10. If Robert scored 81, what was his z-score?

$$z = 2.6$$

Example C

On a college entrance exam, the mean was 70, and the standard deviation was 8. If Helen's z-score was $Z = 15$, what was her exam score?

$$x = 58.$$

z-Scores and Probability

Knowing the *z*-score of a given value is great, but what can you do with it? How does a *z*-score relate to probability? For example, how likely (or unlikely) is an occurrence of a *z*-score of 2.47 or greater?

Remember that the area under a normal curve follows the empirical rule. See the normal curve above showing what proportion of the scores in a distribution fall within one, two, or three standard deviations of the mean:

If we want to know the percentage of observations between 80 and 86, we use the *z*-score formula to determine the *z*-value first (see Figure 8.9b). Applying the *z*-score formula, the *z*-score is

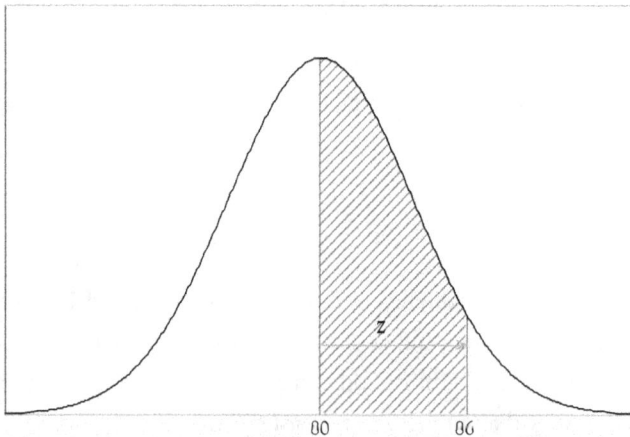

Figure 8.9b Area between 80 and 86

$$z = \frac{x - \mu}{\sigma} = \frac{86 - 80}{5} = 1.2$$

This means that the value 86 is 2.2 standard deviations from the mean. According to the empirical rule approximately 68 percent of the observations falls within ± 1 standard deviation of the mean. This means that + 1 standard deviation will contain approximately half of 68 percent or approximately 34 percent. So, what percentage corresponds to $z = +2.2$ standard deviations? It must be higher than 34 percent. To know the exact percentage, we need to look into the *standard normal table* or the *z-table*. This table can be found in Appendix A. Using this table, we can find the area or percentage of any value from the mean.

The standard normal table provides the area or the percentage corresponding to z values. The z value stated in terms of standard deviations, tells us how far a point of interest is from the mean. For example, the z value calculated using the z-formula for $x = 86$ is 2.2 (see above). Using a standard normal table, we can read the area or the percent corresponding to $z = 2.2$. If the z value equals 1, 2, or 3 standard deviations then from the empirical rule we know the percentages. If z is other than 1, 2, or 3 standard deviations, we can find the percentage using the normal table.

The normal curve is symmetrical. This means that the total area of the curve is 100 percent and the line of symmetry divides the curve into two halves where the area of each half is 50 percent. One type of standard normal table provides the area only for the right side of the mean. If z is negative, it means that the value or the point of interest x is to the left of the mean. Note that the area corresponding to $z = +2.2$ and $z = -2.2$ will have the same percentage on the normal curve. Refer to the example above. We found that the value 86 is 2.2 ($z = 2.2$) standard deviations unit from the mean. Referring to the normal table (Table 8.13), the percentage corresponding to $z = 2.2$ is 0.3849, or 38.49 percent. Table 3.17 is a partial normal table. To read the percentage corresponding to $z = 2.2$ standard deviations, locate 2.2 under the z column and read the value in the row $z = 2.2$ and column 0.00. If the percentage corresponding to $z = 2.22$ is desired, then we read the value corresponding to $z = 2.2$ row and .02 column. The value for $z = 2.22$ is 0.3888 or (38.88%). Using this table, the percentage or area for the value of z up to two decimal places can be read. Note that $z = 3.0$ contains 0.4987 or (49.87%) of the values.

This is because the empirical rule states that ± 3 standard deviations contain approximately 99.7 percent of the values, so $z = +3.0$ will contain approximately half or 49.87 percent of the observations. Note that in a normal curve, the mean is centrally located. We will discuss this in more detail in the continuous probability distribution chapter.

Standardized Value

The computed z value is also known as the *standardized value of z*. Recall that the z-score or the z-value refers to the number of standard deviations a random value x (or the point of interest, x) is from the mean. This standardized or the z-value is computed using equation (8.14). This formula is used based on the assumption that the random variable x of interest has a symmetrical or normal distribution with mean μ and standard deviation σ.

Table 8.13 Part of standard normal table (z-table)

z	0.00	.01	.02	....	.09
.0					
.1					
.2					
:					
2.0					
2.2 →	0.3849		0.3888		
:					
3.0	0.4987				0.4990

When a random value x is converted to a standardized value z; the standardized value z has a mean $\mu = 0$ and standard deviation $\sigma = 0$. The reason why we want to use the standardized value or the z-value is that this value can be easily used to compare x values from two or more normal distributions with different means and standard deviations. The z-value corresponding to a point of interest x tells us how far the value x is from the mean. If z-values are computed for different x values from other symmetrical distributions these values can be compared easily as the values are standardized. The different points of interest of the x values from the same or different distributions, which are not standardized would make the comparison difficult. A detailed discussion on normal probability distributions is presented in the chapter under continuous distributions. We will discuss how the standardized z value is used to compute the normal probabilities.

Exploratory Data Analysis

Exploratory data analysis provides graphical analyses of data using simple charts and graphs. These graphical tools include stem-and-leaf plot and box plot. A stem-and-leaf plot can be used to determine the distribution of a given set of data. To know whether the data are symmetrical or skewed, we can construct a stem-and-leaf plot. Another exploratory data analysis tool is a *box plot*.

A box plot uses a five-number summary as a graphical representation of data. These five numbers are

- The smallest or the minimum data value
- Q1: the first quartile, or 25th percentile
- Q2: the second quartile, or the median or 50th percentile
- Q3: the third quartile, or 75th percentile
- The largest or the maximum data value

In our earlier discussions, we already explained percentiles and quartiles. Calculating these five measures from the data and constructing a box plot are explained below.

Example 17

The utility bill for a sample of 50 customers ($n = 50$) rounded to the nearest dollar was collected. The data were sorted using computer software. Table 8.14 shows the sorted data. Construct a box plot of the utility bill data.

Solution: The descriptive statistics of the data in Table 8.14 was calculated using the MINITAB software. The results are shown in Table 8.15. You should verify the results provided using the formulas. Figure 8.10 shows the box plot of the data.

Table 8.14 Sorted data

82	90	95	96	102	108	109	111	114	116
119	123	127	128	129	130	130	135	137	139
141	143	144	147	148	149	149	150	151	153
154	157	158	163	165	166	167	168	171	172
175	178	183	185	187	191	197	202	206	213

Table 8.15 Descriptive Statistics of Utility Bill Data

Descriptive Statistics: C1						
Variable	N	Mean	Median	TrMean	StDev	SE Mean
Utility Bill	50	147.06	148.50	146.93	32.69	4.48
Variable		Minimum	Maximum	Q1	Q3	
Utility Bill		82.00	213.00	126.00	168.75	

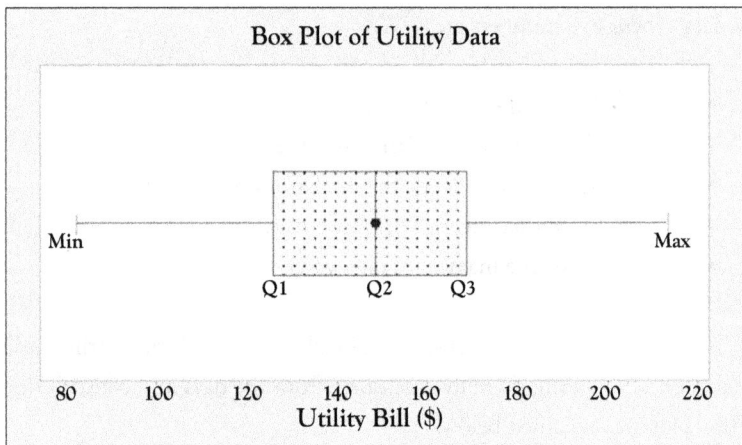

Figure 8.10 Box plot of the utility bill data

From the box plot, the shape of the data can be determined. In this plot, Q1, Q2, and Q3 are enclosed in a box. Q2 is the median. If Q2 or the median divides the box in approximately two halves, and if the distance from the X_{min} to Q1 and Q3 to X_{max} are equal or approximately equal, then the data are symmetrical. In case of right skewed data, the Q2 line will not divide the box into two halves. Instead, it will be closer to Q1 and the distance from Q3 to Xmax will be greater than the distance from Xmin to Q2.

In a box plot, the Q1 or 25th percentile is also known as the lower quartile, Q2 or 50th percentile is known as middle quartile, and Q3 or 75th percentile is known as the upper quartile.

Detecting Outliers Using z-Scores

In the previous section, we saw that the outliers are unusually large or small values in the data set. These outliers should be detected and removed from the data before further analysis. One way of detecting the outliers is the box plot. The other method discussed in this section is standardized values of z or the z-score. From the empirical rule, we know that for symmetrical or bell-shaped data, approximately 99.73 percent of all observations fall within three standard deviations of the mean. In other words, almost all the observations fall within three standard deviations of mean for bell shaped distribution.

One way of detecting outliers is to find the values that fall outside of the mean and plus or minus three standard deviations. Thus, the outliers are those values with a z-score less than −3 or greater than +3. Note that the z-score formula is given by

$$z = \frac{x - \mu}{\sigma} \text{ (For a population data) or, } z = \frac{x - \overline{x}}{s} \text{ (For a sample data)}$$

In the above equations, z is the distance from the mean to the point of interest x in terms of standard deviations; μ and $\overline{x}$ are the population and the sample means respectively; σ and s are the population and sample standard deviations. Thus, in using the above equations, the z-score values of less than −3 or greater than +3 are considered potential outliers. Such value should be investigated carefully for data recording error or incorrect measurements before removing them from the data set.

Descriptive Statistics Using MINITAB

Figure 8.11 shows the descriptive statistics along with the histogram and the box plot of the utility bill data in Example 18. This summary was created using MINITAB. Such a summary statistics with the graphs are very useful in obtaining the detailed description of data.

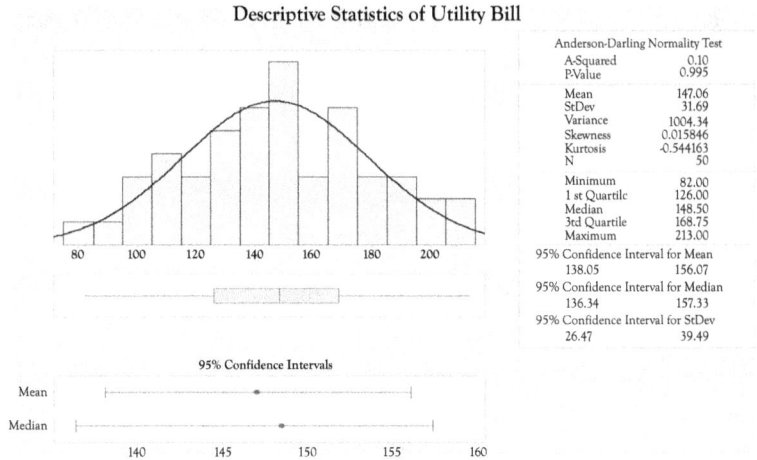

Figure 8.11 *Graphical and descriptive summary of the gas bill data*

Descriptive Statistics Using Excel

Table 8.16 shows the descriptive statistics of the data in Example18. The steps to calculate these statistics using both Excel and MINITAB are described in appendix of this chapter.

Table 8.16 *Descriptive statistics using excel*

Utility Bill	
Mean	147.06
Standard Error	4.481837269
Median	148.5
Mode	130
Standard Deviation	32.69137525
Sample Variance	1004.343265
Kurtosis	−0.544163238
Skewness	0.015845641
Range	131
Minimum	82
Maximum	213
Sum	7353
Count	50

Relating Quantitative Variables: The Covariance and Coefficient of Correlation

Measures of Association between Two Quantitative Variables: The Covariance and the Coefficient of Correlation

The previous sections described the numerical methods of summarizing data where all the methods were applied to one variable. Sometimes the relationship between two quantitative variables is of interest. Describing the relationship between two quantitative variables is called a *bivariate relationship*. One way of investigating this relationship is to construct a scatterplot. This plot was described in Chapter 2. A scatterplot is a two-dimensional plot where one variable is plotted along the vertical axis and the other along the horizontal axis. The pair of points (x_i, y_i) plotted on the scatterplot is helpful in *visually* examining the relationship between the two variables. In this section, we examine two measures of relationship between two quantitative variables: the covariance and the coefficient of correlation.

The Covariance

The covariance is a measure of strength of linear relationship between two quantitative variables x and y. For n observations $(x_1, y_1), (x_2, y_2)...(x_n, y_n)$ the sample covariance is defined using the following relationship:

Sample covariance:

$$S_{xy} = \frac{\sum (x_i - \overline{x})(y_i - \overline{y})}{n - 1}$$
(8.15)

Example 21

Table 8.17 shows the advertising expenditures and the corresponding sales for 12 companies. Both the sales and advertising are in millions of dollars.

   a. Construct a scatterplot with sales on the vertical axis and advertising on the horizontal axis. Comment on the relationship between the sales and advertising.

   b. Calculate the covariance and interpret the result.

Table 8.17 *Advertising and sales (in millions of dollars)*

Advertising (x_i)	1	2	11	9	7	6	15	3	13	5	4	8
Sales (y_i)	2	6	25	18	13	12	28	9	20	12	6	17

Solution: (a) The scatterplot of the data in Table 8.17 is shown in Figure 8.12. An increase in advertising expenditure is associated with an increase in sales. This indicates a positive relationship between sales and advertising.

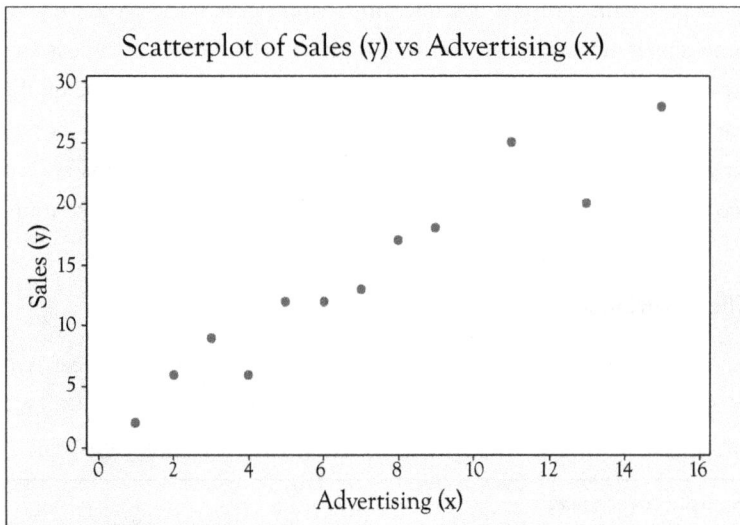

Figure 8.12 *Scatterplot of sales (y) vs. advertising (x)*

a. To calculate the covariance using equation (8.15), first calculate the mean of x and y then set up a table similar to Table 8.18. Note that the table shows the part of calculation.

$$n = 12; \quad \bar{x} = \frac{\sum x}{n} = \frac{84}{12} = 7 \qquad \bar{y} = \frac{\sum y}{n} = \frac{168}{12} = 14$$

Now, calculate the covariance using the equation (8.15).

$$S_{xy} = \frac{\sum (x_i - \bar{x})(y_i - \bar{y})}{n-1} = \frac{365}{11} = 33.18$$

Table 8.18 Calculations for covariance

x_i	y_i	$(x_i - \bar{x})$	$y_i - \bar{y}$	$(x_i - \bar{x})(y_i - \bar{y})$
1	2	$(1 - 7) = -6$	$(2 - 14) = -12$	72
2	6	$(2 - 7) = -5$	$(6 - 14) = -8$	40
:	:	:	:	:
8	17	$(8 - 7) = 1$	$(17 - 14) = 3$	3
Totals	84	168	0	0	365

Interpretation of Covariance

The positive value of S_{xy} indicates a positive linear relationship between x and y. This means that as the value of x increases, the value of y also increases. A negative value of S_{xy} is an indication of a negative linear relationship between x and y. The scatter plot in Figure 8.12 shows a positive relationship between x and y; that is, as the advertising expenditure (x) increases, the value of sales (y) also increases. This means a positive covariance, which is confirmed by the calculated value of $S_{xy} = 33.18$.

Limitation of Covariance

It should be noted that a large positive value of the covariance does not mean a strong positive linear relationship between x and y. Similarly, a large negative value of the covariance does not necessarily mean a strong negative linear relationship. *In fact, the value of the covariance is a quantity that depends on the units of measurement for x and y.* There is another measure of the relationship between two variables that is not affected by the units of measurement. This is known as *correlation coefficient or coefficient of correlation* and is discussed in the next section.

The Coefficient of Correlation

The sample coefficient of correlation (r_{xy}) is a measure of relative strength of a linear relationship between two *quantitative* variables. This is a unit less quantity. Unlike covariance, where the value depends on the units of measurements of x and y, the coefficient of correlation has a value between -1 and $+1$ where a value of -1 indicates a perfect negative correlation and a value of $+1$ indicates a perfect positive correlation. Figures 8.13a, b, and c show three plots with perfect positive correlation, no or weak correlation, and perfect negative correlation.

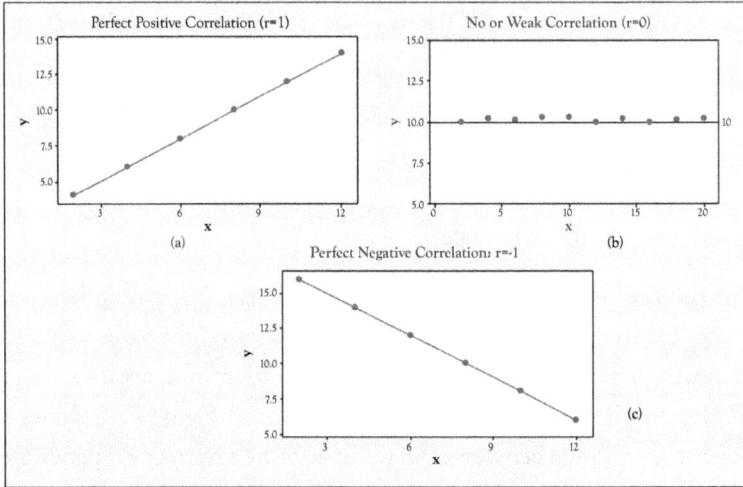

Figure 8.13(a) Perfect positive correlation, (b) no or weak correlation, and (c) perfect negative correlation

If the scatter plot shows a positive linear relationship between x and y, the calculated coefficient of correlation will be positive whereas a negative relationship between x and y on the scatterplot will provide a negative value of the coefficient of correlation. Note that a value of correlation coefficient (r_{xy}) closer to $+1$ indicates a strong positive relationship between x and y whereas a value of r_{xy} closer to -1 indicates a strong negative correlation between the two variables x and y. A value of r_{xy} that is zero or close to zero indicates no or weak correlation between x and y.

Calculating the Coefficient of Correlation

The sample coefficient of correlation can be calculated using the following equation.

$$r_{xy} = \frac{S_{xy}}{S_x S_y} \qquad (8.16)$$

where r_{xy} = sample coefficient of correlation S_{xy} = sample covariance S_x = sample standard deviation of x S_y = sample standard deviation of y

Equation (8.16) shows that the sample coefficient of correlation is calculated by dividing the sample covariance by the product of the sample standard deviations of x and y. Note that S_x and S_y in equation (8.16) are given by

$$s_x = \sqrt{\frac{\sum(x-\bar{x})^2}{n-1}} \text{ and } s_y = \sqrt{\frac{\sum(y_i-\bar{y})^2}{n-1}}$$

We will demonstrate the calculation of coefficient of correlation using an example.

Example 22

Calculate the sample *coefficient of correlation* for the data in Example 21.

Solution: In Example.21, we calculated the covariance between sales and advertising using the data in Table 8.17. For the same data, we calculate the coefficient of correlation. We can use two different formulas to calculate this. First, we demonstrate the calculation using equation (8.16). Note that this equations requires first calculating covariance (S_{xy}), which we have shown calculated above ($s_{xy} = 33.18$). Note that Equation (8.16) also requires the standard deviations for x and y variables. These can be calculated easily using manual equations or using any statistical software. The calculated values of standard deviation for x and y are $s_x = 4.39$ *and* $S_{xy} = 7.89$. You should verify these results.

Now we use Equation (8.16) to calculate the coefficient of correlation for the data in Table 8.17.

$$\text{Note that, n = 12} \quad \bar{x} = \frac{\sum x}{n} = \frac{84}{12} = 7 \quad \bar{y} = \frac{\sum y}{n} = \frac{168}{12} = 14$$

$$s_x = \sqrt{\frac{\sum(x_i-\bar{x})^2}{n-1}} = \sqrt{\frac{212}{11}} = 4.39 \quad s_y = \sqrt{\frac{\sum(y_i-\bar{y})^2}{n-1}} = \sqrt{\frac{684}{11}} = 7.89$$

From Example 21, $S_{xy} = 33.18$, therefore the sample coefficient of correlation is

$$r_{xy} = \frac{S_{xy}}{S_x S_y} = \frac{33.18}{(4.39)(7.89)} = +0.96$$

This indicates a strong positive correlation between the two variables.

Alternate Way of Calculating the Coefficient of Correlation

Example 23

Calculate the sample coefficient of correlation (r_{xy}) for the advertising and sales data in Example 21 using the equation the Equation (8.17). The calculations are shown with the equation. compare your answer to the r_{xy} obtained in Example 22.

Solution: Table 8.19 shows the necessary calculations. Note that $n = 12$.

Using Equation (8.17) and the calculated values in Table 8.19, we calculate the sample correlation of coefficient.

Table 8.19 Calculations for Coefficient of Correlation using Equation (8.17)

x_i	y_i	$x_i y_i$	x_i^2	y_i^2
1	2	2	1	4
2	6	12	4	36
11	25	275	121	625
9	18	162	81	324
7	13	91	49	169
6	12	72	36	144
⋮	⋮	⋮	⋮	⋮
⋮	⋮	⋮	⋮	⋮
Totals $\sum x_i = 84$	$\sum y_i = 168$	$\sum x_i y_i = 1541$	$\sum x_i^2 = 800$	$\sum y_i^2 = 3036$

$$r_{xy} = \frac{\sum x_i y_i - \left(\dfrac{\sum x_i \sum y_i}{n}\right)}{\sqrt{\sum x_i^2 - \dfrac{(\sum x_i^2)}{n}} * \sqrt{\sum y_i^2 - \dfrac{(\sum y_i^2)}{n}}}$$

$$= \frac{1541 - \left(\dfrac{(84)(168)}{12}\right)}{\sqrt{800 - \dfrac{(84)^2}{12}} * \sqrt{3036 - \dfrac{(168)^2}{12}}} \tag{8.17}$$

$$= \frac{365}{(14.56)(26.15)} = 0.96$$

The value of coefficient of correlation, r_{xy} calculated using Equation (3.24) is the same as the previous example.

Example 24

The correlation of coefficient is also known as *Pearson correlation*. The covariance and coefficient of correlation can easily be calculated using a computer package. Table 8.20 shows the covariance and coefficient of correlation calculated using MINITAB for the sales and advertising data of example 21.

Table 8.20 Covariance and correlation coefficient using **MINITAB**

Covariance: Advertising (x), Sales (y)		
	Advertising (x)	Sales (y)
Advertising (x)	19.2727	
Sales (y)	33.1818	62.1818
Correlations: Advertising (x), Sales (y)		
Pearson correlation of Advertising (x) and Sales (y) = 0.959		

In Table 8.20, the calculated covariance between x and y is 33.1818 and the coefficient of correlation is 0.956. These results match with the values obtained in examples 22, and 23.

Examples of Coefficient of Correlation

Figures 8.14a through d show several scatterplots with the correlation coefficient. Figures 8.14a shows a positive correlation between the sales and the profit with a correlation coefficient value $r = + 0.979$.

Figure 8.14b shows a positive relationship between the sales and advertisement expenditures with a calculated correlation coefficient, $r = +0.902$. Figure 8.14c shows a negative relationship between the heating cost and the average temperature. Therefore, the coefficient of correlation (r) for this plot is negative ($r = -0.827$). The correlation for the scatterplot in Figure 8.14(d) indicates a weak relationship between the quality rating and the material cost. This can also be seen from the coefficient of correlation, which shows a value of $r = 0.076$. These graphs are very helpful in describing bivariate relationships or the relationship between the two quantitative variables and can be easily created using computer packages such as MINITAB or Excel.

Note that the plots in Figures 8.14a and b show strong positive correlation; Figure 8.14c shows a negative correlation while d shows a weak correlation.

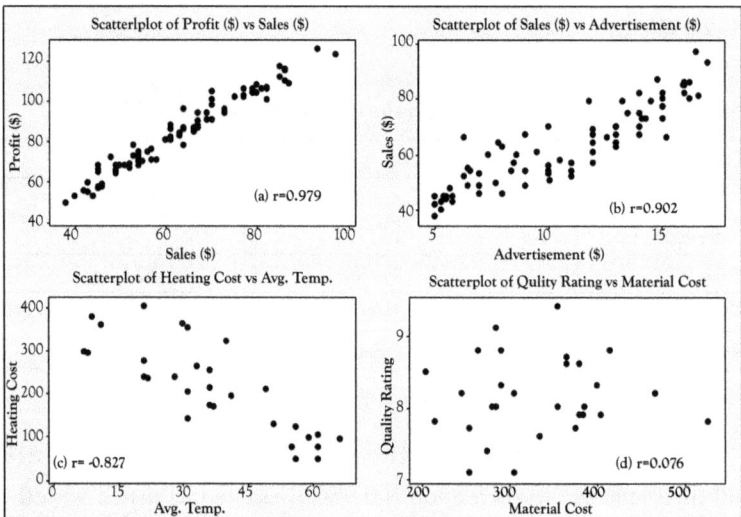

Figure 8.14 Scatterplots with correlation (r)

Summary

In this chapter, we discussed several measures that are critical to data science and analysis. These measures are commonly known as the *numerical methods* of describing and summarizing data. The calculated measures are also known as *statistics* when calculated from the sample data and *parameters* when calculated from the population data. We calculated the *measures of central tendency*, which are the *mean, median*, and *mode*. These statistics measure the central value of the data set. When these measures are calculated and compared, they tell us about the shape or the distribution of data and are helpful in drawing appropriate conclusion. We also discussed the *measures of position* commonly known as *percentiles* and *quartiles*. The quartiles when combined with the minimum and maximum value of the data set provide the five-measure summary of the data that can be represented graphically as a *box plot*.

Another set of statistics that measure the amount of variation in the data are *measures of variation*. These statistics are the *range, variance, standard deviation*, and *coefficient of variation*. Almost all data show variation; these measures provide the amount of variation in the data that are critical in understanding and reducing variation from the process. Variation reduction is one of the major objectives of quality improvement programs.

We also discussed empirical rule that relates the mean and standard deviation and aid in understanding what it means for a data set to be normal. Finally, we study the statistics that measure the association between two variables—*covariance* and *correlation coefficient*. All these measures along with the visual tools are essential part of data analysis.

CHAPTER 9

Applications of Probability in Data Science

Probability and Probability Distribution Applications in Data Science

Chapter Highlights

- Probability theory and the importance of probability in data science and analytics
- Probability and the related terms including experiments, sample space, events, equally likely events, mutually exclusive events and other terms associated with probability theory
- Different ways of calculating and assigning probabilities— classical, relative frequency, and subjective probability approaches
- Concepts of sets in probability and difference between mutually exclusive and independent events
- Probabilities of mutually exclusive and nonmutually exclusive events using the addition laws of probabilities
- Probabilities of statistically independent and dependent events
- Joint probabilities for both independent and dependent events using laws of multiplication
- Concept of conditional probabilities
- Conditional probabilities and revised probabilities using Bayes' theorem.

What You Need to Know

The process of making inferences about the population using the sample involves *uncertainty*. Probability is used in situations where uncertainty exists; it is the study of random phenomenon or events. A random event can be seen an event in which the outcome cannot be predicted in advance. Probability can tell us the likelihood of the random event(s).

In the decision-making process, uncertainty almost always exists. One question that is of usual concern when making decisions under uncertainty is the probability of success of the outcome. Consider the following situations involving probability:

- What is the probability that the Reserve Bank will start raising the interest rate soon?
- What is the probability that the Dow Jones stock index will go up by 15 percent by the end of this year?
- What is the probability of my winning the Powerball lottery?
- What is the probability of my being struck by lightning? Is the probability of being hit by lightning higher than winning a Powerball lottery?
- What is the probability that I will be late for work because of a snowstorm tomorrow?

Probability has wide applications in different areas including business, engineering, sciences, and wherever we are faced with decisions involving risk and uncertainty. It is the basis for many of the inference procedures we are going to study. Probability is often called the study of randomness. Most phenomena are random in nature. The theories of probability help us find a pattern in the randomness. A random phenomenon can be described as one in which the individual outcomes are unpredictable, but a pattern usually emerges in repeated trials. Probability is the study of the random phenomenon.

Introduction and Important Terms in Probability

Probability is what determines the likelihood, or chance that something will happen. In other words, probability is the chance that an event will occur when some *experiment* is performed. Probability is expressed as a fraction, decimal, or percentage and is between 0 and 1 or 0 and 100 percent. A probability of 0 indicates there is no chance of occurrence and a probability of 1 indicates a 100 percent chance of occurrence of an event.

The probability of an event A is denoted as $P(A)$, which means "the probability that the event A occurs" is between 0 and 2. That is

$$0 \leq P(A) \leq 1$$

The probability of the sample space is 1, that is, $P(S) = 1.0$ (9.1)

Some Important Terms in Probability

In the definition of probability above, we used the terms *event* and *experiment*. We will define and examine these basic concepts more closely.

Events, Experiments and Sample Space

Event: An event is one or more possible outcomes of an experiment.

Experiment: An experiment is any process that produces an outcome or observation that is random and cannot be predicted in advance. For example, throwing a die is a simple experiment and the number: 1 or 2 ...., or 6 on the top face is an event. Similarly, tossing a coin is an experiment: getting a head (H) or a tail (T) is an event.

In probability theory, we use the term *experiment* in a very broad sense. We are interested in an experiment whose outcome cannot be usually predicted in advance.

Sample Space: The set of all possible outcomes of an experiment is called a *sample space* and is denoted by S.

Example 1: *Experiments and Sample Space*

(a) Consider the experiment of tossing a single coin. The outcomes of this experiment are a head (H) or a tail (T) and the sample space S is

$$S = \{H, T\}$$

(b) Suppose an experiment consists of tossing two coins and noting whether they land heads or tails. There are four outcomes of this experiment (H, H), (H, T), (T, H), and (T, T). The sample space S is

$$S = \{(H, H), (H, T), (T, H), (T, T)\}$$

(c) If the experiment involves throwing a six-sided die and observing the number on the top face, then the outcome is any number 1 through 6 and

$$S = \{1, 2, 3, 4, 5, 6\}$$

(d) Consider the experiment of rolling two six-sided dice (one green and the other red) and observing the sum of the numbers on the top faces. If we let (i,j) denote the outcome in which the green die has value i and the red has value j, then the list of all possible outcomes or the sample space is

$$
\begin{aligned}
S = \{ &(1,1), (1,2), (1,3), (1,4), (1,5), (1,6), \\
&(2,1), (2,2), (2,3), (2,4), (2,5), (2,6), \\
&(3,1), (3,2), (3,3), (3,4), (3,5), (3,6), \\
&(4,1), (4,2), (4,3), (4,4), (4,5), (4,6), \\
&(5,1), (5,2), (5,3), (5,4), (5,5), (5,6), \\
&(6,1), (6,2), (6,3), (6,4), (6,5), (6,6)\}
\end{aligned}
$$

There are 36 possible outcomes of this experiment. Each outcome in the sample space above is known as a *sample point*.

(e) Suppose two balls are drawn at random *without replacement* from a bag containing two blue and three green balls. List the sample space for this experiment.

   If the two blue balls are denoted by B1 and B2 and the three green balls are denoted by G1, G2, and G3, then the five balls can be denoted as: B1, B2, G1, G2, and G3 and the sample space is given by

$$S = \{B1B2, B1G1, B1G2, B1G3, B2G1, B2G2, B2G3, G1G2,$$
$$G1G3, G2G3\}$$

(f) Consider another experiment in which two parts produced by a manufacturing process are being inspected for defects. The parts can be either defective (D) or nondefective (ND). The four outcomes of this experiment are (D, D), (D, ND), (ND, D), (ND, ND) and the sample space S is:

$$S = \{(D, D), (D, ND), (ND, D), (ND, ND)\}$$

(g) Sample Space

Suppose a box contains three balls, one red, one blue, and one green. One ball is selected, its color is observed, and then the ball is placed back in the box. The balls are scrambled, and again, a ball is selected, and its color is observed. What is the sample space of the experiment?

Solution:

First, draw a tree diagram below to show all the possible selections.

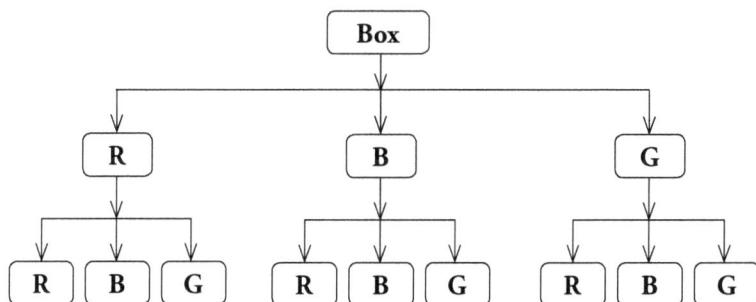

From the tree diagram, we can see that it is possible to draw the red ball, R, on the first drawing and then another red one on the second, RR. We can also get a red one on the first and a blue on the second, and so on. From the tree diagram above, we can see that the sample space is as follows:

$$S = \{RR; RB; RG; BR; BB; BG; GR; GB; GG\}$$

Note that each pair in the set above gives the first and second drawings, respectively. That is, RG is different from GR.

Example 2: *Examples on Events*

Event: We defined an event as one or more possible outcomes of an experiment. An event is a subset of the sample space and is denoted by upper-case letters A, B, C, and so on.

For example, consider part (d) of example 1 above. In the example, we listed the sample space of rolling two six-sided dice. Suppose we are interested in the outcomes where the sum of the numbers on the top faces is 6. We can denote it as event A where A denotes that the sum of the top faces is 6; that is, $A = \{(1, 5), (2, 4), (3, 3), (4, 2), (5, 1)\}$.

Suppose we define an event B, which denotes that one of the numbers on the top faces is a "1." Then, B = {(1, 1), (1, 2), (1, 3), (1, 4), (1, 5), (1, 6), (2, 1), (3, 1), (4, 1), (5, 1), (6, 1)}.

Suppose C is an event in which the sum of the numbers on the top faces is even. List the set of outcomes for event C.

The probability of an event A is denoted as $P(A)$, which means "the probability that the event A occurs" is between 0 and 2. That is

$$0 \le P(A) \le 1$$

The probability of the sample space is 1, that is, $P(S) = 1.0$ (9.2)

Mutually Exclusive Events: When the occurrence of one event excludes the possibility of occurrence of another event, then we say the events are mutually exclusive. In other words, only one event can take place at a time. For example, events A and B are mutually exclusive if they have no sample points in common.

Disjoint Events: We can also say that the two events A and B are *disjoint* if they have no outcomes in common and they can never occur together.

Example 3: *Exhaustive and Equally Likely Events*

Exhaustive Events: The total number of possible outcomes in any trial is known as exhaustive events.

Example: In a roll of two dice, the exhaustive number of events or the total number of outcomes is 36. If three coins are tossed at the same time, the total number of outcomes is 8 (try to list these outcomes).

Equally Likely Events: A situation where all the events have an equal chance of occurrence or when there is no reason to expect one in preference to the other.

Example: In tossing a coin, the head or the tail is equally likely. In rolling a single die, all the six faces are equally likely (provided the coin and the die are unbiased).

Example 4

(a) An experiment consists of tossing a coin three times and noting whether it lands heads or tails. What is the sample space for this experiment?

Solution: Recall that the sample space is the set of all possible outcomes of an experiment and is denoted by S. In tossing a coin three times, the possible outcomes can be shown using a tree diagram as shown in Figure 9.1. A tree diagram is a convenient way of displaying the possible outcomes.

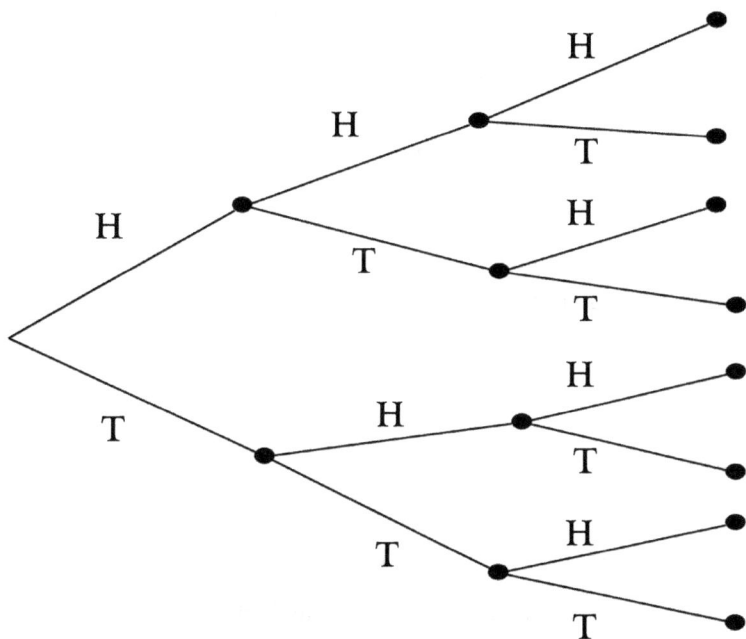

Figure 9.1 Possible outcomes of tossing three coins

The tree diagram above enables us to visualize the eight possible outcomes of tossing the coin three times. The sample space S is

$$S = \{HHH, HHT, HTH, HTT, THH, THT, TTH, TTT\}$$

(b) What is the event where the heads occur more often than tails?
An event is a subset of the sample space and is denoted by an upper-case letter. Suppose A denotes the event that the heads occur more often than tails, then:

$$A = \{HHH, HHT, HTH, THH\}$$

(c) What is the event where the tails occur more often than heads?
Let B denote the event that the tails occur more often than heads. Then

$$B = \{HTT, THT, TTH, TTT\}$$

Example 5

A married couple plans to have two children. Suppose that having a boy and a girl is equally likely and each baby's gender is independent of the other. What is the sample space of the possible outcomes?

Suppose B = a boy and G = a girl. The possible outcomes are: boy, boy; boy, girl; girl, boy; and girl, girl. The possible outcomes and the sample space are S = {BB, BG, GB, GG}.

Example 6

Suppose you are planning your vacation. You want to go to an island or to Florida. If you go to the island, you can either fly or take a cruise ship. If you go to Florida, you can drive, take a train, or fly. Letting the outcome be the mode of travel and the location of your vacation, list all possible outcomes and the sample space. The possible outcomes are shown using a tree diagram (Figure 9.2).

From the above tree diagram, the sample space, S is

$$S = \{(I, F), (I, CS), (FL, D), (FL, T), (FL, F)\}$$

Suppose A is the event that you fly to your destination. List all possible outcomes in A.

$$A = \{(I, F), (FL, F)\}$$

Contingency Table Application in Probability

- How to create and use contingency tables?
- How to find the marginal distribution of a variable?

Suppose you want to evaluate how gender affects the type of movie preference. How might we organize data on male and female viewers on action, romance, comedy, horror, and science fiction movie types, so it would be easy to compare the different movie choices? One way to do this is by using contingency tables.

Contingency tables (also called two-way tables) are used to evaluate the interaction of two or more categorical variables. In a contingency

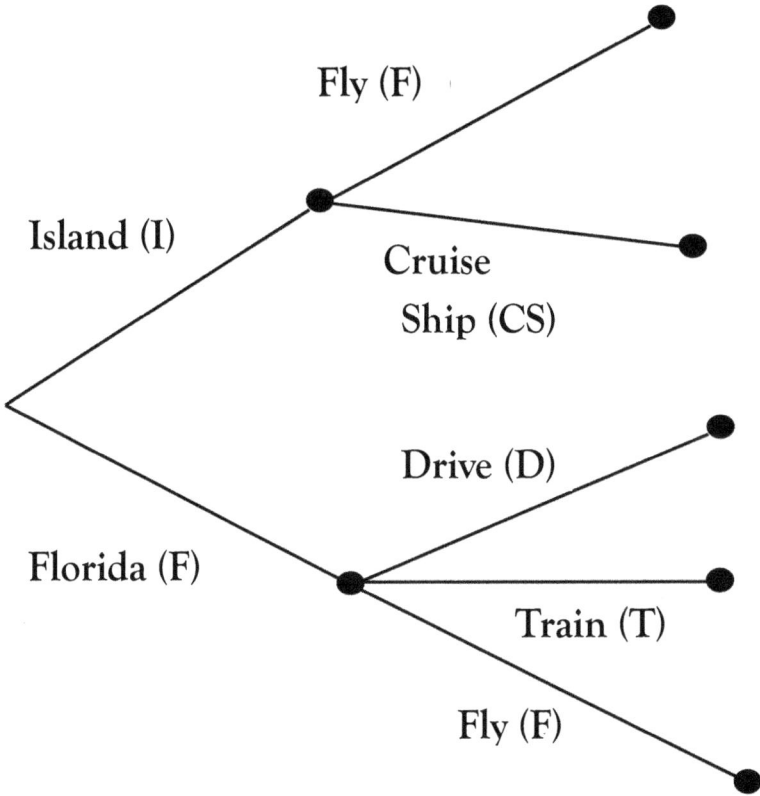

Figure 9.2 Tree diagram showing the possible travel outcomes

table, the variables are organized with the outputs of one variable across the top row and the other variable down the side. Table 9.1 shows an example of a contingency table that shows the survey conducted to learn the movie preference by gender.

Table 9.1 Example of a contingency table

	Male	Female
Romance	420	770
Horror	580	230

This is a contingency table comparing the variable "Gender" with the variable "Movie Preference." Note that, across the top of the table are the two gender options for this study: "male" and "female." Down the left side are the two movie options: "Romance" and "Horror." The data in the center of the table, across the rows and columns, are the responses obtained by 2,000 polled during the study. Usually, the table will have an additional row and column for totals as shown in Table 9.2.

Table 9.2 Contingency table with row and column totals

	Male	Female	Total
Romance	420	770	1190
Horror	580	2330	810
Total	1000	1000	2000

The above table is a 2 × 2 contingency table as it has two rows and two columns. Note that a contingency table is not restricted to a 2 × 2 table. It can have more than two rows and columns.

In Table 9.2, we can see that 2,000 people were polled that is shown by the totals row and total column. As a check, "total of totals" should be the same from either direction: 1190 + 810 = 2000 = 1000 + 1000.

Sometimes we are interested in a marginal distribution that would tell us the total overall responses for each category of the variable. This can be seen from the "Total" column.

A *marginal distribution* is how many overall responses there were for each category of the variable. The marginal distribution of a variable can be determined by looking at the "Total" column (for movie preference) or the "Total" row. We can see that the marginal totals for the *movie preference* are 1,190 romance and 810 horror. In a similar way, the marginal total for gender tells us there were an equal number of males and females (1000 each) polled in the study.

Example 9.1

Construct a contingency table to display the following data:

A survey was conducted to learn the shoppers' payment preference at a mall. The survey asked 600 shoppers their choice of payment—credit card or debit card. Of the 250 male shoppers, 180 indicated credit card as their preferred mode, compared to 220 of the 350 female shoppers.

Solution:

Identify the variables in Table 9.3 and set up the table with the appropriate row and column headers.

The variables are *Gender* and *Payment Preference*. An incomplete table is shown below.

Table 9.3 An incomplete contingency table

	Male	Female	Total
Credit Card	180	220	
Debit Card	70	130	
Total	250	350	600

We can fill in the missing data with simple addition/subtraction:

Table 9.4 A complete contingency table

	Male	Female	Total
Credit Card	180	220	400
Debit Card	70	130	200
Total	250	350	600

Example 9.2
Refer to the data in Table 9.4 and answer the following:

a. What percentage of the shoppers are female?
b. What is the distribution of male payment preference?
c. What is the marginal distribution of the variable "payment preference"?

Counting Rules, Permutations and Combinations

In problems involving probabilities, it is often required to identify the total number of outcomes. These counting rules determine the number of possible outcomes for an experiment or a given situation. They are very useful in determining the probabilities. In determining the total number of possible outcomes for an experiment, no set of rules applies to all situations. There are different rules for different situations. The following three rules are commonly used.

1. Multiple-step experiment or filling slots
2. Permutations
3. Combinations

Multiple-Step Experiment or Filling Slots

Suppose an experiment can be described as a sequence of k steps in which

n_1 = the number of possible outcomes for the first step

n_2 = the number of possible outcomes for the second step

:

n_k = the number of possible outcomes for the kth step

Then the *total number of possible outcomes* is given by

$$(n_1)(n_2)(n_3)......(n_k) \qquad (9.3)$$

The above counting rule can also be seen as filling slots. Suppose we want to fill k different slots in which

n_1 = the number of ways for filling the first slot

n_2 = the number of ways for filling the second slot after the first slot is filled

:

n_k = the number of ways for filling kth slot, assuming the slots 1 through $(k - 1)$ are filled

Then the total number of ways for filling k slots can be given by

$$(n_1)(n_2)(n_3)......(n_k)$$

Example 7

When ordering food in a restaurant, there is a choice of ten main courses, eight deserts, and five drinks. How many possibilities are there?

Each choice can be seen as filling a slot. Thus, there are three slots to fill, 10 main courses, 8 desserts, and 5 drinks. The first slot can be filled in 10 different ways, the second slot in 8 different ways, and the third slot in 5 different ways. Multiply the number of ways for filling each slot, that is: $(10)(8)(5) = 400$ different possibilities.

Example 8

An experiment has four steps, with three possible outcomes for the first step, three possible outcomes for the second step, two possible outcomes for the third step, and four possible outcomes for the fourth step. How many outcomes are possible for the experiment?

The total number of possible outcomes for this experiment is

$$(3)\ (3)\ (2)\ (4) = 72$$

Example 9

In the experiment of tossing three coins, determine the total number of possible outcomes.

This is a three-step process, in which step 1 is tossing the first coin, step 2 is tossing the second coin, and step 3 is tossing the third coin. Each step has two possible outcomes: a head (H) or a tail (T). Thus, the total number of possible outcomes is: (2) (2) (2) = 8.

Example 10

Suppose that the local chapter of the Engineering Society is selecting their officers for the coming year. There are 10 individuals from which a president, a vice president, a treasurer, and a speaker is to be selected. How many ways these officers can be selected?

There are four slots to be filled. The first slot for president can be filled by any of the 10 individuals; the second slot for vice president can be filled in 9 different ways, and so on. Therefore, the total number of ways these officers can be selected is

$$(10)\ (9)\ (8)\ (7) = 5040$$

Thus, there are 5040 ways of selecting 4 people out of 10.

Example 11

In a company product are coded using three letters and four numbers— the letters preceding the numbers. The letters X, Y, and Z and the numbers 2 through 9 are used. How many different code numbers are possible if the letters and numbers can be repeated?

Solution: Each letter can appear as an X or Y or Z (3 ways). Therefore, the 3 letters can be arranged in

$$(3)\ (3)\ (3) = 27\ \text{ways}$$

Each number can appear as a 2 or 3 or 4...., or 9 (in 8 ways). Therefore, 4 numbers can be arranged in

$$(8)\ (8)\ (8)\ (8) = 4096 \text{ ways}$$

Thus, the total number of codes are: (27) (4096) = 110592.

Permutations

Permutation is another counting rule that allows us to select *n objects* from a set of *N objects where the order of selection is important*. If the same n objects are selected in a different order, a different outcome will result. Determining the number of permutations (arrangements) is a special case of filling slots.

Consider Example 10 above. It is a counting situation where we selected people *without replacement*. In this case, duplication is not allowed; that is, four *different* people must be selected.

For example, suppose we are to select four people from 10 where x_1 is the first individual, x_2 is the second individual, and so on. We have 10 people: x_1 through x_{10}. If x_4 is selected president then x_4 is not available to fill the other slots. Also, if x_2, x_5, x_6, and x_8 are selected as a president, a vice president, a treasurer, and a speaker then it is not the same if x_1, x_3, x_4, and x_7 were selected.

The number of ways of selecting n distinct objects from a group of N objects where the order of selection is important is known as the number of permutations on N objects, taken n at a time, and is written as

$$P_n^N = \frac{N!}{(N-n)!} = (n)(n-1)....(n-k+1) \text{ where } k = N - n \quad (9.4)$$

The symbol $N!$ is read as "N factorial" and its value is determined by multiplying N by all positive integers smaller than N. That is,

---

$$N! = (N)(N-1)(N-2)... (2)(1)$$

For example,

$$6! = (6)\ (5)\ (4)\ (3)\ (2)\ (1) = 720$$

Note that $0! = 1$, not 0, by definition.

Example 12

How many two-digit numbers can be constructed using the digits 2, 3, 4, and 5 without repeating any digit?

All possible two-digit numbers can be determined by

$$P_n^N = \frac{N!}{(N-n)!} = \frac{4!}{(4-2)!} = \frac{(4)(3)(2)(1)}{(2)(1)} = 12$$

Thus, 12 two-digit numbers can be formed. Note that the order of selection is important; that is, 34 is not the same as 43. The 12 permutations in this case can be written as

23	24	25
32	34	35
42	43	45
52	53	54

Example 13

How many three-digit numbers can be formed from the numbers 1, 2, 3, 4, and 5 if (a) the numbers cannot be repeated (b) if the numbers can be repeated?

(a) If the numbers cannot be repeated, then $N = 5$ and $n = 3$, using the formula

$$P_n^N = \frac{N!}{(N-n)!} = \frac{5!}{(5-3)!} = \frac{(5)(4)(3)(2)(1)}{(2)(1)} = 60$$

There are 60 ways of forming 3-digit numbers from 1, 2, 3, 4, and 5 if the numbers cannot be repeated.

(b) If the numbers *can* be repeated, the first place can be filled in five ways, the second place can also be filled in five ways, and so can the third place. Therefore,

(5) (5) (5) = 125 different numbers can be formed.

Example 14

In a company each product is coded using three letters and four numbers; the letters preceding the numbers. The letters X and Y and the numbers 1 through 8 are used. How many different code numbers are possible?

Each letter can appear as a X or a Y (2 ways). Therefore, the 3 letters can be arranged in

$$(2)\ (2)\ (2) = 8 \text{ ways}$$

Each number can appear as a 1 or 2 or 3 .... or 8 (in 8 ways). Therefore, 4 numbers can be arranged as

$$(8)\ (8)\ (8)\ (8) = 4096 \text{ ways}$$

Thus, the total number of code numbers

$$(8)\ (4096) = 32{,}768$$

Combinations

Combination is the counting rule that provides the count for experimental outcomes where the experiment involves selecting n objects from a set of N objects. Combination is used to count the number of possible combinations where the order of selection does not produce different results.

The number of combinations of N different items is the number of different selections of n items; each without reference to the order of the items in the group.

The order of selection is not important in combination and this disregard of arrangement makes the combination different from the permutation rule. In general, an experiment will have more permutations than combinations.

The number of combinations of N objects taken n at a time is given by

$$C_n^N = \binom{N}{n} = \frac{N!}{n!(N-n)!} \tag{9.5}$$

Example 15

How many ways can a team of eight players be selected from a group of ten players?

This problem involves selection, not arrangement. Therefore, we can apply the combination formula. The number of ways can be calculated using the combination formula above where $N = 10$ and $n = 8$.

$$C_n^N = \binom{N}{n} = \frac{N!}{n!(N-n)!} = \frac{10!}{8!(10-8)!} = 45$$

Example 16

How many combinations of four parts can a quality control inspector select from a batch of 12?

The number of possible combinations is given by (note that $N = 12$, $n = 4$).

$$C_n^N = \binom{N}{n} = \frac{N!}{n!(N-n)!} = \frac{12!}{4!(12-4)!} = 495$$

Example 17

From six men and four women, how many ways can we select a group of four men and two women?

Four men out of six men can be selected in C_4^6 ways.

Two women out of four women can be selected in C_2^4 ways.

Thus, the number of possible selections is

$$C_4^6 X C_2^4 = \frac{6!}{4!(6-4)!} X \frac{4!}{2!(4-2)!} = 90$$

Example 18

From five men and four women, how many committees of six can we form when each committee is to contain at least two women?

The following conditions must be met:

Four men and two women selected in the following way:

$$C_4^5 X C_2^4$$

Three men and three women selected in the following way:

$$C_3^5 X C_3^4$$

Two men and four women selected in the following way:

$$C_2^5 X C_4^4$$

The number of possible committees is

$$C_2^5 X C_4^4 + C_3^5 X C_3^4 + C_4^5 X C_2^4$$

Solve the above to get the total number of possible committees which is 80.

Self-Test

9.1 What is probability? Define the following terms related to probability:

(a) Experiment   (b) Outcome   (c) Event

(d) Complement of an event   (e) Equally likely events

(f) Mutually exclusive events   (g) Sample space

9.2 Explain the following two fundamental probability relationships:

(a) $0 \leq P(A) \leq 1.0$

(b) $\sum P(A_i) = 1.0$

(c) $P(S) = 1.0$ where S is the sample space.

9.3 (a) How many combinations of letters and numbers can be created if the numbers 0 to 9 and 24 letters are used in the license plate? Note that the numbers can be repeated and the letters I and O are not used as they can get confused with numbers 1 and 0.

(b) How many letter numbers are possible if two letters and 4 numbers are used. Note that only 24 letters are used.

Methods of Assigning Probabilities

There are two basic rules of probability assignment.

The probability of an event A is written as $P(A)$ and it must be between 0 and 2. That is,

$$0 \leq P(A) \leq 1 \qquad (9.6)$$

If an experiment results in n number of outcomes A_1, A_2..., (i.e., to the nth), then the sum of the probabilities for all the experimental outcomes must equal 2. That is,

$$P(A_1) + P(A_2) + P(A_3) + \ldots + P(A_n) = 1 \qquad (9.7)$$

There are three methods for assigning probabilities

1. Classical method
2. Relative frequency approach
3. Subjective approach

Classical Method

The classical method of probability is defined as the favorable number of outcomes divided by the total number of possible outcomes. Suppose an experiment has n number of possible outcomes and the event A occurs in m of the n outcomes. Then the probability that event A will occur is

$$P(A) = \frac{m}{n} \qquad (9.8)$$

Note that $P(A)$ denotes the probability of occurrence of event A. The probability that the event A will not occur is given by $P(\overline{A})$, which is read as P (not A) or "A complement." Thus

$$P(A) + P(\overline{A}) = 1 \qquad (9.9)$$

Equation (9.9) means that the probability that event A will occur plus the probability that event A will not occur must be equal to 2.

The classical definition of probability (Equation (9.8)) assumes that *n possible* outcomes are equally likely or have the equal chance of occurrence. If this condition is not satisfied, the classical definition does not apply. For example, the probability that a student will pass a course is usually not 50 percent since the two possible outcomes—pass and fail—may not be equally likely. The classical probability also fails if the exhaustive or total number of outcomes in a trial is infinite.

Example 19

(a) What is the probability of getting a head on a single toss of a coin?

$$P(A) = \frac{1}{2} \text{ or, } 50\%$$

There are two possible outcomes, and there is one way of getting a head. Hence, according to classical definition, the probability of getting a head is ½ or 50 percent.

(b) What is the probability of getting a 4 if a six-sided die is rolled?

$$P(4) = \frac{1}{6}$$

Example 20

Suppose that a person is equally likely to be born on any day of the week. What is the probability that a baby is born on [a] on a Sunday?

$P(S) = 1/7$

(b) On a day beginning with the letter T, P(Tuesday or Thursday) = 2/7. These are examples of classical probability.

Relative Frequency Approach

Probabilities are also calculated using the relative frequency. In many problems, we define probability by relative frequency. Using this approach, we define probability as

2   We calculate the relative frequency of an event in a very large number of trials (note that relative frequency is calculated by dividing the frequency by the total number of observations). For example, suppose that a researcher has determined that 70 out of 20,000 males in the age group 70 to 80 years have a chance of getting a rare type of blood disease. Then the probability or chance of getting this type of disease is

$$70/20,000 = 0.0035 \text{ or } 0.35\%$$

2   In a relative frequency approach, we calculate the proportion of times an event has occurred in the long run when conditions are stable.

If the relative frequency approach is used without using sufficient data or outcomes, it won't provide reliable results. For example, in the single toss of a coin, we know that there is an equal chance of getting a head and a tail. If you take a coin and toss it 10 times, there is a good chance you will not get five heads and five tails. But if you toss the coin 500 times and count the outcomes, you will get closer to getting heads half of the time and the tails half of the time.

Subjective Probability

Subjective probability is used when the events occur only once or very few times and when little or no relevant data are available. In assigning subjective probability, we may use any information available, such as our experience, intuition, or expert opinion. In this case, the experimental outcomes may not be clear and relative frequency of occurrence may not be available. Subjective probability is a measure of our belief that an event will occur. This belief is based on any information that is available for determining the probability.

For example, suppose a decision is to be made regarding the construction of a nuclear plant at a location where there is some evidence of geological fault. The decision to locate the nuclear plant at this site will depend upon how high the probability of a nuclear accident at this location is. In such a case, there may not be any past data available. The decision or the likelihood of a nuclear accident must be determined based on the judgment or expert opinion.

Basic Concepts of Probability Using Sets

In this section we define set, complement of a set, union, and intersection of sets, and Venn diagrams. These concepts are important in evaluating different probabilities.

Set: A set is an aggregate or collection of objects and is denoted by using upper-case letters A, B, and C. Members of set A are called the elements of A. If x is an element of set A then we write $x \in A$. The symbol $\in$ means "element of." Thus, x is an element of A or is contained in A. If x is not an element of A then $x \notin A$.

For example: Set A, whose elements are all even numbers between 0 and 10, is written as

$$A = \{2, 4, 6, 8, 10\}$$

Here, 2, 4, 6, 8, 10 are elements of set A where $6 \in A$ but $9 \notin A$.

Universal Set: The universal set is a set of all objects under consideration. A universal set is denoted by U. A set is contained within the universal set.

Null Set or Empty Set: A Null set is a set that contains no elements and is denoted by ϕ.

Equality of Sets: If the set $A = \{x, y, z\}$ and the set $B = \{z, x, y\}$, then $A = B$ (order is immaterial).

Venn Diagrams

A Venn diagram is often used to represent a universal set and the sets contained in that universal set. When we are dealing with two or more events, we can illustrate these events by means of a Venn diagram. In a Venn diagram, the universal set is represented by a rectangle and the set or the event is represented by a circle. This is illustrated in the Figure 9.3.

In the figure above, the universal set is shown by a rectangle and A is the set contained in the universal set.

Complement of a Set A

The complement of set A is denoted by $\bar{A}$ (read as A-bar) or A^c and is the set made up of the elements of U that do not belong to A. In other

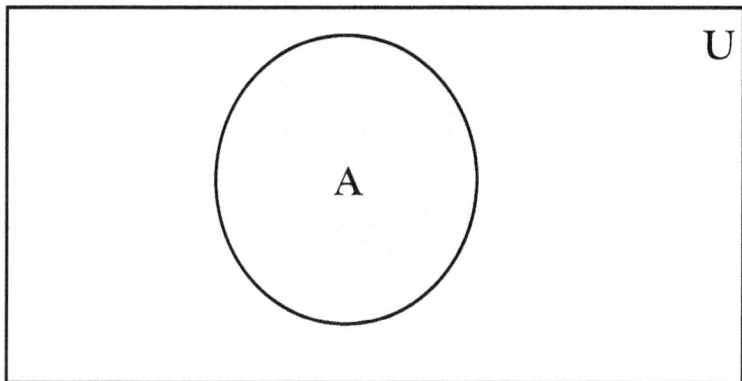

Figure 9.3 Example of a venn diagram

words, the complement of set A is everything but A (with respect to the universal set).

In Figure 9.4, A^c (complement of A) is the shaded area.

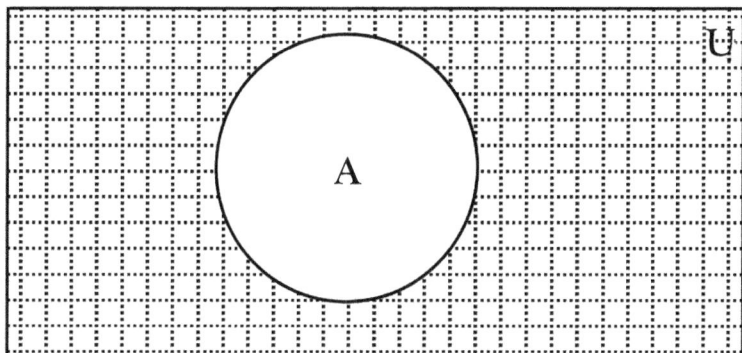

Figure 9.4 Complement of a set.

Union of Sets A and B

Union of Sets A and B is denoted by $A \cup B$ (read as "A union B") and is a set of elements that belong to at least one of the sets A or B. In other words, $A \cup B$ contains all the elements of A and all the elements of B where the common elements are not repeated.

In the above Figure 4.5, $A \cup B$ is shaded.

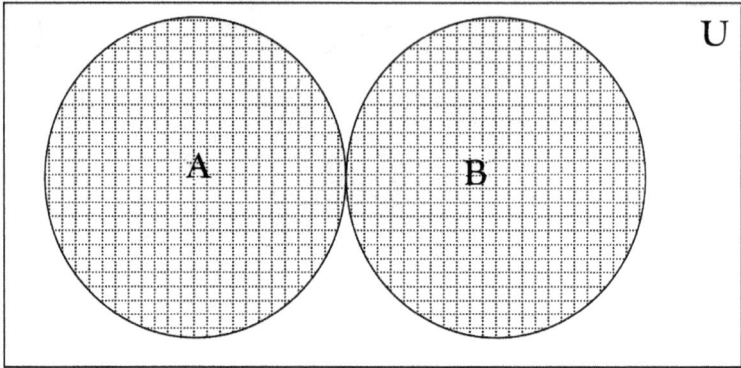

Figure 9.5 Union of two sets A and B

Intersection of Two Sets A and B

Intersection of two sets A and B is denoted by $A \cap B$ (read as "*A* intersection *B*"). This is the set of elements that belong to both *A* and *B* or the elements that are common to *A* and *B*. Figure 9.6 shows the intersection of *A* and *B*.

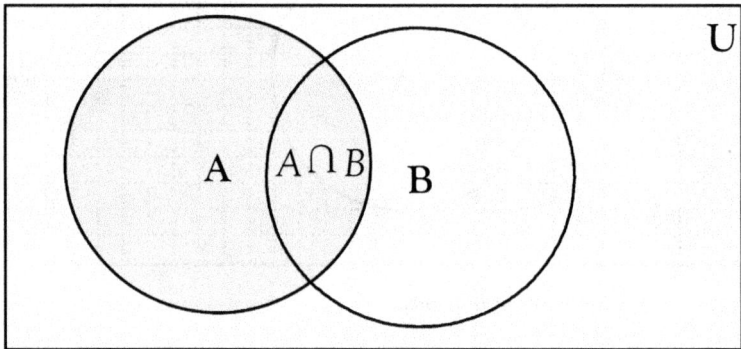

Figure 9.6 Intersection of two sets A and B

Example 20

Suppose the universal set $U = \{1, 2, 3, 4, 5, 6, 7, 8, 9\}$ and three sets A, B, and C defined as

$$A - \{1, 2, 4, 5, 8\}$$

$$B = \{4, 6, 8, 9\}$$

$$C = \{1, 3, 5, 7, 8\}$$

Find A complement, $\overline{A}$ or A^c, $A \cup B$, $A \cup C$, $B \cup C$, $A \cap B$, $A \cup C$

$$\overline{A} = \{3, 6, 7, 9\}$$

$$A \cup B = \{1, 2, 4, 5, 6, 8, 9\}$$

$$A \cup C = \{1, 2, 3, 4, 5, 7, 8\}$$

$$B \cup C = \{1, 3, 4, 5, 6, 7, 8, 9\}$$

$$A \cap B = \{4, 8\}$$

$$A \cap C = \{1, 5, 8\}$$

Addition Law for Mutually Exclusive Events

Mutually Exclusive Events: When the occurrence of one event excludes the occurrence of another event, the two events are mutually exclusive. In other words, one and only one event can take place at a time.

In this section, we will discuss how to calculate the probabilities for events that are mutually exclusive and for events that are nonmutually exclusive.

Note that when events are mutually exclusive, then they cannot occur simultaneously—only one can occur at a time.

If we have two events A *and B that are mutually exclusive*, then the probability that A or B will occur is given by

$$P(A \cup B) = P(A) + P(B) \qquad (9.10)$$

Note that the "union" sign is used for "or" probability that is, $P(A \cup B)$ is the same as $P(A$ or $B)$. Equation (9.10) is the addition law for mutually exclusive events because if events A and B are mutually exclusive, the probability that A or B will occur is calculated by adding the probabilities of occurrence of events A and B. This rule can be extended to three or more mutually exclusive events. If three events A, B, and C are mutually exclusive then the probability that A or B or C occurs is:

$$P(A \cup B \cup C) = P(A) + P(\overline{B}) + P(C) - P(A \cap B) - P(A \cap C)$$
$$- P(B \cap C) + P(A \cap B \cap C)$$

Addition Law for Nonmutually Exclusive Events

If two events A and B are *nonmutually exclusive,* then they can occur together. If the events A and B are nonmutually exclusive, the probability that A or B will occur is given by

$$P(A \cup B) = P(A) + P(B) - P(A \text{ and } B)$$
$$\text{or, } P(A \cup B) = P(A) + P(B) - P(A \cap B) \qquad (9.12)$$

Note that $P(A$ or $B)$ is same as $P(A \cup B)$ and $P(A$ and $B)$ is same as $P(A \cap B)$ or $P(AB)$. Note the difference between Equations (9.10) and (9.12). The equations for calculating "or" probabilities are different when the events are *mutually exclusive* and *nonmutually exclusive.*

The Venn diagram (Figure 9.7) is a situation when A and B both occur. In this case, there is a common area between A and B (intersection of A and B) when the events A and B are nonmutually exclusive. And if we want to find $P(A$ or $B)$, we cannot find it by adding $P(A) + P(B)$ because in Figure 9.7, in adding $P(A) + P(B)$ the area $P(A$ and $B)$ is added twice. We need to subtract $P(A$ and $B)$ to obtain the actual area corresponding to $P(A$ or $B)$.

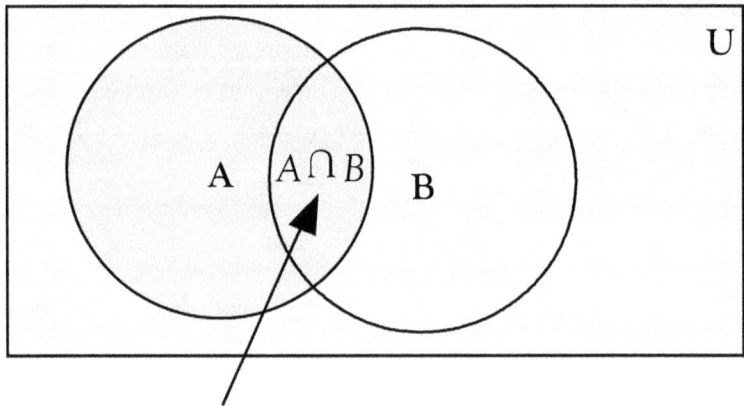

Both A and B

Figure 9.7 Simultaneous occurrence of two events A and B

Equation (9.12) can be extended to three or more nonmutually exclusive events. If events A, B, and C are nonmutually exclusive, then the probability that A, B, or C will occur,

$$P(A \cup B \cup C) = P(A) + P(B) + P(C) - P(A \text{ and } B) - P(A \text{ and } C) -$$
$$P(B \text{ and } C) + P(A \text{ and } B \text{ and } C)$$

or,

$$P(A \cup B \cup C) = P(A) + P(B) + P(C) - P(A \cap B) - P(A \cap C) -$$
$$P(B \cap C) + P(A \cap B \cap C) \quad (4.12)$$

Example 23

Given $X = \{1,3,5,6,7,8,9\}$, $Y = \{2,4,7,9\}$, $Z = \{1,2,3,4,6,7\}$

Find the following:

$$X \cup Z, X \cap Z, X \cup Y \cup Z, X \cap Y \cap Z, (X \cup Y) \cap Z$$

Solution:

$$X \cup Z = \{1,2,3,4,5,6,7,8,9\}$$
$$X \cap Z = \{1,3,6,7\}$$
$$X \cup Y \cup Z = \{1,2,3,4,5,6,7,8,9\}$$
$$X \cap Y \cap Z = \{7\}$$
$$(X \cup Y) \cup Z = \{1,2,3,4,5,6,7,8,9\} \cap \{1,2,3,4,6,7\} = \{1,2,3,4,6,7\}$$

The operations within the parentheses are performed first.

Example 24

Two dice, one green and the other red are rolled. Let A be the event where the sum of the numbers on the top faces is odd, and B is the event where at least one of the faces is a "2."

(a) Describe the sample space.
The sample space of rolling two dice is shown below.

$$S = \{(1,1), (1,2), (1,3), (1,4), (1,5), (1,6),$$
$$(2,1), (2,2), (2,3), (2,4), (2,5), (2,6),$$
$$(3,1), (3,2), (3,3), (3,4), (3,5), (3,6),$$
$$(4,1), (4,2), (4,3), (4,4), (4,5), (4,6),$$
$$(5,1), (5,2), (5,3), (5,4), (5,5), (5,6),$$
$$(6,1), (6,2), (6,3), (6,4), (6,5), (6,6)\}$$

(b) Describe the events A, B, $\bar{B}$ (B-complement), $A \cup B$, and find their probabilities, assuming all 36 sample points have equal probabilities.

A = the event that the sum of the numbers shown by the two dice is odd. Therefore,

$$A = \{(1,2), (2,1), (1,4), (2,3), (3,2), (4,1), (1,6), (2,5), (3,4),$$
$$(4,3), (5,2), (6,1), (3,6), (4,5), (5,4), (6,3), (5,6), (6,5),\}$$

The probability that A will occur

$$P(A) = \frac{18}{36} = \frac{1}{2} \; or, \; 50\%$$

B = the event that at least one face is "2." Therefore,

$$B = \{ (1,1), (1,2), (1,3), (1,4), (1,5), (1,6),$$
$$(2,1), (3,1), (4,1), (5,1), (6,1) \} \text{ and}$$

$$P(B) = \frac{11}{36}$$

$\bar{B}$ = the event that each face obtained is not an ace or number "1"

$$\bar{B} = \{(2,2), (2,3), (2,4), (2,5), (2,6), (3,2), (3,3), (3,4), (3,5), (3,6),$$
$$(4,2), (4,3), (4,4), (4,5), (4,6), (5,2), (5,3), (5,4), (5,5), (5,6),$$
$$(6,2), (6,3), (6,4), (6,5), (6,6)\}$$

and,

$$P(\bar{B}) = \frac{25}{36}$$

$A \cup B$ = the elements common to A and B or the event that the sum is odd and least one face is a "1"

$$A \cup B = \{(1,2), (2,1), (1,4), (2,3), (3,2), (4,1), (1,6),$$
$$(2,5), (3,4), (4,3), (5,2), (6,1), (3,6), (4,5), (5,4), (6,3),$$
$$(5,6), (6,5), (1,1), (1,3), (1,5), (3,1), (5,1)\}$$

and,

$$P(A \cup B) = \frac{23}{36}$$

(c)] Describe the events $(A \cap B), (A \cup \bar{B})$. What are their probabilities?

$A \cap B = \{(1,2).(2,1)(1,4),(4,1)(1,6)(6,1)\}$

$$P(A \cap B) = \frac{6}{36} = \frac{1}{6}$$

$A \cap \bar{B} = \{(2,3),(2,5),(3,2),(3,4),(3,6),(4,3),(4,5),(5,2),$
$(5,4),(5,6),(6,3),(6,5)\}$

$$P(A \cap \bar{B}) = \frac{12}{36} = \frac{1}{3}$$

Example 25

If two dice are thrown, what is the probability that the sum is (a) greater than 8, and (b) neither 7 or 11?

(a) Suppose S denotes the sum of the number on the top faces. We want to find the probability that the sum is greater than 8; that is, $P(S > 8)$.

The required event takes place when the sum $S = 9$, or $S=10$, or $S=11$, or $S=12$. Note that when two dice are thrown, the events are mutually exclusive. When two events are mutually exclusive, the probability of their occurrence is given by the sum of the probabilities of individual events. For example, if A and B are mutually exclusive, then the probability that A or B will happen is

$$P(A \cup B) = P(A) + P(B)$$

Therefore, the probability that the sum is greater than 8 is

$$P (S=9) \text{ or } P(S=10) \text{ or } P(S=11) \text{ or } P(S=12)$$

or,

$$P (S=9) + P(S=10) + P(S=11) + P(S=12)$$

or,

$$P(Sum > 8) = P(9) + P(10) + P(11) + P(12)$$

The next step is to find the probability that the sum is 9, 10, 11, and 12 and then add the probabilities. These probabilities can be evaluated as

$$\text{Sum} = 9$$

$$(3, 6), (6, 3), (4, 5), (5, 4)$$

$$P (S=9) = 4/36$$

$$\text{Sum} = 10$$

$$(4, 6), (6, 4), (5, 5)$$

$$P(S=10) = 3/36$$

$$\text{Sum} = 11$$

$$(5, 6), (6, 5)$$

$$P(S=11) = 2/36$$

$$\text{Sum} = 12$$

$$(6, 6)$$

$$P(S=12) = 1/36$$

The probability that the sum is greater than 8 is,

$$P(S>8) = P(S=9) \text{ or } P(S=10) \text{ or } P(S=11) \text{ or } P(S=12)$$

$$= P(S=9) + P(S=10) + P(S=11) + P(S=12)$$

$$= 4/36 + 3/36 + 2/36 + 1/36$$

$$= 10/36 \text{ or } 27.8\%$$

(b) Find the probability that the sum is neither 7 nor 12.

Suppose in rolling two dice; A is the event where the sum is 7 and B is the event that the sum is 12. Then, the sum of 7 can be obtained in the following way:

$$(1, 6), (6, 1), (2, 5), (5, 2), (3, 4), (4, 3) \text{ and}$$

$$P(7) = 6/36 \text{ or } 1/6$$

The sum of 11 can be obtained in the following way:

$$(5, 6), (6, 5) \text{ and}$$

$$P(11) = 2/36 \text{ or } 1/18$$

The probability that the sum is neither 7 nor 11 is

$$P(\bar{A} \cap \bar{B}) = 1 - P(A \cup B) = 1 - [P(A) + P(B)]$$
$$= 1 - [1/6 + 1/18]$$
$$= 7/9 \text{ or } 77.8\%$$

Example 27

A survey of 10,000 business professionals found that 20 percent of all professionals use the Internet, 40 percent use cell phones, and 12 percent use both Internet and cell phone.

(a) What is the probability that a randomly selected business professional uses the Internet?

Let I = event that the professional uses the Internet then

$$P(I) = 0.20$$

(b) What is the probability that a randomly selected business professional uses cell phone?

C = event that the professional uses cell phone then

$$P(C) = 0.40$$

(c) What is the probability that a randomly selected business professional uses the Internet or cell phone?

In this case, we need to calculate "or" probability. Note that there are two events—I and C—these are not mutually exclusive because there are professionals who use both the Internet and cell phone. Recall that if two events A and B are nonmutually exclusive, then the probability that A or B will occur is given by

$$P(A \cup B) = P(A) + P(B) - P(A \text{ and } B)$$
$$or, P(A \cup B) = P(A) + P(B) - P(A \text{ and } B)$$

In this case, we have events I and C where $P(I) = 0.20$, $P(C) = 0.40$, and $P(I \text{ and } C) = 0.12$. Therefore, required probability,

$$P(I \cup C) = P(I) + P(C) - P(I \cap C) = 0.20 + 0.40 - 0.12 = 0.48$$

Note that $\cup$ is "or" and $\cap$ is "and." Also, it is given that

$$P(I \cup C) = 0.12$$

(d) What is the probability that a randomly selected business professional uses the Internet or the cell phone but not both?

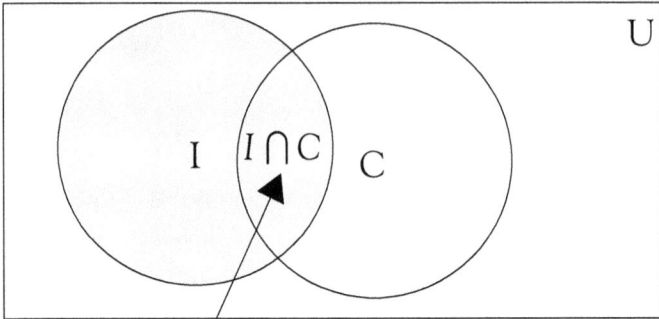

Both I and C

From the above figure,

$$P(I \cup C) \text{ but not both} = P(I \cup C) - P(I \cap C) = 0.48 - 0.12 = 0.36$$

(e) What is the probability that a randomly selected business professional uses neither the Internet nor the cell phone?

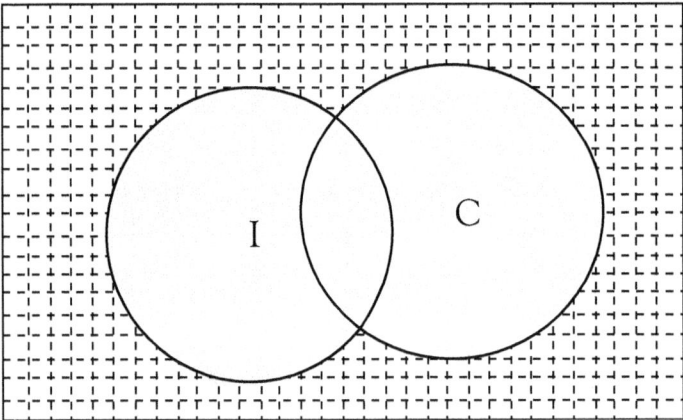

From the above figure, note that the shaded area (area outside both the circles) is the area where business professionals do not use the Internet and the cell phone. Therefore,

$$P(\bar{I} \cap \bar{C}) = 1 - P(I \cup C) = 1 - 0.48 = 0.52$$

Example 28

The survey of credit cards in a certain city revealed that 26 percent of the people carry a Visa card, 48 percent carry a Master Card, and 18 percent carry both. What is the probability that a randomly selected person will have at least one of these cards?

Let V denote the event that a person has a Visa card, M be the event that a person has a Master Card. Then

$$P(V) = 0.26$$

$$P(M) = 0.48 \text{ and}$$

$$P(V \cap M) = 0.18$$

The probability of carrying at least one of the cards is

$$P(V \cup M) = P(V) + P(M) - P(V \cap M)$$

$$= 0.26 + 0.48 - 0.18 = 0.56 \text{ or } 56\%$$

Example 30

Two dice are rolled. Find the probabilities that the numbers on the top faces are (i) five, (ii) eight?

The 36 possible outcomes of rolling two dice are shown in Example 24. Let A be the event that the sum of the numbers is five while B denotes the event that the sum is eight. Then

$$A = \{(1, 4), (2, 3), (3, 2), (4, 1)\} \text{ therefore,}$$

$$P(A) = \frac{4}{36} = \frac{1}{9}$$

Similarly, $B = \{(2, 6), (3, 5), (4, 4), (5, 3), (6, 2)\}$
Therefore,

$$P(B) = \frac{5}{36}$$

Self-Test

9.4   What is a set? Give an example.

9.5   Describe the union and intersection of two sets. If $A = \{2,4,67\}$ and $B = \{1,3,5\}$. What is $(A \cup B)$?

9.6   If $A = \{3,4,6,8,9\}$ and $\{3,5,7,8\}$, find $A \cap B$?

9.7   What is a Venn diagram? What is the purpose of Venn diagrams?

9.8   What is meant by the complement of a set A? Draw a Venn diagram to illustrate the concept of the complement of a set A.

9.10   Using the Venn diagram in problem 4.25, show that

$$P(B \mid A) = \frac{P(A \cap B)}{P(A)} = \frac{P(A \text{ and } B)}{P(B)} = 0.4286$$

$$P(R) = P(A \mid B)P(R) + P(S \mid R)P(R)$$

$$P(B \mid A)$$
$$P(R \mid D)$$
$$P(R \mid S)$$

9.11   Draw Venn diagrams to illustrate the following: (a) Probability of events A and B or $P(A \cap B)$

(b) Probability of events A or B or $P(A \cup B)$

(c) Probability of mutually exclusive events A and B.

9.12   A survey of the women engineers showed that 68 percent of all women engineers 28 to 50 years of age are employed. The survey also indicated that 56 percent of the women engineers in that age group are married and 47 percent are both employed and married.

(a) What is the probability that a randomly selected woman engineer is employed or is married? (b) What is the probability that a randomly selected woman engineer is employed or is married but not both? (b) a randomly selected woman engineer is neither employed nor married?

Probabilities Under Statistical Independence and Dependence

In the previous sections, we calculated probabilities using the classical and relative frequency approach. We also calculated probabilities when the events were mutually exclusive, nonmutually exclusive, and equally likely. There are instances where the events we are interested in may be dependent or independent of each other. In this section, we will first define what is meant by independent and dependent events, and then describe ways of calculating probabilities for independent and dependent cases.

Probabilities Under Statistical Independence

When two events occur, the occurrence of the first event may or may not have an effect on the occurrence of the second one. More simply put, the events may be either dependent or independent.

Statistical Independence

When two or more events occur, the occurrence of one event has no effect on the probability of occurrence for any other event. In this case, the events are considered independent. The probabilities under statistical independence are shown in Figure 9.8.

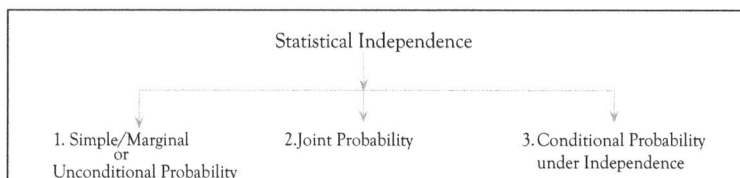

Figure 9.8 diagram:

Statistical Independence

1. Simple/Marginal or Unconditional Probability   2. Joint Probability   3. Conditional Probability under Independence

Figure 9.8 Probabilities for independent events

Simple probability is also known as marginal or unconditional and is the probability of occurrence for a single event; say A and is denoted by $P(A)$.

Example 31

Toss a single coin. The probability of getting a head and a tail is

$$P(H) = 0.5$$
$$P(T) = 0.5$$

The above is true for every toss, no matter how many tosses are made. In tossing a coin, the two outcomes are independent. Every toss stands alone and is no way connected with any other toss. The other example is rolling a six-sided die. There are six outcomes in this case and each is independent of the other.

Joint Probability under Statistical Independence

Joint probability is the probability of occurrence of two or more events together or in succession. It is also known as "and" probability.

Suppose we have two events A and B, which are independent. Then the joint probability, $P(AB)$ is the probability of occurrence of both A "and" B and is given by

$$P(AB) = P(A) \cdot P(B) \qquad (9.13)$$

Equation (4.13) means that the probability of two independent events that occur together, or in succession is *the product of their marginal or simple probabilities*. Note that

$P(AB)$ = probability of event A and B occurring together. This is known as ***joint probability***

$P(AB)$ is the same as $P(A$ and $B)$ or $P(A \cap B)$ where, $P(A)$ = marginal probability of event A, $P(B)$ = marginal probability of event B. Equation (9.13) is also written as

$$P(A \cap B) = P(A) \cdot P(B)$$

where events A and B are independent and can be extended to more than two events. For example,

$$P(ABC) = P(A) \cdot P(B) \cdot P(C) \qquad (9.14)$$

Note that $P(ABC)$ is same as $P(A$ and B and $C)$ and is also written as $P(A \cap B \cap C)$.

Equation (9.14) is the probability of three independent events, A, B, and C, and can be calculated by taking the product of their marginal or simple probabilities.

Example 32

Toss a coin twice. What is the probability of getting a head on the first toss, and a head on the second toss?

Suppose: H_1 = probability of getting a head on the first toss, and

H_2 = probability of getting a head on the second toss, then the probability of a head on the first toss *and* the probability of a head on the second toss is

$$P(H_1 H_2) = P(H_1) \cdot P(H_2) = (0.5)(0.5) = 0.25$$

This follows from Equation (9.13). Here the events are statistically independent because the probability of any outcome is not affected by any preceding outcome. Since the probability of a head on any toss is 0.5, the probability of head on the first toss is 0.5 and so is the probability of head on the second toss. Therefore, the probability of a head on the first toss and on the second toss is 0.5 times 0.5, which is 0.25 or 25 percent. In a similar way, the probability of getting three heads in three successive tosses is

$$P(H_1 H_2 H_3) = P(H_1) \cdot P(H_2) \cdot P(H_3) = (0.5)(0.5)(0.5) = 0.125$$

Thus, there is a 12.5 percent chance of getting three heads in succession if we toss a coin three times.

Example 33

Note that in tossing a coin three times, the sample space is S = {HHH, HHT, HTH, HTT, THH, THT, TTH, TTT}. Thus, there are eight outcomes and these are independent of each other. Suppose we want to calculate the following probabilities: (a) the probability of getting a tail on the first toss, a head on the second toss, and a tail on the third toss.

$$P(THT) = P(T)P(H)P(T) = (0.5)(0.5)(0.5) = 0.125$$

(b) The probability of at least one tail on three tosses = $1 - P(HHH)$ = $1 - 0.125 = 0.875$ or from the sample space, the required probability is 7/8 or 0.875.

3. Conditional Probability under Statistical Independence

The conditional probability is written as $P(A \mid B)$ and is read as the probability of event A, given that B has already occurred, or the probability of A, given B. If two events A and B are *independent,* then

$$P(A \mid B) = P(A) \qquad (9.15)$$

This means that if the events are independent, the probabilities are not affected by the occurrence of each other. The probability of occurrence of B has no effect on the occurrence of A. That is, the condition has no meaning if the events are independent.

Example 34

Toss a coin twice. What is the probability of getting a head on the second toss if the first toss resulted in a head?

Let

H_2 = probability of a head on the second toss,

H_1 = probability of a head on the first toss

The probability of a head on the second toss, given that the first toss resulted in a head, can be written as $P(H_2 \mid H_1)$. Since the result of the first toss has no effect on the result of the second toss, we can write

$$P(H_2 \mid H_1) = P(H_2) = 0.5$$

Probabilities under Statistical Dependence

When two or more events occur, the occurrence of one event has an effect on the probability of the occurrence of any other event. In this case, the events are dependent. The probabilities when the events are dependent are shown in Figure 9.9.

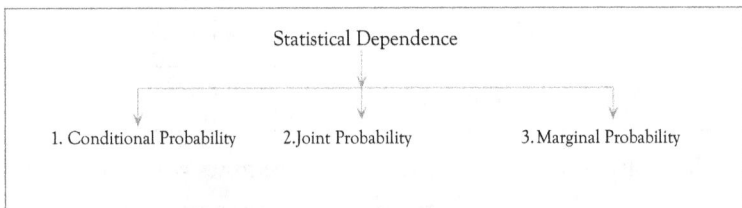

Figure 9.9 *Probabilities under statistical dependence*

Conditional Probability Under Statistical Dependence

The probabilities discussed so far relate to the entire sample space. Sometimes we are interested in evaluating the probability of events where the event is *conditioned* on some part or subset of the sample space. Consider the following example:

Suppose there is a group of 100 people, out of which 40 are college graduates, 30 are businessmen, and 15 are both college graduates and businessmen.

If we define A = set of businessmen and B = set of college graduates

Then $A \cap B$ = set of college graduates and businessmen.

This can be shown using the Venn diagram in Figure 9.10.

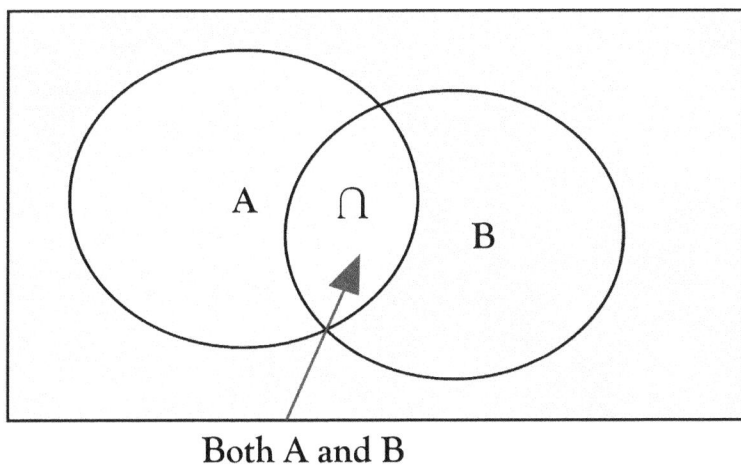

Both A and B

Figure 9.10 Venn diagram

The Venn diagram shows the entire sample space. Suppose from this group of 100 people, a person is randomly selected. Then the probability that the person is a businessman is

$$P(A) = \frac{30}{100} = 0.30$$

The probability that the person is a college graduate,

$$P(B) = \frac{40}{100} = 0.40$$

and the probability that the person is both a college graduate and a businessman,

$$P(A \cap B) = \frac{15}{100} = 0.15$$

The above probabilities are calculated using the entire sample space.

Now, suppose we select a person from the group who we know is a college graduate. What is the probability that the person is a businessman?

The probability that we want to calculate is a conditional probability and is written as

$$P(A \mid B)$$

The above probability statement is read as probability of A given that B is known. Since we know that the person belongs to the college graduate group, so we need to look only in the college graduate group. In other words, the sample space is now reduced (see Figure 9.11). Note that A is the set of businessmen and B is the set of college graduates.

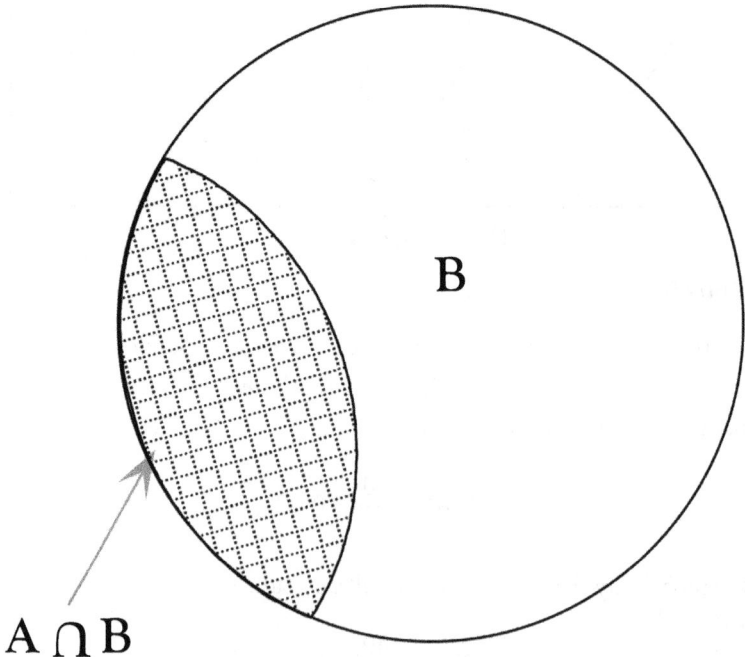

Figure 9.11 The reduced sample space

The sample space is reduced in which only college graduates are considered, and the probability is given by

$$P(A \mid B) = \frac{P(A \cap B)}{P(B)} = \frac{P(A \text{ and } B)}{P(B)} \qquad (9.16)$$

Equation (4.16) above defines the conditional probability.

Example 35

A bag contains 50 balls, of which 15 are red and dotted, 5 are red and striped, 10 are green and dotted, and 20 are green and striped. Suppose a red ball is drawn from the box. What is the probability that the ball is dotted? What is the probability that it is striped?

For this type of problem, it is easier to calculate the probabilities if we construct a joint probability table. We will first show how to use the given information to construct a joint probability table and then calculate the required probabilities. First, put the information in a table form, as shown below.

	Dotted (D)	Striped (S)	Marginal Probability Totals
Red (R)	15	5	20
Green (G)	10	20	30
Marginal Probability Totals	25	25	50

From the above table, we can calculate the following relative frequency probabilities:

$$P(R \text{ and } D) = 15/50 = 0.30$$
$$P(R \text{ and } S) = 5/50 = 0.10$$
$$P(G \text{ and } D) = 10/50 = 0.20$$
$$P(G \text{ and } S) = 20/50 = 0.40$$

Note that the above probabilities are *joint* probabilities. Joint probabilities are *"and"* probabilities. Similarly, we can calculate the simple or marginal probabilities as

$$P(R) = 20/50 = 0.40$$

$$P(G) = 30/50 = 0.60$$

$$P(D) = 25/50 = 0.50$$

$$P(S) = 25/50 = 0.50$$

Now, we can use the above probabilities to construct a *joint probability table*. The table is shown below.

	Dotted (D)	Striped (S)	Total
Red (R)	0.30	0.10	0.40
Green (G)	0.20	0.40	0.60
Total	0.50	0.50	2.00

This table contains the joint ("and") probabilities and also the marginal or simple probabilities. We want to find the following probabilities:

[a] Suppose a red ball is drawn from the box, what is the probability that the ball is dotted?

This is a conditional probability because we know that the ball drawn is a red one. The required probability can be written as $P(D|R)$.

The probability is calculated using Equation (4.16). Note that D and R is same as R and D. Since we know that the ball drawn is a red one, the sample space is reduced and we divide by $P(R)$ and *not* by the entire sample space. Try to construct a Venn diagram for the problem. In order to solve for the required probability, obtain the values in the numerator and denominator—from the joint probability table.

$$P(D \mid R) = \frac{P(D \cap R)}{P(R)} = \frac{0.30}{0.40} = 0.75$$

[b] Suppose a red ball is drawn from the box. What is the probability the ball is striped?

$$P(S \mid R) = \frac{P(S \cap R)}{P(R)} = \frac{0.10}{0.40} = 0.25$$

[c] Try calculating the following probabilities, using the information in the joint probability table and Equation (4.16).

$$P(G \mid D)$$
$$P(R \mid D)$$
$$P(R \mid S)$$

Example 36

Let A and B be two events, such that $P(A) = 0.7$, $P(B) = 0.3$, and P (A and B) = 0.2. Find

$$P(A \mid B), P(B \mid A)$$

$$P(A \mid B) = \frac{P(A \cap B)}{P(B)} = \frac{0.1}{0.3} = 0.333$$

$$P(B \mid A) = \frac{P(B \cap A)}{P(A)} = \frac{0.1}{0.7} = 0.1429$$

Example 37

In a certain manufacturing plant, 40 percent of the workers are skilled, 70 percent of the workers are full time, and 30 percent of the workers are skilled and full time. If a full-time worker is selected at random, what is the probability that he or she is skilled?

Let S = skilled, F = full time. Then $P(S) = 0.40$, $P(F) = 0.70$, $P(S \cap F) = 0.30$

We want to find $P(S \mid F) = ?$

The probability can be calculated as:

$$P(S \mid F) = \frac{P(S \cap F)}{P(F)} = \frac{0.30}{0.70} = 0.4286$$

Joint Probability under Statistical Dependence

The joint probability under statistical dependence can be calculated using the formula of conditional probability in Equation (9.16). Refer to Equation (9.16), which is the conditional probability

$$P(A \mid B) = \frac{P(A \cap B)}{P(A)} = \frac{P(A \, and \, B)}{P(B)} \qquad (9.17)$$

$$P(B \mid A) = \frac{P(B \cap A)}{P(A)} = \frac{P(B \, and \, A)}{P(A)} \qquad (9.18)$$

Notice the difference between Equations (9.17) and (9.18). Equation (9.17) is *the probability of event A when B has already occurred*. Equation (4.18) is *the probability of event B when A has occurred*. In these equations, (A and B) is same as (B and A) but the denominator is different, depending upon what we are calculating.

We always divide by the event after the vertical bar in Equations (9.17) and (9.18). Also, using Equations (9.17) and (9.18), we can calculate the joint probabilities. Recall that the joint probability is the probability of occurrence of two or more events together or in succession. The joint probability is "and" probability. The joint probabilities from Equations (9.17) and (9.18) can be written as

$$P(A \cap B) = P(F \mid S) = 0.90 P(B)$$

$$\text{or, } P(A \, and \, B) = P(A \mid B)P(B) \qquad (9.19)$$

From Equation (9.18), we can write

$$P(B \cap A) = P(B \mid A)P(A)$$

$$\text{or, } P(B \, and \, A) = P(B \mid A)P(A) \qquad (9.20)$$

Equations (9.19) and (9.20) are the joint probabilities under statistical dependence.

Example 38

In a certain manufacturing plant, 40 percent of the workers are skilled, 70 percent of the workers are full time, and 90 percent of the skilled workers are full time. If a full-time worker is selected at random, what is the probability that he or she is a skilled full-time employee?

Let S = skilled, F = full time, then $P(S) = 0.40$, $P(F) = 0.70$, $P(F \mid S) = 0.90$. We want to find $P(S$ and $F)$ or $P(F$ and $S)$. This probability can be calculated as

$$P(F \cap S) = P(F \mid S)P(S) = (0.90)(0.40) = 0.36$$

Marginal Probability under Statistical Dependence

The marginal probability is the probability of occurrence for a single event. Under statistical dependence, the calculation of marginal probability can be demonstrated using the joint probability table of Example 35. The joint probability table is reproduced below.

	Dotted (D)	Striped (S)	Total
Red (R)	0.30	0.10	0.40
Green (G)	0.20	0.40	0.60
Totals	0.50	0.50	2.00

Suppose we want to calculate the probability of a ball being red; that is, $P(R)$. From the joint probability table, this probability is 0.40 and can be calculated by adding the two joint probabilities; $P(D$ and $R)$ plus $P(S$ and $R)$. Therefore, we can write

$$P(R) = P(D \text{ and } R) + P(S \text{ and } R)$$

The expressions on the right-hand side of the above equation are "and" or "joint" probabilities and under statistical dependence, the joint probabilities are calculated using equations (9.19) or (9.20). Thus, $P(R) = P(D$ and $R) + P(S$ and $R)$ or,

$$P(R) = P(D \mid R)P(R) + P(S \mid R)P(R) \qquad (9.21)$$

Equation (9.21) is the expression for marginal probability under statistical dependence. This formula is useful in revising probabilities.

Bayes' Theorem

In calculating conditional probability, we use the information about the occurrence of one event to determine the probability of another event. For example, in determining $P(A \mid B)$ we determine the probability of an event *A* when *B* is known, or *B* has already occurred. This concept can be extended to *revise* probabilities as new information become available. In determining probability, we often have initial estimates for specific events of interest. These initial estimates are known as *prior probability* estimates. Next, we are interested in determining the probability of these events, having been given some new information. With the new information available, we update the prior probability values by calculating revised probabilities. These revised probabilities are known as *posterior probabilities* and are always conditional probabilities. These probability calculations are often made using *Bayes' theorem* (named after the English priest and mathematician).

Summary

Probability is used in situations where uncertainty exists; it is the study of random phenomenon or events. A random event can be seen as an event in which the outcome cannot be predicted in advance. Probability can tell us the likelihood of the random event(s). In the decision-making process, uncertainty almost always exists. One question that is of usual concern when making decisions under uncertainty is the probability of success of the outcome. This chapter provided several ways of calculating probability with examples and applications.

CHAPTER 10

Discrete Probability Distributions Applications in Data Science

Chapter Highlights

- Discrete probability distributions that are critical to decision making in data analysis.
- Random variables, the concept of probability distribution, and discrete distribution
- The expected value or the mean, variance, and standard deviation of discrete probability distributions
- Problems involving binomial distributions using the binomial formula, binomial table, and computer packages
- Problems involving Poisson distributions using the Poisson distribution formula, table, and computer packages
- Introduction to the other discrete distributions: Hypergeometric negative binomial, geometric, and discrete uniform distributions

Introduction: What You Need to Know

The fast food business is very competitive. The speed of service and accuracy of order are major concerns. In order to improve customer service, the fast food chains often study the customer arrival pattern. In one of the studies, the customer arrival pattern at a drive through was studied. The number of arrivals (x) per 5-minute period during the lunch hour between 11:30 a.m. and 1:30 p.m. on selected days were recorded.

From the number of arrivals, the probabilities, $p(x_i)$ associated with the number of arrivals were also calculated. These are shown in the table below.

x	1	2	3	4	5	6	7	8	9	10
p(x)	0.08	0.18	0.17	0.15	0.12	0.08	0.07	0.06	0.05	0.04

In the above table, the number of customer arrival (x) is a random variable because it is a chance phenomenon and cannot be predicted in advance. When the random variable can assume only a *countable* number of values, it is called a *discrete random variable*. The customer arrival (x) along with the probability, p(x) associated with each outcome describes the probability distribution of the customer arrival at the drive through. *The above example describes the probability distribution in a table form. This probability distribution can also be represented in a graphical form as shown in Figure 10.1.*

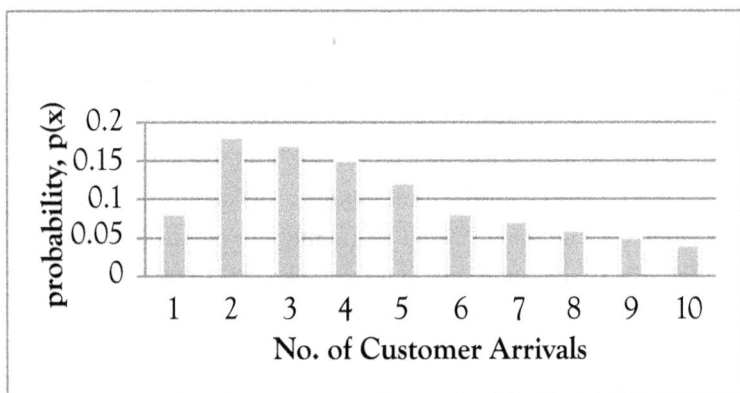

Figure 10.1 Distribution of customer arrival

The probability distribution can be helpful in studying the drive through process. In particular, the distribution of the customer arrival and service are used to model and study this type of process. Using the customer arrival distribution, the average number of customer arrival, and the probabilities of interest can be calculated to make appropriate decisions.

This chapter introduces the concepts of probability distributions and focuses on a class of distributions known as the *discrete probability distributions.* Several of the widely used probability distributions including the binomial, Poisson, and hypergeometric are studied in this chapter.

In this chapter, we advance the concept of probability by studying another important topic: probability distributions. The concept and understanding of probability distributions is critical in modeling and decision making in statistics and data science. There are two categories of probability distributions: *discrete and continuous* probability distributions. This chapter focuses on the discrete probability distributions.

A probability distribution is described using a *graph*, a *table*, or a *formula*. The probability distribution assigns probabilities to each value of a *random variable*. A variable is usually denoted using a letter (for example: X, Y, A, B, x, y, etc.) and can take any specified set of values.

A random variable is a variable that can take numerical values that are associated with the random outcomes of an experiment. A random variable is usually an outcome of a statistical experiment or a process that generates random outcomes. All statistical experiments have three things in common: (a) the experiment has one or more than one possible outcome; (b) each outcome can be specified in advance; and (c) the outcome of the experiment depends on chance. Thus the outcome of a random variable cannot be predicted in advance.

When a probability distribution is described in a tabular form, it requires that we list the possible values or outcomes of the random variable and the probability associated with each value. A probability distribution can also be presented in a graphical form. The graphical display helps define the features or the patterns of the distribution that are usually not apparent from just looking at a table describing the probability distribution. In plotting the graph of a probability distribution, the random variable is plotted along the x-axis, and the corresponding probability is plotted along the y-axis. The probability distribution can also be described using a formula. For example, consider rolling a single die. In this case, any of the six numbers has equal chance of appearing on the top face and therefore, the probability distribution of rolling a single die can be written as:

$$P(X = i) = \frac{1}{6} \text{ for } i = 1, 2, 3, 4, 5, 6$$

In the above experiment of rolling a single die, each outcome, 1 through 6 is random with a probability of 1/6 for each outcome.

A random variable can be *discrete* or *continuous*. A random variable that can assume only a *countable* number of values is called a *discrete random variable* for example: 2, 4, 6, and 8 are examples of discrete values. Some of the examples of discrete random variables are as follows:

- The number of emergency calls received by an ambulance service: $x = 0,1,2,3,\ldots.$
- The number of customers arriving every 5 minutes to a grocery store checkout counter, $x = 0,1,2,3,\ldots.$
- The number of planes arriving and departing every hour from the Salt Lake City international airport: $x = 0,1,2,3,\ldots.$
- Number of cars rented by Avis Car Rental chain on a given day: $x = 0,1,2,3,\ldots.$
- The number of customers waiting to be served at the Burger King fast food restaurant: $x = 0,1,2,3,\ldots.$

Note that in all the above cases, the random variables described are discrete because the values are integers or counts.

The random variables that are not countable but correspond to the points in an interval are known as *continuous random variables*. Continuous random variables are infinite and uncountable. An example of a continuous variable would be the time it takes to assemble a computer. If x is a random variable that denotes the assembly time, then x can take values greater than 0 or $x > 0$. We will study the continuous variables in the next chapter.

Discrete Probability Distributions and Their Properties

The major objective of this chapter is to gain an understanding of several of the discrete probability distributions and their properties. A good knowledge and understanding of probability distributions is critical in being able to apply these distributions in data analysis, decision making, modeling, quality, and computer simulation. In this chapter, we will discuss the following topics:

Probability distributions, discrete probability distribution, and widely used probability distribution are the mean or expected value and the variance of a discrete probability distribution.
- Probabilities from several discrete distributions.

Binomial distribution
- Understand the binomial distribution and its applications.

Poisson distribution
- Understand the Poisson distribution and be able to calculate the Poisson probabilities.

Other important discrete distributions
- Hypergeometric distribution.
- Negative binomial or Pascal distribution.
- Geometric distribution.
- Discrete uniform distribution.

Random Variables and Discrete Probability Distributions

The concepts of random variables and discrete probability distributions are important in statistical decision making and data analysis. A *random variable* is a variable that takes on different values as a result of the outcomes of a random experiment. It is a variable that assumes numerical values governed by chance so that a particular value cannot be predicted in advance. When the outcome of an experiment results in numerical values that are random, then the list of the possible values of the random variable and their probabilities provides a probability distribution. The random variable can be both *discrete* and *continuous*. If the random variable x is either finite or countably infinite, it is a *discrete random variable*. On the other hand, if a random variable takes any value within a given range, it is a *continuous random variable*.

The distribution of a discrete random variable is a list of all possible outcomes of a random variable X and their probabilities. There are three methods of describing a discrete random variable: (1) list each value of X—the outcome, and the corresponding probability of x in a table form, (2) use a histogram that shows the outcomes of an experiment x on the *x*-axis and the corresponding probabilities of the outcomes on the *y*-axis, and (3) use a function (or a formula) that assigns a probability to each outcome, *X*.

Using a function, that is, an algebraic formula that assigns a probability to each discrete random variable is a very convenient way of describing the probability distribution of a discrete random variable. The function that assigns a probability to each value of the random variable *X* is called a probability mass function (PMF). Thus, PMF for a discrete random variable *X* is a list of all possible values of *X* and its associated probabilities, or [*x*, *P*(*X* = *x*)]. For a function to be a valid probability mass function, the following two conditions in Equation (10.1) must be satisfied. The probability mass function is commonly referred to as the probability distribution of a discrete random variable.

---

1. *P*(*x*) is between 0 and 1 (both inclusive) for each *x*, and
2. $\Sigma P(x) = 1.0$ (10.1)

The probability mass function (pmf) is a way of describing a discrete probability distribution. The pmf is a function that assigns a probability to each value of *x* if the random variable *x* of interest is a continuous random variable, the term probability density function is used to describe the continuous probability distribution.

What Is a Probability Distribution?

The probability distribution is a model that relates the value of a variable with the probability of occurrence of that value. The probability distribution describes the frequencies that occur theoretically whereas the relative frequency distribution describes the frequencies that have actually occurred.

Consider rolling two dice and observing the sum of the numbers on the top faces. Suppose *x* is a *random variable* that denotes the sum of the numbers on the top faces. The theoretical probability distribution of this experiment is known and is shown in Table 10.1. This is an example of a discrete probability distribution. Note that in a discrete distribution, the outcomes x_1 are integers or whole numbers.

Table 10.1 Probability distribution of throwing to dice

x	2	3	4	5	6	7	8	9	10	11	12
P(x)	1/36	2/36	3/36	4/36	5/36	6/36	5/36	4/36	3/36	2/36	1/36

In Table 10.1, the outcome *x* (which is the sum of the numbers on the top faces) is a *random variable* as it takes on different values in the population according to some random mechanism. As indicated above, a random variable is a variable that takes on different values as a result of the outcomes of a random experiment. It can also be a variable that assumes numerical values governed by chance so that a value cannot be predicted in advance. Rolling two dice is a random experiment. We know that the sum of the numbers in rolling two dice will vary from 2 through 12, but the exact sum cannot be predicted in advance. The outcome in each throw of two dice is a random phenomenon and assumes values 2 through 12 randomly governed by chance.

The probability distribution describes the probability of occurrence of any value *x* in the population. The probability distribution is the outcomes x, and the probabilities for these outcomes $P(X_i)$ can be shown both in a tabular or a graphical form. Table 10.1 shows the probability distribution in a table form. Figure 10.2 shows the probability distribution graphically.

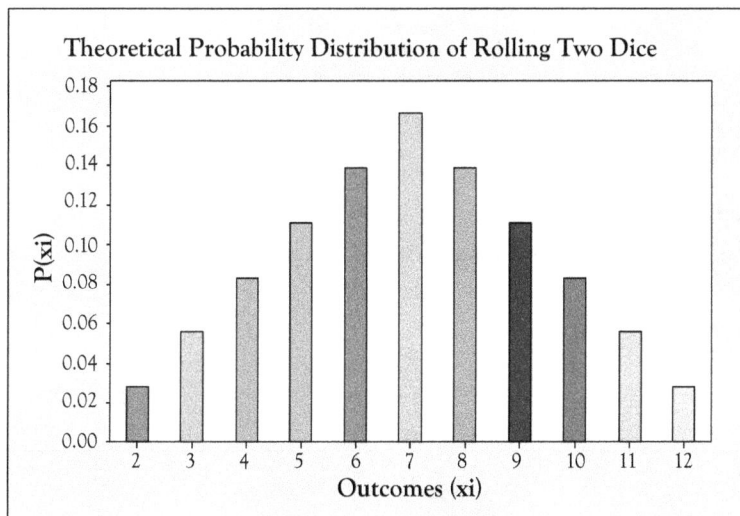

Theoretical Probability Distribution of Rolling Two Dice

Figure 10.2 Probability distribution of rolling two dice

Expected Value, Variance, and Standard Deviation of a Discrete Distribution

The mean or the expected value of a discrete random variable denoted by μ, or $E(x)$ is the average value observed over a long period. The variance and standard deviation σ^2 and σ are the measures of variation of the random variable.

In this section, we will demonstrate how to calculate the expected value, variance, and standard deviation for a discrete probability distribution. We will use the concept of the mean or expected value and variance in the next section.

Background

The mean for a discrete random variable is defined mathematically as the expected value and is written as

$$\mu_x = E(X) = \sum x_i P(x_i) \tag{10.2}$$

The variance of a discrete random variable is defined as

$$\sigma^2 = \sum (x_i - \mu)^2 P(x_i) \tag{10.3}$$

$$\sigma^2 = \sum x^2 P(x) - \mu^2 \tag{10.4}$$

$$\text{The standard deviation, } \sigma = \sqrt{\sigma^2} \tag{10.5}$$

Example 2

Suppose we want to determine the *mean* and *variance* of the discrete probability distribution for the data in the table below. The table is the distribution of calls received by a fire department on a given day and their probabilities given below:

x	0	1	2	3	4	5
$P(x)$	0.10	0.30	0.25	0.20	0.10	0.05

Calculation of the mean or expected value

x	P(x)	x*P(x)
0	0.10	0.00
1	0.30	0.30
2	0.25	0.50
3	0.20	0.60
4	0.10	0.40
5	0.05	0.25
		2.050

For this example,

$$\mu_x = E(X) = \Sigma x_i P(x_i) = 2.050$$

This is the mean or expected value of this discrete distribution.

Calculation of the Variance and the Standard Deviation

Note that you need to calculate the mean or the expected value of the distribution before you can calculate the variance. The variance is calculated using the following formula:

$$\sigma^2 = \Sigma(x_i - \mu)^2 P(x_i)$$

For this example,
$\sigma^2 = (0 - 2.050)^2 (0.10) + (1 - 2.050)^2 (0.30) + ... + (5 - 2.050)^2 (0.05)$
$= 2.7475$
and the standard deviation, $\sigma = \sqrt{1.7475} = 1.32$

Self-test

10.1   Describe a random variable? What is a probability distribution?

10.2   Distinguish between a discrete and continuous probability distribution.

10.3   Classify each of the following random variables as either discrete or continuous. In each case, state what values the random variable can assume.

(a) Outcomes of a roll of a single six-sided die.
(b) The number of calls coming to a call center between 10 and 11:00 a.m. on a given day
(c) The number of passengers arriving at the check-in counter of an airport
(d) Waiting time (in minutes) of the patients at the hospital emergency clinic
(e) Time to serve customers at a fast food drive-through restaurant.

Some Important Discrete Distributions: Bernoulli Process and Binomial Distribution

The binomial distribution is a very widely used discrete distribution that describes discrete data resulting from an experiment known as a Bernoulli process.

Bernoulli Trials and Bernoulli Distribution

In many situations, the experiment or the process under study consists of n number of trials. Each trial has only two possible outcomes: success (S) and failure (F). We can denote this as

$$x_j = 1 \qquad \text{if the experiment results in a success (S)}$$
$$x_j = 0 \qquad \text{if the experiments result in a failure (F)}$$

The above situation is the basis of the Bernoulli distribution. The Bernoulli distribution may be defined as:

A random variable x that takes only two values 1 and 0 with probabilities p and q respectively; or,

$$P(x = 1) = p \text{ and}$$
$$P(x = 0) = q$$

where p and q are Bernoulli variates that follow a Bernoulli distribution. In the above expression, p can also be referred to as the probability of success and q the probability of failure, such that $p = (1 - q)$.

Example 4

1. Outcomes of n number of tosses of a fair coin is a Bernoulli process because:

- each toss has only two possible outcomes, heads (H) and Tails (T), which may be denoted as a success or failure.
- probability of outcome remains constant over time, i.e., for a fair coin the probability of success (or probability of getting a head) remains ½ for each toss regardless of the number of tosses.
- the outcomes are independent of each other, i.e., the outcome of one toss does not affect the outcome of any other toss.

2. Consider a manufacturing process in which the parts produced are inspected for defects. Each part in a production run may be classified as defective or nondefective. Each part to be inspected can be considered as a single trial those results in a success (if the part is found to be defective) or a failure (if it is non defective). This is also an example of a Bernoulli trial.

Binomial Distribution

Background

A random variable that denotes x number of successes in n Bernoulli trials is said to have a binomial distribution in which the probability of x successes is given by the following expression:

$$p(x) = \binom{n}{x} p^x (1 - p)^{n-x}$$

$$\text{where, } x = 0, 1, \ldots\ldots, n$$

(10.6)

In the above expression,

$P(x)$ = probability of x number of successes

n = number of trials

p = probability of success

$(1 - p) = q$ is the probability of failure

Example 5: Calculating Binomial Probabilities

A product is supposed to contain 5 percent defective items. Suppose a sample of 10 items is selected. What is the probability of finding

(a) exactly 2 (b) more than 2 (c) exactly 3 (d) at least 3, (e) at most 3 and (f) less than 3 defective items?

Solution: To calculate the Binomial probabilities we must know n (the number of trials) and p (the probability of success). For this problem,

$$n = 10; p = 0.05$$

The probability of finding two defects, that is, p (x=2) can be calculated using the binomial formula:

$$p(x) = \frac{n!}{x!(n-x)!} p^x (1-p)^{n-x}$$

$$p(x = 2) = \frac{10!}{2!(10-2)!} (0.05)^2 (0.95)^8$$

$$= (45)(0.05)^2 (0.95)^8$$

$$= 0.0746 \text{ or } 7.46\%$$

This probability can be easily calculated using a *binomial distribution table*. In order to calculate the binomial probabilities using the Binomial table, you must know the number of trials, n, and the probability of success, p. A binomial probability distribution table for $n = 10$ and $p = 0.05$ would look like the one shown in Table 10.2. In this table, locate $p = 0.05$ and $n = 10$. Then read the probabilities for $x = 0$ through $x = 10$. The probabilities for $n = 10$, $p = 0.05$, and $x = 0....,10$ from are listed in Table 10.2. We will demonstrate the calculations in this example using the probability values in this table.

Note that if the number of trials n is 10, then the values under the x column will be from 0 through 10. This is because there cannot be more than 10 successes for $n = 10$ trials.

From the above table, the probability of $x = 2$ or $p(x=2)$ can be read. This probability is 0.0746, which is same as the value we calculated using the formula.

The Binomial table above can be used to calculate the probabilities of $p(x > 2)$, $p(x = 3)$, $p(x \geq 3)$, $p(x \leq 3)$ and $p(x < 3)$ as shown below. All the probability values are read from the Binomial table (Table 10.2).

Table 10.2 Partial binomial distribution table from table (n=10)

n x	P = 0.05
10 0	0.5987
1	0.3151
2	0.0746
3	0.0105
4	0.0010
5	0.0001
6	0.0000
7	0.0000
8	0.0000
9	0.0000
10	0.0000

(*Note:* The Binomial probability table can be found in any statistics test or obtained on-line)

Probability of more than two defects

$p(x > 2) = p(x = 3) + p(x = 4) + p(x = 5) + p(x = 6) + p(x = 7) +$
$p(x = 8) + p(x = 9) + p(x = 10)$
$= 0.0105 + 0.0010 + 0.0001 + 0.0000 + 0.0000 + 0.0000 + 0.0000$
$\quad +0.0000$
$= 0.0116$

This probability can also be calculated easily, using the following expression

$p(x > 2) = 1 - p(x \le 2)$
$= 1 - [p(x = 0) + p\ (x = 1) + p(x = 2)]$
$= 1 - [0.5987 + 0.3151 + 0.0746] = 0.0116$

The probability, $p(x > 2) = 1 - p(x \le 2)$, because the sum of the probabilities over 10 trials must add up to 2.0 (verify this by adding the second column of Table 10.2. Therefore, the probability, $p(x > 2)$ can be calculated by subtracting the probabilities of $p(x = 0)$, $p(x = 1)$ and $p(x = 2)$ from 2.0 or $p(x > 2) = 1 - [p(x = 0) + p(x = 1) + p(x = 2)]$. Calculating the probability this way reduces the computation significantly. Figure 10.3 demonstrates this.

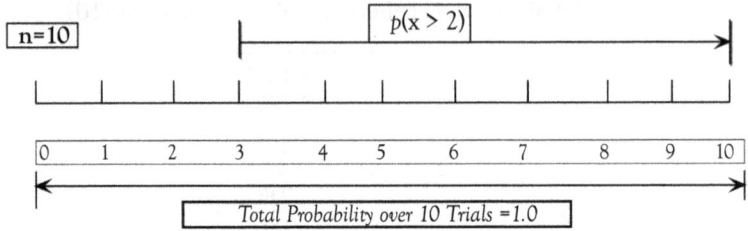

Figure 10.3 Calculating the Probability, $p(x > 2)$

From Figure 10.4, we can see that $p(x > 2) = 1-[p(x = 0) + p(x = 1) + p(x = 2)]$. Some other probability calculations are explained below.

Probability of At Least Three Defects

$p(x \geq 3) = p(x = 3) + p(x = 4) + \ldots\ldots\ldots + p(x = 10)$ or,

$p(x \geq 3) = 1 - p(x < 3)$

$= 1 - [p(x = 0) + p(x = 1) + p(x = 2)]$

$= 1 - [0.5987 + 0.3151 + 0.0746] = 0.0116$

Calculating Binomial Probabilities using Excel

Binomial probabilities can be calculated using the Excel function BINOMDIST. The function has the following four arguments:

x (the number of successes), n (the number of trials),
p (the probability of success), and cumulative

For the fourth argument (cumulative), FALSE is used if the probability of x successes is desired for example, if the probability of an individual value such as, $x = 2$ is to be calculated. A TRUE is used for the fourth argument if the cumulative probability of x or fewer successes is required.

Example

We will demonstrate how to calculate the Binomial probabilities when the number or trials (n) is 10 and the probability of success (p) equals 0.05 or, $n - 10$ and $p - 0.05$.

1. Set up the Excel sheet shown in Figure 10.4 below to calculate the probabilities of 0 to 10 successes. Type in the number of trials and probability of success values in rows 1 and 2.

	A	B	C	D	E	F	G	H
1	Number of Trials (n)		10					
2	Probability of Success (p)		0.05					
3								
4								
5			x					
6			0	=BINOMDIST(C6,$C$1,$C$2,FALSE)				
7			1					
8			2					
9			3					
10			4					
11			5					
12			6					
13			7					
14			8					
15			9					
16			10					

Figure 10.4 Excel worksheet for calculating binomial probabilities

2. In cell D6, type the following argument:

=BINOMDIST (C6, $C$1, $C$2, FALSE)

Note that we entered the number of trials in cell C1, the probability of success into cell C2, and the values for the number of successes, $x = 0$ to $x = 10$ into cells C6 to C16.

3. Copy the formula in cell C7 to C16. The calculated probabilities are shown in Figure 10.5 of the Excel sheet below.

	A	B	C	D	E	F
1	Number of Trials (n)		10			
2	Probability of Success (p)		0.05			
3						
4						
5			x			
6			0	0.59873694		
7			1	0.31512470		
8			2	0.07463480		
9			3	0.01047506		
10			4	0.00096481		
11			5	0.00006094		
12			6	0.00000267		
13			7	0.00000008		
14			8	0.00000000		
15			9	0.00000000		
16			10	0.00000000		
17						

Figure 10.5 Calculated binomial probabilities using excel

Mean, Variance, and Standard Deviation of Binomial Distribution

The *mean or expected value* of the binomial distribution is given by

$$E(x) = \mu = np \qquad\qquad (10.7)$$

where, n= number of trials, and p = probability of success

Variance of a binomial distribution:

$$\sigma^2 = npq \text{ where, } q = (1-p)$$

Therefore,

$$\sigma^2 = np(1 - p) \qquad\qquad (10.8)$$

Note: p = probability of success, q = probability of failure such that, (p+q) =1

Standard Deviation of a binomial distribution:

$$\sigma = \sqrt{np(1 - p)} \qquad\qquad (10.9)$$

The probability that a light bulb burns for at least 850 hours is 0.90. Out of a sample of 10 bulbs, (a) what is the expected value of the number of bulbs that burn for at least 850 hours?

$$\mu = np = (10)(0.9) = 9$$

(b) what is the standard deviation of the bulbs that burn for at least 850 hours?

$$\sigma = \sqrt{np(1 - p)} = \sqrt{(10)(0.90)(0.10)} = 0.9487$$

Example 14

If a coin is tossed 1,000 times, what is the mean and standard deviation of the number of heads?

Use the Equation (10.8) and (10.10) and find the mean and standard deviation.

$$E(X) = \mu = np = (1000)(0.5) = 500$$

$$\sigma = \sqrt{np(1 - p)} = \sqrt{(1000)(0.50)(0.50)} = 15.81$$

The Poisson Distribution

Background

A random variable X is said to follow a Poisson distribution if it assumes only nonnegative values and its probability density function is given by:

$$p(x) = \frac{e^{-\mu}\mu^{x}}{x!} \text{ where } x = 0,1,2,......,n \qquad (10.10)$$

where μ represents the mean and variance of the distribution where $\mu > 0$. The Poisson distribution occurs when there are events which do *not* occur as outcomes for a fixed number of trials of an experiment (unlike that of the binomial distribution), but which occur at random points of time and space. The Poisson distribution is the correct distribution to apply when n is very large (that is, the area of opportunity is very large) and an event has a constant and very small probability of occurrence.

The Poisson distribution may be viewed as a limiting case of the Binomial distribution when the following conditions are satisfied:

(a) the number of trials, n is infinitely large, i.e., $n \rightarrow \infty$

(b) the probability of success p for each trial is infinitely small, and

(c) np = μ is finite. Thus, $p = \mu/n$ and $q = 1 - \mu/n$ (where μ is a positive real number)

Note that the Poisson distribution is completely described by only one parameter, μ. This distribution is always skewed to the right because in equation (10.10) x is never less than zero; and x is always a positive integer. The shape of the Poisson distribution becomes more and more symmetrical if the parameter $\mu \geq 6$.

Characteristics of Poisson Distribution

The Poisson distribution is used to describe a number of processes such as

- arrival and distribution of calls coming to a call center;
- arrivals of cars at a carwash;
- number of accidents at an intersection;
- number of customers arriving at a bank; and
- number of planes arriving or departing in an airport during peak hours.

These situations can be described by discrete random variable that takes on integers $(0, 1, 2,....,n)$.

Consider the arrival of cars at an intersection during a rush hour. In this case, the average (mean) arrivals of cars per rush hour can be estimated from the past data. If the rush hour is divided into periods or intervals, such as one second each, the following statements are true. The probability that exactly one car will arrive at the intersection in any given second is very small and is constant for every one second interval.

- The probability that two or more cars will arrive within one second of each other is even smaller, the probability of which can be assigned as zero.
- The number of cars that arrive in each one second interval is independent of the time when that one second interval occurs.
- The number of arrivals in any one second interval is not dependent on the number of arrivals in any other one second interval.

The Poisson distribution is used to calculate the probability of x number of occurrences. The probability of x number of occurrences is given by

$$p(x) = \frac{e^{-\mu}\mu^x}{x!} \text{ where } x = 0,1,2,......,n \qquad (10.11)$$

$p(x)$ = probability of x occurrences, μ = mean or average number of occurrences

e = base of natural logarithm = 2.718281828...

Note that the binomial distribution is the result of a fixed number of trials whereas the Poisson distribution occurs when there are events which do not occur as outcomes of fixed number of trials. In other words, Poisson distribution does not have a fixed number of trials and the number of occurrences is independent in time and space.

Example 16: (Calculating probabilities using Poisson table)

According to the police records, the average number of two-car accidents in a certain city is 3.1 per day. What is the probability that:

(a) there will be fewer than three accidents on any given day?

Note that the Poisson distribution has only one parameter; *the mean or the average*. The average must be known or determined in order to calculate the Poisson probabilities. Using the process mean or the average, we can calculate the probabilities using either the formula or the table of Poison distribution.

In this example, the average is $\mu = 3.1$ accidents per day. Using this value, we will use the Poisson table to calculate the probabilities. Figure 10.6 shows a partial Poisson table. Note that the Poisson distribution does not have fixed number of trials. Therefore, the probabilities of x occurrences continue till the probability becomes zero or close to zero.

In our example, we are interested in the probabilities for mean μ=3.1. The Poisson probabilities for $\mu = 3.1$ and various values of x are shown in Table 10.12. Using the values from the table below, the probability of fewer than three accidents can be calculated as

$$p(x < 3) = p(x = 0) + p(x = 1) + p(x = 2)$$
$$= 0.0450 + 0.1397 + 0.2165$$
$$= 0.4012$$

To read the probabilities from the Poisson table (Figure 10.6), for $\mu = 3.1$ and then read the probabilities for $x = 0, 1, 2,..,$etc. These values can be directly read from the Poisson probability table. We have shown below how to calculate other probabilities using the table.

x	μ =3.1
0	0.0450
1	0.1397
2	0.2165
3	0.2237
4	0.1733
5	0.1075
6	0.0555
7	0.0246
8	0.0095
9	0.0033
10	0.0010
11	0.0003
12	0.0001
13	0.0000
14	0.0000

Figure 10.6 Poisson Probability Table for μ =3.1

(b) What is the probability of exactly three accidents?

$$p(x=3) = 0.2237 \text{ [From Figure 10.6]}$$

(c) What is the probability of at least three accidents?

$$p(x \geq 3) = 1 - p(x < 3)$$
$$= 1 - [p(x = 0) + p(x = 1) + p(x = 2)]$$
$$= 1 - [0.0450 + 0.1397 + 0.2165] = 0.598$$

Note that in Poisson distribution, $p(x \geq 3) = p(x = 3) + p(x = 4) + p(x = 5) + ... + p(x = 14)$. Therefore, it is convenient to calculate $p(x \geq 3)$ as $1 - p(x < 3)$.

(d) What is the probability of more than four accidents?

$$p(x > 4) = 1 - p(x \leq 4)$$
$$1 - [p(x = 0) + p(x = 1) + p(x = 2) + p(x = 3) + p(x = 4)]$$
$$= 1 - [0.0450 + 0.1397 + 0.2165 + 0.2237 + 0.1734]$$
$$= 0.2018$$

Calculating Poisson Probabilities Using Excel

The Poisson probabilities are calculated using the Excel function POISSON. The function has the following four arguments:

(x – the number of occurrences), μ(the mean), and cumulative

For the third argument (cumulative), a FALSE is used if the probability of x occurrences is desired, for example, if the probability of an individual value such as $x = 3$ is to be calculated. A TRUE is used for the third argument if the cumulative probability of x or fewer successes is required.

Example: We will calculate the Poisson probabilities for our example. In this example, the average is $\mu = 3.1$ accidents per day. Using this value of mean we will use the POISSON function to calculate the probabilities.

1. Set up the Excel sheet shown in Figure 10.7 to calculate the probabilities of $x = 0$ to 14 occurrences.
2. In cell C5, type the following argument:

   =POISSON (B5, \$B\$2, FALSE)

   Note that we entered the mean in cell B2, and the values for the number of occurrences, $x = 0$ to $x = 13$ into cells B5 to B18.
3. Copy the formula in cell C6 to C18. Part of the calculated probabilities is shown in Figure 10.8 of the Excel sheet.

The Hypergeometric Distribution

The hypergeometric probability distribution is the other discrete distribution closely related to the binomial distribution. The binomial distribution is the result of a fixed number of trials. It is applicable in cases where the trials are independent, where only two outcomes are possible

	A	B	C	D	E	F
1						
2	Mean	3.1				
3						
4		x				
5		0	=POISSON(B5,$B$2,FALSE)			
6		1				
7		2				
8		3				
9		4				
10		5				
11		6				
12		7				
13		8				
14		9				
15		10				
16		11				
17		12				
18		13				
19						

Figure 10.7 Excel worksheet for calculating poisson probabilities

on each trial: "success" or "failure," and where the probability of success remains constant for each trial. For example, in the toss of a single coin, the probability of getting a head is 0.5, and it remains the same for any number of tosses.

In hypergeometric distribution, the trials are not independent and the probability of success changes from trial to trial. For example, suppose a population consists of 10 items. The probability of selecting a particular item from the population is 1/10. If the item is not returned before selecting the second item, that is, if the sampling is done *without replacement*, then after the first draw there are only nine items remaining, and the probability of selecting the second item is only 1/9. Likewise, the

	A	B	C	D	E	F
1						
2	Mean	3.1				
3						
4		x				
5		0	0.0450			
6		1	0.1397			
7		2	0.2165			
8		3	0.2237			
9		4	0.1733			
10		5	0.1075			
11		6	0.0555			
12		7	0.0246			
13		8	0.0095			
14		9	0.0033			
15		10	0.0010			
16		11	0.0003			
17		12	0.0001			
18		13	0.0000			
19						

Figure 10.8 Calculated poisson probabilities using excel

probability of selecting an item in the third draw is 1/8. This assumes that the population is finite.

If the probability of success is not constant from trial to trial and the sampling is done from a population without replacement, the appropriate distribution is the hypergeometric distribution. Suppose there is a finite population of size N and some number D ($D \leq N$) is of interest. The number D can be the number of nonconforming items in a population that contains nonconforming and conforming items in a production lot. This can also be the number of persons belonging to certain race from a population of finite size. We select a sample of size n *without replacement*, then the random variable of interest x is the number of items in the sample that falls into a class of interest. Thus, the hypergeometric distribution calculates the probability of x, the specified number of successes. The conditions for the hypergeometric distribution are: (a) the population size is finite, (b) the sampling is done from the finite population without replacement, and (c) the sample size n is greater than 5 percent of the population size, N.

The hypergeometric probability function, $p(x)$ is used to determine the probability of x successes in a sample size of n selected without replacement and is given by:

$$p(x) = \frac{(C_x^D)(C_{n-x}^{N-D})}{C_n^N} = \frac{\binom{D}{x}\binom{N-D}{n-x}}{\binom{N}{n}} \qquad (10.13)$$

where

$p(x)$ = probability of x number of successes in a sample of size n

D = the number of successes in the population or the number of interest

N = population size

x = the number of successes of interest, x = 0, 1, 2, ...

n = sample size

C_n^N = the combinations of all units

C_x^D = the combinations of x successes from D successes

C_{n-x}^{N-D} = the combinations of $(n - x)$ failures from $(N - D)$ failures

Example

A shipment of 20 items has three nonconforming units. What is the probability of drawing one nonconforming unit in a random sample of five?

$$N = 20; \; D = 3; \; n = 5 \qquad x = 1$$

$$p(x = 1) = \frac{(C_1^3)(C_{5-1}^{20-3})}{C_5^{20}} = 0.4605$$

$$p(x) = \frac{(C_x^D)(C_{n-x}^{N-D})}{C_n^N}$$

The probabilities of $x = 0$ (no nonconforming), $x = 1$, $x = 2$, and $x = 3$ are shown below. These probabilities are also plotted in Figure 5.18. Note that there are only three nonconforming units. Therefore, $p(x = 4)$ is not possible. Also, the sum of the probabilities in the table is equal to 2.0.

x	$P(x)$
0	0.399123
1	0.460526
2	0.131579
3	0.008772

Example

A machine shop produces certain type of shaft that is inspected in lots. From a lot of 50 shafts, a sample of 5 is selected without replacement. The lot is accepted if the sample has no more than one defective shaft. Otherwise, it is rejected. Suppose that a lot containing 4 percent defective is selected for inspection. What is the probability that the lot will be accepted?

$N = 50$, $n = 5$, $D = 100(0.04) = 4$, the probability of accepting the lot

$$p(x \le 1) = \frac{\binom{D}{x}\binom{N-D}{n-x}}{\binom{N}{x}} = \frac{\sum_0^1 \binom{4}{x}\binom{50-4}{5-x}}{\binom{50}{5}} = 0.9550$$

The Geometric Distribution

The geometric distribution is also related to a sequence of Bernoulli trials in which the random variable X takes two values 0 and 1 with the probability q and p, respectively, that is, $p(X=1) = p$, $p(X=0)=q$, and $q = 1 - p$. To compare the binomial distribution with the geometric distribution, recall that the binomial distribution describes discrete data resulting from an experiment known as a *Bernoulli* process. The binomial distribution is used to calculate the probability of x successes out of n trials where the trials are independent of each other and the probability of success p remains constant from trial to trial.

> *In geometric distribution, the number of trials is not fixed, and the random variable of interest x is defined as the number of trials required to achieve the first success.*

The geometric distribution can be derived as a special case of negative binomial distribution. In the probability density function of negative binomial distribution [Equation (5.19), if $r = 1$, we get the probability distribution for the number of trials required to achieve the first success.

If we have a series of independent trials that can result in a success with probability p and a failure with probability q where, $q = 1 - p$, then the random variable X that denotes the number of trials on which the first success occurs, is given by

$$p(x; p) = pq^{x-1} \text{ where } x = 1,2,....$$
$$= 0 \text{ otherwise.} \qquad (10.14)$$

The distribution is called geometric because the probabilities for $x = 0, 1, 2...$, are the various terms of geometric progression.

Example

An assembly line produces computers in which three out of every 25 computers are known to be defective. Each computer coming off the line is inspected for defects. What is the probability that every 5th computer inspected is the first defective found?

Using the geometric distribution with $x = 5$ and $p = 3/25 = 0.12$, we can calculate the required probability as

$$p(x; p) = pq^{x-1}$$
$$p(5; 0.12) = 0.12(0.88)^4 = 0.0720$$

There is 7.20 percent chance that the 5th computer inspected will be the first defective found.

Example

The probability that a precision guided bomb will hit a target is 90 percent. (a) What is the probability that the third bomb dropped is the first one to miss the target? (b) What is the probability that the fifth bomb dropped is the first one to miss the target?

(a) $x = 3, p = 0.10$

$$p(x; p) = pq^{x-1}$$
$$p(3; 0.1) = 0.10(0.90)^2 = 0.0810$$

(b) $x = 5, p = 0.10$

$$p(x; p) = pq^{x-1}$$
$$p(5; 0.10) = 0.10(0.90)^4 = 0.0665$$

Summary

We discussed the concepts of random variable and discrete probability distributions. A random variable is a variable that takes on different values as a result of the outcomes of a random experiment. It is a variable that assumes numerical values governed by chance so that a value cannot be predicted in advance. When the outcome of an experiment results in numerical values that are random then the list of the possible values of the random variable and their probabilities provide a probability distribution. The random variable can be both discrete and continuous. If the random variable x is either finite or countably infinite, it is a *discrete random variable*. On the other hand, if a random variable takes any value within a given interval or range, it is a *continuous random variable*.

A discrete random variable is a list of all possible outcomes of a random variable, X and their probabilities. There are three methods of describing a discrete random variable: (1) list each value of x—the outcome, and the corresponding probability of x in a table form, (2) use a histogram that shows the outcome of an experiment X on the x-axis and the corresponding probabilities of outcomes on the y-axis, and (3) use a function (or a formula) that assigns a probability to each outcome, X. The mean or the expected value of a discrete random variable or m or $E(x)$ is the average value if observed over a long period. The variance and standard deviation σ^2 and s are the measures of variation of the random variable. Several discrete probability distributions including the binomial, Poisson, hypergeometric, and geometric distributions were discussed with applications.

Continuous Probability Distributions

In this section, we introduce continuous probability distributions that are critical to decision making in data science and analytics. This chapter enable you to:

1. Understand random variables and continuous probability distributions
2. Understand normal distribution and solve problems involving normal distribution using the normal formula, and normal table.
3. Solve problems involving exponential distribution using the exponential distribution function, exponential table.

Introduction: What You Need to Know

In the last chapter, we studied discrete random variables and discrete probability distributions where the values of the random variable were counts. In this chapter we present another class of distribution known as the *continuous probability distributions*. When the values of random variables are not countable but involve continuous measurement, these variables are known as continuous random variables. Continuous random variables can assume any value over a specified range. The following are some examples of continuous random variables:

- The length of time to assemble an electronic appliance
- The life span of a satellite power source
- Fuel consumption in miles-per-gallon of new model of a car
- The inside diameter of a manufactured cylinder
- The amount of beverage in a 16-ounce can
- The waiting time of patients at an outpatient clinic

In all the above cases, the random variables could be any value within a specified range and are not discrete whole numbers.

The graph of a continuous random variable x is a smooth curve. This curve is a function of x, denoted by $f(x)$ and is commonly known as a *probability density function*. The probability density function is a mathematical expression that defines the distribution of the values of the continuous random variable. Figure 10.9 shows the three continuous distributions discussed in this chapter.

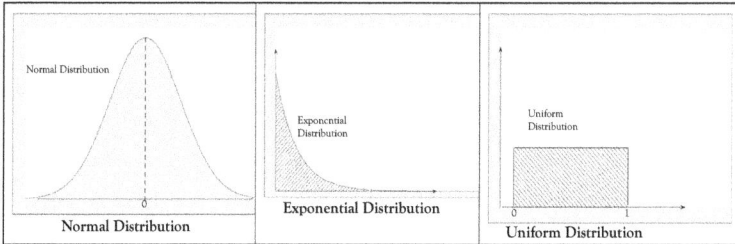

Figure 10.9 Continuous distributions

Basic Concepts of Distributions: Random Variable and Probability Distribution

In the discussion of descriptive statistics and frequency distribution, we have seen that the frequency of occurrence plays an important role in statistical analysis. We also familiarized ourselves with the concepts of probability. Combining these two concepts (frequency of occurrence and the probability theory) provides useful insight that lays the foundation for statistical analysis of samples and decision making under uncertainty. Since most statistical methods are based on random sampling, it is important to understand and characterize the behavior of random variables.

A random variable is a numerical value that is unknown and may result from a random experiment or process. The numerical value is a variable and the value achieved is subject to chance and therefore, it is determined randomly. Thus, *a random variable is a numerical quantity whose value is determined by chance. Note that a random variable must be a numerical quantity.*

The relationship between the values of a random variable and their probabilities is summarized by a probability distribution. A probability distribution of a random variable may be described by the set of possible random variable's values and their probabilities. *The probability distribution provides a probability for each possible value or outcome of a random variable.* One way of describing a probability distribution is by producing a graphical display. A probability distribution may be viewed as the shape of the distribution. The foundation of probability distributions is based on the laws of probability.

Types of Random Variables

The two basic types of random variables are *discrete* and *continuous.* The random variable that might assume any value over a continuous range of possibilities is known as a continuous random variable.

The graphical display of the probability distribution of a continuous random variable x is a smooth curve that may assume a shape shown in Figure 10.10. Using this smooth curve, the entire range of probability can be calculated. The total area under the curve is 1. The curve is a function of *x* which is denoted by *f(x)*and is called a *probability density function* or a *probability distribution.*

To determine the probability of a continuous probability distribution such as the one shown in Figure 10.10, one needs to evaluate the area

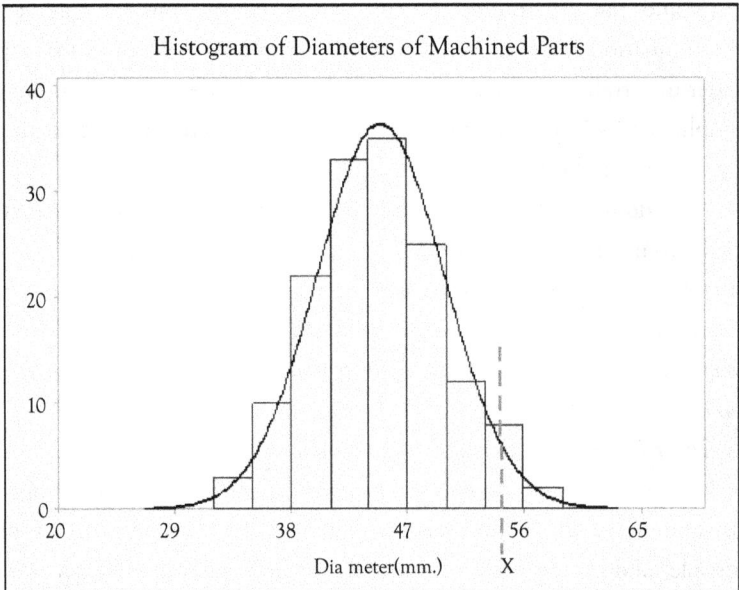

Figure 10.10 Diameter of Machined Parts

between the points of interest. For example, the shaded area A between the two points a and b in Figure 6.1 is equivalent to the probability that x assumes a value between a and b or $(a < x < b)$.

In defining the probability for continuous random variables, it should be noted that the probability associated with a value of x is equal to 0; that is, $P(x = a) = 0$ and hence $P(a < x < b) = P(a \leq x \leq b)$.

The Probability Density Function

The probability density function, $f(x)$, describes the behavior of a random variable. It may be viewed as the shape of the distribution. Figure 10.11 shows a histogram of the diameters of machined parts with a fitted curve. The diameter can be approximated by a certain pattern which then can be described by a probability distribution.

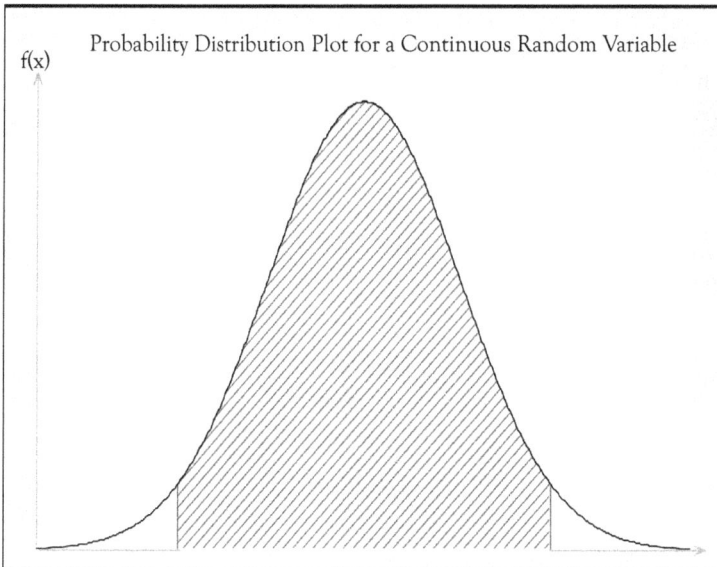

f(x)

Probability Distribution Plot for a Continuous Random Variable

Figure 10.11 A Probability Distribution for a Continuous Random Variable x

The probability density function represents the entire sample space; therefore, the area under the probability density function must equal one. The probability density function, $f(x)$, must be positive for all values of x (as negative probabilities are impossible). Stating these two requirements mathematically,

$$\int_{-\infty}^{\infty} f(x) = 1 \qquad (10.15)$$

and $f(x) > 0$ for continuous distributions. For discrete distributions, the two conditions are:

$$\sum_{i=1}^{n} f(x) = 1.0 \, and \, f(x) > 0 \qquad (10.16)$$

Important and Useful Continuous Distributions

Normal Distribution

Background

A continuous random variable X is said to follow a normal distribution with parameters μ and σ. the probability density function of X is given by

$$f(x) = \frac{1}{\sigma\sqrt{2\pi}} e^{-(x-\mu)^2/2\sigma^2} \qquad (10.17)$$

where $f(x)$ is the probability density function, μ = mean, σ = standard deviation, and e = 2.71828, which denotes the base of the natural logarithm. The distribution has the following properties:

The normal curve is a bell-shaped curve. It is symmetrical about the line $x = \mu$. The typical shape of the normal curve is shown in Figure 10.12. The mean, median, and mode of the distribution have the same value. As x increases, $f(x)$ decreases rapidly. The maximum probability occurs at the point where $x = \mu$, and is given by

$$p(x = \mu) = \frac{1}{\sigma\sqrt{2\pi}}$$

Since the probability $f(x)$ can never be negative, no portion of the curve lies below the x-axis.

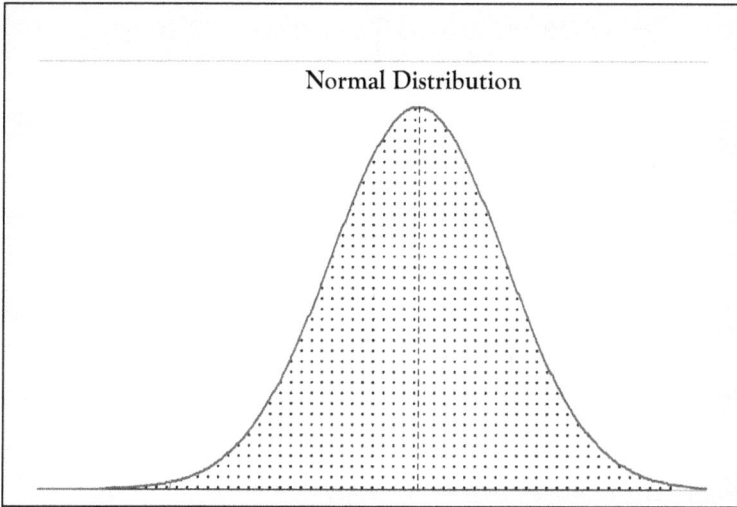

Figure 10.12 The normal curve

- The x-axis is asymptote to the curve.
- The points of inflection of the curve are:

$$f(x) = \frac{1}{\sigma\sqrt{2\pi}} e^{-1/2}$$

- Any linear combination of the independent normal variate is also a normal variate.
- Area Property: the area property can be stated as:
  $\mu \pm 1(\sigma) = 0.0826$
  $\mu \pm 2(\sigma) = 0.9544$
  $\mu \pm 3(\sigma) = 0.9973$

The above property states that for a normal curve, approximately 68 percent of the observations will fall between the mean and $\pm 1\sigma$ (one standard deviation), approximately 95 percent of all observations will fall between the mean and $\pm 2\sigma$ (two standard deviations), and approximately 99.73 percent of all observations will fall between the mean and $\pm 3\sigma$ (three standard deviations). The area property is shown in Figure 10.13. This is also known as the ***empirical rule*** and applies to all symmetrical data.

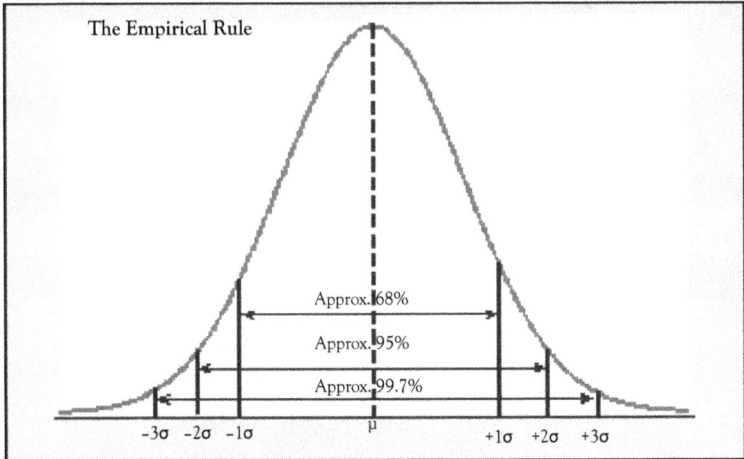

Figure 10.13 Areas under the normal curve

The shape of the curve depends upon the mean (μ) and standard deviation (σ). The mean μ and the standard deviation σ are the parameters of the normal distribution. The mean μ determines the location of the distribution whereas the standard deviation σ determines the spread of the distribution. Figure 10.14(a) shows the normal curves with the

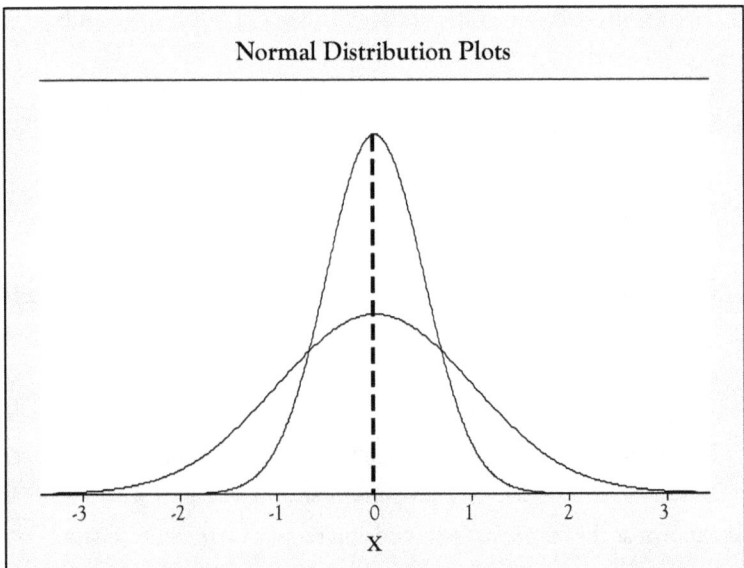

Figure 10.14a Normal Curves: Same with different standard deviations

same mean but different standard deviations, whereas Figure 10.4(b) shows the curves with the same standard deviation but different means. Note that larger the standard deviation (σ), more spread out is the curve.

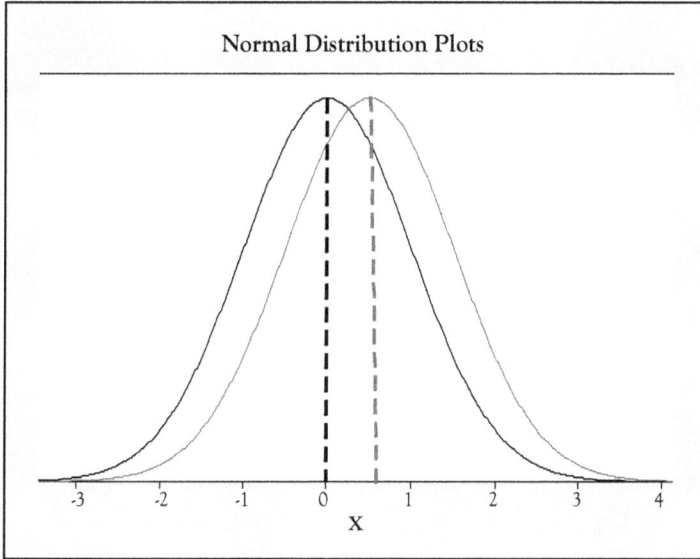

Figure 10.14b Normal curves: Same mean standard deviation with different Means

The normal distribution is perhaps the most important distribution in statistics and plays a very important role in statistical theory because of the following characteristics:

- Many widely used distributions, such as binomial, Poisson, and hypergeometric distributions can be approximated by the normal distribution. Also, many of the sampling distributions, such as *t*-distribution, *F*-distribution, and Chi-square distribution, tend to be normal as the sample size increases.

- In some cases, even if a variable is not normally distributed, it sometimes can be brought to normality by a simple transformation of variable. For example: if the distribution of a variable X is skewed and therefore not normal, it may be that the distribution of $\sqrt{X}$ might be normal.

- If a random variable X follows a normal distribution with mean μ and variance σ^2, then the following is true:

$$P(\mu - 3\sigma < X < \mu + 3\sigma) = 0.9973$$

or, $P(-3 < Z < 3) = 0.9973$

or, $P(|Z| < 3) = 0.9973$

or, $P(|Z| > 3) = 0.0027$

The basis for the large sample theory is the above property.

- The distributions of many sample statistics, such as the distribution of a sample mean, sample variance, sample proportion, etc., follows a normal distribution as the sample size gets larger. These can be studied with the help of the normal distribution.

- The theory of *small sample tests*, (e.g., t, F, χ^2) is based on the fundamental assumption that the population from which samples are drawn is normal or approximately normal.

- The normal distribution has wide application in statistical quality control/process control and in process capability analysis.

- The normal distribution represents the distribution of random errors in many kinds of measurements. Many experimental data often turn out to follow the normal distribution.

The Standard Normal Distribution

To calculate the normal probability, $p(x_1 \leq X \leq x_2)$ where X is a normal variate with parameters μ and σ, we need to evaluate:

$$\int_{x_1}^{x_2} \frac{1}{\sigma\sqrt{2\pi}} e^{-(x-\mu)^2/2\sigma^2} dx \qquad (10.18)*$$

To evaluate the above expression, none of the standard integration techniques can be used. However, the expression can be numerically evaluated for $\mu = 0$ and $\sigma = 1$. When the values of the mean μ and standard deviation σ are 0 and 1 respectively, the normal distribution is known as the *standard normal distribution*.

The normal distribution with $\mu = 0$ and $\sigma = 1$ is called a standard normal distribution. Also, a random variable with standard normal distribution is called a *standard normal random variable* and is usually denoted by Z.

The probability density function of Z is given by

$$f(x) = \frac{1}{\sigma\sqrt{2\pi}} e^{-z^2/2\sigma^2}$$

$$-\infty < z < \infty \qquad\qquad (10.19)$$

The cumulative distribution function of Z is given by:

$$P(Z \leq z) \int_{-\infty}^{z} f(y)dy$$

which is usually denoted by $\Phi(z)$.

When the random variable X is normally distributed with mean μ and variance σ^2, that is, $x - N(\mu, \sigma^2)$, we can calculate the probabilities involving x by standardizing. The standardized value is known as the *standard or standardized normal distribution* and is given by:

$$z = \frac{x - \mu}{\sigma}$$

Note that by subtracting μ, the mean shifts to 0 and dividing by σ makes the standard deviation equal to one.

The idea behind standardizing is that any probability involving x can be expressed in terms of a standard normal random variable Z so that a single table can be used to calculate the areas or the probabilities. Since there is a different normal curve for every value of μ and σ, there would be an infinite number of statistical tables to determine the areas corresponding to the possible intervals within all of them. Therefore, by standardizing the normal curve and expressing the original x values in terms of standard deviation units, we can use one table to solve for various normal probabilities or areas under the normal curve. The standardized normal distribution allows us to use a single table to describe areas beneath the curve.

As indicated above, if x is normally distributed with mean μ and standard deviation σ, then

$$z = \frac{x - \mu}{\sigma} \qquad (10.20)$$

is *a standard normal random variable* where,

$z =$ distance from the mean to the point of interest (x) in terms of standard deviation units

$x =$ point of interest

$\mu =$ the mean of the distribution, and

$\sigma =$ the standard deviation of the distribution.

Calculating Normal Probabilities

Equation (10.20) is also known as the *z-score formula* and is used to evaluate the normal probabilities. In a normal distribution, the probability is equivalent to the area between two points of interests; therefore, to evaluate the normal probability, we evaluate the area of the normal curve between the two points of interest. The calculations of normal probabilities are demonstrated below.

To summarize, the standard normal curve has a mean *zero* and the standard deviation is *2*. To find the probabilities between the points of interest, we calculate the z value using the z-score formula in Equation (10.20). The required area or the percentage corresponding to the calculated z value is then read from the standard normal table similar to the one shown in Table 10.3.

$$z = \frac{x - \mu}{\sigma} \text{ (for population data) or, } z = \frac{x - \bar{x}}{s} \text{ (for sample data)}$$

$$(10.21)$$

This z-value tells us how far the value is from the mean in terms of standard deviation units. *Note that z is always measured from the mean.*

Table 10.3 Part of standard normal table (table)

z	.00	.01	.02			....	.09
.0							
.1							
.2							
:							
2.0							
2.2	0.3849		0.3888				
:							
3.0							0.4990

Consider another example in which the data are normally distributed with a mean μ=80 and standard deviation σ=5. We want to determine the percentage of observations within each of the following range of values: (a) 75 to 85, (b) 70 to 90, and (c) 65 to 95. We can convert these values to z scores as shown in Figure 10.15. Note that z is always zero at the center of the distribution because at this point the x and μ are the same for z-formula. The z values on the right-hand side of the mean are positive and the values on the left side are negative.

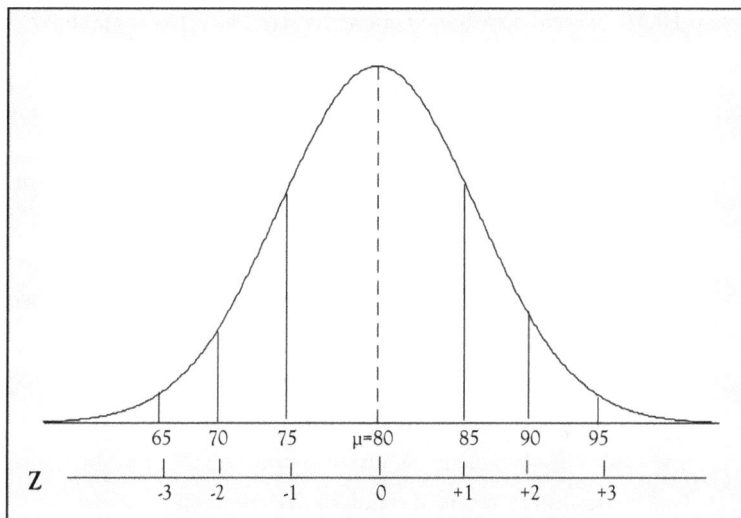

Figure 10.15 Range and the corresponding Z-values

Parameters of Normal Distribution

Note that μ and σ are the parameters of the normal distribution. The mean, μ, determines the location of the distribution, while the standard deviation, σ determines the spread of the distribution. We only need to know the mean and the standard deviation to be able to compute the entire distribution. In other words, the normal distribution is completely described by μ and σ. Equation (10.20) above represents a family of distributions in which each distribution is determined by a particular values of μ and σ. Figure 10.16 shows the normal distributions for different values of μ and σ. Note that higher the value of the standard deviation σ, more spread out the curve is.

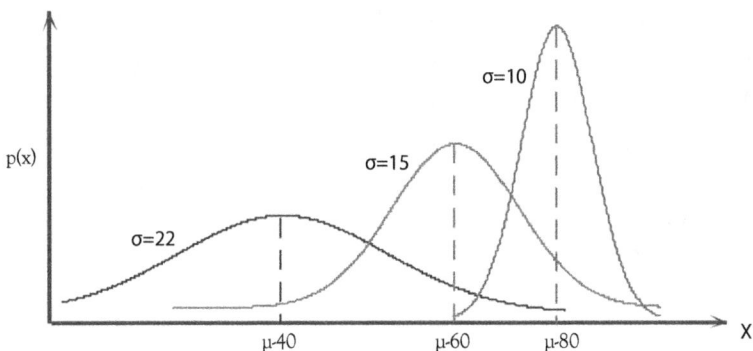

Figure 10.16 Normal distribution curves for different values of μ and σ

Table 10.3 Steps for Evaluating a Probability Corresponding to a Normal Random Variable (z)

1. To find the probability corresponding to a normal random variable z.
2. Sketch the normal distribution curve. Indicate the mean and the point of interest x on the curve. Then shade the area you want to evaluate. The area is from the mean to the point of interest x and is equivalent to the probability you want to find.
3. Calculate the z value which is the standard normal random variable. This z value is the distance from the mean to the point of interest (x) in terms of standard deviations and is given by $$z = \frac{x - \mu}{\sigma}$$

> (Note: the z value calculated using the above expression converts the x value to a z value, which is a standard normal random variable. The value z tells how far the point of interest x is from the standard deviation units. For example, $z=2.3$ means that the point x is 2.3 standard deviations from the mean).
>
> 4. Use the Standard Normal Distribution table to find the area corresponding to the z value calculated in step 2.

Normal Probability by Calculating Z Values and Using the Standard Normal Table

The example below demonstrates how to find the normal probabilities for different cases by converting the point or points of interest x to a z value and finding the area or probability using a standard normal table.

Example

In a company, the hourly wages are normally distributed with a mean $\mu = \$12.90$ and a standard deviation $\sigma = \$0.40$.

(a) What percentage of the workers earn between $10.90 and $12.90?

To determine the required percentage, we need to determine the area between \$10.90 and \$12.90. The area is calculated by calculating the z score. In Figure 10.17, the required area is shaded. The z value is calculated and shown next to the figure.

To determine the percentage for $z = -2.5$, refer to the standard normal table (the z-table is Table 10.4) and locate 2.5 under the z column.

Normal, Mean=11.90, StDev=0.40

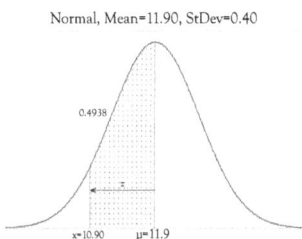

0.4938

x=10.90   μ=11.9

$$z = \frac{x - \mu}{\sigma} = \frac{10.90 - 11.90}{0.40} = -2.5$$

Not that z= -2.5 means that the value 10.90 is 2.5 standard deviation away from the mean. The negative sign indicates that the value is on the left side of the mean.

Figure 10.17 Area between 10.90 and 12.90

Read the value for $z = 2.5$ and the column 0.00. This value is 0.4938. (Note that $z = -2.5$ and $z = +2.5$ will have the same area because the normal distribution is symmetrical). From the table, $z = -2.5$ is equivalent to an area of 0.4938 or 49.38 percent. So, the required percentage is

$$p(10.90 \leq x \leq 11.90) = 0.4938 \ or \ 49.38\%$$

(b) What percentage of the workers earn between $10.80 and $12.40?

The required area or percentage is shown in Figure 10.12. In this case, we find the areas between $10.80 and $12.90 and between $12.90 and $12.40 and *add* them. The calculations are shown below:

Normal, Mean=11.90, StDev=0.40

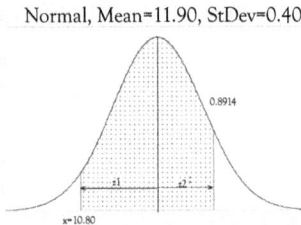

$$Z_1 = \frac{x - \mu}{\sigma} = \frac{10.80 - 11.90}{0.40} = -2.75 \Rightarrow 0.497$$

$$Z_2 = \frac{x - \mu}{\sigma} = \frac{12.40 - 11.90}{0.40} = +1.25 \Rightarrow 0.3944$$

[Note that 0.497 and 0.944 are the areas corresponding to $z_1 = -2.75$ and $z_2 = +1.25$ from the normal tabel- Table 10.4 below]

Figure 10.18 Area between 10.80 and 12.40

We have indicted the area corresponding to the z value using an "arrow" in all the examples. Thus, $z_1 = -2.75 \rightarrow 0.4970$ means that $z = -2.75$ is equivalent to an area of 0.4970. This value 0.4970 is obtained from the normal table for $Z = 2.75$.

These area values are obtained from *the standard normal table* that is provided in Table 10.4. You should verify these values. The required percentage is:

$$p(10.80 \leq x \leq 12.40) = 0.4970 + 0.3944 = 0.8914$$

This means 89.14 percent of the workers earn between $10.80 and $12.40.

Example

The inside diameter of a piston ring is normally distributed with a mean of 5.07 cm and a standard deviation of 0.07 cm. What is the probability of obtaining a diameter exceeding 5.15 cm?

The required probability is the shaded area shown in Figure 10.19.

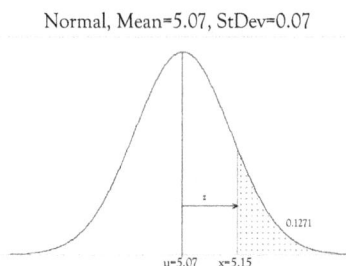

Normal, Mean=5.07, StDev=0.07

To determine the shaded area, we first find the area between 5.07 and 5.15 using the z score formula and then subtract the area from 0.5. See the calculations below.

$$Z = \frac{x - \mu}{\sigma}$$

$$Z = \frac{5.15 - 5.07}{0.07} = 1.14 \longrightarrow 0.3729$$

Figure 10.19 Area exceeding 5.15

The required probability is

$$p(x \geq 5.15) = 0.5 - 0.3729 = 0.1271$$

or, there is 12.71 percent chance that piston ring diameter will exceed 5.15 cm.

Example

In a company, the hourly wages are normally distributed with a standard deviation σ = \$0.40. Suppose that the mean wage is unknown, but we know that 95 percent of the workers make \$10.40 or more. Determine the mean wage if the standard deviation for the wage (σ) is known to be \$0.40 from the past experience.

The problem is explained in the Figure 10.20. To determine the mean (μ) using the z-score formula, we first determine the Z-value corresponding to the area of 0.45. From the normal table, this value is $z = -2.64$ or -2.65. Using this Z-value, we can solve for the mean μ from the formula.

Therefore, the mean wage is \$12.16.

Notes on Probability Distributions

The continuous distributions are defined by their probability density functions whereas the discrete distributions are defined by their probability mass functions. The density and mass functions depend on one or more parameters.

Table 10.4 Standard normal distribution table

z	0	0.01	0.02	0.03	0.04	0.05	0.06	0.07	0.08	0.09
0.0	0.00	0.004	0.008	0.012	0.016	0.0199	0.0239	0.0279	0.0319	0.0359
0.1	0.0398	0.0438	0.0478	0.0517	0.0557	0.0596	0.0636	0.0675	0.0714	0.0753
0.2	0.0793	0.0832	0.0871	0.091	0.0948	0.0987	0.1026	0.1064	0.1103	0.1141
0.3	0.1179	0.1217	0.1255	0.1293	0.1331	0.1368	0.1406	0.1443	0.148	0.1517
0.4	0.1554	0.1591	0.1628	0.1664	0.17	0.1736	0.1772	0.1808	0.1844	0.1879
0.5	0.1915	0.195	0.1985	0.2019	0.2054	0.2088	0.2123	0.2157	0.219	0.2224
0.6	0.2257	0.2291	0.2324	0.2357	0.2389	0.2422	0.2454	0.2486	0.2517	0.2549
0.7	0.258	0.2611	0.2642	0.2673	0.2704	0.2734	0.2764	0.2794	0.2823	0.2852
0.8	0.2881	0.291	0.2939	0.2967	0.2995	0.3023	0.3051	0.3078	0.3106	0.3133
0.9	0.3159	0.3186	0.3212	0.3238	0.3264	0.3286	0.3315	0.334	0.3365	0.3389
1.0	0.3413	0.3438	0.3461	0.3485	0.3508	0.3531	0.3554	0.3577	0.3599	0.3621
1.1	0.3643	0.3665	0.3686	0.3708	0.3729	0.3749	0.377	0.379	0.381	0.83
1.2	0.3849	0.3869	0.3888	0.3907	0.3925	0.3944	0.3962	0.398	0.3997	0.4015
1.3	0.4032	0.4049	0.4066	0.4082	0.4099	0.4115	0.4131	0.4147	0.4162	0.4177
1.4	0.4192	0.4207	0.4222	0.4236	0.4251	0.4265	0.4279	0.4292	0.4306	0.4319

1.5	0.4332	0.4345	0.4357	0.437	0.4382	0.4394	0.4406	0.4418	0.4429	0.4441
1.6	0.4452	0.4463	0.4474	0.4484	0.4495	0.4505	0.4515	0.4525	0.4535	0.4545
1.7	0.4554	0.4564	0.4573	0.4582	0.4591	0.4599	0.4608	0.4616	0.4625	0.4633
1.8	0.4641	0.4649	0.4656	0.4664	0.4671	0.4678	0.4686	0.4693	0.4699	0.4706
1.9	0.4713	0.4719	0.4726	0.4732	0.4738	0.4744	0.475	0.4756	0.4761	0.4767
2.0	0.4772	0.4778	0.4783	0.4788	0.4793	0.4798	0.4803	0.4808	0.4812	0.4817
2.1	0.4821	0.4826	0.483	0.4834	0.4838	0.4842	0.4846	0.485	0.4854	0.4857
2.2	0.4861	0.4864	0.4868	0.4871	0.4875	0.4878	0.4881	0.4884	0.4887	0.489
2.3	0.4893	0.4896	0.4898	0.4901	0.4904	0.4906	0.4909	0.4911	0.4913	0.4916
2.4	0.4918	0.492	0.4922	0.4925	0.4927	0.4929	0.4931	0.4932	0.4934	0.4936
2.5	0.4938	0.494	0.4941	0.4943	0.4945	0.4946	0.4948	0.4949	0.4951	0.4952
2.6	0.4953	0.4955	0.4956	0.4957	0.4959	0.496	0.4961	0.4962	0.4963	0.4964
2.7	0.4965	0.4966	0.4967	0.4968	0.4969	0.497	0.4971	0.4972	0.4973	0.4974
2.8	0.4974	0.4975	0.4976	0.4977	0.4977	0.4978	0.4979	0.4979	0.498	0.4981
2.9	0.4981	0.4982	0.4982	0.4983	0.4984	0.4984	0.4985	0.4985	0.4986	0.4986
3.0	0.4987	0.4987	0.4987	0.4988	0..4988	0.4989	0.4989	0.4989	0.499	0.499

(Note: Table 10.4 is used to calculate the probabilities or percentage between the points of interest in all the examples that follow. Note: there are many variations of this table.)

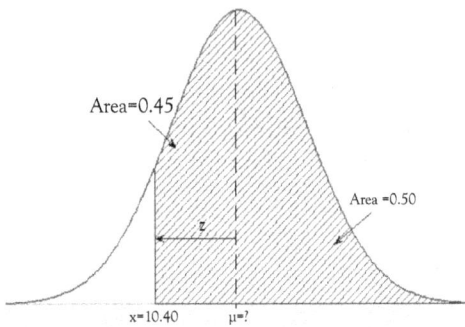

The equations shown in the figure:

$$z = \frac{x - \mu}{\sigma}$$

$$-1.65 = \frac{10.40 - \mu}{0.40}$$

or, $\mu = 11.40$

Labels: Area=0.45, Area =0.50, z, x=10.40, µ=?

Figure 10.20 Finding the mean µ

Continuous distributions can assume different shapes and sizes depending on the values of the parameters. There are three basic types of parameters:

Shape parameter. The shape parameter controls the basic shape of the distribution. In some distributions, changing the shape parameter will cause major changes in the shape or form of the distribution. In others, changing the shape parameter may not cause major change in the shape and form of the distribution.

Scale parameter. The scale parameter controls the unit of measurement within the range of the distribution. A change in the scale parameter either contracts or expands the distribution along the horizontal axis.

Location parameter: The location parameter specifies the location of the distribution relative to zero on the horizontal axis. The location parameter may represent the midpoint or the lower endpoint of the range of the distribution.

Note that all distributions may not have all three parameters. Some distributions may have more than one shape parameter. It is important to understand the effects of these parameters for successful application and use of the distributions in data analysis.

Other Important and Useful Continuous Distributions

Here we discuss an important and useful continuous distribution that is used in simulation, modeling and quality. One such distribution is *exponential distribution*, and the *uniform distribution*.

The Exponential Distribution

The exponential distribution has wide applications in modeling. In the previous chapter we discussed the Poisson distribution, which is often used to describe the *number* of arrivals (or occurrences) over a specified time period. The exponential distribution is used to describe such phenomenon as the time between failures of components, the time between arrivals of customers, or telephone calls, or the lifetime of certain types of components in a machine. This distribution is widely used in reliability engineering to describe the time to failure of certain types of components.

If X is the random variable that represents the *number* of arrivals over a specified period T, then X is said to follow a Poisson distribution, and if Y represents the *time between successive arrivals*, then Y will follow an exponential distribution. Thus, the Poisson and exponential distributions are closely related.

The exponential distribution is an appropriate model to use when the *failure rate is constant*. For example, the time between failures of a computer chip is a continuous random variable and the failure rate is assumed to be a constant.

Probability Density of an Exponential Distribution

If the random variable X follows an exponential distribution, then the probability density function is given by:

$$f(x) = \frac{1}{\mu} e^{-x/\mu} \text{ where, x > 0 and } \mu > 0 \qquad (10.22)$$

Cumulative Probabilities for exponential distribution are given by:

$$p(x \leq x_0) = 1 - e^{-x/\mu} \quad \text{for } x > 0 \qquad (10.23)$$

The mean and standard deviation of the exponential distribution are equal and given by:

$$\text{Mean} = \mu$$
$$\text{Standard deviation, } \sigma = \mu \qquad (10.24)$$

The parameter $1/\mu$ in Equation (10.22) is often referred to as the *failure rate (time between failures)* and is related to the Poisson distribution. Consider another example where the *number of arrivals per unit time* in the Poisson distribution and the *time between arrivals* in the exponential distribution can both be used to describe the same thing. For example, if the number of arrivals per unit time follows a Poisson distribution with mean or average of 10 arrivals per hour, then we can say that the time between arrivals is exponentially distributed with mean time between arrivals being $1/10 = 0.1$ hour or 6 minutes.

Unlike the normal distribution which is described by its location and shape parameters (μ and σ respectively), exponential distribution is described by only one parameter, μ. Each value of μ determines a unique exponential distribution. The distribution has no shape or location parameter; it is described by a scale parameter, which is ($1/\mu$). In the section that follows, we will investigate the shapes of the exponential distribution.

Investigating the Exponential Distribution

Objective

Investigate the general shape of the exponential distribution and observe how the shape of the distribution changes as we change the characteristic scale parameter (μ) of the distribution. Figure 10.21 shows the plot of the density functions of the exponential distribution for different values of $\mu = 0.5, 0.67, 1.0, 2.0$.

From Figure 10.21, it can be seen that the exponential distribution curve steadily decreases as the value of the random variable x increases. The larger the value of x, the probability of observing a value of x at least this large decrease exponentially. Note also that the distribution is not symmetrical and unlike the normal random variable, the exponential random variable is always greater than zero.

Finding Exponential Probabilities

The probabilities for exponentially distributed random variables are found by evaluating the areas between the points of interest of the exponential

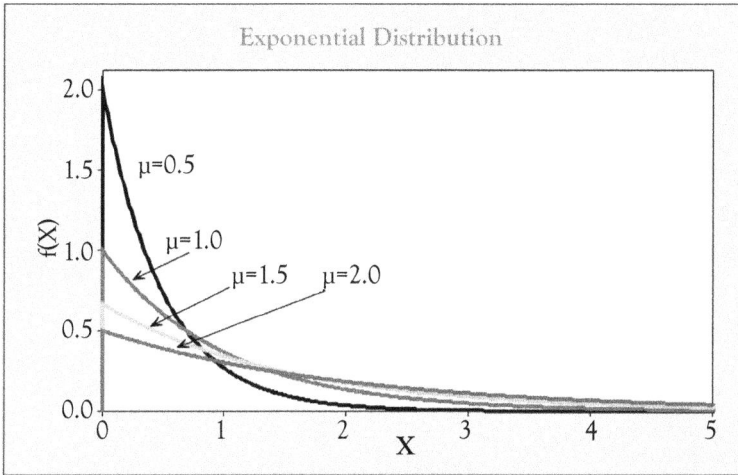

Figure 10.21 *Graph of exponential distribution for different values of μ*

curve described in Figure 6.39. Suppose X is an exponentially distributed random variable with parameter μ then

$$P(X \leq x) = e^{-x/\mu} \quad \textbf{for } x \geq 0 \qquad (10.25)$$

$$P(X \leq x) = 1 - e^{-x/\mu} \textbf{ for } x > 0 \qquad (10.26)$$

$$P(x_1 \leq X \leq x_2) = e^{-x_1/\mu} - e^{-x_2/\mu} \quad \textbf{for } x_1, x_2 > 0 \qquad (10.27)$$

The above equations are used to find the probability between the points of interest in exponential distribution.

Summary

This part of the chapter dealt with important continuous distributions. One of the most important continuous distribution is the normal distribution. This has wide applications in data analysis and decision making. Several applications of the distribution were demonstrated through examples. The other distribution with applications in modelling is the exponential distribution. This has a number of applications in product reliability and reliability engineering.

CHAPTER 11

Sampling and Sampling Distributions: Central Limit Theorem

Chapter Highlights

- Sampling techniques and the importance of sampling distribution in data science
- Importance of sampling and different types of samples including the probability and nonprobability sampling
- Sampling techniques including the simple random, systematic, stratified, cluster, judgment sampling, and other sampling methods
- Concepts of standard error for both finite and infinite populations
- Sampling distribution and how it is used to draw conclusions about the population
- Sampling distributions of two statistics: sample mean and sample proportion
- Central limit theorem and the distribution of sample means using this theorem

What You Need to Know

According to a July 2014, Gallop poll report on the status of healthcare insurance, the United States uninsured rate declined by 13.4 percent in the second quarter of 2014. The uninsured rate fell 2.2 points in the second quarter, evidently due to a surge in the percentage of Americans who completed their enrollment in healthcare plans just before the mid-April deadline. The uninsured rate has since been flat at about

13.4 percent, suggesting that there won't be further reductions in the rate until after the open enrollment period for 2015 begins on November 15. Although Medicaid has added to the increase in health insurance coverage as more states have adopted expansion provisions over the past few months, it remains unclear how many Americans were previously insured and moved to Medicaid to reduce costs. Throughout the enrollment period for 2014, the Obama administration increased outreach efforts to young Americans, including 26- to 34-year-olds, and Hispanics. It is likely that these groups will be targeted again in the months leading up to the enrollment period for 2015 as they are the subgroups with the highest uninsured rates.

The above poll and several others on current issues are conducted by Gallup polls using sample data; these polls usually use a survey. The survey methods explained by the poll are outlined below.

Survey Methods

Results are based on telephone interviews conducted as part of the Gallup-Heathway's Well-Being Index survey from April 1 to June 30, 2014, with a random sample of 45,125 adults, aged 18 and older, living in all 50 U.S. states and the District of Columbia. For results based on the total sample of national adults, the margin of sampling error is ±1 percentage point at the 95 percent confidence level.

Samples are weighted to correct for unequal selection probability, nonresponse, and double coverage of landline and cell users in the two sampling frames. They are also weighted to match the national demographics of gender, age, race, Hispanic ethnicity, education, region, population density, and phone status (cellphone only, landline only, both, and cellphone mostly). Demographic weighting targets are based on the most recent Current Population Survey figures for the aged 18 and older U.S. population. Phone status targets are based on the most recent National Health Interview Survey. Population density targets are based on the most recent U.S. census. All reported margins of sampling error include the computed design effects for weighting.

In addition to sampling error, wording in questions and practical difficulties in conducting surveys can introduce error or bias into the findings of public opinion polls.(*Source*: http://gallup.com/poll/172403/uninsured-rate-sinks).

Need for Sample(s)

In sampling, we need to consider several factors and answer questions such as why do we use samples? Why do we need to have a homogeneous sample? What are different ways of taking samples? What is a sampling distribution and what is the purpose of it?

One of the obvious reasons of using samples in statistical analysis is because in most cases the population can be huge, and it is not practical to study the entire population. Samples are used to make inferences about the population, and this can be done through a sampling distribution.

In previous chapters we discussed probability distributions of discrete and continuous random variables and studied several of the distributions. The understanding and knowledge of these distributions are critical in decision making. This chapter extends the concept of probability distribution to that of sample statistics. Note that the *sample statistics* are measures calculated from the sample data to describe the data. The commonly used sample statistics are the sample size (n), sample mean ($\bar{x}$), sample variance (s^2), sample standard deviation (s), and sample proportion ($\bar{p}$). If these measures are calculated from the population data, they are known as the *population parameters*. These parameters are population size (N), population mean (μ), population variance (σ^2), population standard deviation (σ), and population proportion (p).

It is important to note that a population parameter is always a constant whereas a sample statistic is a random variable. Like other random variables, each sample statistic can be described using a probability distribution.

In this chapter, we discuss the probability distributions of two widely used statistics: the sample mean ($\bar{x}$) and the sample proportion ($\bar{p}$). The probability distribution of a sample statistic is called its *sampling distribution*. We will also study the *central limit theorem* and how the amazing results produced by it are used in reaching conclusions in sampling theory.

The concepts of sampling distribution form the basis for the inference procedures we will study in the coming chapters. Before studying the sampling distribution, we discuss the fundamental concepts behind sampling and explain the terms related to sample and sampling. Some of the common terms used in sampling theory are sample, census, sampling error or the margin of error, sampling bias, and the types of samples— probability and nonprobability sampling.

Differentiate Between a Census and a Survey or Sample

A sample is a part or subset of a population. Census, on the other hand, involves studying every unit in the population being studied. If we really want to learn about a population, we would conduct a census and study every unit in the population. Thus, the only way to be truly sure is to conduct a census and measure survey every unit. For example, a polling agency conducting an opinion poll about the upcoming national election, they would have to ask every single American voter his or her opinion. This process is going to be impractical, expensive, and very time consuming. By the time the poll results are produced, the event may be over. These are some obvious reasons why a census is not a practical approach to learn about a population.

In addition, a census has the potential to be destructive to the population being studied as in case of a manufacturing company conducting census to test all its products. For example, a manufacturer of light bulbs tests each bulb it produced to determine the average life of the bulb. For this they test the bulbs they burn out. If they did this with every bulb, at the end of testing, they would have none left to sell!

Sampling and Its Risks

Because of the obvious problems associated with a census, a more practical approach is sampling that involves studying the part of a population. Sampling is a systematic way of selecting a few items from the population. Sample or samples are then analyzed to draw conclusion about the entire population. In the sections that follow, we discuss several ways of drawing sample from a population along with their merits and drawbacks.

Drawing sample or samples requires a lot of planning. Even the most carefully planned sample will be subject to random variation. Due to this variation, that is due to chance causes the difference between the population parameter and the corresponding sample statistic. This is called *sampling error*. Many polling agencies conducting opinion polls, like Gallup polls refer to this as *margin of error*.

It is important to note that it is often difficult to obtain a sample that accurately reflects the total population. It is also possible to make mistakes in selecting the sample and collecting the information. These problems can lead to nonrepresentative sample resulting into wrong conclusions.

Sampling Bias

In general, sampling bias refers to the methods used in selecting the sample. The sampling frame is the term we use to refer to the group or listing from which the sample is to be chosen. If you wanted to study the population of students in your school, you could obtain a list of all the students from the office and choose students from the list. This list is also sampling frame.

Sampling and Sampling Techniques

It is important to note that the *population* denotes the entire measurements that are theoretically possible (or the universe). It is the totality of items or things under consideration. A *sample* is a part of the population. In most statistical studies, we collect sample data to draw a conclusion about the population. *Sampling* is a systematic way of selecting a few items from the population. The purpose of sampling is to draw a conclusion or make a decision about the population parameters using the information contained in the sample statistics. Recall that a population is described by its parameters.

The sample mean, $\bar{x}$ (x-bar)is used to estimate the population mean, μ. In general, sample statistics are used to estimate population parameters. Note that in most cases, we don't know the population parameters (for example, the population mean, μ) and therefore, the population mean, μ must be estimated using the sample statistic, $\bar{x}$. The process of estimating population parameters using sample statistics comes under the broad category of *inferential statistics* (or statistical inference).

There are many ways of taking samples from the population of interest. Different types of samples are described in Figure 11.1. Sampling can be divided into two broad categories: probability sampling and nonprobability sampling. In probability sampling techniques, the probability or chance plays a role. For example, every sample has an equal probability or chance of being selected. Here is a breakdown of categories.

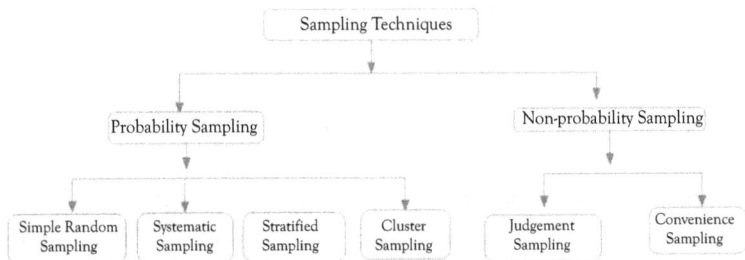

Figure 11.1 Sampling methods

Probability Sampling Methods

Simple random sampling is a sampling technique in which every sample has equal probability of being selected and every item in the sample has equal probability of being selected. This means that when using a simple random sample (or a random sample) you will need to make sure that every selected sample of size n has the same chance of being selected. The random samples can be drawn from a population of interest using the following methods:

- Using a table of random numbers (computer generated); or
- Using computer software such as Excel or MINITAB

The random number table is a table of randomly generated numbers. These numbers are usually a computer-generated list of random digits. Table 11.1 shows a partial table of random numbers with five-digit numbers.

To illustrate the process of generating samples using the random number table, consider a situation in which you are asked to select a random sample of 15 checking accounts from a list of 1,000 accounts where the accounts are numbered sequentially from 1 to 1,000. For this procedure to work, it is important to list sequentially all of the population elements from 1 to 1,000. Once it is done, you can use the table of random numbers (Table 11.1) as explained below.

Table 11.1 Table of random numbers

Row	Col1	Col2	Col3	Col4	Col5	Col6	Col7	Col8
1	12785	99985	46746	51452	50406	61229	63378	86436
2	40951	11508	76859	58093	20288	11376	20435	82228
3	15208	21791	78527	61821	32491	73946	36750	30036
4	25209	5633	822	55887	88145	13777	8927	44126
5	50556	79612	92213	35982	28416	78567	18095	29057
6	4562	15620	13855	79475	79669	17115	23956	62566
7	10316	34927	82992	27844	56148	11981	80583	98368
8	48962	8931	77251	16916	33614	7187	86386	12402
9	36287	52928	70684	41051	23529	3722	9069	72202
10	83418	90623	78304	4007	52705	82505	21244	36507
11	71480	52958	62868	55371	85155	38450	92304	36651
12	29945	24758	86671	77813	44851	85208	13148	99626
13	3665	75510	85123	75042	67234	8711	83912	20031
14	5463	41437	61181	63693	85952	19573	96066	76250
15	5204	94929	36820	12299	7427	65740	96865	72323

To draw a random sample of 15 ($n = 25$) from a population of 1,000 accounts ($N = 1,000$), follow the steps below.

- Start in any position, such as row 8 and column 3.
- Select a list of 15 random numbers by reading either across the row or down the column.
- Read across the row, start in row 8 and column 3 and the first set of five-digit numbers is 77252. Place a decimal between the third and fourth digits and round this value to the nearest integer. For our example, the number would be 772.51, which would become 773 after rounding. Thus, account number 773 is the first account selected for our sample. The next set of five digits is 16916, which would be 169 after rounding. Continuing in this manner, a sample of 15 accounts selected for our sample would be

773, 169, 336, 719, 864, 124, 363, 529, 707, 411, 235, 372, 907, 722, and 834

Other Probability Sampling Techniques

Systematic Sampling

Systematic sampling is another method of drawing samples. In a systematic sampling

- Samples are drawn at a prespecified number or at some prespecified time.
- The N items in the population are partitioned into groups of m items by dividing the size of the population N by the desired sample size n. That is,

$$m = \frac{N}{n}$$

where m is rounded to the nearest integer. To obtain a systematic sample, the first item to be selected is chosen at random from m items in the first partitioned group in the population frame, and the rest of the samples are obtained by selecting every mth item thereafter, from the entire population frame listing. This method is more convenient and practical than simple random sampling.

Stratified Sampling

In this method of drawing samples,

- The population is divided into different groups or *strata*, according to some common characteristic (e.g., department, age, income level, industry type, location, etc.).
- A simple random sample is taken from each group and the results from the separate simple random samples are then combined.

This technique is more efficient than simple random sampling or systematic sampling because it ensures representation of individuals or items across the entire population, which in turn ensures a greater precision in estimating the population parameters.

Cluster Sampling

In cluster sampling:

- the N individuals or items in the population are divided into several *clusters*, such that each cluster is representative of the entire population.
- a random sampling of clusters is then taken and all individuals or items in each selected cluster are then studied.

Some applications are area sampling where clusters are city blocks or other well-defined areas

---

Statistical Inference and Sampling Techniques

Statistical Inference: The objective of statistical inference is to draw conclusions or make decisions about a population based on the samples selected from the population. To be able to draw conclusion from the sample, the distribution of the samples must be known. Knowledge of sampling distribution is very important for drawing conclusion from the sample regarding the population of interest.

Sampling Distribution

Sampling distribution is the probability distribution of a sample statistic (sample statistics are a sample mean $\bar{x}$, sample variance s^2, sample standard deviation s, or sample proportion,$(\bar{p})$).

As indicated earlier, in most cases the true value of the population parameters is not known. We must draw a sample or samples and calculate the sample statistic to estimate the population parameter. The sampling error of the sample mean is given by

$$\text{Sampling error} = x - \mu$$

Suppose we want to draw a conclusion about the mean of certain population. We would collect samples from this population, calculate the mean of the samples, and determine the probability distribution (shape) of the sample means. This probability distribution may follow a normal or a t-distribution, or other distribution. The distribution will then be used to draw conclusion about the population mean.

Sampling Distribution of the Sample Mean and Sample Proportion

Sampling distribution of the sample mean $\bar{x}$ is the probability distribution of all possible values of the sample mean, $\bar{x}$.

Sampling distribution of sample proportion, $\bar{p}$ is the probability distribution of all possible values of the sample proportion, $\bar{p}$. The process of sampling distribution for the sample mean, $\bar{x}$, is illustrated below:

As indicated, sampling distribution is the probability distribution of a sample statistic, such as a sample mean $\bar{x}$.

As indicated earlier, in most cases the true value of the population parameters is not known. We must draw a sample or samples and calculate the sample statistic to estimate the population parameter. The sampling error of the sample mean is given by

$$\text{Sampling error} = \bar{x} - \mu$$

Suppose we want to draw a conclusion about the mean of certain population. We would collect samples from this population, calculate the mean of the samples and determine the probability distribution (shape) of the sample means. This probability distribution of the population may follow a normal or a t-distribution, or any other distribution. The distribution will then be used to draw conclusion about the population mean.

- *Sampling distribution of the sample mean ($\bar{x}$) is the probability distribution of all possible values of the sample mean, $\bar{x}$.*
- *Sampling distribution of sample proportion, $\bar{p}$ is the probability distribution of all possible values of the sample proportion, $\bar{p}$.*

The process of sampling distribution is illustrated in Figure 11.2.

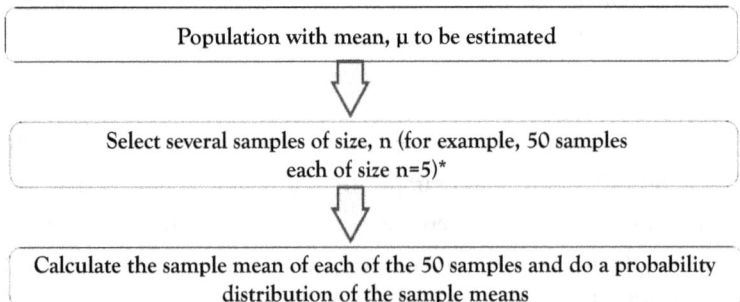

Population with mean, μ to be estimated

⬇

Select several samples of size, n (for example, 50 samples each of size n=5)*

⬇

Calculate the sample mean of each of the 50 samples and do a probability distribution of the sample means

Figure 11.2 Sampling distribution process

Fifty samples each of size $n = 5$ means that 50 different samples are drawn, where each sample will have five items in it. Also, a probability distribution is similar to a frequency distribution through which the distribution or the shape of the sample means is determined]. The procedure is illustrated below with an example.

Example: Examining the Distribution of the Sample Mean, x

The assembly time of a particular electrical appliance is assumed to have a mean, $\mu = 25$ minutes, and a standard deviation, $\sigma = 5$ minutes.

1. Draw 50 samples each of size 5 ($n = 5$) from this population using MINITAB statistical software or any other statistical package.
2. Determine the average or the mean of each of the samples drawn.
3. Draw a histogram of the sample means and interpret your findings.
4. Determine the average and standard deviation of the 50-sample means. Interpret the meaning of these.
5. What conclusions can you draw from your answers to (3) and (4)?

Solution to (1): Table 11.2 shows 50 samples each of size 5 using MINITAB.
Solution to (2): The last column shows the mean of each sample drawn. Note that each row represents a sample of size 5.

Table 11.2 Fifty samples of size 5 (n = 5)

Sample						Mean, $\overline{x}$
1	30.50	24.27	33.33	22.54	22.63	26.45
2	25.87	27.84	23.17	25.52	27.09	25.90
3	18.03	24.11	26.94	26.63	26.81	24.51
4	28.44	28.87	20.90	27.51	24.34	26.01
5	24.45	23.14	28.04	22.47	22.84	23.79
6	23.73	25.32	24.84	22.87	23.89	23.93
7	25.84	24.04	30.87	20.64	26.11	25.50
8	26.63	22.50	26.85	32.51	25.49	26.60
9	26.02	28.94	25.19	24.24	22.99	25.28
10	24.91	27.00	25.47	26.34	24.21	25.59
:						
48	19.24	23.47	22.69	22.85	26.59	22.97
49	18.66	28.18	22.92	20.98	22.54	22.45
50	27.89	22.28	22.27	32.06	25.72	25.44

Solution to (3): Figure 11.3 shows the histogram of the sample means shown in the last column of Table 11.2. The histogram shows that the sample means are normally distributed. Figure 11.3 is an example of the sampling distribution of the sample means $\bar{x}$.

In a similar way, we can do the sampling distribution of other statistics such as, the sample variance or the sample standard deviation. As we will see later, the sampling distribution provides the distribution or the shape of the sample statistic of interest. This distribution is useful in drawing conclusions.

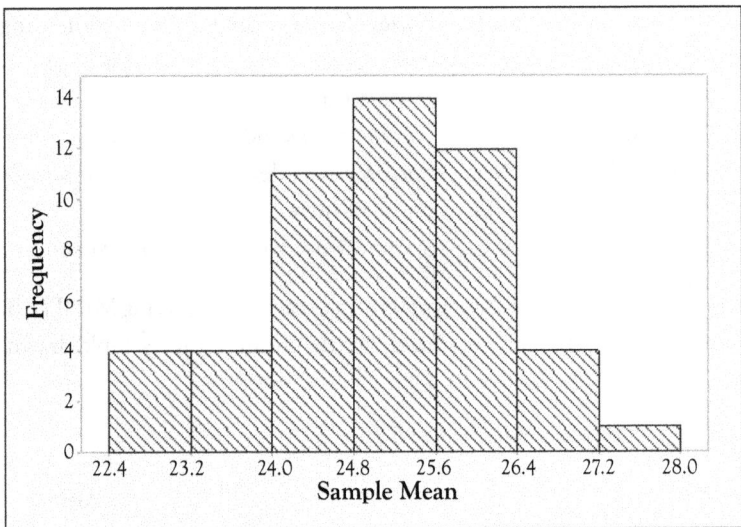

Figure 11.3 Sampling distribution of the sample means

Solution to (4): The mean and standard deviation of the sample means shown in the last column of Table 11.2 were calculated using a computer package. These values are shown in Table 11.3.

Table 11.3 Mean and standard deviation of sample means

Descriptive Statistics: Sample Mean	
Mean	StDev
25.0942	2.1035

The mean of the sample means is 25.0942, which indicates that $\bar{x}$ values are centered at approximately the population mean of $\mu = 25$.

However, the standard deviation of 50 sample means is 2.1035, which is much smaller than the population standard deviation, $\sigma = 3$. Thus, we conclude that $\bar{x}$ – or the sample mean values – have much less variation than the individual observations.

Solution to (5): Based on parts (3) and (4), we conclude that the sample mean, $\bar{x}$ follows a normal distribution, and this distribution is much narrower than the population of individual observations, which has a standard deviation, $\sigma = 3$. This is apparent from the standard deviation of $\bar{x}$ value, which is 2.1035 (see Table 11.3). In general, the mean and standard deviation of the random variable $\bar{x}$ are given by

---

Mean of the sample mean, $\bar{x}$ is

$$\mu_{\bar{x}} = \mu \quad \text{or} \quad E(\bar{x}) = \mu \qquad (11.1)$$

The standard deviation of the sample mean $\bar{x}$ is

$$\sigma_{\bar{x}} = \frac{\sigma}{\sqrt{n}} \qquad (11.2)$$

For our example, $\mu = 25$, $\sigma = 5$ and $n = 5$. Using these values

$$\mu_{\bar{x}} = \mu = 25$$

and

$$\sigma_{\bar{x}} = \frac{\sigma}{\sqrt{n}} = \frac{5}{\sqrt{5}} = 2.236$$

From Table B.2, the mean and the standard deviation of 50 sample means were 25.0942 and 2.1035 respectively. These values will get closer to 25 and 2.236 if we take more and more samples of size 5.

Standard Deviation of the Sample Mean or the Standard Error

Both Equations (11.1) and (11.2) are of considerable importance. Equation (11.2) shows that the standard deviation of the sample mean, $\bar{x}$ varies inversely as the square root of the sample size. Since the standard deviation of the mean is a measure of the scatter of the sample means, it provides the precision that we can expect of the mean of one or more samples. The standard deviation of the sample mean $\sigma_{\bar{x}}$ is often called the *standard error of the mean*. Using Equation (11.2), it can be shown that a sample of 16 observations ($n = 16$) is twice as precise as a sample of 4 ($n = 4$). It may be argued that the gain in precision in this case is small, relative to the effort in taking additional 12 observations. However, doubling the sample size in other cases may be desirable.

Figure 11.4 shows a comparison between the probability distribution of individual observations and the probability distributions of means of samples of various sizes drawn from the underlying population.

Note that as the sample size increases, the standard error becomes smaller and hence the distribution becomes more peaked.

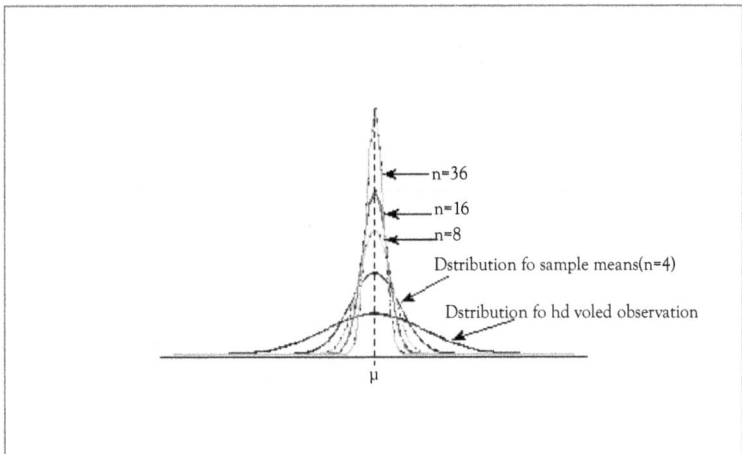

Figure 11.4 Probability distribution of sample means (n = 4, 9, 16, and 36) compared to individual observations

It is obvious from Figure 11.4 that a sample of one does not tell us anything about the precision of the estimated mean. As more samples are taken, the standard error decreases, thus providing greater precision. It should be noted that Equation (11.2) also applies to sampling with replacement for both finite and infinite populations. Sampling from a finite population with replacement is equivalent to sampling from an infinite population.

Two different formulas are used to calculate the *standard error* or the *standard deviation of the sample mean* ($\bar{x}$). Standard deviation of $\bar{x}$, $\sigma_{\bar{x}}$ or the *standard error* is

$$\sigma_{\bar{x}} = \frac{\sigma}{\sqrt{n}} \text{ for an infinite population}$$

$$\sigma_{\bar{x}} = \frac{\sigma}{\sqrt{n}}\sqrt{\frac{N-n}{N-1}} \text{ for a finite population}$$

(*Note*: Infinite population means that the population size is infinitely large and we don't know the population size. In a finite population, we know N, the size of the population).

Example

Suppose for a population, the standard deviation, $\sigma = 25$. Calculate the standard error for the sample size of $n = 50, 100, 150,$ and 200. Comment on your results.

Solution:

$n = 50$ $\sigma_{\bar{x}} = \dfrac{\sigma}{\sqrt{n}} = \dfrac{25}{\sqrt{50}} = 3.54$
$n = 100$ $\sigma_{\bar{x}} = \dfrac{\sigma}{\sqrt{n}} = \dfrac{25}{\sqrt{100}} = 2.50$
$n = 150$ $\sigma_{\bar{x}} = \dfrac{\sigma}{\sqrt{n}} = \dfrac{25}{\sqrt{150}} = 2.04$
$n = 200$ $\sigma_{\bar{x}} = \dfrac{\sigma}{\sqrt{n}} = \dfrac{25}{\sqrt{200}} = 1.77$

The standard error decreases as the sample size n, increases.

Example

a. Suppose the population standard deviation $\sigma = 10$ and the sample size $n = 50$. Calculate the standard error.

   Solution: Using the standard error formula for infinite population.

$\sigma_{\bar{x}} = \dfrac{\sigma}{\sqrt{n}}$	$\sigma_{\bar{x}} = \dfrac{10}{\sqrt{50}} = 1.41$

b. Suppose $n = 50$, $\sigma = 50$, $N = 50{,}000$. Calculate the standard error. The standard error can be calculated using the formula for the finite population.

$$\sigma_{\bar{x}} = \frac{\sigma}{\sqrt{n}} \sqrt{\frac{N-n}{N-1}}$$

Note that

$$\sqrt{\frac{N-n}{N-1}}$$

is the *finite population correction factor* and if $\dfrac{n}{N} \langle 0.05$, do not use this factor.

c. The purpose of this factor is to reduce the error. But if the sample size is too small compared to the population size, the factor becomes almost 2.0 and does not help to reduce the error.

   For our example:

d. If $n = 50$ and $N = 500$, $n/N = 50/500 = 0.1 > 0.05$ therefore, we use the correction factor.

$$\frac{\sigma}{\sqrt{n}} \sqrt{\frac{N-n}{N-1}} = \frac{10}{\sqrt{50}} \sqrt{\frac{500-50}{500-1}} = 1.34$$

The above example shows when to use the finite population correction factor.

Sampling from Different Populations: Sampling Distribution of the Sample Mean

In this section we will draw samples of various sizes from different distributions (normal, exponential, uniform, etc.), calculate the means of all the samples, and do a probability distribution of the sample means ($\bar{x}$). The purpose of this exercise is to observe the shape of the sampling distribution. We would like to know what happens to the shape of the distribution when (a) the samples are drawn from different populations, and (b) the sample size increases. The results will lead to a very important conclusion that is critical to solving problems involving sampling distribution. The following distributions are considered for demonstration purpose: (1) normal, (2) exponential, and (3) uniform.

The steps are outlined below.

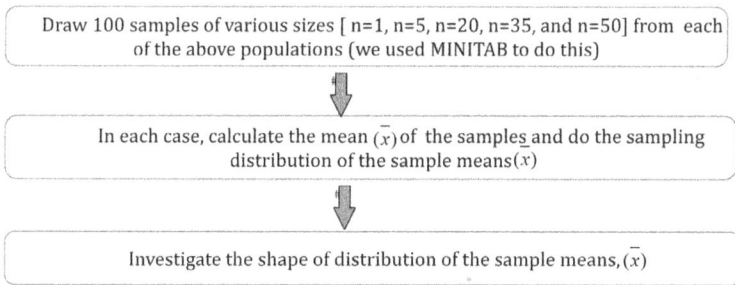

> Draw 100 samples of various sizes [n=1, n=5, n=20, n=35, and n=50] from each of the above populations (we used MINITAB to do this)

> In each case, calculate the mean ($\bar{x}$) of the samples and do the sampling distribution of the sample means ($\bar{x}$)

> Investigate the shape of distribution of the sample means, ($\bar{x}$)

To answer the questions, we performed the experiments explained in the next section.

Sampling from a Normal Distribution

Using a computer package, we generated 150 samples of size $n = 1$, $n = 2$, $n = 5$, $n = 10$, $n = 20$, $n = 30$, and $n = 50$ from the normal distribution with mean $\mu = 20$ and standard deviation $\sigma = 4$. The steps for generating these samples will be discussed later in the computer applications section. The sample mean for each of the samples were calculated and the histograms for the sample means were constructed. We also calculated the descriptive statistics for each sample. From Figure 11.5 you can see that if the samples are drawn from a normal population, the distribution of the sample means also follows a normal distribution and the standard error of the mean (SE Mean) decreases as we increase the sample size.

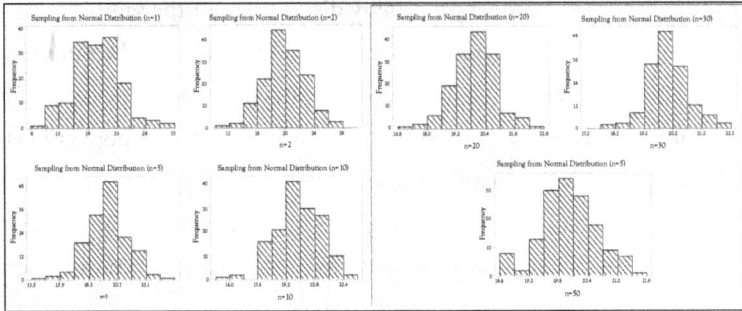

Figure 11.5 Sampling distribution of the sample means (data from a normal distribution)

Sampling from an Exponential Distribution

We generated 500 samples of size $n = 1$, $n = 2$, $n = 5$, $n = 10$, $n = 20$, $n = 30$, and $n = 50$ from an exponential distribution with mean = 2.0. The sample mean for each of the samples were calculated and the histograms for the sample means were generated. From Figure 11.6, you can see that the distribution of the sample mean follows a normal distribution as the sample size increases. Also, the standard error of the mean (SE Mean) will decrease as the sample size increases.

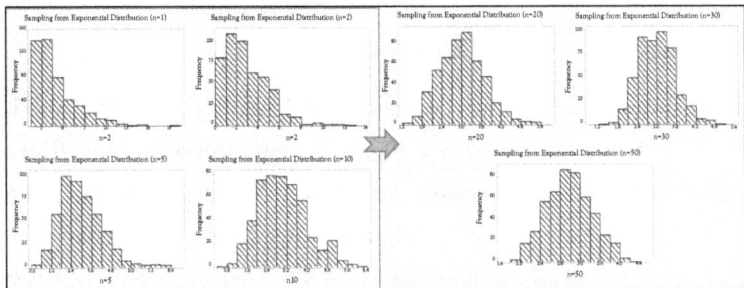

Figure 11.6 Sampling distribution of the sample means (data from an exponential distribution)

Sampling From a Uniform Distribution

In this case, 500 samples of size $n = 1$, $n = 2$, $n = 5$, $n = 10$, $n = 20$, $n = 30$, and $n = 50$ were generated using a uniform distribution with a lower value,

$a = 0.0$ and upper value, $b = 2.0$. The sample mean for each of the samples were calculated and the histograms for the sample means were generated. Figure 11.7 shows the distribution of the sample means. The distribution is very close to a normal distribution as the sample size increases.

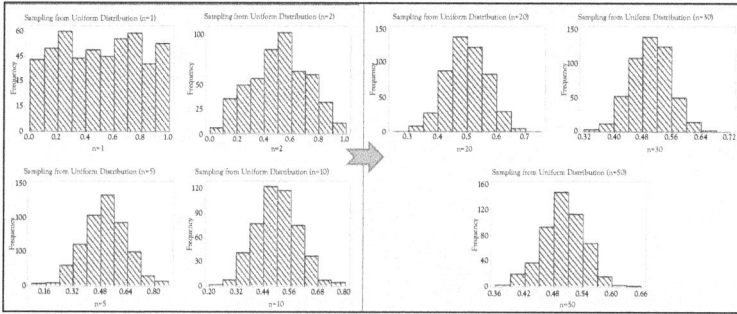

Figure 11.7 Sampling distribution of the sample means (data from a uniform distribution)

If you repeat the above procedure with any other distribution, the distribution of the sample means will approach a normal distribution as the sample size increases. In general, as the sample size gets closer to $n = 30$ or more, the distribution will always be normal, or bell shaped.

Conclusion: No matter what the shape of the distribution is, the distribution of the sample means ($\bar{x}$) approaches a normal distribution as the sample size increases. For a large sample ($n \geq 30$), the shape is almost always symmetrical, i.e., follows a normal distribution.

This leads to an important theorem in statistics known as the central limit theorem discussed below.

Central Limit Theorem

If $\bar{x}$ is the mean of a random sample of size n drawn from a population with mean σ and standard deviation, s then the sampling distribution of the sample mean

$$Z = \frac{\bar{x} - \mu}{\sigma / \sqrt{n}}$$

will approach a normal distribution as the sample size n increases. The normal approximation of the sample mean $\bar{x}$ is good for the sample size, $n \geq 30$. If the population is known to be normal, the sampling distribution of $\bar{x}$ will exactly follow a normal distribution even for small samples. Even when the population is not normal, the distribution of the sample means approaches a normal distribution as the sample size increases. We have demonstrated this using computer simulation above.

The sample size of $n \geq 30$ is considered a large sample.

- The central limit theorem has been proclaimed as "the most important theorem in statistics"[1] and "perhaps the most important result of statistical theory."
- The central limit theorem can be proven to show the "amazing result" that the mean values of the sum of a large number of independent random variables are normally distributed.
- The probability distribution resulting from "a large number of individual effects... would tend to be Gaussian."

Figures 11.8 and 11.9 illustrate the working of central limit theorem. These two figures show how the distribution of sample mean $\bar{x}$ approaches a normal distribution as the sample size n increases. This is true even if the underlying population is not normal. Figure 11.8 demonstrates the distribution of an individual observation ($n = 1$) from a uniform distribution, which is clearly nonsymmetric. When the samples of larger size is drawn from this distribution ($n = 10$ and $n = 30$), the distribution of $\bar{x}$ gets closer to normal. Figure 11.9 shows similar results using an exponential distribution.

These results were demonstrated using computer simulation. It was pointed out using the results of the computer simulations in Figures 11.5 to 11.7, that as the sample size increased, the mean of the sample means $\bar{x}$ gets closer to a normal distribution irrespective of the distribution of the population. We verified this using the computer simulation and demonstrated that even when the samples were drawn

---

[1] Ostle, Bernard and Mensing, Richard W., *Statistics in Research*, Third Edition, The Iowa State University Press, Ames, IA, 1979, p. 76.

from non-normal population (e.g., exponential or uniform distribution), the sampling distribution of the sample mean followed a normal distribution as the sample size increased (see Figures 11.6 and 11.7).

The sampling distribution also showed that as the sample size increases, the standard deviation of $\bar{x}$ or the standard error gets smaller.

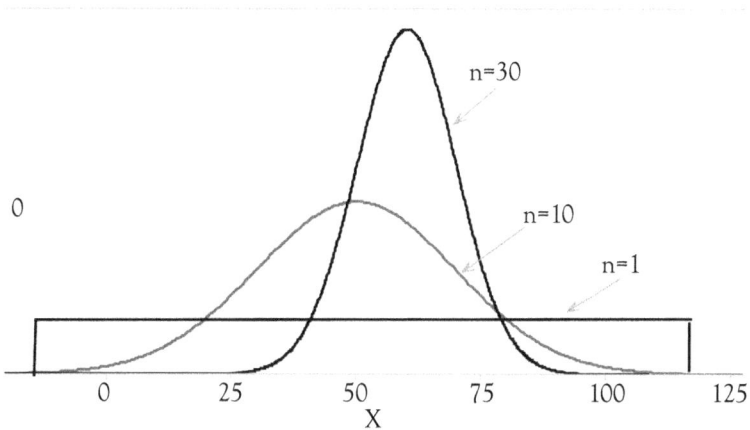

Figure 11.8 *Sampling distribution of the sample mean $\bar{x}$ when the population is uniformly distributed*

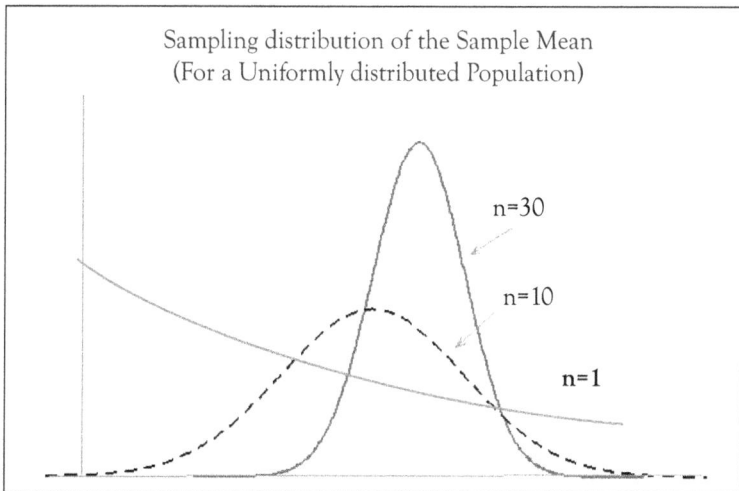

Figure 11.9 *Sampling distribution of the sample mean $\bar{x}$ when the population has an exponential distribution*

How Are the Results from Central Limit Theorem Used in Sampling?

The results of central limit theorem are very useful in drawing conclusions from the data. For a sample size of $n \geq 30$ (large sample), we can always use the normal distribution to draw conclusions from the sample data.

- For a large sample, the sampling distribution of the sample mean ($\bar{x}$) follows a normal distribution and the probability that the sample mean ($\bar{x}$) is within a specified value of the population mean (μ) can be calculated using the following formulas:

$$Z = \frac{\bar{x} - \mu}{\frac{\sigma}{\sqrt{n}}} \text{ (for an infinite population)} \qquad (11.5)$$

or

$$Z = \frac{\bar{x} - \mu}{\frac{\sigma}{\sqrt{n}}\sqrt{\frac{N-n}{N-1}}} \text{ (for a finite population)} \qquad (11.6)$$

Equation (11.5) is for an infinite population, and Equation (11.6) is for a finite population.

Example

The mean price per gallon of regular gasoline sold in the United States was $2.20 (March 1997). Assume that the population mean price per gallon was $\mu = \$2.20$ and the population standard deviation was $\sigma = 0.10$. Suppose that a random sample of 50 gasoline stations is selected and a sample mean price per gallon is computed for the data collected from 50 gasoline stations.

a. Show the sampling distribution of the sample mean $\bar{x}$, where $\bar{x}$ is the sample mean price per gallon for 50 stations.

$$n = 50 \quad \mu = \$1.20 \quad \sigma = 0.10 = \$2.20$$

$$E(\bar{x}) = \mu = \$1.20$$

$$\sigma_{\bar{x}} = \frac{\sigma}{\sqrt{n}} = \frac{0.10}{\sqrt{50}} = 0.014$$

Note: The sampling distribution of $\bar{x}$ will follow a normal distribution as $n > 30$. The normal distribution is described by mean (μ) and $\sigma_{\bar{x}}$.

$$\text{Here, } E(\bar{x}) = \mu \text{ and } \sigma_{\bar{x}} = \frac{\sigma}{\sqrt{n}}$$

b. What is the probability that the simple random sample of size 50 will provide a sample mean within 2 cents or 0.02 of the population mean?

The required probability is the shaded area in figure below. The probability calculations are shown next to the figure.

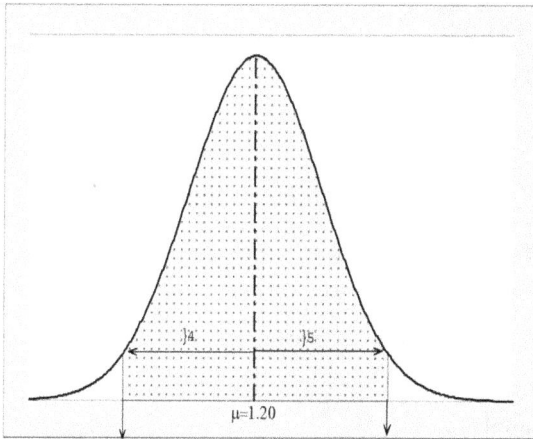

$\bar{x} = 1.18 \; \bar{x} = 1.22$

The required probability:

$$Z = \frac{\bar{x} - \mu}{\frac{\sigma}{\sqrt{n}}} = \frac{1.18 - 1.20}{\frac{0.10}{\sqrt{50}}} = -1.41 \Rightarrow 0.4207$$

$Z_1 = -1.41$ **corresponds to an area of 0.4207 (from the standard normal table)**

$$Z_2 = \frac{x - \mu}{\dfrac{\sigma}{\sqrt{n}}} = \frac{1.22 - 1.20}{\dfrac{0.10}{\sqrt{50}}} = +1.41 \Rightarrow 0.4207$$

Required probability = P (2.18 ≤ $\bar{x}$ ≤ 2.22)
$$= 0.4207 + 0.4207$$
$$= \mathbf{0.8414 \text{ or, } 84.14\%.}$$

c. What is the probability that the simple random sample will provide a sample mean within 1 cent or 0.01, of the population mean?

$$P (2.19 ≤ \bar{x} ≤ 2.21) = 0.5224 \text{ or } 52.24\%$$

Calculations are like part (b).

Concept Questions and Answers

What are population parameters and sample statistics?
A population is described by its parameter while a sample is described by its statistic.

The *population parameters* are:

N: the population size

σ^2: the population variance

μ: the population mean

$\sigma\rightarrow$: the population standard deviation

$\sigma\rightarrow p$: population proportion

A sample is described by its statistic. The *sample statistics* are:

n: the sample size s^2: the sample variance

$\bar{x}$: the sample mean s: the sample standard deviation

$\bar{p}$: sample proportion

What is sampling? Why do we use samples?
Sampling is a systematic way of selecting a few items from the population. Samples are analyzed to draw conclusion(s) about the entire population. In most cases, the parameters of the population are unknown, and we can estimate a population parameter using a sample statistic.

There are several reasons for taking samples. The most obvious reason is that a sample is less expensive than a complete enumeration of the population. The other reasons are:

1. It may be impossible to study all members of the population because of the size.
2. Studying the entire population may be expensive and time consuming.
3. The results of a sample may adequately estimate the population parameter.
4. Some tests are destructive; they destroy the items tested.

What are different types of samples? Describe them briefly.

There are two types of samples: probability sample and nonprobability sample. *Probability sampling*: In a probability sampling, every item of the population has a chance of being selected for the sample. The main type of probability samples are simple random sample, systematic sample, stratified sample, and cluster sample.

Nonprobability Sampling: In a nonprobability sampling, samples are taken based on the judgment or the expert knowledge of someone familiar with the process. This type of sample may lead to biased results.

Sampling is also classified as: convenience sampling (where easiest observations are made), judgment sampling, and random sampling.

What is sampling error?

Sampling error is the difference between the sample statistic and the population parameter. For instance, the sampling error of the mean is given by

$$\text{Sampling error} = \bar{x} - \mu$$

What do you understand by sampling distribution?

Sampling distribution is the probability distribution of a sample statistic; for example, the sampling distribution of the sample means is a probability distribution that shows all possible sample means and their probabilities of occurrence.

The sampling distribution is the probability distribution of a sample statistic (note that a sample statistic may be a sample mean $\bar{x}$, sample variance s^2, sample standard deviation s, sample median, etc.]. Suppose we want to draw a conclusion about the mean of certain population. We would collect samples from this population, calculate the means of the samples, and determine the probability distribution (shape) of the sample means. This probability distribution may be a normal or a t-distribution. The distribution will then be used to draw a conclusion about the population mean.

- *Sampling distribution of the sample mean* ($\bar{x}$) is the probability distribution of all possible values of the sample mean, $\bar{x}$.

The process of sampling distribution is illustrated below.

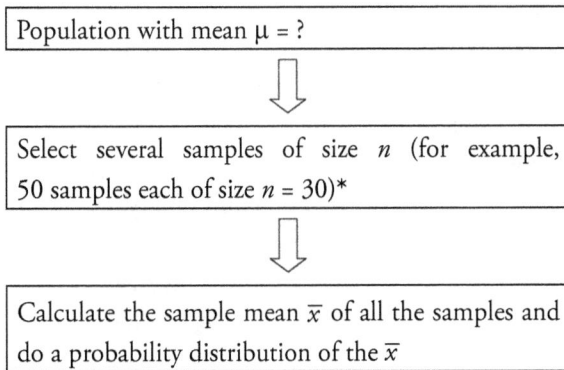

Population with mean μ = ?

⇩

Select several samples of size n (for example, 50 samples each of size $n = 30$)*

⇩

Calculate the sample mean $\bar{x}$ of all the samples and do a probability distribution of the $\bar{x}$

Fifty samples each of size $n = 30$ means that 50 different samples are drawn, where each sample will have 30 items in it. Also, a probability distribution is similar to a frequency distribution. Using the probability distribution, the shape of the sample means is determined.]

For a given sample size, the mean of all possible means selected from a population is equal to the population mean or, $E(\bar{x})$

What is the standard error of the mean?
There is less variation in the distribution of the sample means than in the population. If we take a sample of certain size from the population and do a sampling distribution of the sample mean, and keep increasing the sample size, we would expect to get less variation as we increase the sample size. *The objective is to minimize the error (reduce the variation). One way of doing this is by taking a larger sample.*

The standard error of the mean is the standard deviation of the distribution of sample means. In the sampling study, the smaller the standard error, the closer we are to the population parameter, which is often unknown. The standard error is calculated by the formulas below. It shows that error can be reduced by taking larger samples.

$$\sigma_{\bar{x}} = \frac{\sigma}{\sqrt{n}} \text{ For an infinite population } \sigma_{\bar{x}} = \frac{\sigma}{\sqrt{n}} \sqrt{\frac{N-n}{N-1}} \text{ (For a finite}$$

population)

The factor

$$\sqrt{\frac{N-n}{N-1}}$$

is known as the *finite population correction factor*. If the ratio of the sample size (n) to the population size (N) is < 0.05; that is

$$\frac{n}{N} < 0.05$$

Both standard error formulas will provide the same answer. This means that if the sample size (n) is too small compared to the population size (N), the finite population correction factor does not help to reduce the error.

Describe the central limit theorem and its importance in sampling.

The central limit theorem states that as the sample size (n) increases, the distribution of the sample mean (x) approaches a normal distribution. This means that if samples of large size ($n \geq 30$) are selected from a population, then the sampling distribution of the sample means is approximately normal. This approximation improves with larger samples.

The central limit theorem has major applications in sampling and other areas of statistics. It tells us that if we take a large sample ($n \geq 30$), we can use the normal distribution to calculate the probability and draw conclusion about the population parameter.

- Central limit theorem has been proclaimed as "the most important theorem in statistics"[2] and "perhaps the most important result of statistical theory."

---

[2] Ostle, Bernard and Mensing, Richard W., *Statistics in Research*, Third Edition, The Iowa State University Press, Ames, Iowa, 1979, p. 76.

- The central limit theorem can be proven to show the "amazing result" that the mean values of the sum of a large number of independent random variables are normally distributed.
- The probability distribution resulting from "a large number of individual effects… would tend to be Gaussian."

The above are useful results in drawing conclusions from the data. For a sample size of $n = 30$ (large sample), we can always use the normal distribution to draw conclusions from the sample data.

Suppose we draw samples from each of the following populations:

1. Normal,
2. Exponential,
3. Uniform

The procedure is outlined below.

Discuss the importance of the results of sampling from normal and non-normal populations.

⇩

Draw 100 samples of various sizes ($n = 1$, $n = 5$, $n = 20$, $n = 35$, and $n = 50$) from each of the above population (we used a computer software to do this).

⇩

In each case, calculate the mean ($\bar{x}$) of all the samples and do the sampling distribution of the sample means ($\bar{x}$)

⇩

What distribution the sample mean $\bar{x}$ follows?

You can perform experiments to answer the above question. Suppose 100 samples of size $n = 1$, $n = 2$, $n = 5$, $n = 10$, $n = 20$, $n = 30$, and $n = 50$ was generated using each of the normal, exponential, and uniform distributions. The sample mean for each of the samples was calculated and the histograms for the sample means were generated. *Sampling distribution from each of the normal, exponential, and uniform distributions are shown in simulated Figures 11.5 to 11.7 in the chapter. From these figures above, you can see that the sampling distribution follows a normal distribution (as n increases). This is true no matter what the distribution of the population is.*

Conclusion: No matter what the shape of the distribution is, the distribution of the sample means ($\bar{x}$) approaches a normal distribution as the sample size increases. For a large sample ($n \geq 30$), the shape is almost always symmetrical, that is, follows a normal distribution. This is an important result of the central limit theorem.

What are the formulas for sampling distribution of $\bar{x}$ when the sample size (n) is large?

For a large sample, the sampling distribution of the sample mean ($\bar{x}$) follows a normal distribution, and the probability that the sample mean $\bar{x}$ is within a specified value of the population mean (μ) can be calculated using one of the following formulas:

$$Z = \frac{\bar{x} - \mu}{\dfrac{\sigma}{\sqrt{n}}} \qquad\qquad Z = \frac{\bar{x} - \mu}{\dfrac{\sigma}{\sqrt{n}} \sqrt{\dfrac{N-n}{N-1}}}$$

The first formula is for an infinite population, and the second is for a finite population.

Summary

This chapter introduced the concepts of sampling and sampling distribution. In statistical analysis, we almost always rely on sample to draw conclusion about the population. Sampling can be divided into random and nonrandom or probability and nonprobability sampling. In nonprobability sampling, the probability does not play a role in drawing such samples. The main types of probability sampling techniques discussed are simple random sampling, systematic sampling, stratified sampling, and cluster sampling. We also demonstrated how to draw random samples using a table of random numbers.

We also introduced the concepts of standard error were introduced both for a finite and an infinite population. Sampling distribution and the role of the central limit theorem in sampling distribution was also a major topic of discussion in this chapter. The central limit theorem states that for large samples, the distribution of the sample mean $\bar{x}$ is always approximately normal. The importance of the central limit theorem is that no assumption regarding the shape of the population is required. Through computer simulation, we demonstrated that the sampling distribution of $\bar{x}$ is always normal for large samples regardless of the distribution of population from which the samples are drawn.

CHAPTER 12

Estimation, Confidence Intervals, Hypothesis Testing

Introduction

Estimation and hypothesis testing come under inferential statistics. *Inferential statistics* is the process of using *sample* statistics to draw conclusions about the *population* parameters. *Interference* problems are those that involve inductive generalizations. For example, we use the *statistics* of the sample to draw conclusions about the *parameters* of the population from which the sample was taken. An example would be to use the average grade achieved by one class to estimate the average grade achieved in all ten sections of the same course. The process of estimating this average grade would be a problem of inferential statistics. In this case, any conclusion made about the ten sections would be a generalization, which may not be completely valid so it must be stated how likely it is to be true.

Statistical inference involves generalization and a statement about the probability of its validity. For example, an engineer or a scientist can make inferences about a population by analyzing the samples. Decisions can then be made based on the sample results. Making decisions or drawing conclusions using sample data raises question about the likelihood of the decisions being correct. This helps us understand why probability theory is used in statistical analysis.

Tools of Inferential Statistics

Inferential tools allow a decision maker to draw conclusions about the population using the information from the sample data. There are two major tools of inferential statistics: *estimation* and *hypothesis testing*. Figure 12.1 shows the tools of inferential statistic.

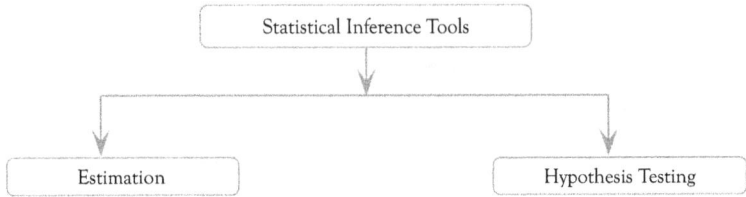

Figure 12.1 Tools of inferential statistics

- *Estimation* is the simplest form of inferential statistics in which a sample statistic is used to draw conclusion about an unknown *population parameter*.
- An estimate is a numerical value assigned to the unknown population parameter. In statistical analysis, the calculated value of a *sample statistic* serves as the estimate. This statistic is known as the estimator of the unknown parameter.
- Estimation or parameter estimation comes under the broad topic of *statistical inference.*
- The objective of parameter estimation is to estimate the unknown population parameter using the sample statistic. Two types of estimates are used in parameter estimation: *point estimate* and *interval estimate.*

The parameters of a process are generally unknown; they change over time and must be estimated. The parameters are estimated using the techniques of estimation theory. Hypothesis testing involves deciding about a population parameter using the information in the sample data. These techniques are the basis for most statistical methods.

Estimation and Confidence Intervals

Estimation

There are two types of estimates: (a) the point estimates, which are single-value estimates of the population parameter, and (b) the interval estimates or the confidence intervals which are a range of numbers that contain the parameter with specified degree of confidence known as the confidence level. Confidence level is a probability attached to a confidence interval that provides the reliability of the estimate. In the discussion of estimation, we will also consider the standard error of the estimates, the margin of error, and the sample size requirement.

Estimation: Point Estimates

Statistical inference is an extremely important area of statistics. Estimation and inference procedures are used to estimate certain unknown parameters of the population and to draw conclusion about a population using the information in the sample data. For example, the unknown population mean, μ or the population standard deviation, σ are estimated using the corresponding sample statistic, the sample mean $\bar{x}$, and the sample standard deviation, s.

The purpose of estimation is to estimate the unknown population parameters. Usually the parameters of the population are unknown and are estimated using sample statistics. The estimates can be a point or an interval estimate. When we calculate a single value, for example, a sample mean, $\bar{x}$; it is a point estimate of the population mean, μ. An interval estimate on the other hand involves estimating a range of values and is known as interval estimate or the confidence interval. The confidence interval is the topic of the next chapter. The table below shows the population parameters and the sample statistics used to estimate them.

Population Parameter	Point Estimator	Formula of the Point Estimator
μ	$\bar{x}$	$\bar{x} = \dfrac{\sum x}{n}$
σ^2	s^2	$s^2 = \dfrac{\sum(x_i - \bar{x})^2}{n-1}$ or, $s^2 = \dfrac{\sum x^2 - \dfrac{(\sum x)^2}{n}}{n-1}$
σ	s	$s = \sqrt{s^2}$
p	$\bar{p}$	$\bar{p} = \dfrac{x}{n}$

Interval Estimate

An interval estimate provides an interval or range of values that is used to estimate a population parameter. To construct an interval estimate, we find an *interval* about the point estimate so that we can be highly confident that it contains the parameter to be estimated. An interval with high confidence means that it has a high probability of containing the unknown population parameter that is estimated.

An interval estimate acknowledges that the sampling procedure is subject to error, and therefore, any computed statistic may fall above or below its population parameter target.

The interval estimate is represented by an interval or range of possible values, so it implies the presence of uncertainty. An interval estimate is represented in one of the following ways:

$$16.8 \leq \mu \leq 18.6$$

or

$$(16.8 \text{ to } 18.6) \text{ or } (16.8–18.6)$$

A formal way of writing an interval estimate is "$L \leq \mu \leq U$" where L is the lower limit and U is the upper limit of the interval. The symbol μ indicates that the population mean μ is estimated. The interval estimate involves certain probability known as the confidence level.

Confidence Interval Estimate

In many situations, a point estimate does not provide enough information about the parameter of interest. For example, if we are estimating the mean or the average salary for the students graduating with a bachelor's degree in business, a single estimate which would be a point estimate may not provide the information we need. The point estimate would be the sample average and will just provide a single estimate that may not be meaningful. In such cases, an interval estimate of the following form is more useful: $L \leq \mu \leq U$.

It also acknowledges sampling error. The end points of this interval will be random variables since they are a function of sample data. To construct an interval, estimate of unknown parameter β, we must find two statistics L and U such that

$$P\{L \leq \beta \leq U\} = 1 - \alpha \qquad (12.1)$$

The resulting interval $L \leq \beta \leq U$ is called a $100(1 - \alpha)$ percent confidence interval for the unknown parameter β. L and U are known as the lower and upper confidence limits respectively, and $(1 - \alpha)$ is known as the confidence level. A confidence level is the probability attached to a confidence interval. A 95 percent confidence interval means that the interval is estimated with a 95 percent confidence level or probability. This means that there is a 95 percent chance that the estimated interval would include the unknown population parameter being estimated.

Interpretation of Confidence Interval

The confidence interval means that if many random samples are collected and a $100 (1 - \alpha)$ percent confidence interval computed from each sample for b, then $100 (1 - \alpha)$ percent of these intervals will contain the true value β.

In practice, we usually take one sample and calculate the confidence interval. This interval may or may not contain the true value, and it is not reasonable to attach a probability level to this specific event. The appropriate statement would be that β lies in the observed interval $[L, U]$ with confidence $100(1 - \alpha)$. That is, we don't know if the statement is true for this specific sample, but the method used to obtain the interval $[L, U]$ yields correct statement $100(1 - \alpha)$ percent of the time. The interval $L \leq \beta \leq d\, U$ is known as a two-sided or two-tailed interval. We can also build one-sided interval. The length of the observed confidence interval is an important measure of the quality of information obtained from the sample. The half interval $(\beta - L)$ or $(U - \beta)$ is called the accuracy of the estimator. A two-sided interval can be interpreted in the following way:

> *The wider the confidence interval, the more confident we are that the interval contains the unknown population parameter being estimated. On the other hand, the wider the interval, the less information we have about the true value of β. In an ideal situation, we would like to obtain a relatively short interval with high confidence.*

Confidence Interval for the Mean, Known Variance s^2 (or s known)

The confidence interval estimate for the population mean is centered around the computed sample mean ($\bar{x}$). The confidence interval for the mean is constructed based on the following:

(a) The size of the sample (n),

(b) The population variance (known or unknown), and

(c) The level of confidence.

Let X be a random variable with an unknown mean μ and known variance σ^2. A random sample of size n ($x_1, x_2 ..., x_n$) is taken from the population. A $100(1 - \alpha)$ percent confidence interval on m can be obtained by considering the sampling distribution of the sampling mean $\bar{x}$. We know that the sample mean $\bar{x}$ follows a normal distribution as the sample size n increases. For a large sample n the sampling distribution of the sample mean is almost always normal. The sampling distribution is given by

$$z = \frac{\bar{x} - \mu}{\dfrac{\sigma}{\sqrt{n}}} \tag{12.2}$$

The distribution of the above is normal and is shown in Figure 12.2. To develop the confidence interval for the population, mean μ, refer to Figure 12.2.

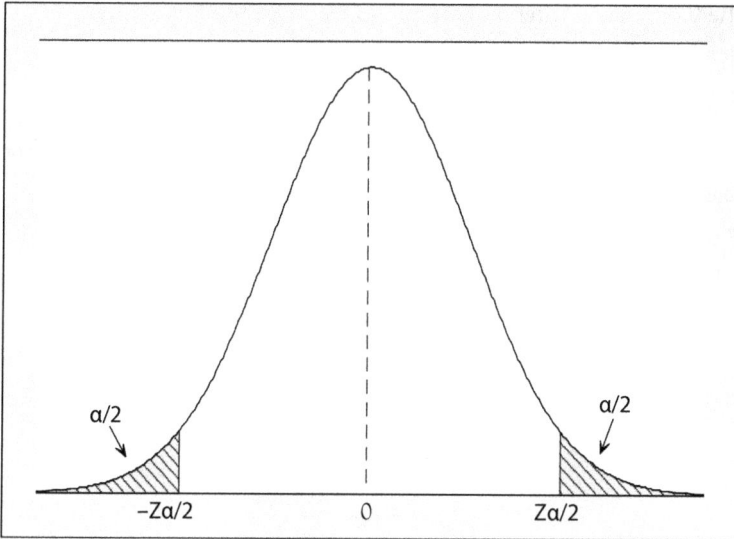

Figure 12.2 Distribution of the sample mean

From the above figure we see that:

$$P\left\{-z_{\alpha/2} \leq z \leq z_{\alpha/2}\right\} = 1 - \alpha$$

or

$$P\left\{-z_{\alpha/2} \leq \frac{\bar{x} - \mu}{\sigma/\sqrt{n}} \leq z_{\alpha/2}\right\} = 1 - \alpha$$

This can be rearranged to give

$$P\left\{\bar{x} - z_{\alpha/2}\sigma/\sqrt{n} \leq \mu \leq \bar{x} + z_{\alpha/2}\sigma/\sqrt{n}\right\} = 1 - \alpha$$

This leads to

$$\left\{\bar{x} - z_{\alpha/2}\sigma/\sqrt{n} \leq \mu \leq \bar{x} + z_{\alpha/2}\sigma/\sqrt{n}\right\} \tag{12.3}$$

Equation (12.3) is a $100(1 - \alpha)$ percent confidence interval for the population mean μ.

The Confidence Interval Formula to Estimate the Population
Mean for Known and Unknown Population Variances or
Standard Deviations

The confidence interval is constructed using a normal distribution. The
following two formulas are used when the sample size is large:

(a) Known population variance (σ^2) or known standard deviation (σ):

$$\bar{x} - z_{\alpha/2} \frac{\sigma}{\sqrt{n}} \leq \mu \leq \bar{x} + z_{\alpha/2} \frac{\sigma}{\sqrt{n}} \tag{12.4}$$

Note that the margin of error is given by

$$E = z_{\alpha/2} \frac{\sigma}{\sqrt{n}} \tag{12.5}$$

(b) Unknown population variance (σ^2) or unknown standard
deviation (s)

$$\bar{x} - t_{n-1,\ \alpha/2} \frac{s}{\sqrt{n}} \leq \mu \leq \bar{x} + t_{n-1,\ \alpha/2} \frac{s}{\sqrt{n}} \tag{12.6}$$

(c) Unknown population variance (σ^2) or unknown standard
deviation (σ)

If the population variance is unknown and the sample size is large, the
confidence interval for the mean can also be calculated using a normal
distribution using the following formula:

$$\bar{x} \pm z_{\alpha/2} \frac{s}{\sqrt{n}} \tag{12.7}$$

In the above confidence interval formula, s is the sample standard
deviation.

Confidence Interval for the Mean When the Sample Size Is Small and the Population Standard Deviation σ Is Unknown

When σ is unknown and the sample size is small, use t-distribution for the confidence interval. The t-distribution is characterized by a single parameter, the number of *degrees of freedom (df)* and its density function provides a bell-shaped curve similar to a normal distribution.

The confidence interval using *t*-distribution is given by

$$\overline{x} - t_{n-1,\alpha/2}\frac{s}{\sqrt{n}} \le \mu \le \overline{x} + t_{n-1,\alpha/2}\frac{s}{\sqrt{n}} \qquad (12.8)$$

where $t_{n-1,\alpha/2}$ = *t*-value from the *t*-table for $(n-1)$ degrees of freedom and $\alpha/2$ where is the confidence level.

Confidence Interval for Estimating the Population Proportion, *p*

In this section, we will discuss the confidence interval estimate for the proportions. A proportion is ratio or fraction, or percentage that indicates the part of the population or sample having a particular trait of interest. Following are the examples of proportions: (1) a software company claiming that its manufacturing simulation software has 12 percent of the market share, (2) a public policy department of a large university wants to study the difference in proportion between male and female unemployment rate, and (3) a manufacturing company wants to determine the proportion of defective items produced by its assembly line. In all these cases, it may be desirable to construct the confidence intervals for the proportions of interest. The population proportion is denoted by *p* whereas, the sample proportion is denoted by $\overline{p}$.

In constructing the confidence interval for the proportion:

1. The underlying assumptions of binomial distribution holds.
2. The sample data collected are the results of counts (for example, in a sample of 100 products tested for defects, six were found to be defective).

3. The outcome of the experiment (testing six products from a randomly selected sample of 100 is an experiment) has two possible outcomes: "success" or "failure" (a product is found defective or not).
4. The probability of success (p) remains constant for each trial.

We consider the sample size (n) to be large. If the sample size is large and

$$np \geq 5, and$$
$$n(1 - p) \geq 5$$

where n is the sample size and p the population proportion; the binomial distribution can be approximated by a normal distribution. In constructing the confidence interval for the proportion, we use large sample size so that normal distribution can be used.

The confidence interval is based on:

(a) The large sample so that the sampling distribution of the sample proportion ($\bar{p}$) follows a normal distribution.
(b) The value of sample proportion.
(c) The level of confidence, denoted by z.

The confidence interval formula is given by

$$\bar{p} - z_{\alpha/2}\sqrt{\frac{\bar{p}(1 - \bar{p})}{n}} \leq p \leq \bar{p} + z_{\alpha/2}\sqrt{\frac{\bar{p}(1 - \bar{p})}{n}} \qquad (12.9)$$

In the above formula, note that p = population proportion and $\bar{p}$ is the sample proportion given by $\bar{p} = x/n$

Sample Size Determination: Sample Size (n) to Estimate μ

Determining the sample size is an important issue in statistical analysis. To determine the appropriate sample size (n), the following factors are considered:

(a) The margin of error, E (also known as tolerable error level or the accuracy requirement). For example, suppose we want to estimate the population means salary within \$500 or within \$200. In the first case, the error, $E = 500$; in the second case, $E = 200$. A smaller value of the error E means more precision is required which in turn, will require a larger sample. In general, smaller the error, E larger the sample size.

(b) The desired reliability or the confidence level.

(c) A good guess for σ.

Both the margin of error, E, and reliability are arbitrary choices that have an impact on the cost of sampling and the risks involved. The following formula is used to determine the sample size:

$$n = \frac{(z_{\alpha/2})^2 \sigma^2}{E^2}$$

(12.10)

E = margin of error or accuracy (or, maximum allowable error), n = sample size.

Sample Size (n) to Estimate p

The sample size formula to estimate the population proportion p is determined similar to the sample size for the mean. The sample size is given by

$$n = \frac{(z_{\alpha/2})^2 \, p(1-p)}{E^2}$$

(12.11)

p = population proportion (if p is not known or given, use $p = 0.5$).

Example

A quality control engineer is concerned about the bursting strength of a glass bottle used for soft drinks. A sample of size 25 ($n = 25$) is randomly obtained, and the bursting strength in pounds per square inch, psi) is recorded. The strength is considered to be normally distributed. Find a 95 percent confidence interval for the mean strength using both t-distribution and normal distribution. Compare and comment on your results.

Data: Bursting Strength (X10 psi)

$$26,\ 27,\ 18,\ 23,\ 24,\ 20,\ 21,\ 24,\ 19,\ 27,\ 25,\ 20,\ 24,$$
$$21,\ 26,\ 19,\ 21,\ 20,\ 25,\ 20,\ 23,\ 25,\ 21,\ 20,\ 21$$

Solution

First, calculate the mean and standard deviation of 25 values in the data. You should use your calculator or a computer to do this. The values are

$$\bar{x} = 22.40$$
$$s = 2.723$$

$$\bar{x} \pm t_{n-1,\frac{\alpha}{2}}\left(\frac{s}{\sqrt{n}}\right)$$

The confidence interval using a t-distribution can be calculated using the following formula:

A 95 percent confidence interval using the above formula

$$22.40 \pm (2.064)\left(\frac{2.723}{\sqrt{25}}\right)$$
$$21.28 \le \mu \le 23.52$$

The value 2.064 is the t-value from the t-table for $n - 1 = 24$ degrees of freedom and $\alpha/2 = 0.025$.

The confidence interval using a normal distribution can be calculated using the formula below.

$$\bar{x} \pm Z_{\alpha 2}\frac{\sigma}{\sqrt{n}}$$
$$22.40 \pm 1.96\left(\frac{2.723}{\sqrt{25}}\right)$$

This interval is

$$21.33 \le \mu \le 23.47$$

The confidence interval using the t-distribution is usually wider. This happens because with smaller sample size, there is more uncertainty involved.

Example

The average life of a sample of 36 tires of particular brand is 38,000 miles. If it is known that the average lifetime of the tires is approximately normally distributed with a standard deviation of 3,600 miles, construct 80 percent, 90 percent, 95 percent, and 99 percent confidence intervals for the average tire life. Compare and comment on the confidence interval estimates.

Solution: Note the following data:

$$n = 36 \qquad \overline{x} = 38,000 \qquad \sigma = 3,600$$

Since the sample size is large ($n \geq 30$), and the population standard deviation σ is known, the appropriate confidence interval formula is

$$\overline{x} \pm z_{\alpha/2} \frac{\sigma}{\sqrt{n}}$$

The confidence intervals using the above formula are shown below.

(a) 80 percent confidence interval

$$38,000 \pm 1.28 \left(\frac{3,600}{\sqrt{36}} \right)$$

$$37,232 \leq \mu \leq 38,768$$

(b) 90 percent confidence interval

$$38,000 \pm 1.645 \left(\frac{3,600}{\sqrt{36}} \right)$$

$$37,013 \leq \mu \leq 38,987$$

(c) 95 percent confidence interval

$$38,000 \pm 1.96 \left(\frac{3,600}{\sqrt{36}} \right)$$

$$36,824 \leq \mu \leq 39,176$$

(d) 99 percent confidence interval:

$$38,000 \pm 2.58 \left(\frac{3,600}{\sqrt{36}} \right)$$

$$36,452 \leq \mu \leq 39,548$$

Note that the z values in the above confidence interval calculations are obtained from the normal table. Refer to the normal table for the values of z. Figure 12.3 shows the confidence intervals graphically.

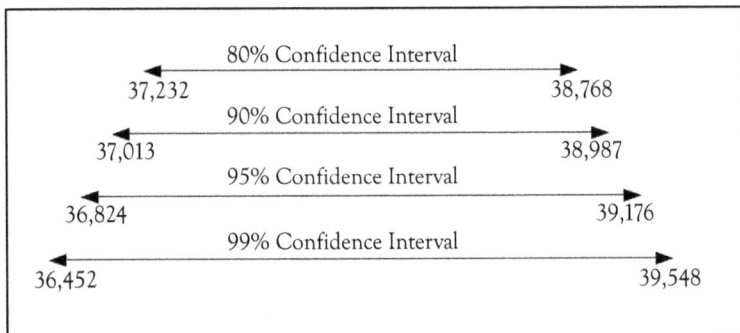

80% Confidence Interval

37,232   38,768

90% Confidence Interval

37,013   38,987

95% Confidence Interval

36,824   39,176

99% Confidence Interval

36,452   39,548

Figure 12.3 Effect of increasing the confidence level on the confidence interval

Figure 12.3 shows that larger the confidence level, the wider is the length of the interval. This indicates that for a larger confidence interval, we gain confidence. There is higher chance that the true value of the parameter being estimated is contained in the interval but at the same time, we lose accuracy.

Example

During an election year, ABC news network reported that according to its poll, 48 percent voters were in favor of the democratic presidential candidate with a margin of error of ±3 percent. What does this mean? From this information, determine the sample size that was used in this study.

Solution: The polls conducted by the news media use a 95 percent confidence interval unless specified otherwise. Using a 95 percent confidence interval, the confidence interval for the proportion is given by

$$\bar{p} \pm 1.96\sqrt{\frac{\bar{p}(1-\bar{p})}{n}}$$

The sample proportion, $\bar{p} = 0.48$. Thus, the confidence interval can be given by

$$0.48 \pm 1.96\sqrt{\frac{0.48(1-0.48)}{n}}$$

Since, the margin of error is ±3 percent, it follows

$$1.96\sqrt{\frac{0.48(1-0.48)}{n}} = 0.03$$

Squaring both sides and solving for n gives

$$n = 1066$$

Thus, 1066 voters were polled.

Example

A pressure seal used in an assembly must be able to withstand a maximum load of 6,000 pounds per square inch (psi) before bursting. If the average maximum load of a sample of seals taken from a shipment is less than 6,000 psi, then the quality control must reject the entire shipment. How large a sample is required if the quality engineer wishes to be 95 percent confident that the error in estimating this quantity is no more than 15 psi, or the probability that the sample mean differs from the population mean by no more than 15 psi is 0.95. From the past experience, it is known that the standard deviation for bursting pressures of this seal is 150 psi.

Solution: The sample size n can be calculated using

$$n = \left(\frac{z_{\alpha/2}\sigma}{E}\right)^2$$

Since $Z_{\alpha/2} = Z_{0.025} = 1.96$, $\sigma = 150$, and the error $E = 15$, the required sample size will be as follows:

$$n = \left(\frac{(1.96)150}{15}\right)^2 \approx 385$$

Confidence Interval on the Difference between Two Means

The confidence interval discussed in the previous sections involved a single population. In many cases, we are interested in comparing two populations. Suppose the average hourly wage of union and nonunion workers are of interest. We are interested to find out whether there is a difference in the wages between the two. In this case, we would construct a confidence interval on the difference between the two means. These intervals depend on what information is available. The different cases are explained below.

Case 1

Assumptions:

- The two populations are independent.
- The population variances are equal.
- The samples n_1 and n_2 are large and population variances σ_1^2 and σ_2^2 are *known* so that normal distribution applies.

If the above assumptions hold, then the confidence interval for the difference between two population means is given by

$$(\bar{x}_1 - \bar{x}_2) \pm z_{\alpha/2} \sqrt{\frac{\sigma_1^2}{n_1} + \frac{\sigma_2^2}{n_2}} \qquad (12.12)$$

or,

$$(\bar{x}_1 - \bar{x}_2) - z_{\alpha/2} \sqrt{\frac{\sigma_1^2}{n_1} + \frac{\sigma_2^2}{n_2}} \leq \mu_1 - \mu_2 \leq (\bar{x}_1 - \bar{x}_2) + z_{\alpha/2} \sqrt{\frac{\sigma_1^2}{n_1} + \frac{\sigma_2^2}{n_2}}$$

$$(12.13)$$

where $\bar{x}_1, \bar{x}_2$ are the sample means from populations 1 and 2
n_1, n_2 = sample size of sample 1 and 2
σ_1^2, σ_2^2 = variances of first and second populations respectively (known in this case)

Case 2

Assumptions:

- The two populations are independent.
- The population variances are equal.

- The samples n_1 and n_2 are large and population variances σ_1^2 and σ_2^2 are *unknown*, which means the normal distribution can be applied.

If the above assumptions hold, then the confidence interval for the difference between two population means is given by

$$(\bar{x}_1 - \bar{x}_2) \pm z_{\alpha/2} \sqrt{\frac{s_1^2}{n_1} + \frac{s_2^2}{n_2}} \qquad (12.14)$$

or,

$$(\bar{x}_1 - \bar{x}_2) - z_{\alpha/2} \sqrt{\frac{s_1^2}{n_1} + \frac{s_2^2}{n_2}} \leq \mu_1 - \mu_2 \leq (\bar{x}_1 - \bar{x}_2) + z_{\alpha/2} \sqrt{\frac{s_1^2}{n_1} + \frac{s_2^2}{n_2}}$$

$$(12.15)$$

where, s_1^2 and s_2^2 = sample variances of first and second sample, respectively
$\bar{x}_1, \bar{x}_2$ = sample means from populations 1 and 2 respectively
n_1, n_2 = sample size of sample 1 and 2.

Case 3

Assumptions:

- The two populations are independent.
- The population variances are equal.
- The samples n_1 and n_2 are small (< 30) and population variances σ_1^2 and σ_2^2 are *unknown* so that *t-distribution* applies.

If the above assumptions hold, then the confidence interval for the difference between two population means is given by

$$(\bar{x}_1 - \bar{x}_2) \pm t_{n_1 + n_2 - 2, \alpha/2} \sqrt{s_p^2 \left(\frac{1}{n_1} + \frac{1}{n_2} \right)} \qquad (12.16)$$

or,

$$(\bar{x}_1 - \bar{x}_2) - t_{n_1 + n_2 - 2, \alpha/2} \sqrt{s_p^2 \left(\frac{1}{n_1} + \frac{1}{n_2} \right)} \leq \mu_1 - \mu_2 \leq (\bar{x}_1 - \bar{x}_2)$$

$$+ t_{n_1 + n_2 - 2, \alpha/2} \sqrt{s_p^2 \left(\frac{1}{n_1} + \frac{1}{n_2} \right)}$$

$$(12.17)$$

where $\bar{x}_1, \bar{x}_2$ = sample means from populations 1 and 2 respectively

n_1, n_2 = sample size of sample 1 and 2

s_1^2, s_2^2 = sample variances of 1st and 2nd sample respectively

$n_1 + n_2 - 2$ = degrees of freedom

s_p^2 is the "pooled" or combined variance, given by

$$s_p^2 = \frac{(n_1 - 1)s_1^2 + (n_2 - 1)s_2^2}{n_1 + n_2 - 2}$$

Note: In this problem, first calculate s_p^2 and then substitute in equation to calculate the confidence interval.

Example

The average hourly wage of union and nonunion workers are of interest. Assume that (i) the populations are independent, and (ii) the variances of the populations are equal ($\sigma_1^2 = \sigma_2^2$). Sample from both groups were taken with the following results:

Union Workers	Nonunion Workers
$n_1 = 15$	$n_2 = 20$
$\bar{x}_1 = 14.54$	$\bar{x}_2 = 15.36$
$s_1 = 2.24$	$s_2 = 2.99$

(a) Find the "pooled" estimate of the variance.

$$S_p^2 = \frac{(n_1 - 1)s_1^2 + (n_2 - 1)s_2^2}{n_1 + n_2 - 2}$$

$$= \frac{(14)(2.24)^2 + (19)(1.99)^2}{33} = 4.41$$

(b) Find a 95 percent confidence interval for the difference in the mean hourly wage.

Confidence interval formula for this case:

$$\left(\bar{x}_1 - \bar{x}_2\right) \pm t_{n_1 + n_2 - 2, \, \alpha/2} \sqrt{Sp^2\left(\frac{1}{n_1} + \frac{1}{n_2}\right)}$$

$$\downarrow$$

$$t_{33, 0.025} - 2.035$$

$$(14.54 - 15.36) \pm (2.035)(0.72)$$
$$-0.82 \pm 1.47$$
$$-2.29 \; to \; 0.65$$

or, $-2.29 \le \mu_1 - \mu_2 \le 0.65$

Note that this interval contains zero (−2.29 to 0.65). This means that the difference is zero at some point in the interval indicating there is no difference in the average wage of union and nonunion workers.

Point and Interval Estimates for the Difference Between Two Population Proportions

Consider two large populations. Let p_1 and p_2 denote the proportions of these two populations that have certain characteristics of interest. Suppose we want to find the difference between the two population proportions. To do this, we will take two random samples of size n_1 and n_2 from the two populations. If x_1 is the number having the characteristic of interest in the first population, and x_2 the number having the characteristic of interest in the second population, then $\bar{p}_1$ and $\bar{p}_2$ are the sample proportions of the two samples that have the characteristic of interest. Note that

$$\bar{p}_1 = \frac{x_1}{n_1} \; and \; \bar{p}_2 = \frac{x_2}{n_2}$$

The point estimate for the difference between the population proportions is given by

$$\text{Point Estimate} = \bar{p}_1 - \bar{p}_2 \qquad (12.18)$$

The confidence interval for the difference between the population proportions is given by

$$(\bar{p}_1 - \bar{p}_2) \pm z_{\alpha/2} \sqrt{\bar{p}(1-\bar{p})(\frac{1}{n_1} + \frac{1}{n_2})} \qquad (12.19)$$

where $\bar{p}$ is the "pooled" or combined proportion given by

$$\bar{p} = \frac{x_1 + x_2}{n_1 + n_2} \; or \; \bar{p} = \frac{n_1 \bar{p}_1 + n_2 \bar{p}_2}{n_1 + n_2}$$

Example

A manufacturer of computer chips has two plants in two different cities. An improved method of producing the chips is suggested by the research and development department, which is expected to reduce the proportion of defective chips. After implementing the new method in one of the plants, the manufacturer wanted to test whether the improved method reduced the proportion of defects. To do this, they collected a sample of 400 chips from the improved method of production, and a sample of 450 chips from the old production method. The numbers of defective chips were found to be 80 and 108 respectively. At a 95 percent confidence, can we conclude that there is a difference in proportion of defective chips?

Proportion of defective using the improved method:

$$\bar{p}_1 = \frac{x_1}{n_1} = \frac{80}{400} = 0.20$$

Proportion of defective using the old method: $\bar{p}_2 = \frac{x_2}{n_2} = \frac{108}{450} = 0.24$

Combined or the "pooled" proportion: $\bar{p} = \frac{x_1 + x_2}{n_1 + n_2} = \frac{80 + 108}{400 + 450} = 0.221$

The confidence interval:

$$(\bar{p}_1 - \bar{p}_2) \pm z_{\alpha/2}\sqrt{\bar{p}(1 - \bar{p})(\frac{1}{n_1} + \frac{1}{n_2})}$$

$$(0.20 - 0.24) \pm (1.96)\sqrt{(0.221)(1 - 0.221)(\frac{1}{400} + \frac{1}{450})}$$

$$-0.04 \pm 0.06$$

Thus, a 95 percent confidence interval is

$$-0.1 \le p_1 - p_2 \le 0.02$$

This interval contains zero which indicates that there is no difference between the improved method and the old method of production.

Hypothesis Testing for One and Two Population Parameters

Hypothesis Testing

A *hypothesis* is a statement about a *population parameter*. This statement may come from a claim made by a manufacturer, a mathematical model, a theory, or design specifications. For example, an automobile manufacturer may claim that they have come up with a new fuel injection system design that provides an improved average mileage of 50 miles a gallon. In such a case, we may want to test the claim by taking sample data. The claim can formally be written as a hypothesis testing problem and can be tested using a hypothesis testing procedure. Several population parameters may be of interest. Sometimes we may be interested in testing the average or the mean. In other cases, we may be interested in testing a variance, a standard deviation, or a population proportion.

Many problems require us to decide whether or not a statement about some parameter is true or false. This statement about the population parameter is called a *hypothesis*.

Hypothesis testing is the decision-making procedure about a statement being true or false. The statement is about a population parameter of interest, such as, a population mean, population variance, or a population proportion. It involves making a decision about a population parameter based on the information contained in the sample data.

Hypothesis testing is one of the most useful aspects of statistical inference because many types of decision problems can be formulated as hypothesis testing problems.

In the chapters that follow, we will see that the control charts used in statistical process control are closely related to the hypothesis testing. The tests are also used in several quality control problems and form the basis of many of the statistical process techniques to be discussed in the coming chapters.

Example: Testing a Single Population Mean

An automobile manufacturer claims that their new hybrid model will provide 60 miles per gallon on the average because of an improved design. A consumer group wants to test whether this claim is correct. They would test a hypothesis stated formally as follows:

H_0: $\mu = 60mpg$
H_1: $\mu \neq 60mpg$

Here, H_0 is known as the null hypothesis and H_1 (also written H_a) is called the alternate hypothesis. The hypothesis written with an "equal to" sign under the null hypothesis and a "not equal to" sign under the alternate hypothesis is known as a two-sided or two-tailed test. A hypothesis can also be one-sided or one-tailed. The alternate hypothesis is opposite of the null hypothesis. To test the validity of above claim,

- The consumer group would gather the sample data and calculate the sample mean, $\bar{x}$ and
- Compare the difference between the hypothesized value of (μ) and the value of the sample mean ($\bar{x}$).
- If the difference is small, there is a greater likelihood that the hypothesized value of the population mean is correct. If the difference is large, there is less likelihood that the claim about the population mean is correct.

In most cases, the difference between the hypothesized population parameter and the actual sample statistic is neither so large that we reject our hypothesis, nor it is so small that we accept it. Thus, in hypothesis testing, clear cut solutions are not the rule.

Note that in hypothesis testing, the decision to reject or not to reject the hypothesis is based on a single sample and therefore there is always a chance of not rejecting a hypothesis that is false or rejecting a hypothesis that is true. In fact, we always encounter two types of errors in hypothesis testing. These are:

$$\text{Type I Error} = \alpha = P\{\text{Reject } H_0 \,|\, H_0 \text{ is true}\}$$
$$\text{Type II Error} = \beta = P\{\text{Fail to reject } H_0 \,|\, H_0 \text{ is false}\} \qquad (12.20)$$

We also use another term known as the power of the test defined as

$$\text{Power} = 1 - \beta = P \{\text{Reject } H_0 \mid H_0 \text{ is false}\}$$

Thus, the type I error, denoted by a Greek letter α ("alpha") is the probability of rejecting a true null hypothesis and the type II error, denoted by a Greek letter β (beta) is the probability of not rejecting a null hypothesis when it is false. In a hypothesis testing situation, there is always a possibility of making one of these errors.

The power of the test is the probability that a false null hypothesis is correctly rejected. The type I error, α, is selected by the analyst. Increasing the type I error α will decrease the type II error β and decreasing the type I α error will increase the type II error β. Thus, the type I error is controlled by the analyst and the type II error is determined based on the type I error. The type II error is a function of the sample size. The larger the sample size n, the smaller is the β.

Type I error α is also known as the level of significance. In hypothesis testing, we specify a value of the type I error or the level of significance and then design a test that will provide a small value of the type II error. Recall that the *type I error is the probability of rejecting a true null hypothesis.* Since we don't want this to happen, α is set to a low value of 1, 5 or 10 percent in general cases. If you set the value of $\alpha = 5$ percent, it means that there is a 5 percent chance of making an incorrect decision, and a 95 percent chance of making a right decision. In a hypothesis testing, there is never a 100 percent chance of making a right decision because the test is based on one sample (large or small).

What Does It Mean To Test a Hypothesis at a 5 percent Level of Significance?

Suppose we want to test a hypothesis about a population mean and the sample size is large ($n \geq 30$) so that the sample mean follows a normal distribution. If the level of significance α is set at 5 percent, it means that we will reject the null hypothesis if the difference between the sample statistic (in this case, $\bar{x}$) and the hypothesized population mean μ is so large that it would occur on the average only 5 or fewer times in every 100 samples.

See Figure 12.4. This figure shows that if the sample statistic falls in the "do not reject" area, we will not reject the null hypothesis. On the other hand, if the sample value falls in the rejection areas, we will reject the null hypothesis. Rejecting the null hypothesis means that the alternate hypothesis is true.

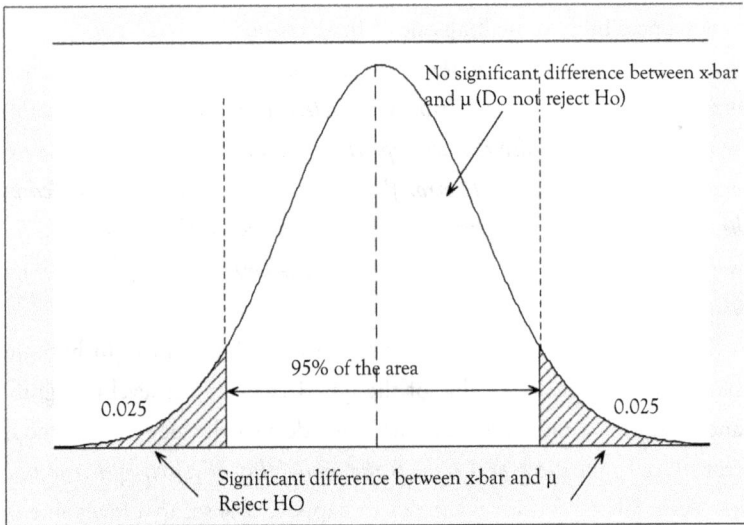

Figure 12.4 *Rejection and nonrejection areas*

It is evident from the figure that by selecting a significance level α, the areas of rejection and non-rejection are determined. In other words, we set the boundaries that determine when to reject and when not to reject the null hypothesis.

Note that the value of α is selected by the analyst and it must be determined before you conduct the test. If we don't have a significance level α, we don't know when to reject and when not to reject a hypothesis.

In a hypothesis testing situation, there is always a possibility of making one of the two types of errors (that is, there is always a chance of rejecting a true null hypothesis; similarly, there is always a chance of accepting a false null hypothesis). In a hypothesis testing, we must consider the cost and the risk involved in making a wrong decision. Also, we would like to minimize the chance of making either a Type I or Type II error therefore, it is desirable to have the probabilities of both type I and type II error to be low.

In quality control, α is also known as *producer's risk* because it denotes the probability of rejecting a good lot. The type II error β is referred as the *consumer's risk* as it indicates the probability of accepting a bad lot.

Testing a Single Population Mean

Testing a population mean involves testing a one-sided or a two-sided test. The hypothesis is stated as:

$H_0 : \mu = \mu_0$	$H_0 : \mu \geq \mu_0$	$H_0 : \mu \leq \mu_0$
$H_1 : \mu \neq \mu_0$	$H_1 : \mu < \mu_0$	$H_1 : \mu > \mu_0$
Two-tailed or	*Left-tailed or*	*Right –tailed or*
Two-sided Test	*Left-sided Test*	*Right-sided Test*

Note that μ_0 is the hypothesized value. There are three possible cases for testing the population mean. The test statistics or the formulas used to test the hypothesis are given below.

Case (1): Testing a single mean with known variance or known population standard deviation s and large sample: in this case, the sample mean $\bar{x}$ follows a normal distribution and the *test statistic* is given as follows:

$$z = \frac{\bar{x} - \mu}{\sigma / \sqrt{n}} \qquad (12.21)$$

Case (2): Testing a single mean with unknown variance or unknown population standard deviation σ and large sample: in this case, the sample mean $\bar{x}$ follows a Normal distribution and the *test statistic* is given by

$$z = \frac{\bar{x} - \mu}{s / \sqrt{n}} \qquad (12.22)$$

Case (3): Testing a single mean with unknown variance or unknown population standard deviation σ and small $(n < 30)$ sample. In this case, the sample mean, $\bar{x}$ follows a *t*-distribution and the *test statistic* is given by

$$t_{n-1} = \frac{\bar{x} - \mu}{s / \sqrt{n}} \qquad (12.23)$$

Note that s is the sample standard deviation and n is the sample size.

There are different ways of testing a hypothesis. These will be illustrated with examples.

Example: Formulating the Correct Hypothesis

A hypothesis test can be formulated as a one-sided or a two- sided test. If we have a one-sided test, it can be a left-sided or a right-sided test.

Example of a Left-Sided Test

Suppose a tire manufacturer claims that the average mileage provided by a certain type of tire is at least 60,000 miles. A product research group has received some complains in the past and wants to check the claim. They are interested in testing whether the average mileage is below 60,000 miles. They would formulate their hypothesis as follows:

$$H_0 : \mu \geq 60000$$
$$H_1 : \mu < 60000$$

The hypothesis is formulated as shown above because the claim of at least 60,000 miles is $\mu \geq 60,000$ and the opposite of this statement is $\mu < 60,000$ miles. Since the null hypothesis is written with an "equal to" sign, and this is the claim made by the manufacturer, the statement $\mu \geq 60,000$ is written under the null hypothesis, and the statement $\mu < 60,000$ is written under the alternate hypothesis.

Note that the alternate hypothesis is opposite of the null hypothesis. This is an example of a left sided test. The left-sided test will reject the null hypothesis (H_0) below a specified hypothesized value of μ.

The alternate hypothesis is also known as *the research hypothesis*. If you are trying to establish certain hypothesis, then it should be written as the alternate hypothesis.

The statement about the null hypothesis contains the claim or the theory. Therefore, rejecting a null hypothesis is a strong statement. This is the reason that the conclusion of a hypothesis test is stated as "*reject the null hypothesis*" or "*do not reject the null hypothesis.*"

Example of a Right-Sided Test

A car manufacturer has made a significant improvement in the fuel injection system that is expected to provide an improved gas mileage.

The average mileage before the modification was 24 miles or less. The research group expects that the modified system will provide significant improvement in the gas mileage. The group would like to test the following hypothesis to show the improvement:

$$H_0 : \mu \leq 24$$
$$H_1 : \mu > 24$$

Example of a Two-Sided Test

A robot welder in an assembly line takes on average 2.5 minutes to finish a welding job. If the average time taken to finish the job is higher or lower than 2.5 minutes, it will disrupt other activities along the production line. Since there has been too much variation in the time it takes to perform the welding job by the robot, the line supervisor wants to take a sample to check if the average time taken by the robot is significantly higher or lower than the average of 2.5 minutes. The supervisor would be testing the following hypothesis:

$$H_0 : \mu = 1.5$$
$$H_1 : \mu \neq 1.5$$

Example

A new production method will be implemented if a hypothesis test supports the conclusion that the new method results in reduced production cost per hour. If the current average operating cost per hour is $600 or more, write the appropriate hypothesis. Also, state and explain the Type I and Type II error in this situation.

(a) Write the appropriate null and alternate hypotheses.
   The appropriate hypotheses to test the claim:

$$H_0 : \mu \geq 600$$
$$H_1 : \mu < 600$$

(b) State and explain the Type I and Type II error in this situation.

Type I error: Reject H_0: $\mu \geq 600$ and conclude that the average production cost is less than \$600 ($\mu < \$600$). Type II error would be to conclude that the average operating cost is at least \$600 when it is not.

Example

In a production line, automated machines are used to fill beverage cans with an average fill volume of 16 ounces. If the mean weight falls above or below this figure, the production line must be stopped, and some remedial action be taken. A quality control inspector samples 30 cans every hour: opens and weighs the content, tests the appropriate hypothesis, and decides whether to shut down the line for making adjustments. Write the appropriate hypothesis to be tested in this situation and perform the hypothesis test. A significance level of $\alpha = 0.05$ is selected for the test. The sample results indicate a sample mean of 16.32 oz. and the standard deviation is assumed to be 0.8 oz.

Solution: For this problem, the given data are:

$$n = 30, \ \alpha = 0.05$$
$$\sigma = 0.8, \ \bar{x} = 16.32$$

1. State the null and alternate hypothesis.

$$H_0 : \mu = 16$$
$$H_1 : \mu \neq 16$$

   Note that this is a two-sided test.

2. Determine the sample size or use the given sample size.

   The given sample size is $n=30$ (large sample)

3. Determine the appropriate level of significance (α) or use the given value of significance, α

   The given level of significance, $\alpha = 0.05$.

4. Select the appropriate distribution and test statistic to perform the test.

   The sample size is large and the population standard deviation is known. Therefore, use normal distribution with the following test-statistic

$$z = \frac{\bar{x} - \mu}{\sigma/\sqrt{n}}$$

5. Based on step 3, find the critical value or values and the area or areas of rejection. Show the critical value(s) and the area or areas of rejection and nonrejection using a sketch.

This is a two-sided test. The level of significance, $\alpha = 0.05$ must be split into two halves for a two-tailed test with each tail area 0.025. The critical value (z-value) for an area of 0.475 is 2.96 from the normal or z table. The sketch is shown in Figure 12.5.

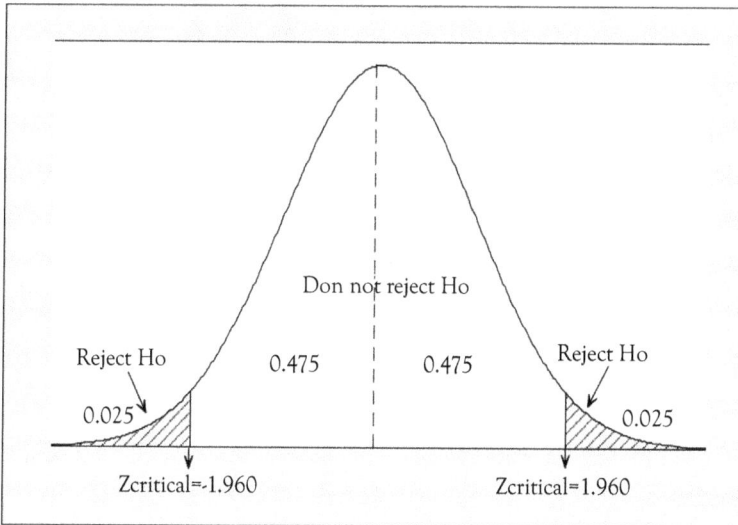

Figure 12.5 Critical values for a two-sided test

6. Write the decision rule

$$\text{Reject } H_0 \text{ if } z > 1.96 \text{ or,}$$
$$\text{if } z < -1.96$$

7. Use the test data (sample data) and find the value of the test statistic.

$$z = \frac{\bar{x} - \mu}{\sigma/\sqrt{n}} = \frac{16.32 - 16}{0.8/\sqrt{30}} = 2.19$$

8. Find out if the value of the test statistic is in rejection or non-rejection region; make appropriate decision and state your conclusion in terms of the problem.

$$z = 2.19 > z_{critical} = 2.96 \text{ therefore, reject } H_0$$

There is an evidence of over filling or under filling. The line should be shut down.

Example

Testing the Hypothesis Using the p-Value Approach

In the z-value approach of testing the hypothesis, we compared the test statistic value to the critical value of z to either reject or not to reject the hypothesis. For example, in the previous example, the critical value z was ± 2.96 and the test statistic value was 2.19. Since the test statistic value of 2.19 is greater than the critical value of +2.96, we rejected the null hypothesis. In this method of testing the hypothesis, we compared the similar terms (test statistics value of z to the critical z value). This method of stating conclusion in the hypothesis test requires a predefined level of significance which may not tell if the computed test statistic value is barely in the rejection region or it is far into the region. In other words, the information may be inadequate sometimes.

To overcome this problem, another approach of testing the hypothesis is suggested which is widely used in testing hypothesis. This is known as *p-value* (probability value) approach. This method compares a probability to the given probability.

You may recall that to test a hypothesis you must have the level of significance α, which is decided by the analyst before conducting the test. This α is the same as the type I probability and is often called the given level of significance. In a hypothesis testing situation, the type I probability is given or known. We then calculate the p value, or the probability based on the sample data. This is also the observed level of significance. We then compare the given level of significance α to the p-value (observed level of significance) to test and draw the conclusion about the hypothesis.

> The p-value is the probability (assuming that the null hypothesis is true) of getting the value of the test statistic at least as extreme as, or more extreme than the value actually observed. The p-value is the smallest level of significance at which the null hypothesis can be rejected. A small p-value for example, p = 0.05 or less is a strong indicator that the null hypothesis is not true. The smaller is the value of p, the greater the chance that the null hypothesis is false.

If the computed p-value is smaller than the given level of significance α, the null hypothesis H_0 is rejected. If the p-value is greater than α then H_0 is not rejected. For example, a p-value of 0.002 indicates that there is less chance that H_0 is true, while a p-value of 0.2356 indicates a less likelihood of H_0 being false. The p-value also provides us insight into the strength of the decision. This tells us how confident we are in rejecting the null hypothesis.

Example: Testing the Hypothesis Using p-Value Approach
We will test the hypothesis using p-value for the following two-sided test:

$$H_0 : \mu = 15$$
$$H_1 : \mu \neq 15$$

The data for the problem: $n = 50$, $\bar{x} = 14.2$, $s = 5$, $\alpha = 0.02$.

Decision Rule for p-value approach

If $p \geq \alpha$, do not reject H_0

If $p < \alpha$; reject H_0

First; using the appropriate test statistic formula, calculate the test statistic value.

$$Z = \frac{\bar{x} - \mu}{s/\sqrt{n}} = \frac{14.2 - 15}{5/\sqrt{50}} = -1.13$$

This test statistic value of $z = -2.13$ will be converted into a probability that we call p-value. This is shown in Figure 12.6.

Area corresponding to $z = 2.13$ is 0.3708 (from z-table).

Probability of $z > 2.13 = 0.5 - 0.3708 = 0.1292$

Probability of $z < -2.13 = 0.5 - 0.3708 = 0.1292$

For a two-sided test, the p value is the sum of the above two values, that is, $0.1292 + 0.1292$.

$= 0.2584$. Since $p = 0.2584 > \alpha = 0.02$; do not reject H_0.

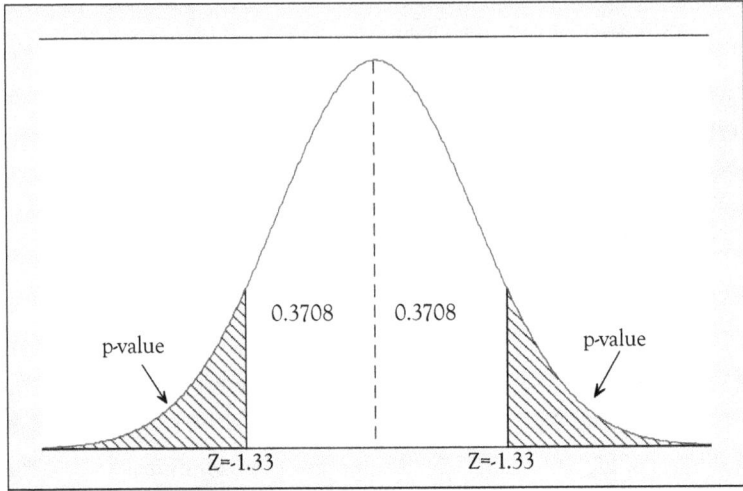

Figure 12.6 p-values for the example problem

Hypothesis Testing Involving Two Population Means

This section extends the concepts of hypothesis testing to two populations. Here we are interested in testing two population means. For example, we may be interested in comparing the average salaries of male and female employees for the same job, or we may be interested in the difference between the average starting salaries of business and engineering majors. In these cases, we would like to test whether the two-population means are equal or there is no difference between the two populations (two-sided test). In other cases, we may want to test if one population is larger or smaller than the other population (one-sided test). The hypothesis testing procedures or steps are very similar to those for testing the single mean but the data structure and the test statistics or the formulas to test these hypotheses are different. In testing hypothesis involving two populations, the samples will be drawn from both populations. The hypotheses tested are explained below.

Hypothesis Testing for the Equality of Two Means or the Differences between Two Population Means

Basic Assumptions:

1. The populations are independent.
2. The population variances are equal ($\sigma_1^2 = \sigma_2^2$).

The hypothesis for testing the two means can be a two-sided test or a one-sided test. The hypothesis is written in one of the following ways:

(a) Test if the two population means are equal or there is no difference between the two means: *a two-sided test.*

$$H_0 : \mu_1 = \mu_2 \text{ or } H_0 : \mu_1 - \mu_2 = 0$$
$$H_1 : \mu_1 \neq \mu_2 \text{ or } H_1 : \mu_1 - \mu_2 \neq 0 \qquad (12.28)$$

(b) Test if one population mean is greater than the other: *a right-sided test.*

$$H_0 : \mu_1 \leq \mu_2 \text{ or } H_0 : \mu_1 - \mu_2 \leq 0$$
$$H_1 : \mu_1 > \mu_2 \text{ or } H_1 : \mu_1 - \mu_2 > 0 \qquad (12.29)$$

(c) Test if one population mean is smaller than the other: *a left-sided test.*

$$H_0 : \mu_1 \geq \mu_2 \text{ or } H_0 : \mu_1 - \mu_2 \geq 0$$
$$H_1 : \mu_1 < \mu_2 \text{ or } H_1 : \mu_1 - \mu_2 < 0 \qquad (12.30)$$

Since we want to study two population means, the sampling distribution of interest is the sampling distribution of the difference between the sample means ($\bar{x}_1 - \bar{x}_2$) and the test statistic is based on the information (data) we have. The following three cases and test statistics are used to test the means. To test two means, the test statistics are based on the following cases:

Case 1: Sample sizes n_1 and n_2 are large (≥ 30) and the population variances σ_1^2 and σ_2^2 are known

If the sample sizes n_1 and n_2 are large (≥ 30) and the population variances σ_1^2 and σ_2^2 are known, then the sampling distribution of the difference between the sample means follows a normal distribution and the test statistic is given by

$$z = \frac{(\bar{x}_1 - \bar{x}_2) - (\mu_1 - \mu_2)}{\sqrt{\dfrac{\sigma_1^2}{n_1} + \dfrac{\sigma_2^2}{n_2}}} \tag{12.31}$$

where, $\bar{x}_1, \bar{x}_2$ = sample means from populations 1 and 2, respectively
n_1, n_2 = sample size of sample 1 and 2
σ_1^2, σ_2^2 = variances of first and second populations respectively (known in this case)

Case 2: Sample sizes n_1 and n_2 are large (≥ 30) and the population variances σ_1^2 and σ_2^2 are unknown

If the sample sizes n_1 and n_2 are large (≥ 30) and the population variances σ_1^2 and σ_2^2 are unknown, then the sampling distribution of the difference between the sample means follows a normal distribution and the test statistic is given by

$$z = \frac{(\bar{x}_1 - \bar{x}_2) - (\mu_1 - \mu_2)}{\sqrt{\dfrac{s_1^2}{n_1} + \dfrac{s_2^2}{n_2}}} \tag{12.32}$$

where, $\bar{x}_1, \bar{x}_2$ = sample means from populations 1 and 2 respectively
n_1, n_2 = sample size of sample 1 and 2
s_1^2, s_2^2 = sample variances of first and second sample respectively

Case 3: Sample sizes n_1 and n_2 are small (≥ 30) and the population variances σ_1^2 and σ_2^2 are unknown.

If the sample sizes n_1 and n_2 are small (≥ 30) and the population variances σ_1^2 and σ_2^2 are unknown, then the sampling distribution of the difference between the sample means follows a t-distribution and the test statistic is given by

$$t_{n_1+n_2-2} = \frac{(\bar{x}_1 - \bar{x}_2) - (\mu_1 - \mu_2)}{\sqrt{s_p^2\left(\dfrac{1}{n_1} + \dfrac{1}{n_2}\right)}} \tag{12.33}$$

where, $\bar{x}_1$, $\bar{x}_2$ = sample means from populations 1 and 2 respectively

n_1, n_2 = sample size of sample 1 and 2

s_1^2, s_2^2 = sample variances of first and second sample respectively

$n_1 + n_2 - 2$ = degrees of freedom (df)

s_p^2 is the "pooled" or combined variance, given by

$$s_p^2 = \frac{(n_1 - 1)s_1^2 + (n_2 - 1)s_2^2}{n_1 + n_2 - 2} \tag{12.34}$$

Important Note:

In Equations (13.32), (13.33), and (13.34) the difference $(\mu_1 - \mu_2)$ is zero in most cases. Also, these equations are valid under the following assumptions:

- The populations are independent and normally distributed.
- The variances of the two populations are equal; that is, $(\sigma_1^2 = \sigma_2^2)$.

The assumption that the two population variances are equal may not be correct. In cases where the variances are not equal, the test statistics formula for testing the difference between the two means is different.

Example

Suppose that two independent random samples are taken from two processes with equal variances and we would like to test the null hypothesis that there is no difference between the means of two processes or the means of the two processes are equal; that is,

$$H_0 : \mu_1 - \mu_2 = 0 \qquad \text{or} \qquad H_0 : \mu_1 = \mu_2$$

$$H_1 : \mu_1 - \mu_2 \neq 0 \qquad \qquad H_1 : \mu_1 \neq \mu_2$$

The data from the two processes are given below:

Sample 1	Sample 2
$n_1 = 80$	$n_2 = 70$
$\bar{x}_1 = 104$	$\bar{x}_2 = 106$
$s_1 = 8.4$	$s_2 = 7.6$
$\alpha = 0.05$	

Note that when n_1, n_2 are large and σ_1, σ_2 unknown, therefore use normal distribution. The test statistic for this problem is

$$z = \frac{(\bar{x}_1 - \bar{x}_2) - (\mu_1 - \mu_2)}{\sqrt{\dfrac{s_1^2}{n_1} + \dfrac{s_2^2}{n_2}}}$$

Solution: The test can be done using four methods which are explained below.

Method (1): z-Value Approach

Critical values: The critical values and the decision areas based on $\alpha = 0.05$ are shown in Figure 12.7. Decision Rule: Reject H_0 if $z > 1.96$

or   if $z < -1.96$

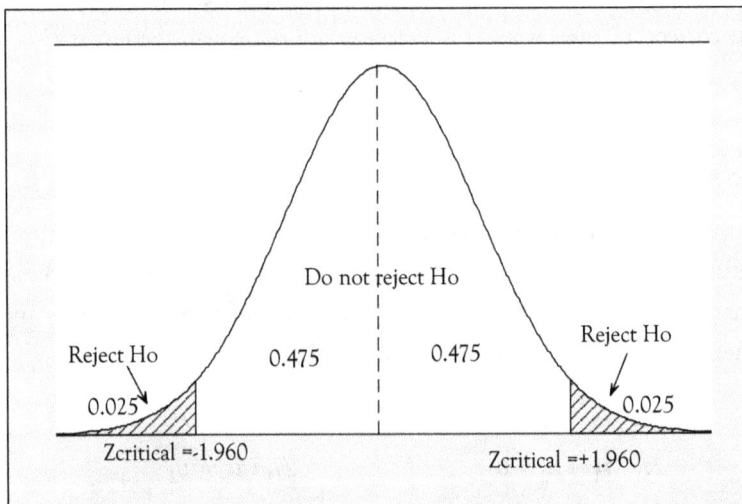

Figure 12.7 Critical values and decision areas

Test Statistic Value:

$$z = \frac{(\bar{x}_1 - \bar{x}_2) - (\mu_1 - \mu_2)}{\sqrt{\dfrac{s_1^2}{n_1} + \dfrac{s_2^2}{n_2}}} = \frac{(104 - 106) - 0}{\sqrt{\dfrac{(8.4)^2}{80} + \dfrac{(7.6)^2}{70}}} = -1.53$$

The test statistic value z, $-2.53 > z_{critical} = -1.96$; do not reject H_0.

Method (2): p-Value Approach

Calculate the p-value and compare it to α. Note that in this method we compare a probability to a probability; that is, we compare the given level of significance α or the type I probability to the probability obtained from the data (or, the observed level of significance). The decision rule and the procedure are explained below.

Decision Rule: If $p \geq \alpha$; do not reject H_0.
                               If $p < \alpha$; reject H_0.

Calculating p-value: the p-value is calculated by converting the test-statistics value into a probability. In method (1), we calculated the test statistic value z. This value was -2.53 or, $z = -2.53$. This test statistics value is converted to a probability (see the Figure 12.8).

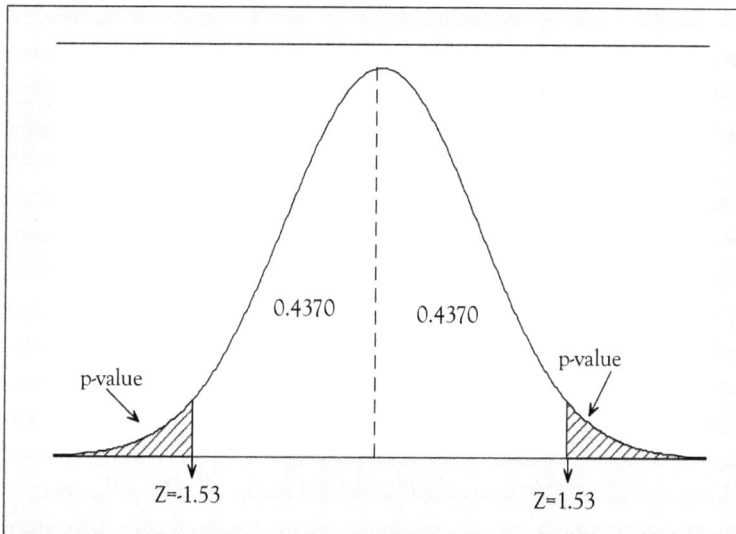

0.4370   0.4370

p-value   p-value

Z=-1.53   Z=1.53

Figure 12.8 p-values

In the above figure, $z = 2.53$ is the test statistic value from method 1 above. From the standard normal table, $z = 2.53$ corresponds to 0.4370. The p-value is calculated as shown below.

$$\text{Probability of } z > 2.53 = 0.5 - 0.4370 = 0.0630$$
$$\text{Probability of } z < -2.53 = 0.5 - 0.4370 = 0.0630$$

In a two-sided test such as, this one the p-value is obtained by adding the probabilities in both tails of the distribution. Thus,

$$p = 0.0630 + 0.0630 = 0.1260$$

Since $p(= 0.1260) > \alpha(= 0.05)$; do not reject H_0.

Testing Two Means for Dependent (Related) Populations or Hypothesis Testing for Paired Samples (Paired t-Test)

In some situations, there may be a relationship between the data values of the samples of two populations and the data values or the sample values from one population may not be independent of the sample values from the other population. The two populations may be considered dependent in such cases.

In cases where the populations are considered related, the observations are paired to prevent other factors from inflating the estimate of the variance. This method is used to improve the precision of comparisons between means. The method of testing the difference between two means when the populations are related is also known as *matched sample* or *the paired test*.

We are interested in testing a two-sided or a one-sided hypothesis for the difference between the two population means. The hypotheses can be written as

$H_0 : \mu_d = 0$	$H_0 : \mu_d \leq 0$	$H_0 : \mu_d \geq 0$
$H_1 : \mu_d \neq 0$	$H_1 : \mu_d > 0$	$H_1 : \mu_d < 0$
Two-tailed or	*Right tailed or*	*Left-tailed or*
Two-sided test	*Right-sided test*	*Left-sided test*

Note: the difference, d can be taken in any order; (sample 1 – sample 2) or (sample 2 – sample 1).

Test Statistic: If the pairs of data values X_{1n} and X_{2n} are related, and are not independent; the average of the differences $(\overline{d})$ follows a *t*-distribution and the test statistic is given by

$$t_{n-1} = \frac{\overline{d} - \mu_d}{s_d / \sqrt{n}}$$

(12.35)

where,

$\overline{d}$ = average of the differences = $\dfrac{\sum d_i}{n}$

S_d = standard deviation of the differences;

$$s_d = \sqrt{\frac{\sum (d_i - \overline{d})^2}{n-1}} = \sqrt{\frac{\sum d_i^2 - \dfrac{\left(\sum d_i\right)^2}{n}}{n-1}}$$

n = number of observations (sample size).

$t_{n-1,\frac{\alpha}{2}}$ = critical *t*-value from the *t*-table for $(n-1)$ degrees of freedom and appropriate α

The confidence interval given below can also be used to test the hypothesis

$$\overline{d} \pm t_{n-1,\frac{\alpha}{2}} \frac{s_d}{\sqrt{n}}$$

(12.36)

Summary

This chapter discussed three important topics that are critical to modelling and regression analysis in data science. We studied estimation and confidence intervals, and hypothesis testing. The concept of sampling theory is important in studying these applications. Samples are used to make inferences about the population, and this can be done through sampling distribution. The probability distribution of a sample statistic is called its *sampling distribution*. We explained the *central limit theorem* and its role in sampling, sampling distribution, and sample size determination. Besides sampling and sampling distribution, other key topics covered in this chapter included point and confidence interval estimates of means and proportions.

Two types of estimates used in inferential statistics were discussed. These estimates include: (a) the *point estimates*, which are single-value estimates of the population parameter, and (b) the interval estimates or the confidence intervals which are a range of numbers that contain the parameter with specified degree of confidence known as the confidence level. Confidence level is a probability attached to a confidence interval that provides the reliability of the estimate. In the discussion of estimation, we also discussed the standard error of the estimates, the margin of error, and the sample size determination.

We also discussed the concepts of hypothesis testing which is directly related to the analysis methods used in regression analysis. Hypothesis testing is one of the most useful aspects of statistical inference. We provided several examples on formulating and testing hypothesis about the population mean and population proportion. Hypothesis tests are used in assessing the validity of regression methods. They form the basis of many of the assumptions underlying the regression analysis to be discussed in the coming chapters.

PART IV

Introduction to Machine Learning and R-statistical Programming Software

CHAPTER 13

Basics of MachLearning (ML)

Chapter Highlights

- Introduction to Machine Learning: What is machine learning?
- Machine Learning and Artificial Intelligence (AI)
- Examples of Some Problems Where Machine Learning Is Applied
- Types of Problems Machine Learning Can Solve
- Supervised Learning: Classification
- Regression
- Unsupervised Learning
- Clustering and Types of Clustering
- Examples of Classification Problems: Examples
- Clustering Problems: Examples
- Programming Languages used in Machine Learning
- R-Statistical Programing Language
- Python Programing Language
- Automating the Machine Learning Problem
- SAS Machine Learning
- Microsoft Auto Machine Learning: Azur

What Is Machine Learning (ML)?

Machine learning is a method of designing systems that can learn, adjust, and improve based on the data fed to them without being explicitly programmed. Machine learning applications are a way of analyzing and creating models from huge amount of data commonly referred to as *big data*.

Machine learning is closely related to artificial intelligence (AI). In fact, it is an application of artificial intelligence (AI).

Machine learning works based on predictive and statistical algorithms that are provided to these machines. The algorithms are designed to learn and improve as more data flows through the system. Fraud detection, e-mail spam, GPS systems are some examples of machine learning applications.

Machine learning applications are based on teaching a computer how to learn. Besides predictive and statistical algorithms, it also uses pattern recognition to draw conclusion from the data.

Machine learning methods are used to develop complex models and algorithms that help to understand and make predictions from the data. The analytical models in machine learning allow the analysts to make predictions by learning from the trends, patterns and relationships in the historical data. Machine learning automates model building. The algorithms in machine learning are designed to learn iteratively from data without being programmed.

According to Arthur Samuel, machine learning gives "computers the ability to learn without being explicitly programmed."[2] Samuel, an American pioneer in the field of *computer gaming* and artificial intelligence, coined the term "machine learning" in 1959 while at IBM.

Machine learning algorithms are extensively used for data-driven predictions and in decision making. Some applications where machine learning has been used are email filtering, detection of network intruders or detecting a data breach, optical character recognition (OCR), learning to rank, computer vision, and a wide range of engineering and business applications. Machine learning is employed in a range of computing tasks. Often designing and programming explicit algorithms that are reproducible and have repeatability with good performance is difficult or infeasible.

Machine Learning Methods and Tasks

At the fundamental level, Machine learning tasks are typically classified into following broad categories depending on the nature of the learning "signal" or "feedback" available to a learning system. These are[20] (1) Supervised learning (2) Unsupervised learning.

Supervised Learning

In supervised learning, the computer is presented with example inputs and their desired outputs by the analyst, and the goal is to create a model to learn a general rule that maps inputs to outputs. The learning involves creating a model by establishing the relationship between inputs or the *features* and the desired output or some *label*. Once this model is established, it can be used to apply labels to new, unknown data to predict future events. The idea is to learn from the past data and apply to new data to make prediction for the future events using the created learning algorithm. The output from the learning algorithm can also compare its output to the known output to find the associated error that helps modify the model. The supervised learning problems can be divided into classification problems and regression problems.

Classification

Classification involves classifying the data into one or the other group. Here the labels are discrete categories where the inputs are divided into two or more classes, and the learner must produce a model that assigns unseen inputs to one or more (multilabel classification) of these classes. This is typically tackled in a supervised way.

Classification is a process of assigning items to pre specified classes or categories. For example, a financial institution may study the potential borrowers to predict whether a group of new borrowers may be classified as having a high degree of risk. Spam filtering is another example of classification, where the inputs are email messages that are classified into classes as "spam" and "no spam."

Classification uses the algorithms to categorize the new data according to the observations of the training set. *Classification is a supervised learning technique* where a training set is used to find similarities in classes. This means that the input data are divided into two or more classes or categories and the learner creates a model that assigns inputs to one or more of these classes. This is typically done in a supervised way. The objects are classified, based on the training set of data. A classification problem is when the output variable is a category, such as e-mails can be classified as "spam" or "no spam" or a test can be classified as "negative" and "positive."

The algorithm that implements classification is known as the classifier. Some of the most commonly used classification algorithms are K-Nearest Neighbor algorithm and decision tree algorithms. These are widely used in data mining. An example of classification would be credit card processing. A credit card company may want to segment customer database based on similar buying patterns.

Some of the commonly uses classification algorithms are:

- Decision trees and random forest
- Support vector machines (SVM) for classification problems
- Bayes classification

Regression

Regression is a supervised problem where the outputs are continuous rather than discrete. Regression problems are used to predict continuous labels. There are several regression models used in machine learning. These are linear and nonlinear regression, logistic regression, and others. Besides these the commonly used algorithms are support vector machines (SVM). These are the most widely used regression algorithms:

- Ordinary least squares regression (OLSR)
- Linear regression
- Logistic regression
- Stepwise regression
- Multivariate adaptive regression splines (MARS)
- Locally estimated scatterplot smoothing (LOESS)

Unsupervised Learning

As the name suggests, in unsupervised learning, no labels are given to the program. Unsupervised learning is where we have only have input data (X) and no corresponding output variables. The learning algorithm is expected to find the structure in its input. The goals of unsupervised learning may be finding hidden pattern in the large data. Thus, unsupervised learning process are not based on general rule of training the algorithms. The commonly used models in unsupervised learning include *Clustering* and *Dimensionality reduction.*

Clustering

In clustering, data is assigned to some number of discrete groups. In this type of problem, a set of inputs is to be divided into groups. Unlike in classification, the groups are not known beforehand, making this typically an unsupervised task.

Clustering technique is used to find natural groupings or clusters in a set of data without prespecifying a set of categories. It is unlike classification where the objects are classified based on pre specified classes or categories. Thus, clustering is an unsupervised learning technique where a training set is not used. It uses statistical tools and concepts to create clusters with similar features within the data. Some examples of clustering are as follows:

- Cluster of houses in a town into neighborhoods based on similar features like houses with overall value of over million dollars.
- Marketing analyst may define distinct groups in their customer bases to develop targeted marketing programs.
- City planning may be interested in identifying groups of houses according to their house value, type, and location.
- In cellular manufacturing, the clustering algorithms are used to form the clusters of similar machines and processes to form machine-component cells.
- Scientists and geologists may study the earthquake epicenters to identify clusters of fault lines with high probability of possible earthquake occurrences.

Cluster analysis is the assignment of a set of observations into subsets (called *clusters*) so that observations within the same cluster are similar according to some prespecified criterion or criteria, while observations drawn from different clusters are dissimilar. Clustering techniques differ in application and make different assumptions on the structure of the data. In clustering, the clusters are commonly defined by some *similarity metric or similarity coefficient* and may be evaluated by *internal compactness* (similarity between members of the same cluster) and *separation* between different clusters. Other clustering methods are based on *estimated density* and *graph connectivity*. It is important to note that clustering is *unsupervised learning*, and commonly used method in *statistical data analysis*. The well-known and used clustering algorithms are K-means clustering, spectral clustering, and Gaussian mixture models.

The goal of Clustering algorithms is to identify distinct groups of data.

Dimensionality Reduction

In machine learning problems involving classification, there are often too many factors or variables originally that need to be considered for classification These variables are commonly referred to as features. A large numbers of features makes it hard to visualize the training set and then work on it. These features may also be correlated that make them redundant. In such cases, dimensionality reduction algorithms are used to reduce the number of variables under consideration. These reduction algorithms help to obtain a set of key variables. Dimensionality reduction consists of feature selection and feature extraction.

Some examples where dimensionality reduction algorithms have been used are credit card fraud detection and spam filtering. These may involve many features that may overlap or are correlated. In such cases, reducing the number of features is very helpful in visualizing the problem. For example, a 3-D classification problem can be reduced to a 2-D problem that can make the visualization easier.

Difference Between Clustering and Classification

Clustering is an unsupervised learning technique used to find groups or clusters of similar instances based on features. The purpose of clustering is a process of grouping similar objects to determine whether there is any relationship between them. Classification is a supervised learning technique used to find similarities in classification based on a training set. It uses algorithms to categorize the new data according to the observations in the training set. Table 13.1 outlines the differences between classification and clustering.

Table 13.1 *Difference between classification and clustering*

Classification	Clustering
Classification is supervised learning technique where items are assigned to pre specified classes or categories. For example, a bank may study the potential borrowers to predict whether a group of new borrowers may be classified as having a high degree of risk.	Clustering is unsupervised technique used to find natural groupings or clusters in a set of data without pre specifying a set of categories. It is unlike classification where the objects are classified based on pre specified classes or categories.
Classification algorithm requires training data.	Clustering does not require training data.
Classification uses predefined instances.	Clustering does not assign pre-defined label to each and every group.
In classification, the groups (or classes) are pre-specified with each training data instance that belongs to a particular class.	In clustering the groups (or clusters) are based on the similarities of data instances to each other.
Classification algorithms are supposed to learn the association between the features of the instance and the class they belong to.	Unlike in classification, the groups are not known beforehand, making this an unsupervised task.
Example: An insurance company trying to assign customers into high risk and low risk categories.	Example: Drop box, a movie rental company may recommend a movie to customers because others who had made similar movie choices in the past have favorably rated that movie.

Other Classes of Machine Learning Problems

There are other classes of machine learning problems that fall in between supervised and unsupervised learning problems. These are semisupervised machine learning algorithms and reinforcement learning.

Semisupervised Machine Learning Algorithms

These algorithms fall in between supervised and unsupervised learning. They are designed with both labeled and unlabeled data for training and may contain typically a small amount of labeled data and a large amount of unlabeled data. These systems may in some cases be more efficient and are able to considerably improve learning accuracy. The semisupervised learning methods are usually used when the labeled data requires skilled resources to train or learn from it. The acquired unlabeled data generally doesn't require additional resources.

Reinforcement learning

In this type of learning, the designed computer program interacts with a dynamic environment in which it has a specific goal to perform. This differs from standard supervised learning as no input/output pairs are provided which involves finding a balance between exploration (of uncharted territory) and exploitation (of current knowledge).[6] Examples of reinforced learning are playing a game against an opponent. In this type of learning, the computer program is provided feedback in terms of rewards and punishments as it navigates its problem space.

Other Applications of Machine Learning

Another application of machine learning is in the area of *deep learning*,[25] which is based on *artificial neural networks*.[6] In his application, the learning tasks may contain more than one hidden layer or tasks with a single hidden layer known as shallow learning.

Artificial Neural Networks

An artificial neural network[6,7] (ANN) learning algorithm, usually called "neural network" (NN), is a learning algorithm that is inspired by the structure and functional aspects of biological neural networks. Computations are structured in terms of an interconnected group of artificial neurons, processing information using a connectionist approach to computation. Modern neural networks are nonlinear statistical data modeling tools. They are usually used to model complex relationships between inputs and outputs, to find patterns in data, or to capture the statistical structure in an unknown joint probability distribution between observed variables.

Deep learning[8]

Falling hardware prices and the development of GPUs for personal use in the last few years have contributed to the development of the concept of deep learning, which consists of multiple hidden layers in an artificial neural network. This approach tries to model the way the human brain processes light and sound into vision and hearing. Some successful applications of deep learning are computer vision and speech recognition.

> *Note: Neural networks use machine learning algorithms whereas machine leaning is an application of artificial intelligence[9] that automates analytical model building by using algorithms that iteratively learn from data without being explicitly programmed.*

Machine Learning and Data Mining

Machine learning and data mining are similar in some ways and often overlap in applications. Machine learning is used for prediction, based on *known* properties learned from the training data whereas data mining algorithms are used for discovery of (previously) *unknown* patterns. Data mining is concerned with knowledge discovery in databases (or KDD).

Data mining uses many machine learning methods. On the other hand, machine learning also employs data mining methods as "unsupervised learning" or as a preprocessing step to improve learner accuracy. The goals are somewhat different. The performance of the machine learning is usually evaluated with respect to the ability to *reproduce known* knowledge. In data mining, which is knowledge discovery from the data (KDD) the key task is the discovery of previously *unknown* knowledge. Unlike machine learning which is evaluated with respect to known knowledge, data mining uses uninformed or unsupervised methods that often outperform compared to other supervised methods. In a typical KDD task, supervised methods cannot be used due to the unavailability of training data. Figure 13.1 outlines the predictive and descriptive data mining learning techniques along with supervised and unsupervised leaning techniques. A number of data mining and machine learning methods overlap in applications. As indicated earlier, data mining is concerned with knowledge discovery from the data (KDD) where the key task is the discovery of previously *unknown* knowledge.

Machine learning, on the other hand, is evaluated with respect to known knowledge. According to Arthur Samuel, machine learning gives "computers the ability to learn without being explicitly programmed."[2]

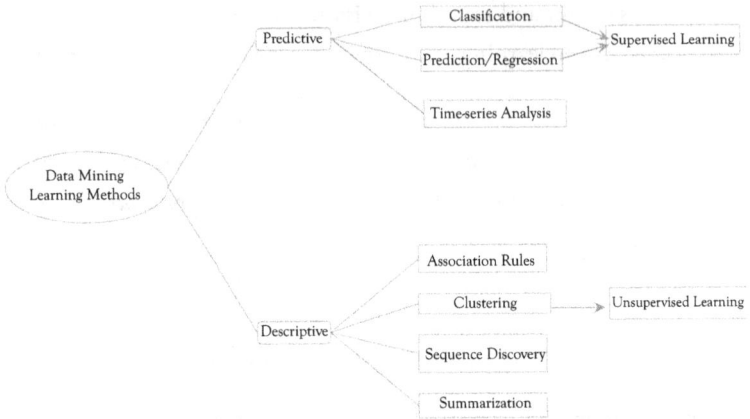

Figure 13.1 Predictive and descriptive data mining

Machine learning methods use complex models and algorithms that are used to make predictions. The machine learning models allow the analysts to make predictions by learning from the trends, patterns, and relationships in the historical data. The algorithms are designed to learn iteratively from data without being programmed. In a way, machine learning automates model building.

Recently, machine learning algorithms are finding extensive applications in data-driven predictions and are a major decision-making tool. Some applications where machine learning has been used are email filtering, cyber security, signal processing, fraud detection, and others. Machine learning is employed in a range of computing tasks. Although machine-learning models are being used in several applications, it has limitations in designing and programming explicit algorithms that are reproducible and have repeatability with good performance. With current research and the use of newer technology, the field of machine learning and artificial intelligence are becoming more promising.

It is important to note that data mining uses unsupervised methods that usually outperform the supervised methods used in machine learning. Data mining is the application of knowledge discovery from the data (KDD) where supervised methods cannot be used due to the unavailability of training data. Machine learning may also employ data mining methods as "unsupervised learning" to improve learner accuracy.

The performance of the machine learning algorithms depends on its ability to *reproduce known knowledge.*

Machine Learning Problems and Tasks: Difference between Supervised and Unsupervised Learning

Machine learning tasks have the following broad categories: supervised learning, unsupervised learning, and reinforced learning. The difference between supervised and unsupervised learning is explained in Table 13.2.

Table 13.2 Supervised and unsupervised learning

Supervised learning	Unsupervised learning
Supervised learning uses a set of input variables $(x_1, x_2, ..., x_n)$ and an output variable, $y(x)$. An algorithm of the form $y = f(x)$ is used to learn the mapping function relating the input to output.	Unsupervised learning uses a set of input variable but no output variable. No labels are given to the learning algorithm. The algorithm is expected to find the structure in its input. The goals of unsupervised learning may be finding hidden pattern in the large data or feature learning. Thus, unsupervised learning can be a goal in itself or a means toward an end that are not based on general rule of teaching and training the algorithms.
This mapping function or the model relating the input and output variable is used to predict the output variable. The goal is to obtain the mapping function that is so accurate that it can use even the new set of data That is, the model can be used to predict the output variable as the new data becomes available.	
The name supervised learning means that in this process the algorithm is trained to learn from the training dataset where the learning process is supervised. In supervised learning process, the expected output or the answer is known. The algorithm is designed to make predictions iteratively from the training data and is corrected by the analyst as needed. The learning process stops when the algorithm provides the desired level of performance and accuracy.	Unlike supervised learning algorithms are designed to devise and find the interesting structure in the data.
	The most used unsupervised learning problems are clustering and association problems.
	In clustering, a set of inputs is to be divided into groups. Unlike classification, the groups are not known beforehand, making this typically an unsupervised task.
The most used supervised problems are regression and classification problems. We discussed regression problems earlier. Time series predictions problems, random forest for classification and regression problems, and support vector machines for classification problems also fall in this category.	*Association*: Association problems are used to discover rules that describe association such as people that buy X also tend to buy Y.

Methods, Various Libraries, and Algorithms Used in Machine Learning

(https://github.com/topics/tensorflow)

Machine learning is the practice of teaching a computer to learn. The concept uses pattern recognition, as well as other forms of predictive algorithms, to make judgments on incoming data. This field is closely related to artificial intelligence and computational statistics.

Python is a dynamically typed programming language designed by Guido van Rossum. Much like the programming language Ruby, Python was designed to be easily read by programmers. Because of its large following and many libraries, Python can be implemented and used to do anything from webpages to scientific research.

TensorFlow is an open source library that was created by Google. It is used to design, build, and train deep learning models.

The Jupyter Notebook is a language-agnostic HTML notebook application for Project Jupyter. Jupyter notebooks are documents that allow for creating and sharing live code, equations, visualizations, and narrative text together. People use them for data cleaning and transformation, numerical simulation, statistical modeling, data visualization, machine learning, and much more.

Scikit-learn is a widely used Python module for classic machine learning. It is built on top of SciPy. There are several Python libraries which provide solid implementations of a range of machine learning algorithms. One of the best known is Scikit-Learn, a package that provides efficient versions of a large number of common algorithms. Scikit-Learn is characterized by a clean, uniform, and streamlined API, as well as by very useful and complete online documentation. A benefit of this uniformity is that once you understand the basic use and syntax of Scikit-Learn for one type of model, switching to a new model or algorithm is very straightforward.

Pandas is Flexible and powerful data analysis / manipulation library for Python, providing labeled data structures similar to R data frame objects, statistical functions, and much more.

Visualization With Matplotlib

Matplotlib is a package for visualization in Python. Matplotlib is a multiplatform data visualization library built on NumPy arrays and designed to work with the broader SciPy stack. It was conceived by John Hunter in 2002, originally as a patch to IPython for enabling interactive MATLAB-style plotting via gnu plot from the IPython command line.

NumPy

NumPy (short for *Numerical Python*) provides an efficient interface to store and operate on dense data buffers. In some ways, NumPy arrays are like Python's built-in list type, but NumPy arrays provide much more efficient storage and data operations as the arrays grow larger in size. NumPy arrays form the core of nearly the entire ecosystem of data science tools in Python, so time spent learning to use NumPy effectively will be valuable no matter what aspect of data science interests you.

Deep learning is an AI function and subset of machine learning, used for processing large amounts of complex data.

Neural networks: Artificial neural networks (ANN) are computational systems that "learn" to perform tasks by considering examples, generally without being programmed with any task-specific rules.

Summary

Machine learning is a method of designing systems that can learn, adjust, and improve based on the data fed to them without being explicitly programmed. Machine learning is used to create models from huge amount of data commonly referred to as *big data*. It is closely related to artificial intelligence (AI). In fact, it is an application of artificial intelligence (AI). Machine learning algorithms are based on teaching a computer how to learn from the training data. The algorithms learn and improve as more data flows through the system. Fraud detection, e-mail spam, GPS systems are some examples of machine learning applications.

Machine learning tasks are typically classified into two broad categories: supervised learning and unsupervised learning. In supervised learning, the computer is presented with example inputs and their desired outputs by the analyst, and the goal is to create a model to learn a general rule that maps inputs to outputs. The supervised learning problems are divided into classification and regression problems. A classification problem is when the output variable is a category, such as e-mails can be classified as "spam" or "no spam" or a test can be classified as "negative" and "positive." Most commonly used classification algorithms are K-Nearest Neighbor and decision-tree algorithms. Regression problems are used to predict continuous labels. There are several regression models used in machine learning. Unlike the supervised learning, no labels are given to the data in unsupervised learning. Unsupervised learning is where there is input data (X) and no corresponding output variables. The commonly used models in unsupervised learning include clustering and dimensionality reduction.

Clustering is an unsupervised learning technique used to find groups or clusters of similar instances based on features. The purpose of clustering is a process of grouping similar objects to determine whether there is any relationship between them. Classification is a supervised learning technique used to find similarities in classification based on a training set. It uses algorithms to categorize the new data according to the observations in the training set.

There are other classes of machine learning problems that fall in between supervised and unsupervised learning problems. These are semisupervised machine learning algorithms and reinforcement learning. Other application of machine learning is *deep learning*,[25] which is based on *artificial neural networks*.[6] Machine learning also has applications in data mining. Machine learning methods use complex models and algorithms that are used to make predictions. The machine learning models allow the analysts to make predictions by learning from the trends, patterns, and relationships in the historical data. The algorithms are designed to learn iteratively from data without being programmed. In a way, machine learning automates model building. To aid in the model building process in Machine Learning several libraries and algorithms are used. Microsoft Azur and SAS machine learning are designed to automate the process.

CHAPTER 14

R Statistical Programing Software for Data Science

R for Data Analysts

Introduction

Here we introduce R and provide an overview of this statistical programming language. R is a powerful and widely used software for data analysis and machine learning applications. It is free and can be downloaded easily. This chapter introduces the software, provides the basic statistical features, and instructions on how to download R and R studio. The software can be downloaded to run on all major operating systems including Windows, Mac OS X, and Unix.

R statistical analysis programming language was designed for statistical computing and graphics and is widely used by statisticians, data mining[36] and data science professionals for data analysis. R is perhaps one of the most widely used and powerful programming platforms for statistical programming and applied machine learning.

This software is available in public domain and can be downloaded for free. This is one of the preferred statistical application software for data analysis and ranks 8th in popularity. It is supported by R Foundation for Statistical Computing.[6]

The R software environment is written primarily in C, Fortran, and R itself. It has a command line interface, there are several third-party graphical user interfaces, such as RStudio, an integrated development environment, and Jupyter notebook interface.[13]

R was created by Ross Ihaka and Robert Gentleman[17] at the University of Auckland, New Zealand, and is developed by the *R Development Core Team* (of which, as of August 2018[update], Chambers was a member).[18] R is named partly after the first names of the first two R authors and partly as a play on the name of S.[19] The project was conceived in 1992, with an initial version released in 1995 and a stable beta version (v2.0) on 29 February 2000.[20, 21, 22] (https://en.wikipedia. org/wiki/R_(programming_language)).

R provides access to thousands of free add-on packages that are downloadable. These packages are contributed by users from different areas. Currently, there are thousands of user-contributed R applications are available (http://r-project.org). R can transfer data, read from, and write to most of the popular statistical packages including Excel, Minitab, SAS, SPSS, Stata, and others.

Statistical Features

R and its libraries implement a wide variety of statistical and graphical techniques. A few of the applications include descriptive and inferential statistics tools and classical statistical tests including independent t-test, paired t-tests, Chi-square goodness of fit tests, Chi square test of independence, hypothesis tests, regression models, ANOVA, time-series analysis, classification, clustering, linear and nonlinear modeling, nonparametric tests, and many others.

Many of R's standard functions are written in R itself. For computational tasks, C, C++, and Fortran code can be linked and called at run time. For advanced applications, users can write C, C++,[23] Java,[24] .NET,[25] or Python code to manipulate R objects directly.[26] With use of user-submitted packages for specific functions or specific areas of study, R can be highly extensible and can be adapted for wide range of statistical applications. The R system is very versatile and can be used to produce publication-quality graphics.

Download R and R-Studio

As mentioned above, R is available in public domain and can be downloaded for free. Here we outline the steps for downloading and installing a working copy of R for windows. Go to the following website:

http://r-project.org/

On the left-hand margin, you will see "Download" and CRAN.

Click on the CRAN link. This will take you to a page with a list of hosts called CRAN mirrors (arranged by geographic location).

CRAN *Mirrors*

The Comprehensive R Archive Network is available at the following URLs, please choose a location close to you. Some statistics on the status of the mirrors can be found here: main page, windows release, and windows old release.

Click on the location closest to you for a faster download. Depending on whether you use Windows or Mac OS, follow the steps accordingly. We provide the steps for Windows.

For Windows users:

- Click on Download for Windows
- On the next screen, click on base

The following screen will show:
Download R 4.0.2 for Windows (84 megabytes, 32/64 bit)

- Installation and other instructions
- New features in this version

i. Click on the Download R4.0.2 for Windows.
ii. Save the file: R4.0.2.-win.exe, double click and follow the onscreen instructions.
iii. When the program is installed successfully, you will see an entry in the All Programs area.
iv. Right Click on R 4.0.2 to place a shortcut R icon on the desktop.
v. Now, you can click on the R icon to start the R program.

Once you have installed R Statistical package, you should also install RStudio. This provides an integrated development environment that works with R to facilitate the running of R. Note that you will need to install RStudio separately. The R program does not include RStudio. Installing R and RStudio makes R more interactive and easier to run. RStudio is also available for free download. To install RStudio, follow the steps below.

Go to the following website:

http://rstudio.com

From the page that is displayed, Click "Download" from the top line selection.

It will take you to Download RStudio screen.

Scroll down to display:

RStudio Desktop

Open Source License

Free

Click on the "Download" box.

Click on

RStudio-2.3.1056.exe
and Save the File.
Follow the onscreen instructions to install the RStudio

Follow the onscreen instructions to install the RStudio

Make sure to install R before installing RStudio.

You can drag the R icon from the list of the programs to the desktop. Click on the R icon to start the R program. Your screen should resemble the one shown in Figure 14.1.

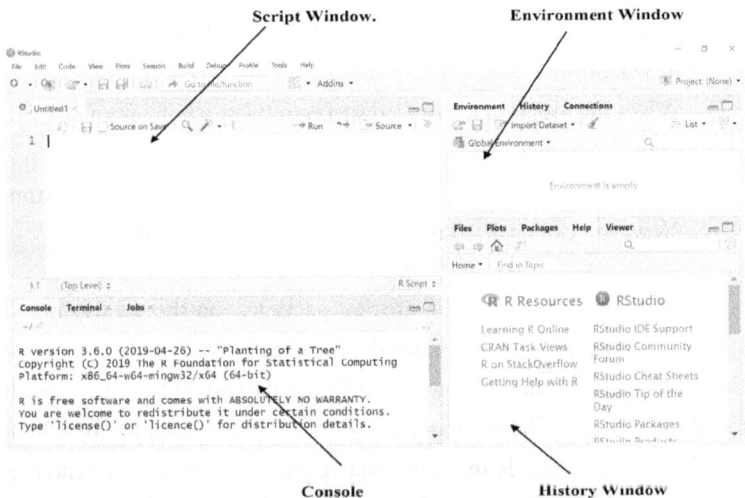

Figure 14.1 *Different Windows in R*

Working in RStudio Environment

RStudio looks displays the windows above when you open it up. There are four main windows. Each window is explained below.

Script Window

1. The upper left window is the Script window. Initially it is blank. If you don't see the Script window, you can open a new script. Click the down arrow next to the + sign just below the top row and select R Script to open a new script window. You can have multiple scripts open at the same time.

Console Window

Below the script window is the Console that has list of every line of code submitted and the output.

The console window can be used to carry out any algebraic calculation by just entering it in the console.

Using the Console window might be good for performing basic calculations line by line. But if there is lots of codes to execute, they should be submitted in the Script window.

Environment Window

The environment widow stores all the objects in the current workspace. This window has two other tabs: *History* and *Connections*. Next to the Environment tab that's called *History*, which lists the lines of code you've submitted.

Below the *History* there are three tabs: Files, Plots, Packages, Help, and Viewer.

This *Files* tab shows the current working directory that you're in right now.

The Plots window will produce any requested plot you ask R to do. It also keeps record of all the plots generated.

Then, we've got the *Packages*, which shows what's been loaded and what has been installed.

The Help window, which will display the help topics for which you are seeking help.

The *Viewer* tab is not used much as most versions of RStudio don't have this *Viewer* tab.

Summary

R is a powerful and widely used software for data analysis and machine learning applications. This chapter introduced the software and provided the basic statistical features, and instructions on how to download R and R studio. The software can be downloaded to run on all major operating systems including Windows, Mac OS X, and Unix. It is supported by R Foundation for Statistical Computing.[6] R statistical analysis programming language was designed for statistical computing and graphics and is widely used by statisticians, data mining,[36] and data science professionals for data analysis. R is perhaps one of the most widely used and powerful programming platforms for statistical programming and applied machine learning. It is widely used for data science and analysis application and is a desired skill for data science professionals. This software is available in public domain and can be downloaded for free. We have proved the steps to download R and R-studio. Both software work together. This is one of the preferred statistical application software for data analysis and ranks eighth in popularity. We provided basic functionality of the software. There are several resources, and tutorials available to learn and use the software effectively.

Online References

1. https://en.wikipedia.org/wiki/Unstructured_data
2. Leek, J. December 12, 2013. "The Key word in "Data Science" is not Data, it is Science." *Simply Statistics*. Archived from the original on 2 January 2014. (accessed January 1, 2014).
3. International Data Group - Wikipedia
4. EMC Corporation. December 2012. "EMC News Press Release: New Digital Universe Study Reveals Big Data Gap: Less Than 1% of World's Data is Analyzed; Less Than 20% is Protected." www.emc.com.
5. "Trends | Seagate US." Seagate.com. (accessed October 1, 2018).
6. https://forbes.com/sites/louiscolumbus/2014/11/26/computerworlds-2015-forecast-predicts-security-cloud-computing-and-analytics-will-lead-it-spending/#441abfb421a0
7. Computerworld - Wikipedia
8. https://en.wikipedia.org/wiki/Unstructured_data
9. Data analysis - Wikipedia
10. ACM SIGKDD. April 30, 2006. "Data Mining Curriculum." (accessed January 27, 2014).
11. Christopher, C. 2010. "Encyclopædia Britannica: Definition of Data Mining." (accessed December 9, 2010).
12. Hastie, T., R. Tibshirani, J. Friedman. 2009. "The Elements of Statistical Learning: Data Mining, Inference, and Prediction." Archived from the original on November 10, 2009. (accessed August 07, 2012).
13. Han, J., M. Kamber, and J. Pei. 2011. *Data Mining: Concepts and Techniques*, 3rd ed. Morgan Kaufmann. ISBN 978-0-12-381479-1
14. Jump up to:[a][b][c] Fayyad, U., and G. Piatetsky-Shapiro, and P. Smyth. 1996. "From Data Mining to Knowledge Discovery in Databases" (PDF). (accessed December 17, 2008).
15. Big data - Wikipedia
16. Machine learning - Wikipedia
17. Data science - Wikipedia
18. Turing Award - Wikipedia
19. https://sisense.com/blog/data-science-vs-data-analytics/
20. Jump up to: [a][b][c][d][e][f][g][h] Donoho, D. September 2015. "50 Years of Data Science." (PDF). Princeton NJ: Based on a Talk at Tukey Centennial Workshop, Archived (PDF) from the original on June 19, 2018. (accessed May 11, 2018).

21. Barlow, M. 2013. *The Culture of Big Data*. O'Reilly Media, Inc.

22. Chambers, J.M. December 1, 1993. "Greater or Lesser Statistics: A Choice for Future Research." *Statistics and Computing* 3, no. 4, 182–184. doi:10.1007/BF00141776. ISSN 0960-3174

23. What Is Data Science, and What Does a Data Scientist Do? (innoarchi tech.com).

24. Davenport, T.H., and D.J. Patil. October 1, 2012. "Data Scientist: The Sexiest Job of the 21st Century." *Harvard Business Review*. ISSN 0017-8012. (accessed April 3, 2020).

25. *Donoho, D. September 18, 2015.* "50 years of Data Science" (PDF). (accessed April 2, 2020).

26. Pham, P. n.d. "The Impacts of Big Data That You May Not Have Heard of." *Forbes*. (accessed April 3, 2020).

27. Jump up to:[a][b][c] Martin, S. September 20, 2019. "How Data Science will Impact Future of Businesses?" *Medium*. (accessed April 3, 2020).

28. Wu, C.F.J. n.d. "Statistics=Data Science?" (PDF). (accessed April 2, 2020).

29. https://en.wikipedia.org/wiki/Business_intelligence#cite_note-14

30. Robert, S, Statistics with R: A beginner's Guide, ISBN 978-1-4739-2489-5, Sage publications, Inc., 2455 Teller Road, Thousand Oaks, CA 91320

31. Hyatt, Saleh, Machine Learning Fundamentals, ISBN 978-1-78980-355-6, 2018 Packet Publishing

32. https://edureka.co/blog/what-is-tableau What is Tableau? Visualizing Data Using Tableau, Edureka, 2019.

33. Martin, S. September 20, 2019. "How Data Science will Impact Future of Businesses?" *Medium*. (Accessed April 3, 2020).

34. *Shell, M Scott (24 September 2019). "An introduction to Python for scientific computing"* (PDF). *Retrieved 2 April 2020.*

Additional Readings

Albright, S.C., and W. Wayne. 2015. *Business Analytics: Data Analysis and Decision Making*. 5th Edition © 2015 Cengage Learning.

Albright, S.C., W. Wayne, L. Zappe, and J. Christopher. 2011. *Data Analysis and Decision Making*, 4th Edition © 2011 South Western, Cengage Learning.

Anderson, D.R., D.J. Sweeny, and T.A. William. 2003. *An Introduction to Management Science – Quantitative approaches to Decision Making*, 10 th ed. © South Western.

Müller, A.C., and S. Guido. N.d. "Introduction to Machine Learning with Python: A Guide for Data Scientists." 1st ed. https://amazon.com/Introduction-Machine-Learning-Python-Scientists/dp/1449369413?tag=hackr-20&geniuslink=true

Benisis, A. 2010. "Business Process Management: A Data Cube To Analyze Business Process Simulation Data For Decision Making." VDM Verlag Dr. Müller e.K. p. 204 pp. ISBN 978-3-639-22216-6

Bowerman, B., and M. O'Connell. 2017. "Business Statistics in Practice Using Data, Modeling, and Analytics." 8th Edition, © 2017, Published by McGraw-Hill Education, 2 penn Plaza, New York, NY 10121.

Box, G.E.P., and G.M. Jenkins. 1976. *Time Series Analysis: Forecasting and Control*, 2nd ed. San Francisco, CA.

Camm, C., et al. 2015. *Essentials of Business Analytics*, 1st ed. © Cengage Learning.

Shan, C., W. Chen, H. Wang, and M. Song. June 19, 2015. "The Data Science Handbook: Advice and Insights from 25 Amazing Data Scientists Paperback." https://amazon.com/Data-Science-Handbook-Insights-Scientists/dp/0692434879?tag=hackr-20&geniuslink=true

Eppen G.D., F.J. Gould, C.P. Schmidt, J.H. Moore, and L.R. Weatherford. 1998. *Introductory Management Science – Decision Making with Spread Sheets*, 5th ed. © Prentice Hall

EMC Education Services (Editor). n.d. "Data Science and Big Data Analytics: Discovering, Analyzing, Visualizing and Presenting Data." 1st ed. https://amazon.com/Data-Science-Big-Analytics-Discovering/dp/111887613X?tag=hackr-20&geniuslink=true

Provost, F., and T. Fawcett. N.d. "Data Science for Business: What You Need to Know about Data Mining and Data-Analytic Thinking." 1st ed. https://amazon.com/Data-Science-Business-data-analytic-thinking/dp/1449361323/ref=zg_bs_3654_2?tag=hackr-20&geniuslink=true

Schniederjans, M.J., D.G. Schniederjans, and C.M. Starkey. 2014. *Business Analytics Principles, Concepts, and Applications with SAS,* © Pearson Education, Inc. Upper Saddle River, New Jersey 07458

Bruce, P. n.d. "Andrew Bruce, Practical Statistics for Data Scientists." https://hackr.io/blog/data-science-books

Russell, R.S., and B.W. Taylor. 2014. *Operations and Supply Chain Management* © 2014 Wiley.

Stevenson, W.J. 2015. *Operations Management,* © McGraw Hill.

Sahay, A. 2017. *Data Visualization, Volume I – Recent Trends and Applications Using Conventional and Big Data,* © Business Expert Press, LLC 222 East 46th Street, New York, NY 10017. https://amazon.com/Data-Visualization-Applications-Graphical-Improving/dp/1631573357/ref=sr_1_6?dchild=1&keywords=Amar+Sahay&qid=1615434250&sr=8-6

Sahay, A. 2017. *Data Visualization, Volume II – Uncovering the Hidden Pattern in Data Using Basic and New Quality Tools,* © Business Expert Press, LLC 222 East 46th Street, New York, NY 10017. https://amazon.com/Data-Visualization-II-Uncovering-Pattern/dp/163157731X/ref=sr_1_3?dchild=1&keywords=Amar+Sahay&qid=1615434306&sr=8-3

Sahay, A. 2019. *Business Analytics, A Data Driven Decision Making Approach for Business: Volume II,* published by Business Expert Press (BEP), New York. https://amazon.com/Business-Analytics-II-Decision-Approach/dp/1631574795/ref=sr_1_2?dchild=1&keywords=Amar+Sahay&qid=1615434416&sr=8-2

Sahay, A. 2016. *Applied Regression and Modeling – A computer Integrated Approach,* © Business Expert Press, LLC 222 East 46th Street, New York, NY 10017. https://amazon.com/Applied-Regression-Modeling-Computer-Integrated-ebook/dp/B01FRK74BK/ref=sr_1_4?dchild=1&keywords=Amar+Sahay&qid=1615434542&sr=8-4

Sahay, A. 2018. *Statistics & Data Analysis Concepts for Business With Computer Applications, 4e* – Published by QMS Global LLC, A.M.T. Printing Digital Solutions, Inc. A Data-Driven Decision Making Approach for Business, Volume I, © 2018 Business Expert Press, LLC 222 East 46th Street, New York, NY 10017. https://amazon.com/Statistics-Analysis-Concepts-Business-Applications/dp/0985044675/ref=sr_1_12?dchild=1&keywords=Amar+Sahay&qid=1615434625&sr=8-12

Sahay, A. 2016. *Business Analytics – A Data-Driven Decision Making Approach for Business, Volume I,* © Business Expert Press, Salt Lake City, U.S.A. https://amazon.com/Business-Analytics-Data-Driven-Decision-Approach-ebook/dp/B07GT8CW8Q/ref=sr_1_1?dchild=1&keywords=Amar+Sahay&qid=1615434710&sr=8-1

Sahay, A. 2010. *Assisting Higher Education in Assessing, Predicting, and Managing Issues Related to Student Success: A Web-based Software using Data Mining and Quality Function Deployment.* Academic and Business Research Institute Conference, Las Vegas.

Stephanie, D.H. 2017. Evergreen, *Effective Data Visualization*, © 2017, Sage Publications, Inc., U.S.A., United Kingdom, India, Singapore.

Swaroop, P. January 2009. Dr Bruce Golden, University of Maryland, College Park, Data Mining: Introduction, and a Health Care Application.

Tufte, E.R. 2001. *The Visual Display of Quantitative Information.* Graphics Press.

About the Author

Dr. Amar Sahay is a professor engaged in teaching, research, consulting, and training. He has a BS in production engineering (Birla Institute of Technology, India), MS in industrial engineering and a PhD in mechanical engineering, both from University of Utah, USA. He has taught and is teaching at several Utah institutions including the University of Utah (school of engineering and management), SLCC, Westminster college, and others. Amar is a certified Six Sigma Master Black Belt and holds expert-level certification in lean manufacturing and lean management. He has contributed over 30 research papers in national and international conferences. Amar is the author of more than 10 professional books and textbooks. Among his recent publications are *Six Sigma Quality–Concepts and Cases, Statistics and Data Analysis Concepts, Managing and Improving Quality, Applied Regression and Modeling, Data Visualization,* and *Business Analytics/Business Intelligence.* He is also associated with QMS Global LLC; a company engaged in the areas of data visualization, analytics, lean six sigma, data analytics, manufacturing, and services systems analysis. Amar is a senior member of Institute of Industrial & Systems Engineers, and a senior member of American Society for Quality (ASQ). Salt Lake City, Utah, USA.

amar@xmission.com
amar@realleansixsigmaquality.com

Index